NATRAJ PUBLISHERS
Rajpur Road, Dehra Dun.

# WAR IN HIGH HIMALAYA

# War in High Himalaya

## The Indian Army in Crisis, 1962

Major General **D.K. PALIT** VrC

**LANCER INTERNATIONAL**
C. HURST & CO. PUBLISHERS LTD., LONDON
ST. MARTIN'S PRESS, INC., NEW YORK

© D.K. Palit, 1991

First Published in India by Lancer International, B-3 Gulmohar Park, New Delhi-110049 in association with C. Hurst & Co, (Publishers) Ltd., UK and St. Martin's Press, Inc., USA.

ISBN 81-7062-138-0

*Printed in India at* Tarun Offset Printers

This copy for sale in India, Bangladesh, Pakistan, Nepal, Bhutan, Sri Lanka, Burma only

p 202 Karag Frontier Div
p 239 Namka-Chu
p 31 Aksai Chin
p 35 Ladakh & Aksai Chin

# CONTENTS

# MAPS

# PREFACE

Some four years ago a senior research officer of the Indian Ministry of Defence's Historical Section telephoned me to seek an interview. The Government of India, he said, had decided to publish an official history of the Sino-Indian war of 1962. Since I had been the Director of Military Operations at the time, would I be agreeable to provide him with details of operational moves and General Staff deliberations leading up to the hostilities? When I told him that the information he sought was available in the files of General Staff Branch, he replied that that was not so: he had approached Army Headquarters, but was told that most General Staff records of that period had been destroyed – hence his request. I expressed my reluctance to be drawn into any form of discussion on the Sino-Indian war because I held strongly critical views, which I was not prepared to share. Furthermore, I had started to write my own memoir of that period and until I decided whether or not to publish it I did not wish to disclose any part of its contents. However, I said that if he sent me a list of questions regarding the facts he was seeking, I would answer them as best as I could.

It is unusual, to say the least, for the General Staff to destroy operational records of a critical period of military operations. At the same time, having been only too aware of government attempts at a cover-up immediately after the end of the Sino-Indian war, I was not overly surprised.

Very few of the facts of that episode have ever been made public; even parliament has on occasion been misinformed. There was a deal of criticism of government bungling in the press and elsewhere at the time, but much of it was based on wrong or inadequate information. To this day there is no authoritative account of the manner in which the crisis was handled by the government and Army Headquarters, or of the reasons for waging an unwinnable war in high Himalay. Assuming that the Defence Ministry's official history would reflect the old cover-up line, I made up my mind to publish my memoir and make public the facts of the case as I knew them.

I did feel some concern that I might be guilty of breach of security. The Government of India has never passed a Freedom of Information Act or similar legislation, and since there has been no move to declassify old documents, virtually everything once marked secret remains so for ever. I decided to self-impose a 30-year rule on the information published in my memoir in order to be morally certain that I would not be disclosing any secrets.

In November 1962, shortly after the end of the Chinese war, the newly appointed Army Chief, J.N. Chaudhuri, required me to write a detailed *Summary of Events and Policies* that culminated in the debacle along the Himalayan border. For reasons I have explained in my memoir, I retained a copy of that review, with the tacit approval of the Army Chief. I had also maintained a personal diary during critical periods of political and military activity. The original copy of the review was, on General Chaudhuri's wishes, transferred from Military Operations Directorate and filed in his secretariat, and thus may have escaped destruction. My diaries are of course a personal record, written in long-hand, and in my possession. Together they provide the framework of my book and I have quoted long passages from both.

There are passages I can read as clearly from the scrolls of my memory. My recollections of those momentous and harrowing events are so vivid that many of them stand out in high relief where, at this distance, much else often seems shrouded in mist. This has proved a blessing because not many of the major participants in these events are still alive; even those who are, are reluctant to talk. Only

Generals Moti Sagar (then Chief of the General Staff), Surendra Singh (then in Military Operations Directorate), Niranjan Prasad (who commanded 4 Infantry Division at Towang) and his staff officer, Colonel Shamsher Singh, have allowed me access to the recesses of their memory.

There are both advantages and disadvantages in writing about events long after they occur. Distance in time has the virtue that viewpoint distortions of contemporary events can be straightened out as they acquire perspective, and as emotion and prejudice recede. The passage of years also makes available others' views and opinions which help to modulate subjective judgments formed under the stress of immediate reactions. Thus, provided written records are available to prevent a memoir from straying from facts, hindsight judgment can result in greater objectivity.

Time has drawbacks too. A memoir is a subjective record, a mix of fact and opinion, and time can play tricks with opinions. It is one thing to form an objective judgment with the advantage of hindsight; it is quite another matter to allow the years to blur the difference between opinions held then and opinions held now. Hindsight must not be manipulative. I have on occasion caught myself subconsciously assuming that an opinion I hold now is also one I held thirty years ago. To allow that impression to remain would be patently dishonest and I have meticulously endeavoured to avoid that pitfall.

Some incidents in my memoir seem so incredible, grotesque even, that readers may have difficulty believing them. All I can do is to assure them that I have nowhere fabricated or manipulated facts or, indeed, been conscious of exaggeration. It is possible that after thirty years of critical reflection I may on occasion have overstressed an incident or observation, but that is a different thing from fiction or hyperbole. Unlike some of the other participants in this tale, I had no need to seek vindication or justification for my own action. My role throughout was that of a staff officer, whose job was not to formulate policies or issue orders but to process them and to offer advice. It is the commanders in the chain who carried responsibility and were accountable for failures and disasters.

Although this is a memoir and not a history, I have

accepted the advice of friends who suggested that I provide factual background material to enable those not familiar with the Sino-Indian border dispute to follow the narrative without having constantly to consult references. I have therefore included a brief history of the northern border disputes and the attempts of the erstwhile British-Indian government to come to an agreement with the Chinese – and the doubts and variables that the government of independent India inherited.

For those unfamiliar with British-Indian military history and tradition, I have also included an introductory assessment of the history and the unique character of the Indian army, its renown, its strengths and also its many shortcomings. The failure of politico-military appraisal and the crisis of generalship in 1962 is more easily comprehensible if the reader is aware of the ethos of the unique military force the British created and passed on to us and its post-independence status in the administration.

I have not felt the need to undermine the readers' entertainment by inflicting a plethora of notes, glosses and other editorial insertions in my narrative. I am aware that nowadays such garnishings are regarded as hallmarks of erudition and scholarship, but I have so often found the flow of my own reading pleasure thwarted by the unwelcome intrusions of the card-index that I decided to keep mine out of reach whenever I sat down to write.

Nor do I apologise for using older forms of spellings for names of places and persons. I have used Peking when I meant Peking and Chou En-lai when I wished to refer to the then Chinese prime minister. Those are the forms by which they were known at the time and I preferred to adhere to them. As for the matter of abbreviations, in order to avoid repeatedly using long and cumbersome military and other designations, I have used popularly known abridgements. For those unfamiliar with them, I have included a Glossary of Abbreviations at the beginning of the book.

I acknowledge my grateful thanks to Mr K. Subrahmanyam, former Director of the Institute for Defence Studies and Analyses New Delhi, who more than any other encouraged me to record this memoir. He also read through the draft

and made many valuable suggestions. Others who have
helped me with their comments are General Sir John
Chapple, Chief of the General Staff of the United Kingdom,
Pamela Burdick, Mr John Lall and Lieutenant Colonel
Tony Mains, late of my Regiment, to all of whom I am
deeply indebted. For the maps I record my gratitude to
my niece Abha Chaudhuri. Very special thanks are due to
Mr Serbjeet Singh for his kind permission to reproduce the
spectacular panorama of the Namka-chu valley and Thag-la
ridge, which he was still painting, perched on a hill
overlooking the battlefield, when the Chinese launched their
attack on 20 October 1962.

# GLOSSARY OF ABBREVIATIONS

| | |
|---|---|
| ADC | Aide-de-Camp |
| AG | Adjutant General |
| AIR | All India Radio |
| a.m. | ante meridiem |
| AVM | Air Vice Marshal |
| BGS | Brigadier General Staff |
| BM | Brigade Major |
| BRDB | Border Roads Development Board |
| Brig Adm | Brigadier in charge of Administration |
| CAO | Chief Administrative Officer |
| CAS | Chief of the Air Staff |
| CENTO | Central Treaty Organisation (Middle East) |
| CGDP | Controller General of Defence Production |
| CGS | Chief of the General Staff |
| CIA | Central Intelligence Agency (USA) |
| CIGS | Chief of the Imperial General Staff (UK) |
| C-in-C | Commander-in-Chief |
| CNS | Chief of the Naval Staff |
| COAS | Chief of the Army Staff |
| DAA&QMG | Deputy Assistant Adjutant & Quarter Master General |
| DBO | Daulet Beg Oldi |
| DCGS | Deputy Chief of the General Staff |
| D-Day | The date on which an attack commences |
| DIB | Director of the Intelligence Bureau |
| DMI | Director of Military Intelligence |
| DMO | Director of Military Operations |
| DSD | Director of Staff Duties |
| DSO | Distinguished Service Order (British military award) |
| ECO | Emergency Commissioned Officer |
| FD | Frontier Division (of NEFA) |

| | |
|---|---|
| FPO | Field Post Office |
| FS | Foreign Secretary (Senior Bureaucrat, not Minister) |
| GHQ | General Headquarters |
| GOC | General Officer Commanding |
| GOC-in-C | General Officer Commanding-in-Chief |
| GOI | Government of India |
| GR | Gorkha Rifles |
| GS | General Staff |
| H-Hour | The exact time at which an attack commences |
| HMG | His (or Her) Majesty's Government (UK) |
| HP | Himachal Pradesh |
| HQ | Headquarters |
| IB | Intelligence Bureau |
| ICS | Indian Civil Service |
| IDC | Imperial Defence College (UK, later renamed Royal College of Defence Studies) |
| IDSA | Institute for Defence Studies and Analyses, New Delhi |
| IDSM | Indian Distinguished Service Medal (British-Indian gallantry award for Other Ranks) |
| IMA | Indian Military Academy, Dehra Dun |
| INA | Indian National Army (Japanese-inspired Indian force under Subhas Chandra Bose) |
| IOM | Indian Order of Merit (British-Indian gallantry award for VCOs) |
| JIC | Joint Intelligence Committee |
| J&K | Jammu and Kashmir |
| KCO | King's Commissioned Officer |
| l of c | line-of-communication (road or rail) |
| MA | Military Advisor (or Attaché) |
| MC | Military Cross (British gallantry award for officers) |
| MGO | Master General of Ordnance |
| MI | Military Intelligence |
| MO | Military Operations |
| MS | Military Secretary |
| MT | Motor Transport; or Military Training |
| NEFA | North Eastern Frontier Agency |
| NWFP | North-West Frontier Province (of British India) |
| OBE | Officer of the Order of the British Empire (award for civilians and military officers) |
| Ops | Operations |
| PLA | People's Liberation Army (of China) |
| PM | Prime Minister |
| PSO | Principal Staff Officer (at Army HQ, New Delhi) |
| Pt | Point |
| QMG | Quarter Master General |

| | |
|---|---|
| recce. | Reconnaissance |
| RN | Royal Navy |
| TAC | Tactical Air Command |
| UK | United Kingdom |
| UP | Uttar Pradesh |
| USA | United States of America |
| VC | Victoria Cross (Britain's highest gallantry award) |
| VCO | Viceroy's Commissioned Officer |
| VIP | Very Important Person |
| VrC | Vir Chakra (Indian gallantry award) |

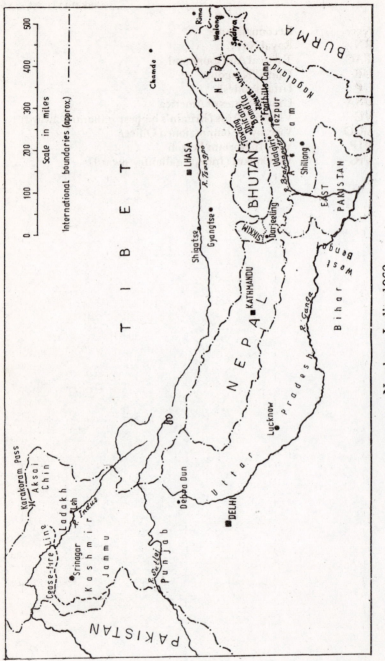

Northern India, 1962

# 1
# THE INDIAN ARMY:
# ITS ETHOS AND CHARACTER

This memoir is a personal account of India's border war against the Chinese in the early 1960s. It records the inept handling of political and military affairs by the government and the army during that crisis – so inept that it verged on the bizarre. Admittedly it was the first time since independence that India had to contend with conflict outside the sub-continental experience, but even so the unqualified bungling by the highest authorities is inexplicable. After an initial stage of diplomatic manoeuvre, during which the Indian Prime Minister, Pandit Nehru, exercised a degree of conflict control, restraint was abandoned, despite a warning by the Intelligence Bureau of likely retaliation by the Chinese. Procedures of democratic government through which policies are formulated and decisions taken were discarded in preference for emotional posturings and untenable assumptions. Nor did the army high command live up to expectation. Its strategic perceptions were unsound; it failed to withstand or moderate ministerial directives that patently foreboded disaster; and it abjectly accepted political over-reach in operational supervision.

It is incomprehensible that a government headed by so highly regarded a statesman as Jawaharlal Nehru could have made such gross misjudgments and breaches of

1

established procedure. As for the army, its senior commanders and staff inexplicably allowed themselves to be cajoled or browbeaten into futile and implausible deployments along the Karakoram and Himalayan ranges.

To this day there is continuing criticism of the handling of the 1962 crisis, much of it uninformed because of the veil of cover-up that was hastily drawn across the whole episode soon after the ceasefire. The government has never published all the facts about that war or about the events and policies that led up to it, presumably because they would reveal the waywardness and lack of sophistication of the politicians involved, besides the weakness of military leadership. Furthermore, the existence of a structured gap in communication between the government and the military has never been brought out. This was an organic deficiency that played a crucial role in the mismanagement of the war. I hope that within the limited confines of this introductory chapter I shall be able partly to explain how such a state of disruption could have existed within a democratic system. Nehru's role in permitting this schism between the political and the professional to continue is difficult to explain; I can only attempt to analyse the matter from the military point of view.

Colonial attitudes and practices have for two centuries shaped the Indian military ethos. Although the Indian Army has a glorious record of service going back nearly two hundred years, it was not until the First World War, when Indian troops fought against Germans and Turks in three continents, that Indian military prowess was first drawn into the international limelight, although the Indian Army was not then regarded as being truly representative of the country because it was officered entirely by the British.

Regular commissions began grudgingly to be granted to Indians in the early 1920s, but it was not till Hitler's war that Indian officers came into their own. Although the highest field command given to an Indian during that war was a brigade – and that also as an exception – thousands of us fought for the British against Germans, Italians and Japanese; and external observers for the first time began to regard the Indian Army as being truly representative of its country. When India gained independence, the same army became the army of independent India. Most of its British officers left to go home, but the army retained the reputation it had earned during the British era. It also preserved most of the practices and rituals of the British, such as regimental traditions, mess customs and social habits. Thus, except for the replacement of British officers by Indians, the army remained much the same in form and character after independence.

Unfortunately it also remained unchanged in another important aspect, even if that aspect has escaped the notice of most contemporary observers.

The national government in Delhi, after half a century of independence, continues to preserve modes and procedures of colonial rule in many of its precepts and practices. This is not by itself exceptionable, because some aspects of *raj* administration were both proven and adaptable by a liberal successor-government. At the same time, it is retrograde and restrictive to perpetuate procedures or usages designed specifically to serve imperial overlordship and ill-suited to democratic government. A glaring example of this is the Indian government's treatment of its military instrument.

It would be natural to assume that in a democratic system the military is an integral part of the policy-making and executive agency called government, but if you were to make such an assumption about the governmental system in India you would be quite wrong. However efficient, professional and effective the Indian armed forces may be, within the Indian political system they exist largely in a vacuum. At the top they have little contact with the government (either with political leaders or even with bureaucrats in the ministries) and underneath, they are kept out of contact with the people. The Indian armed forces contradict the *cliché*: they are not an expression of the society from which they issue; they never have been. Even so, many years after independence, neither their purpose nor their conduct is necessarily determined by what Indian society wants from it. Rather, they remain encapsulated in a cosy, cloistered cocoon, separated from the realities of political and social challenges. Clearly, such a sweeping statement needs to be validated. Since it is the army among the three services that has taproots reaching deep into the

British period, it would be appropriate to examine its growth and development during that period.

The four main historical factors that influenced the evolution of the Indian Army and its ethos and character are: the ancient military tradition of the Hindus; caste and regional insulation in the British-Indian Army; the British inspiration, and a reluctant change to 'Indianisation'[1]; and the naivety of India's political leaders at independence.

Alone of all the civilisations that reach back into antiquity, it was the Indo-Aryan that early in its history formalised and accorded a lustrous role in society to the warrior caste, a group solely devoted to the profession of arms. As early as in the *Rig Veda* period the concept of the *kshatrya dharmam*, the code of the warrior, assigned him social rank next to the Brahmin in the Hindu caste system. During the later *Atharva Veda* and in the post-vedic periods, the warriors' code was specifically laid down in the *Dharma-shastras*, the *Dhanur-veda* and even in Kautilya's *Artha-shastra* – strict rules of discipline, drill and the use of arms in chivalric modes. The result of centuries of this tradition was, on the one hand, to restrict skill-at-arms and martial values such as valour, obedience and loyalty to a small section of society and, on the other, to make that section, the military caste, almost totally apolitical. It was contrary to the warrior's code to undertake any professional activity other than military. He could not govern, or administer, or instruct – those roles were the Brahmin's; he could not buy and sell, or participate in any form of commerce – that was for the middle caste; he could not even till the soil – that was for the Sudra. It is because of this tradition – of a high-caste military coterie that took little interest in anything outside the profession of arms – that Hindu history does not provide any notable example of a *coup d'état* by the military against its ruler or government.

The bravery of Indian warriors was legendary, sometimes carried to implausible extremes of deathwish self-destruction, like the Rajput *ghol* tradition. When faced with certain defeat, Rajput warriors would make a suicidal charge at the enemy in tightly knit massed formation, preferring the sacrifice of their lives to surrendering or fleeing from the battlefield. Despite these traditions of valour and professionalism, history also records that armies of Indian rulers were not always steadfast to the end; they were never totally dependable. In normal circumstances they fought staunchly and without fear, but if their king or chief were to fall in battle (or were thought to have fallen) generals and soldiers alike would lose heart. There have been instances when armies disintegrated and melted away, even at the moment of victory, simply because one man fell (or thoughtlessly dismounted) from his command elephant.

The main reason for this seeming lack of resoluteness was socio-economic. According to the Moghul system the emperor (or king) owned everything over which he ruled, including the land, the personal possessions and the very homes of his subjects. Everything the nobles or the generals or the warriors possessed was his because it was a gift of the king, who also was every man's heir; upon their death, all wealth and property reverted to him. If the king died in battle, what was there left to fight for? Until a new succession had been established, allegiance was held in abeyance.

A contributory reason for the undependability of armies of Indian kings was that they lacked an organised system of regular, permanent officers at lower levels. A large proportion of middle- and lower-rank officers were petty nobles and courtiers, not professionals. Few trained or administered their charges, and they did not always lead them in battle. Quite often a large body of troops fought as a cohesive mass directly under a general; and generals are too remote from the men in the ranks to restore morale in a crisis.

It was Britain's East India Company that elicited the full potential from India's martial traditions. When the presidencies needed to raise battalions of native sepoys in the war against the French,[2] they found a sub-continent of high-caste and peasant warriors willing to flock to the colours because that was their tradition (or because they simply needed the jobs). Whatever the reason, the British found them willing and obedient, skilful with their weapons and steadfast in battle. Later, as the army expanded and an organised officering system was introduced, bonds of mutual respect, loyalty and even affection were established between British officers and their sepoys. In the British army class prejudices and mutual suspicions precluded bonds of camaraderie between the upper-class English officers and the lower classes, particularly the urban soldiery. Discipline often had to be enforced with brutality; floggings and other forms of violent and humiliating punishment were common. No such retribution was necessary, or permitted, in the Indian armies.

The Indians in their turn found in their British officers a new definition of what an officer was supposed to represent: a visible superior who trained them in peace and led them in war – and saw to it that they were paid regularly, in both peace and war. There was something in the social system of Britain – the oligarchical base of the 'establishment' and its inhibiting rituals; the all-masculine environment of the educational system that inured its young men to physical hardship, obedience to orders and acceptance of responsibility from an early age; and a fetish of non-intellectuality – that bred a high proportion of excellent officers at company and battalion level (just as it failed to produce many good generals). Their leadership qualities found full expression in command of Indians because, unlike in their own army, they mixed freely with their well-born (if uneducated) warrior soldiers. They trained them in peace and led them in war, and they did not run in battle. The combination of British officer and Indian warrior established the fighting reputation of the Indian Army; and it was the Indian Army that made it possible for the East India Company to change its role from commerce to conquest, and eventually to Empire. (At no time were there sufficient British regiments in India to undertake the imperial venture by themselves.) In a society in which nationalism was unknown, the sepoy armies of the three presidencies served the British purpose loyally for nearly two centuries. The Queen's regiments and the Company's European troops were there mainly to act as a racial counterbalance.

The British ensured that the Indian sepoy was protected from all social and political influences. His loyalty to the Crown was ensured by keeping him segregated from his own countrymen. For example, the widespread disaffection of the peasantry in the mid-nineteenth century (caused by the East India Company's enforcement of harsh agricultural policies that ruined the subsistence economy of many parts of India) did not really affect him. Even in 1857, what saved the British in north India from total disaster was the lack of common cause between the sepoy rebels and the insurgent landlords of the middle Gangetic valley. A degree of co-ordination between them could have altered the course of history at Delhi and Lucknow.

For the officers and men of the army, the government provided military colonies of barracks and training grounds away from the populace, keeping them not only physically segregated but also confined in cantonments of the mind. The Indian army reached neither upward nor downward in the socio-political chain; it was content to be kept insulated from India's social and political tensions. To some degree that circumstance continues to prevail in independent India today. Almost as a corollary to that policy, the military has been kept excluded from the machinery of government. Despite the fact that the army is now more than a million strong and recruits from a much more educated and socially conscious base, it continues to remain out of the mainstream of national awareness. The government of free India has not thought fit (nor have the generals of the Indian Army demanded) any change in that colonial culture of governance.

Another important factor of Hindu history that greatly affected attitudes and arrangements in the Indian Army was the caste and tribal framework of Indian society. The British at first disregarded prescriptive caste prerogatives but later relied heavily on this system. In the earlier armies of the two southern presidencies all classes and castes were enlisted in mixed units. In the Madras Army even the lowest, the untouchable, was recruited and the experiment was successful. Unfortunately, this policy of integration of castes was discarded in Bengal after Clive's victory at Plassey in 1757 – the start of the era of imperial conquest. When the Bengal Army was raised, the men were recruited mainly from the higher castes of the mid-Gangetic valley; it was homogeneous in composition, not broken up into tribes and sub-castes.

In the aftermath of the uprising of 1857 (in which it

was principally the Bengal Army that rebelled) a series of royal commissions were appointed by the British government to inquire into conditions in the presidency armies and to offer suggestions for evolving a recruiting pattern that would ensure greater loyalty and dependability in the 'Native Army'. As Sir Charles Wood, the Secretary of State for India, wrote to India's Commander-in-Chief, General Sir Hugh Rose, in 1862, he wanted a different army with a 'rivalry between regiments, so that Sikh might fire into Hindu, Goorkha into either, without any scruple. . . .'

The Peel Commission (under the British Secretary of State for War) recommended:

As we cannot do without a large Native army in India, our main object is to make that army safe; and next to the grand counterpoise of a sufficient European force, comes the counterpoise of Natives against Natives. At first sight, it might be thought that the best way to secure this would be to mix up all the available military races of India in each and every regiment, and to make them all General Service Corps. But excellent as this theory seems, it does not bear the test of practice. It is found that different races mixed together do not long preserve their distinctiveness. . . . To preserve that distinctiveness which is so valuable, and which, while it lasts, makes the Muhammadan of one country despise, fear or dislike the Muhammadan of another, corps should in future be provincial. . . . Let all races, Hindu or Muhammadan, of one province be enlisted in one regiment and no others, and having thus created distinctive regiments, let us keep them so against the hour of need. . . . By the system thus indicated, two great evils are avoided: firstly, that community of feeling throughout the Native Army, and that mischievous political activity and intrigue which results from association with other races and travel in other Indian provinces; and, secondly, that thorough discontent and alienation from the service which has undoubtedly sprung up since extended conquest has carried our Hindustani soldiers so far from their homes in India proper.

This logic resulted in the raising of segregated caste and class regiments, and in the transfer of the recruiting base of the Bengal Army from the Gangetic basin to the middle-caste peasants of the Punjab and Nepal who had fought on the British side against Indians during the rebellion of 1857. Sikhs and Gorkhas (and those who had remained neutral, such as Jats, Mahrattas and Rajputs) replaced the high-caste Hindus of Oudh, Hindustani Muslims and south Indian classes. As most of the former were middle-caste entrants and not of the warrior caste, a new term was devised for them: the 'martial races', a catch-all phrase that continues in vogue to the present time.

The Eden Commission of 1879, appointed under the Lieutenant-Governor of Bengal to examine the problems connected with forming a single army in India, stressed the continuing necessity of observing the 'great principle of *divide et impera*'. As a consequence, the recruitment systems in all three presidency armies were brought under the policy of 'pure caste' regiments, largely Punjabi. By the time the three armies were finally combined, in 1894, the Indian Army came to be composed of a disparate collection of one-class (or class-composed) tribal units. There was little possibility of an integrated national or even regional ethos evolving among those segregated groups of soldiery. Thus was it ensured that the sepoy army would remain firmly loyal to the British.

The Punjabisation of the army served yet another purpose. Recruitment from the unsophisticated (and mostly illiterate) middle-caste yeomen peasants of north India assured a greater social and cultural gap between the British officers and the Indian ranks than was evident in the old Bengal Army, where a degree of egalitarianism and intercultural exchange had existed. There was to be no return to the old camaraderie. The new relationship ensured not mutual respect but complete dependence of the sepoy on the British officer for his welfare, economic well-being and social status.

From these 'reforms' an army gradually emerged that was unique in character among contemporary armies. It was composed of strictly sectional groups – multi-partite and mutually contentious regiments – each possessed of a fierce personal loyalty that was something different from a political commitment. The Indian sepoy was ready to serve and lay down his life in battle, not so much for Britain or India or any abstract political cause as for his British officer, to whom he was tied by 'bonds of fidelity and devotion that was human and dog-like at the same time'. It was a society within a society (or, expressed pejoratively, a parasite on Indian society).

Just before the First World War, the theory of the loyal martial races received a considerable jolt. Political agitation for home rule had by then spread from Maharashtra and Bengal to the Punjab, where a marked feature was the large-scale participation of Sikhs. Through them the movement spread world-wide to Indians in South-east Asia, China, Canada and the United States.

In the early years of the twentieth century, large numbers of Punjabis had been driven out by widespread economic depression and had emigrated to oriental Asia and the west coasts of Canada and the United States. It was in these countries that the *ghadar* (revolutionary) movement was born. Inspired by the example of Japan's victory over Russia in 1905, emigrant Indians in Malaya, Siam, Singapore and Hong Kong – mainly Sikhs – organised themselves into revolutionary bodies headquartered in a *gurdwara* (Sikh temple) in Bangkok. The movement had attracted the attention of the Germans even before the start of the Great War and they set up an Indian Revolutionary Society in Berlin to supply the *ghadarites* with arms and equipment. Their aim was to foment anti-British uprisings in South-east Asia, which in turn would precipitate a general revolt in India. This was no flash-in-the-pan movement but an organised political drive with plans for a territorial attack on India. In the United States thousands of Indians volunteered as guerrilla fighters and large sums of money were collected for the cause. A 'provisional government of India' was set up in Kabul.

Fresh impetus for the *ghadarites* came in November 1915 with Britain's declaration of war against Turkey (and, thus, against the Caliphate). Many Muslims were induced to join the revolutionaries. In February 1915 the garrison battalion in Singapore, 5 Light Infantry, composed entirely of north Indian Muslims (Pathans and Punjabis), mutinied and killed all garrison officers (including their own) and local officials. This was part of a larger plan for a general uprising. It was put down only after Russian, Japanese and French warships came to Britain's rescue.

Meanwhile the *ghadarites* had also received setbacks. Immediately after the outbreak of war in August 1914 they hired a number of ships from Japan to transport revolutionaries to India. About five or six thousand landed in Calcutta and Madras with plans to stir up rebellion in every corner of the country, but it was an amateurish and over-ambitious attempt. The plans were betrayed to British-Indian intelligence and most of the *ghadarites* were rounded up at the two ports. When in 1917 the United States came into the war on the Allied side, the *ghadar* movement lost its main impetus.

Although these episodes were played down and even hushed up by the British, a temporary reversal of the army's recruiting policy became inevitable. Large numbers of men were thereafter enlisted from eastern and southern India and from low-caste communities such as the Mahars and Mazhabi (low-caste) Sikhs. The new system, however, did not long survive the end of the war. The British had too much invested in the Punjab to countenance an all-India army as a permanent measure. By the late 1920s wartime practices were discarded and recruitment was again made primarily from the 'martial races'. It was the Second World War that finally put an end to north India's near-monopoly of army service.

Between the two wars the Indian Army's strategic role had been considerably reduced and it figured low on Britain's priority list for mechanisation. Besides stationing a few battalions abroad for imperial policing duties, the Indian Army's main tasks were to keep the peace on the North-west Frontier and to maintain internal security. It was a limited horizon, but there was in the Army little military ambition or visionary urge to widen it. The largely amateurish, sports-oriented British (and Indian) officers and the semi-literate, rugged men of the so-called martial races were not the bedrock from which an inspiration for modernism and technological progress could flow. As late as in the second year of the Second World War the Indian Army still operated with horsed cavalry regiments and relied on mules and mule-carts for unit and station logistics. Only after the fall of France was it thought necessary to modernise the Indian Army for an imperial role.

As the army embarked on an expansion programme that was to convert a para-police force of 144,000 into a modern volunteer army two-and-a-half million strong, it became obvious that neither quantitatively nor qualitatively would the martial base suffice for wartime manpower requirements. The need to absorb new techniques and technology demanded a higher standard of education and a more progressive mental approach than the rugged men from the north could provide. Fortunately India had a liberal and progressive British officer as commander-in-chief. Field-Marshal Sir Claude Auchinleck opened recruitment to. the whole of India and took pains to attract new castes and classes with higher technological potential. Even in the fighting arms there was for the first time a notable influx from the east and the south. Regiments of infantry were raised from Assam, Bihar and other regions never before considered suitable as recruiting areas. There was even a regiment of Chamars, whose very untouchability was their most compulsive incentive to prove worthy of military service.

It is likely that after the war the British would again have reverted to their play-safe policy of recruiting from north India, but this time they were given neither the time nor the opportunity. After independence in 1947 Indian political leaders took an early decision to abolish recruitment by caste in all arms and services. Recruitment was thrown open to all Indians, but the policy could be only partially implemented because of strong opposition from many die-hard senior Indian officers to changes in class composition, particularly in the infantry and the armoured corps. Brainwashed by long years of service under British officers, they firmly believed in the efficacy of tribal *esprit de corps* and many were still convinced of the martial races theory.

If India had enjoyed a period of peace after independence it is possible that an integrated manpower policy would have been enforced by the government in all services. As it was, the war in Kashmir in 1947–8 and subsequent years of Indo-Pakistani hostility and Sino-Indian confrontation inhibited the government from enforcing radical changes in the organisation of the fighting arms. though other corps and services and all new raisings (such as the Parachute Regiment and new battalions in the Brigade of Guards) were constituted on a casteless, all-India basis. However, it is the fighting arms that are the cynosure of all eyes, and so the image (and, to an extent, the reality) remains: that the Indian Army still recruits mainly from middle-caste peasants of north India; and that it resists the mixing of castes and classes. The officer corps is of course recruited and posted on a secular, integrated basis, but the policy for the men still focuses on regional, racial and religious differences. This is the colonial legacy. Not only does this counteract the government's efforts at national integration, it inhibits serving soldiers by hedging them about with provincial and territorial prejudices – which were so evident during the deployments in Assam and the North East Frontier Administration in the 1960s.

Class observance in recruiting other ranks was not the only manifestation of separatism in the pre-independence army. From the regional grouping of sepoys the policy spread to the racial grouping of officers. In the period between the two world wars, when Indians were at last granted King's Commissions, Britain's Indianisation policy in the army eventually led to institutionalised racial segregation of British and Indian officers. Unlike the civilian services, in which there was a degree of social and cultural interaction between British and Indian members, in the army officers of the two races lived and worked in virtual isolation from each other. Even within the narrow confines of cantonment society, British and Indian officers rarely met and there were few friendships. More remarkably, even professional association was minimal.

For one who had been to school and college in England, where there was little racial discrimination in those days, joining one's regiment in India came as something of a culture shock. Images of the past have since softened, and the waves of sentimental *raj* nostalgia that swept through Britain in the 1970s and 1980s have created myths about Indo-British co-partnership. The stark truth is that British officers (collectively and individually) held their Indian 'colleagues' in racial contempt and pushed the policy of officer-duality almost to the limit.

Racial discrimination in officer ranks was a fairly recent phenomenon and could well have stemmed from career insecurity (the fear of being replaced by Indians after two centuries of prescriptive privileges and rights). When the

East India Company's native armies were first raised, battalions were officered by 'native commandants' and other Indian officers, the British commandant serving mainly in a training and supervisory capacity. In those days there was general recognition of the Indian as a product of an ancient culture, and his way of life was freely adopted by the British traders of the East India Company (whence the term 'Nabob'). Subsequently, after the passing of the Evangelical Act in Britain (1803) and the influx of missionaries to India, the same Indian began to be regarded as an inferior being, a 'bloody heathen'. The born-again Christian zeal of the early Victorian era, the advent of the *memsahibs* on the scene and, finally, the rebellion of 1857 all combined to put an end to any semblance of acceptance of Indians as equals. The Indian Army was transformed from an inter-racial association to a dependency of illiterate peasant soldiers. As a cardinal principle of that system, no Indian was allowed to intervene between the British officer and his devoted vassal, not even the Indian officer of Viceroy's commissioned rank (*subedar* or *jemadar*). Although the latter held a gazetted commission, he was in fact little more than an elderly peasant-ranker, respected and cosseted but not regarded as an interloper, because the sum total of his interest and experience lay within the confines of the unit. His limited education and power of command provided no threat to the British officers' need to represent absolute authority.

Although during the nineteenth century several recommendations were made by eminent Britons to open the officer ranks of the army to Indians, it was not until just before the First World War that King's Commissions were granted to Indians, but limited to medical officers and to a handful of 'Indian gentlemen' from the Imperial Cadet Corps, mainly princelings from the native states. (The latter were granted a limited form of King's Commission for service in 'His Majesty's Native Indian Land Forces'.) At the same time, as a reward for the sacrifices made by Indian soldiers in fighting Britain's war in Europe, Africa and the Middle East, promises were made that regular King's Commissions to Indians would be granted after the war, a pledge that was not immediately honoured. Eventually, a few cadets were sent to the Royal Military Academy, Sandhurst, and a number of commissions were granted to graduates of the Cadet College, Indore. Unfortunately, officers from the Indore intake did not create a favourable impression. The selection procedure had been lax; besides, many were unhappy with or unsuitable for regimental life in the unyielding westernised ambience of British cantonments. Although the Indore cadets produced one president (Iskandar Mirza of Pakistan) and one commander-in-chief (Field-Marshal Cariappa), only a few others survived.

Indianisation was seriously considered only after India's political leaders began to apply pressure on the government to grant more regular commissions to Indians. Following a resolution passed by the Legislative Assembly, a military committee set up under Commander-in-Chief Rawlinson agreed to begin Indianisation in earnest, with the professed aim of eventually replacing all British officers with Indians. The number of Indian entrants to Sandhurst was increased, though not by much. It was also decided that a military academy on the lines of Sandhurst would be established in India to increase the flow of Indian officers into the army. It was these measures that first alerted the British officer cadre to the fact that their careers were under threat, and from then on every effort was made to contain (if not thwart) the Indianisation process.

The first insidious step was to isolate the Indians. They were uprooted from their former regiments and allotted to six selected infantry and two cavalry units earmarked for Indianisation. At the second stage (mid-1930s), when increased numbers of Indians were expected to join the army following the opening of the Indian Military Academy, six other units were added to the Indianised list; the fear soon grew that even these new units would eventually be filled up and more and more regiments would require to be Indianised. (Some die-hard in General Headquarters calculated that in forty-two years all the regiments would be Indianised and the British would have nowhere to go!)

The obvious alternative was never contemplated because that would eventually lead to British officers having to serve under Indians, and the very idea of this was by then abhorrent. GHQ produced a wily solution: newly joining

Indian officers would be appointed not to rifle companies but to command platoons in their battalions and thus replace Viceroy's Commissioned Officers (VCOs). (King's Commissioned Officers in the Indian Army joined directly as company officers.) The plot resulted in a threefold increase in the officer holdings of Indianised units and thus slowed down the pace of replacement of British officers in the army. GHQ beguiled Indian political leaders by the specious argument that the proposal for officers to command platoons would increase the efficiency of Indianised battalions and bring them up to the level of British regiments (in which platoons were commanded by officers). It was not explained why, also in the interests of military efficiency, a similar reform was not enforced in the British-officered battalions.

British generals of the Indian Army were not perceptive enough to foresee the potential corrosiveness of the racial policy of Indianisation. It was one thing to segregate the *men* into caste and regional groups – the British officers remained the all-important link that effectively knit the different groups together. The racial separation of *officers* held a different connotation altogether: British officers themselves became a part of the isolating process. They were painting themselves into a corner.

A lone voice among the senior British officers that resisted the Indianisation fiasco was that of (then) Major General Claude Auchinleck. His evidence to various committees always refuted the wisdom of the policy of segregation but, in the face of its almost total acceptance by a dim-sighted GHQ at Delhi, he found himself unable to stem the tide of prejudice.

By limiting the yearly officer intake from the Indian Military Academy to only twenty-five or thirty, Indianisation was deliberately kept a slow process. Even so, if the war had not intervened, the proportion of Indian officers to British would have been sufficiently large by the end of the 1940s for the divisiveness in the officering system to have become a serious problem. It was the Second World War that saved the Indian Army from that misfortune.

First, war-expansion raisings created a demand for more and more regular officers to be posted to new units. No longer could large numbers of trained Indians be kept bottled up in unit ghettoes. By mid-1940 they were being sent out of Indianised units to become adjutants and quartermasters in newly raising battalions. Second, a large number of young Englishmen, fresh from schools and colleges in England and unburdened by colonial inhibitions, came out to India as Emergency Commissioned Officers (ECOs) to fill the gaps in junior ranks. It was they with whom the Indian officers, particularly the younger ones, began to establish easy, relaxed friendships. They came to our homes, ate our types of food, listened to our music – none of which had happened before. (In pre-war Indian Army messes, the only concession to Indian culture was the Sunday morning curry lunch.)

Meanwhile, as thousands of Indians were granted emergency commissions, the proportion of Indians to British in the army increased greatly. Although senior command and key staff appointments were still preserved as a total monopoly of the British, in many fighting units Indian officers equalled or overtook the British in numbers. British officers, regular and emergency, served under Indians, in home stations as well as in active operations, and there were no problems. The smoothness with which the change from Indianisation to an emancipated officer system took place can in large measure be attributed to the cathartic role unconsciously played by the wartime amateur officers from Britain. It was association and rapport with the British ECOs that slowly made many Indian officers think of Britain's war as theirs, of Britain's enemies as theirs, of a British victory as theirs. It would not be an exaggeration to say that before the arrival of the ECOs many Indian officers had regarded British officers as no less hostile than an unknown and abstract enemy from Italy or Germany. Indian prisoners-of-war in Malaya who joined Subhas Chandra Bose's Indian National Army to take up arms against the king-emperor could regard their defection not as treason but as a gesture of rebellion against British injustices. Such was the legacy of the racial discrimination the British called Indianisation.

Much would have been forgiven if the British had given even a handful of senior Indian officers the training and experience necessary to prepare them for the responsibilities they would have to bear at independence; but British officers possessed neither the resolve nor always the competence to fulfil this obligation.

Before the war Indians had proved their capability as regimental officers, but GHQ appointed very few to command or other key posts. Even during the latter part of the war, when senior Indians from Sandhurst had twenty or more years of service, none except the lone brigade commander in Burma (Thimayya) was given an opportunity to acquire command or managerial skills at levels higher than regimental.

Nor was the professionalism of the pre-war British officers of such a calibre that Indians could learn from them by precept and association. Their qualities of leadership (courage, reliability, fair play) were undeniable. But pre-eminent in their make-up was a disdain for professionalism – 'shop', they called it, with an amateur's sneer for the 'pro'. They drew their inspiration not from professional zeal but from the social and academic affectations of their upper-middle-class, public school upbringing. While in service, one could learn as much or as little of professional or technical matters as one liked. Opportunities for not learning were considerable, while those for learning were difficult to find and not always encouraged. The over-eager and the intellectual were suspect. A handicap at polo or a place in the regimental hockey team had a higher rating than a proclivity for professional study. There were regiments that openly boasted that they never sent their officers to Staff College.

Since many senior pre-war Indians adopted this British characteristic, their attitudes were an additional obstacle to professional competence. Younger graduates from the Indian Military Academy were better trained and more professionally zealous than their seniors from Sandhurst, but even they often found it more congenial to fall in line with their seniors. When independence came, senior Indians, with only a few exceptions, proved unqualified to provide the vision and the comprehension needed to fashion a new ethos for the military arm of free India. Adherence to the old order was ingrained in the pre-independence officer cadre.

The retarded development of Indian generalship after

independence cannot be entirely explained away by the lack of experience of senior Indian officers. There have been other breakaway armies in history, but in none has there been such a marked reluctance either to evolve an empirical, indigenous philosophy of warfare or to introduce orthodox precepts of military science. No zeal or momentum appears to have impelled the officers left over from the *raj*. Clearly the seniors among them preferred to perpetuate British affectations of amateurism; their criteria for generalship were confined to a flair for leadership and battlefield panache.

Nor did they encourage their juniors to acquire professional knowledge. On the contrary, officers who studied or wrote about professional subjects were dubbed 'theoretical' – as though theory were something that must be avoided in the pursuit of practice. It is not surprising, in these circumstances, that the first trial in the field, the Kashmir war of 1947–8, was fought more as a series of lieutenant-colonels' battles than by strategic perception or management of force balances. The approach to war was reactive and mechanical – an *à la carte* method of weapons and deployments, with no overview of defence policy and strategic doctrine based on national and international potentialities.

The inspiration could have come from the politicians, but that did not happen either. The freedom struggle had not provided even the giants among them with a comprehensive grasp of the role of the military in government. Although a few had interested themselves in defence matters, their concerns focused mainly on mechanical aspects such as budget-cutting to reduce military expenditure, reforms in recruiting systems, demands for Indianisation and like matters. There was little consciousness of the need to dovetail the military into the governmental system, or of the full potential of militarism in statecraft and the need to develop military power as a lever of state.

The only pre-war Indian political· leader who had understood the significance of armed power as a concomitant of modern politics was Subhas Chandra Bose. It was partly for that reason that Gandhi, in 1938, had him manoeuvred out of the presidency of the Congress Party and thus ensured the succession of the more pliant Nehru. Had Bose remained at the head of the Congress, in all probability he would have been a strong contender for the post of prime minister in 1947. If that had happened Bose could well have provided the necessary afflatus for a reconstruction of the Indian armed forces as an integrated military instrument identified with and welded into the governmental system. Also, it is unlikely that in December 1948 he would have thrown away India's chances of forcing a decision on the Kishenganga-Jhelum riverline – as did Nehru when, against the advice of his field commanders, he stopped the fighting in Kashmir and naively appealed to the UN.

Nehru the international idealist rejected the notion of militarism as a desirable or even necessary instrument in the promotion of a national movement. Moral force, disarmament, *panchsheel*, non-alignment, these were the ingredients of the Nehru formula, not military power. As early as 1928, in a presidential address to the Kerala Provincial Conference of the Congress Party, he had spelled out his international assessments: 'No danger threatens India from any direction; and even if there is any danger we shall cope with it [politically].' He justified his views in simplistic terms: Western European powers like Germany, France and Italy were 'too far away for effective action', Japan was preoccupied with the USA, and the danger from Russia was 'largely imaginary'. He concluded that an independent India, once weaned from British imperial policy, would occupy a favourable position in the world, secure from the threat of invasion.

Immediately following partition in 1947, Nehru continued to ignore military considerations in dealing with political issues. The British General Sir Rob Lockhart, first Commander-in-Chief of free India's armed forces, was left in no doubt by his Prime Minister when he went to him with a Defence Paper, asking for a formal policy directive on defence. Nehru glanced through Lockhart's paper but was not in the least amused. 'Rubbish! Total rubbish!', the Prime Minister exploded (according to Lockhart). 'We don't need a defence policy. Our policy is *ahimsa* (non-violence). We foresee no military threats. As far as I am concerned you can scrap the army – the police are good enough to meet our security needs'.[3]

Perhaps Nehru nursed a lurking suspicion about the

potential of the military mind to subvert rational policy. It is likely that the political indoctrination of Nehru and his contemporaries was excessively influenced by the prolonged and unseemly clash between Viceroy Curzon and Commander-in-Chief Kitchener at the turn of the century, a clash from which the military gained constitutional ascendancy. This could have been the reason for Nehru's desire to downgrade the military potential rather than to assimilate it into the machinery of government.

It is true that Nehru was not greatly impressed by the majority of senior Indian officers whom, with good reason, he regarded as shallow, westernised and British-aping products of the *raj*, who had taken little interest and no part in the freedom movement. Subsequently, as armies of newly independent nations all around him fell prey to military ambitions, he and some of his cabinet colleagues began to view the Indian Army and its leaders with alarm and suspicion. Without any justification, a deep-rooted paranoia plagued Indian politicians. A number of mindless measures were taken to downgrade the status and influence of the army, and in particular of the generals. That insecurity persists today, and one illogical consequence is that the army is still kept at a distance from policy-making councils of government. Neither Nehru's daughter nor his grandson were perceptive enough to close the gap between the politicians and the military. They failed to fashion a governmental organisation that could overlay colonial procedures and break out of the shell of a restrictive past. The military continues to be kept at a distance. Consultation with the General Staff is not considered a prerequisite of political decision-making today any more than it was at independence.

## NOTES

1. The term signified the declared policy of the gradual replacement of British officers by Indians.
2. Strictly speaking it was the French who first recruited sepoy forces but their experiment, although successful, was short-lived.
3. From the unpublished reminiscences of Major General A.A. Rudra, Military Secretary at Army HQ after partition and a close friend of General Lockhart.

# 2
# THE HIGH FRONTIERS

The Central Asian landmass is a vast high-montane wilderness which geographically links three ancient civilisations. It is also the greatest physical obstacle in the world outside the polar ice-caps. Extensive areas of it are uninhabited, barren and desolate, visited only occasionally by nomadic graziers. In such a region space does not have a grudging quality. The nations that share it have lived as neighbours for thousands of years without being obsessed with defined borders or a compelled to demarcate their territorial extent. For the ancient Hindus of India it was sufficient to know that the great range of Himalay, revered as the throne of the gods, was the eternal barrier that enclosed them to the south while excluding all else to the north. Traders and religious travellers who voyaged across the high ranges sometimes marked the crossings – a prayer-flag here, a cairn there, at places a rude shelter of gathered flints – but the towering presence of Himalay (the Abode of Snow) pre-empted any doubts about where India's marches ran.

It was not until the mid-nineteenth century, when the expanding empire created by Britain's East India Company reached the Himalayan frontier,[1] that the necessity arose to determine precise borders, particularly in the north-west, where the imperial interests of Britain and Russia clashed, beyond Himalay, among the high Pamirs.

Russian expansion in Central Asia began in the mid-eighteenth century. By 1865 the Tsar's armies had captured Tashkent and Samarkand, reached the borders of Afghanistan and begun to feel their way towards the Pamirs. Britain's interests in the region began in 1846, when the Treaty of Amritsar was signed whereby the British-Indian government agreed to transfer Kashmir from the territories of the Sikh kingdom in the Punjab to Maharaja Gulab Singh. At the same time it arrogated responsibility for the security of the new state, an obligation that brought Kashmir's claimed northern and eastern boundaries (with Sinkiang and Tibet) under Britain's control for the first time. Of the two borders it was the former that was seen to be crucial, because of the perceived threat of Tsarist expansion towards Chinese Sinkiang and the trans-Karakoram territories.

Boundary commissions were set up by the British-Indian government to define Kashmir's borders with Sinkiang and Tibet, but the task proved intractable because the Chinese, uncertain how far south their territory extended, became evasive whenever invited to discuss border matters with a commission. Maps of the area were virtually non-existent; Chinese cartography was primitive; large parts of the frontier were uninhabited, and, to compound matters, a distinction was seen to exist between demographic control and territorial possession. (For instance, the Chinese claim of overlordship of nomadic tribes such as the Kirghiz did not necessarily accord them rights over territory the wandering graziers happened to be in at any given time.)

The traditional northern border of Kashmir was regarded as lying along the Mustagh-Karakoram range, extending eastward to the Karakoram pass (5,645 metres or 18,400 feet). From there the range takes a sharp turn south-east and thereafter forms the divide between the Aksai Chin and Ladakh. It is at this point that the extent of the Maharaja's domains, both northwards and eastwards, raised doubts and has been a matter of claim and counter-claim from the mid-nineteenth century to the present day.

Unlike Great Himalay, the Karakoram range constitutes a genuine watershed between the Indic and Central Asian river systems and eminently qualifies as a natural boundary.

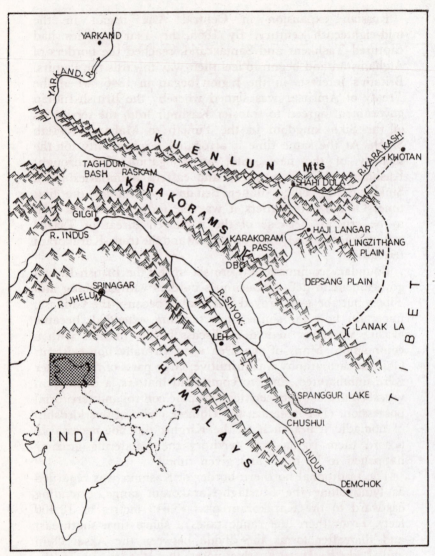

Kuenlun, Karakoram and Himalayan ranges

The difficulty was that after the capture of Ladakh by Maharaja Gulab Singh in 1842 (when he was governor of Kashmir under the Sikhs) Kashmiri forces had advanced beyond the Karakorams and crossed the Karakash valley to the southern slopes of the Kuen Lun mountains to occupy Shahidula, an important staging post on the Leh-Yarkand trade route. The Chinese, preoccupied with a Muslim rebellion in Sinkiang, had not protested. In 1863, the Muslims threw the Chinese out of Shahidula and during the ensuing decade and a half of Muslim rule, they and the British tacitly accepted the Kuen Lun range as the boundary between them. In 1878, even the Chinese, when they returned to re-establish their New Dominion in Sinkiang, declared that they had 'no concern with what lay beyond the [Kuen Lun] mountains'. Accordingly, they kept their customs post located to the north of Shahidula. Unfortunately the government in Calcutta took no steps to ensure that a commonly accepted border was ratified, content to treat the area between the two ranges as a sort of no-man's-land.

At about that time British opinion on the border question began to be divided. One school of thought, strongly influenced by Ney Elias, Joint Commissioner at Leh and an authority on trans-Karakoram territories, reverted to the watershed theory. He recommended to the government in Calcutta that in order to avoid a possible dispute with China, the Maharaja of Kashmir be prohibited from reoccupying Shahidula. He argued that as it was nearly 400 km from Leh, with five major passes on the way, it could not be effectively defended. In 1885, the government accordingly advised the Maharaja not to re-establish his outpost. The other school of thought (advocates of what might be termed a 'forward policy') argued that Shahidula was not merely Kashmir's problem; its occupation was necessary as an imperial strategic move to form a co-terminous border with the New Dominion of China and thus present a joint front to a possible Russian advance into the Yarkand-Karakash valleys across the Little Pamir. Unfortunately a vacillating Foreign Department at Simla brushed the problem aside without taking a decision, thus losing a golden opportunity of arriving at an agreed border.

The Chinese put an end to the vacillation by a series

of bold *démarches*. In the winter of 1890 they occupied Shahidula. The only reaction of the Foreign Department to this unexpected incursion was one of passive acceptance. In a despatch to the Secretary of State for India in Whitehall, it stated: 'We are inclined to think that the wisest course would be to leave them in possession . . . it is evidently to our advantage that the tract of territory intervening between the Karakoram and Kuen Lun mountains should be definitely held by a friendly power like China.' The British were building their security on China's assumed friendship, though the latter had given no evidence of any such accommodation. On the contrary, two years later they took advantage of Britain's lack of protest to move down further, to the Karakoram pass, and erect a boundary mark which proclaimed that the territory was 'under the sway of the Khakan, the Chinese emperor'. Again the Chinese *démarche* went unchallenged: the Government of India advised its Resident in Kashmir that it saw 'no occasion to remonstrate with the Chinese government on account of the erection of these boundary marks'. Although the note contained a rider to the effect that such boundary marks would not be regarded as 'having any international value' unless they have been erected with the concurrence of both powers', in effect the British had, through their diplomatic ineptitude, virtually acquiesced in China's claim that all territory north of the Karakorams was theirs – *without being required to acknowledge that everything south and west was Kashmir's*.

Britain's remissness resulted in the surrender of the Karakash valley without any reciprocal concession from the Chinese. Nor was it any different further westwards, along the Mustagh range (which is in effect an extension of the Karakorams). At the point where the Taghdumbash Pamir slopes into the Yarkand valley (through which now runs the China-Pakistan Karakoram Highway) an area north of the range had long been claimed by the Mir of Hunza, a dependent state of Kashmir, by virtue of tributes and taxes paid by the Kirghiz tribesmen of the valley to the Mir. Further east along the valley is an area known as Raskam, where the Mir also claimed territorial rights, based on occupation, cultivation and grazing rights for more than a hundred years.[2]

The argument over Hunza's trans-Karakoram territorial claims moved from Calcutta to Whitehall to Peking, and finally to the Russian capital at St Petersburg, but in the end the British again gave in. Pusillanimously Curzon, the Viceroy, minuted on the file: 'While on the one hand it is desirable to get the Kanjuts [Hunza] into Raskam in order to keep the Russians out, on the other hand, should the latter seize Kashgar, they may claim Hunza as a subject state.' In 1899 the Government of India yielded Hunza's territorial rights in Raskam (as it had done in Taghdumbash a year or two earlier).

The British had surrendered Hunza's rights without obtaining even the smallest concession from the Chinese on any of the disputes between the Pamirs in the west and the Ladakh-Tibetan border at Demchok in the south-east. Of the three powers involved, the Chinese were by far the weakest, but they conducted negotiations with considerable diplomatic sophistication, playing off Britain against Russia and deriving every advantage without conceding a single point.

One would have imagined that Kashmir's south-eastern border with Tibet would have been more easily negotiable, but here also there were considerable obstacles to an agreement, the main one being that the Tibetans, like the Chinese, kept asserting that boundaries already existed – 'fixed of old' – and there was no need to negotiate new ones. Who can blame them? To them a boundary was not a matter of trijunctions, or longitudes and latitudes, or boundary posts on barren hillsides, but traditional crossing points from one allegiance to another, crossings that could sometimes claim seasonal alternatives, loosely interpretable by individual travellers.

The boundary commissions appointed by the British after the handover of Kashmir to Maharaja Gulab Singh did arrive at fairly definite conclusions in the inhabited Indus valley sector in the south-east, but the conclusions were unilateral because the Tibetan governor at Gartok would not be drawn into negotiations. He pleaded that he was empowered neither to allow members of the commission into Tibetan territory nor to conduct border talks with them, on pain of death. In the circumstances, the best the commissioners could do was to try to identify places, particularly in inhabited areas, which were customarily recognised as trading or crossing points between contiguous Tibetan and Ladakhi districts. Clearly, a series of such points supported by geographical or scientific evidence would provide an indication of a mutually acceptable alignment which might eventually be recognised as an international border. With this aim in mind, the Great Trigonometrical Survey of India, one of the most ambitious scientific projects undertaken anywhere during the nineteenth century, launched its operations along the high frontiers. A whole generation of young British explorers and surveyors criss-crossed the desolate mountains and plateaux on the 'roof of the world' to help fill gaps in geographical knowledge.

Boundary Commissioner Vans Agnew and his assistant, Captain Alexander Cunningham, were among the pioneers. Agnew's proposal for the boundary was eventually the most westerly of the many variants. It linked Chushul, Demchok and Lanak-la (at the head of Changchenmo valley). Northwards it was assumed that the border ran along the general line of the Karakoram range and included the valleys of the Shyok, Galwan and Chip Chap rivers, to Karakoram pass. Agnew's delineation was the first attempt to define the north-eastern boundary of Kashmir by a responsible officer of the Government of India. At this point, however, an unexpected complication intervened: the Aksai Chin or the White Desert, the unexplored and forbidding desolation that stretches eastwards from the Ladakhi Karakorams.

One of the surveyors who had pioneered mapping operations in Kashmir in the mid-1850s was a junior civilian sub-assistant named W.H. Johnson. Since the whole substance of India's title to the Aksai Chin derives from Johnson's claim on behalf of Kashmir, it is necessary to inquire into his character and circumstances. Johnson was a positive, determined and energetic surveyor with a deal of initiative; yet, being Indian-born (the son of a sub-contractor), he would have been considered by the British to be of inferior status, a permanent under-dog. He could not in those days aspire either to commissioned rank or to high civilian status in the Survey Department. It is not unlikely therefore that he was a disgruntled official on the look-out for ways to improve his prospects outside his chosen line, for instance, under the Kashmir *durbar*, which had treated him kindly (and which eventually employed him in an exalted rank).

The turmoil in Khotan following the eviction of the Chinese by the Muslims in 1863 had provided Maharaja Ranjit Singh of Kashmir with an opportunity of sending troops to the Kuen Lun to occupy Shahidula. At that time Johnson happened to be in Leh, where the Governor (Wazir) Mehta Mangal was the person entrusted with arranging frontier operations. Johnson had previously crossed the Kuen Lun range and visited Shahidula. He must have noted the difficulty of maintaining Kashmiri control of Shahidula, given the difficult Karakoram pass that separated it from the rest of Kashmir. It is likely that after logistical difficulties compelled Mehta Mangal to withdraw the Kashmiri garrison from Shahidula, he and Johnson discussed the matter to find a solution to the problem of maintaining a Kashmiri garrison in the Karakash valley.

That, of course, can only remain conjecture, but it is substantiated by the circumstances attending Johnson's subsequent expedition to Khotan and the benefits that accrued to the Maharaja, derived from Johnson's extravagant claim on his behalf.

In Leh, Johnson gave out that his fame as an explorer had earned him an invitation from the Khan of Khotan. If nobody else believed him at least the Governor of Leh did, for he promptly set up an expedition for Johnson, providing him with his requirement of porters and pack animals and even a lone escort from the Maharaja's army, help never before offered to a British surveyor. Johnson started his voyage up the Changchenmo valley, but instead of taking the normal route (Nischu, Lingzhithang, Kizil Jilga, Karakash valley to Shahidula) he veered eastwards, crossed the bleak and uninhabited wilderness vaguely known as the Aksai Chin, and thence northwards by a little-known route across the Kuen Lun to Khotan, where the Khan received him kindly and treated him generously. On his return from Khotan, Johnson prepared a map of the area bounded by Khotan in the north, the Changchenmo valley in the south, the Karakoram range in the west and Tibet's Changthang plateau in the east. He claimed the entire area as part of the Maharaja of Kashmir's province of Ladakh.

There was much controversy about every aspect of Johnson's geographical and other claims. He had completed the journey to Khotan in such a hurry (travelling at an average of 30 km a day, without a halt: an astounding achievement) that he could have spared little time for survey work. His superiors at the Survey of India criticised his map harshly and eventually re-drew it from information available in their own records. It was also alleged that Johnson had misappropriated a consignment of silver ingots the Khan had sent as gifts to 'the Lord Sahib' in India. Johnson himself made contradictory statements about the circumstances of his expedition and, all in all, seems to have become a considerable embarrassment to his superiors. He was passed over for promotion, whereupon he resigned and took service with the Kashmiri Maharaja, where eventually he rose in rank to become governor of Leh – a not inconsiderable recompense for the legacy he left for the state: a British surveyor's claim on its behalf to an extra 18,000 sq km of uninhabited territory. The interesting point is that though the British regarded Johnson's claim with scepticism, their policy at the time was to be accommodating to the Kashmiri ruler. Hence in most of the maps they produced during that period (as also in a published atlas) the Aksai Chin, including the whole Karakash basin, is depicted as part of the Maharaja's domain.

Aksai Chin is loosely used as a geographical term. In its extended interpretation it includes the whole of the vast and lofty wilderness enclosed by the Kuen Lun mountains in the north and the Changchenmo range in the south, and by the Karakorams in the west and Tibet's Changthang plateau is the east. It is a high-altitude geographical oddity, a piece of ocean-bed heaved skywards as the continents clashed and folded in the mesozoic age, forming a lacustrine desert at an average altitude of 5,300 metres (17,200 feet). It is one of the most desolate places on earth, a vast howling wilderness with no form of support for human or animal existence.

As the Sino-Indian war of 1962 was fought largely over disputes arising out of claims of ownership of this windswept desolation, it would be interesting to make a more detailed

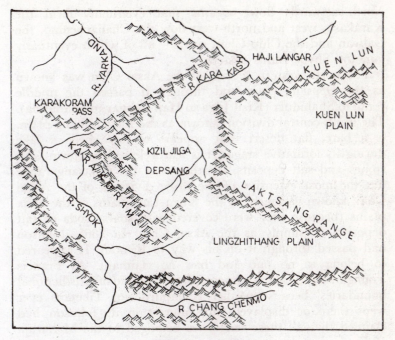

The Aksai Chin

examination of its geographical characteristics. Johnson in his hurried dash to Khotan had made only a cursory record of its main features. It was Frederic Drew (Governor of Leh in 1870–1) who first prepared a detailed map of the Aksai Chin and highlighted aspects of its geographical features that have a bearing on subsequent claims and disputes.

Drew's map was based on his own explorations as well as those of Hayward, Shaw, Forsyth and others. According to him the high-altitude plateau east of the Karakoram range was divided into three distinct parts by a low mountain range known as the Laktsang mountains. This range connects the Kuen Lun with the Karakorams and also sends an offshoot south-eastwards towards Lanak-la. Although the Laktsang mountains rise barely 100 metres above the plateau, in Shaw's opinion they constituted the true watershed between the Indus and the Central Asian river systems.

North-eastwards flow streams that eventually form the Karakash; west and north-west flow the Changchenmo, the Galwan and the Chip Chap rivers – all of which eventually join the Shyok-Indus system.

The north-western section of the Aksai Chin was known as the Depsang plain and through it passed the middle route to Shahidula (Kizil Jilga to Haji Langar to Shahidula). The south-central division, known as the Lingzhithang plain, is a bare, flat desert that appears to have been a lake during its formative stage. It is featureless and strewn with stones and salt deposits. North-east of the Laktsang range lies the most extensive of the three divisions of the Aksai Chin, known variously as the Kuen Lun plains or the Soda plains (because they were covered with coarse soda or salt deposits) or simply as the Aksai Chin. In 1865, Johnson had passed through it on his way to Khotan. It appeared to belong to no one and had no claimant. As Francis Younghusband said, it was completely 'devoid of jurisdictional boundaries' because neither Kashmiris nor Tibetans ever went there or displayed any interest in it. Johnson had claimed that all these territories belonged to the Maharaja of Kashmir.

During the next four decades the British depicted the northern and north-eastern borders of Kashmir differently at different times, the line being pushed backwards or forwards according to the degree of perceived threat from Russia. Most often it was the Johnson line, with its extravagant claim right up to the Kuen Lun range and beyond, that was shown on British maps. The Chinese at that time evinced little interest about the border with Kashmir (other than their move down to the Karakoram pass in 1890–2) or about the Aksai Chin.

In 1898 a determined effort was made to come to an agreement with China regarding Kashmir's borders. Viceroy Elgin sent a despatch to Whitehall incorporating India's first comprehensive boundary proposal for the north-western border. The suggested line followed the watershed principle and included the Lingzhithang plain as part of Kashmir; but thereafter it kept west of the Depsang plain to the Karakoram pass and thence went westwards to the Mustagh. Elgin's despatch also suggested that Britain would be willing to surrender Kashmir's rights to the pasturages and tillages in the Yarkand valley if the Chinese dropped their 'shadowy' claim on Hunza. Elgin's line specifically abandoned the Johnson claim, making no attempt to include the empty quarter of north-eastern Aksai Chin, even though such a claim would have posed no problem at that time.

While Elgin's despatch was still under consideration, the War Office in London took a hand in the matter. A memorandum prepared by General Ardagh, Director of Military Intelligence, entitled *The Northern Frontier of India from the Pamirs to Tibet*, totally refuted the watershed principle and advocated a blatantly predatory policy. Decrying any tendency to rely on China as an effective ally in the Great Game, Ardagh recommended that Britain's border in north India be pushed beyond the watershed to include the Yarkand and Karakash valleys, in order to 'retain within our territory the approaches to them on the northern side and the lateral communications between these approaches'. He suggested that this would best be achieved by establishing 'our supremacy and protection [over] the chief of the local tribes, and to assert it by acts of sovereignty . . . and in this manner acquire a title by prescription'. In blunt terms, he wanted first to subjugate the tribals and then use demographic control as a lever to claim territorial possession, thus going further than the Chinese counter-claims. Fantastic as it may seem, he even suggested that this principle 'be applied at a future period to the upper basins of the Indus, the Sutlej and even the Brahmaputra, in the event of a prospective absorption of Tibet by Russia', implying that to forestall a Russian advance into Tibet, Britain should move across the Himalayan range and occupy Gartok, Shigatse and, inevitably, Lhasa!

No one in India supported Ardagh's proposal, so the British minister at Peking was given the go-ahead to present the Elgin proposal to the Chinese government. In March 1899, the first definite boundary proposal (the Elgin proposal) was made by the British to the Chinese, who never bothered to acknowledge it.

The Ardagh proposal did not, however, die a natural death. It long remained a latent inspiration for 'forward policy' hawks, who soon found a champion in the new

Viceroy when Curzon took over from Elgin. As a celebrated explorer of Central Asia and a prominent Russophobe, Curzon threw all the weight of his not inconsiderable prestige behind an aggressive policy, particularly along the Mustagh-Karakoram section, where he was in total disagreement with Elgin's proposal to relinquish Hunza's rights in Taghdumbash and Raskam. In March 1904 he recommended to the British government that the Mir should disavow all relations with China 'and henceforth own suzerainty to Kashmir and the British Government'. In the process Hunza's rights in the Yarkand valley would be restored and, in fact, the areas claimed as a part of Kashmir.

Another hawkish period followed the collapse of the Manchu regime in 1911. Hardinge was the Viceroy. He feared that in the circumstances of Chinese weakness then prevailing, there would be nothing to stop the Russians occupying Sinkiang and other Chinese territories. He therefore suggested reverting to the Ardagh strategy and occupying the Yarkand valley. His recommendation remained under consideration at India Office in London for several years; in Delhi the idea lingered on in official circles long afterwards.

The collapse of the Tsarist regime in 1917 all but removed the threat of Russian invasion, and concern about the north-western border lost its strategic urgency. By the time the British left India in 1947 they still had not decided which lines to select as the northern and western boundaries of Kashmir. Their withdrawal from the sub-continent was unduly hurried and they failed to leave for their successor governments a precise definition of the extent of the territories they had inherited. India and Pakistan found themselves at liberty to delimit their own outer boundaries. In India's case the task extended to nearly 3,000 km of undecided border from the high Pamirs to the Burmese frontier. If the British had made even a suggestion that Kashmir's boundary should follow the only formal proposal ever to have been made to the Chinese government (in 1899 – that is, along the Mustagh-Karakoram-Laktsang line, including the Lingzhithang plain but not the north-eastern Aksai Chin) at that juncture it would have certainly been accepted by the Nehru government. This would have placed the strategic road subsequently built by the Chinese in the

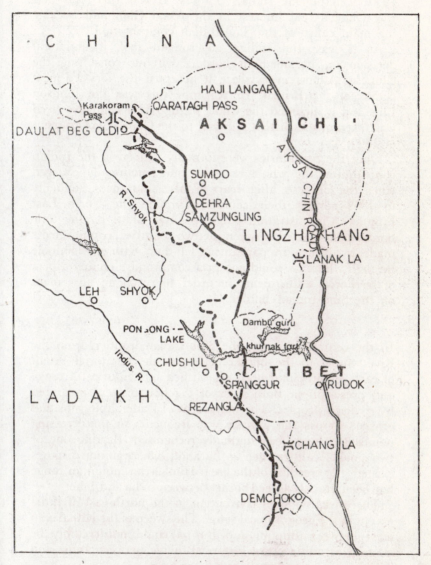

Ladakh and Aksai Chin

1950s well outside India's borders. It was this road that was China's real interest in the Aksai Chin and became the main cause of the Sino-Indian confrontation.

As it was, the Indian government took a unilateral decision on its northern borders without consulting the Chinese. Almost everywhere it accepted the forward-most claims of the British. In Kashmir this was the Johnson Line and it included the whole of the Aksai Chin. No heed was taken of the British proposal to the Chinese government of 1899.

Once the boundaries were formally defined in the Indian constitution, the whole issue became emotionally charged when the Chinese, after years of false assurances, suddenly in 1959 sprang their counter-claims in the North East Frontier Administration and the Aksai Chin. By the time border talks started between the two countries, commitments made by Nehru in parliament left him with no loophole through which he could accept a compromise on any aspect of territorial adjustments in order to reach an agreement on the Sino-Indian border.

In the central sector of the Sino-Indian frontier, from the River Sutlej to the border of Nepal, the territorial extent of each country had been established by centuries of usage and prescription. Both sides of the border were inhabited by civilised peoples. The movement of traders, pilgrims and graziers across the frontier was frequent, so that crossing points had long been mutually recognised. Barring one or two small localities such as Barahoti, where minor disputes existed, the crestline of the great Himalayan mountain range had been a tacitly agreed border between India and Tibet.

There was no such convention in the north-east of India except in the geographical sense. The sweep of the Himalayan crest between Bhutan and Burma could not credibly be claimed as an accepted historical divide between India and Tibet.

Although the western Brahmaputra valley was always part of the ancient Hindu cultural system, during the last two millennia it had not politically formed part of the Indian state. Neither the Asokan nor the Gupta empires extended as far as Kamrup (the old kingdom of western Assam) and Moghul attempts to subjugate Assam had always ended in failure. Hardier races from the east, attracted by the rich tillages of the Brahmaputra valley, established successive rules over the original Hindu inhabitants. The invaders left behind a racial mix of tribes: the Khasis of Cambodian (Khmer) stock; the Nagas, Kukis and Mizos of Tibeto-Burman descent, and the Abors and Miris, remnants of a Mongolian invasion. The last conquerors were a Shan people, the Ahoms of Burma, who invaded Assam in the sixteenth or early seventeenth century and established their kingdom. They eventually came under Hindu influence and colonised the Assam plains; the earlier settlers retained their tribal independence and sought refuge in the mountain fastnesses north and south of the Brahmaputra valley.

In 1819 the Hindu Ahom King, Chandrakant, appealed to the British for help against the depredations of yet another invading Burmese army, an event that eventually led to a two-pronged British campaign against Burma, a sea-borne invasion from Rangoon and an attack by land from Bengal. In 1826, the King of Burma signed the Treaty of Yandabo, ceding Assam, including Assam Himalay, to the British. The wild and unruly tribesmen, neither Tibetan nor Assamese, who inhabited these mountains were described by Military Intelligence as 'the most ruthless savages on the whole northern frontier'. At that time the mountains were of neither strategic nor commercial interest. Not wishing to extend their administrative responsibility to these primitive and plundering tribals, the British contented themselves with occupying the Brahmaputra plains.

To establish the limits of British responsibility two boundary lines were demarcated along the foothills. The Outer Line represented the 'external territorial frontier' and was a jurisdictional or administrative line dividing the rich rice and tea plantations of the plains and the poorer tribal lands to the north. South of this line, at a varying distance of up to 15 km, was the Inner Line representing 'the limits of the Deputy Commissioner's ordinary as distinguished from his political jurisdiction'. British subjects were forbidden to cross the Inner Line without a permit.

Although they did not extend their writ to Assam Himalay (later called the North Eastern Frontier Administration – NEFA) the British nevertheless considered it as geographically falling within their responsibility, if for no other reason than that no other power exercised any form of political or administrative control over it. The Chinese had shown no interest in NEFA before the turn of the century nor begun to depict it as a part of China in their maps. They had no reason to; east of the Sutlej their claims to frontier tracts were at best at secondhand, through Tibet, and in NEFA the Tibetans had no political or territorial ambitions south of the crestline (except at Tawang).

At the eastern and western extremities of the Assam Himalay two mountain trade routes connected Tibet with the Assam plains. In the east the mule-track from Rima, through the Lohit valley and Walong, brought traders from Chamdo to the market fairs of Sadiya. This was an easy approach till the great earthquake of 1951 brought sections of the mountain-side down into the valley and virtually blocked it at places. Along this route there was no significant extension of Tibet's Buddhist belt.

In the west a trade route from Lhasa passed through Tawang, over the Se-la pass, through Dhirang, to the market town of Udalguri. On this route the commercial connection had brought with it an overhang of political and cultural presence. The tribe that inhabited the Towang-Dhirang region was the Mompas, a gentle and progressive people of Bhutanese extraction, ecclesiastically submissive to the Dalai Lama. Furthermore, a large and important monastery, birthplace of the greatly revered Dalai Lama the Fifth, was located at Towang. These cultural links had drawn the Tibetans over the Himalayan crestline, and the Towang salient (including Dhirang) had long been administered by Tibetan *dzongpens*. Even the British regarded the area as belonging to Tibet. (Years after McMahon drew his famous line in 1914, a British political officer touring Kameng Frontier Division during the 1930s described the territory north of the Se-la pass as 'forbidden, because it belonged to Tibet'.)

The Tawang encroachment did not, however, focus China's interest on NEFA. The Manchus had never administered

Tibet, though their claim to suzerainty dated back to a temporary occupation of Lhasa in 1720. As there was no challenge from any other power at that time, they had been content with this vague seigneury. It was not until Younghusband's (*Bayonets to Lhasa*) expedition of 1903–4 that they perceived a direct threat to their claimed suzerainty. The Dalai Lama fled to China at the approach of the British force and the regent *Tri Rimpoche* signed the Anglo-Tibetan convention on his behalf, according Britain permanent rights not only to trade and communication facilities but also to the stationing of British representatives and military escorts within Tibet. Although in the subsequent Anglo-Chinese ratification of this convention (1906) the British agreed 'not to annex Tibetan territory or to interfere in the administration of Tibet', the Manchu imperial government continued to perceive a threat (of Britain replacing it as the suzerain of Tibet).

Determined to assert its rights, the Manchu government appointed General Chao Erh-feng Warden of the Western Marches (of China's Szechuan and Yunnan provinces) with orders to bring all claimed Manchu territories under its administration, a feat the general was largely able to accomplish by ruthless military measures. In 1910 he occupied Lhasa and, for the first time, established Chinese rule there. The Dalai Lama, only recently returned from his self-imposed exile in China, had to flee again, this time to India. It was from that time on that Britain began to feel the pressure of Chinese challenge along the whole Tibetan frontier from Gartok in the west to Rima in the east.

General Erh-feng's campaigns had confirmed China as a military power to be reckoned with and the British, for the first time, became aware of a threat from the north-east. It was time to consider pushing the Outer Line northwards in order to establish a firm, strategic boundary. They set in motion a whole series of explorations to determine the extent of tribal territories and to bring the entire area of Assam Himalay under a loose form of administration.

One of the most successful of the explorers was a Royal Engineers officer, Captain F.M. Bailey, who travelled clandestinely through Tibet, Szechuan and the Assam Himalay. He reported that the Chinese had established themselves in the upper Lohit valley, and were probing south to Walong and beyond and trying to force the Mishmi tribe into submission. As a result of Bailey's report the British mounted an expedition to Walong and established a base there.

Then came the sudden collapse of the Manchu Empire in 1911. Military pressure on Tibet's eastern marches eased and the Dalai Lama returned to Lhasa, but hopes that the establishment of a republican regime in China would relax tensions were soon dashed. The President of the newly proclaimed republic issued a decree that Tibet was thenceforth to be treated as an integral part of China. Although in subsequent meetings with the British envoy at Peking the Chinese Foreign Minister denied that there was any intention of incorporating Tibet as a province of China, no action was taken by his government to rescind the presidential edict and there was no abatement of military pressure on Tibet's borders. The republican government showed every sign of pursuing the imperialist policies of the Manchus. It was then that the British government began to formulate plans for a tripartite conference of British, Chinese and Tibetan representatives to determine trans-Himalayan realities such as the fact of Tibetan autonomy and the nature of Chinese rights in Tibet, the eastern boundaries of Outer and Inner Tibet, the degree of control to be exercised by the Chinese on Inner Tibet and the alignment of the Indo-Tibetan border in the north-eastern sector.

The Chinese at first objected to the presence of a Tibetan representative as an equal participant at the conference, but after some difficulty their objections were overcome. It was agreed that a conference would be convened at Simla in October 1913 under the chairmanship of Sir Henry McMahon, Foreign Secretary to the government of India. The main item, the eastern borders of Outer and Inner Tibet and the degree of Chinese control of Inner Tibet, was taken up first. It dragged on from session to session, the Chinese adamant that all the territories conquered by General Erh-feng as part of China be incorporated in Inner Tibet. Eventually, in March 1914, McMahon prevailed upon the Chinese representative to accept a line on the map drawn by him to indicate the limits of Inner and

Outer Tibet. The map was reluctantly initialled by the Chinese representative, but the government in Peking subsequently refused to ratify the agreement.

It was on the issue of the eastern boundaries of Tibet that the Simla Convention failed, not on the alignment of the Indo-Tibetan border. The latter, the British and Tibetans had agreed, would run along the highest crest of Assam Himalay, from the Bhutan border in the west all the way to the border of Burma with China's Yunnan province. The Chinese representative tacitly accepted the McMahon Line. Interestingly, the Tibetan government agreed to concede the Towang salient, which McMahon had included in India in order to 'have a straight boundary' (and, from the British point of view, to avoid having Tibet and Assam adjoin each other at any point).

During the next four years the war in Europe overshadowed concerns about Assam's borders. McMahon left India to become British Commissioner in Egypt, but his Line was resurrected after the war when an attempt was made to induce China to a conference to finalise them on the map. The Chinese kept postponing it and the whole matter was shelved.

As the proceedings of the Simla Conference had never been published, the government of Assam was not aware of the existence of the McMahon Line (though the government of Burma had been informed of it). Consequently Towang and Dhirang continued to remain under Tibetan administration. (The Tibetans later claimed that Towang was rightfully still theirs because they had agreed to its transfer only as a package deal, that is, only if a satisfactory boundary with China's Szechuan province were agreed to, with McMahon's help.)

The McMahon Line was kept secret and not made public till 1935, whereupon the Survey of India began to mark it on its maps. In 1938 the Assam government sent a British officer of the Assam Rifles with a paramilitary escort to occupy Towang and claim it as British territory. The Tibetan officials were evicted but when Lhasa raised vehement protests, the occupation force was recalled. The dzongpens returned, not to be evicted till thirteen years later, when the government of independent India completed the task the British had let pass.

The Second World War at first distracted attention from India's frontiers but the entry of Japan into the war, the conquest of Burma and the consequent threat to north-eastern India highlighted the necessity of an effective boundary in that region. The McMahon Line was revived and it was resolved to establish posts in the mountains, particularly in the two regions through which routes connected India with Tibet. The Assam government sent contingents of Assam Rifles to set up posts at Walong and Dhirang. Towang was not included in the scheme because there had been some suggestion in the recent past that the McMahon Line be realigned southwards to follow the crest of the Se-la range, with a view to excluding the Towang salient from Indian territory. That was the position when the British handed over power to the government of independent India.

As in Ladakh so also in Assam, the Nehru government, without initiating negotiations with the Chinese, decided on the forward-most British claim as its boundary with Tibet, though at first it did nothing to extend its writ to the Towang salient. Only after the Chinese occupied Tibet was it decided to extend the administration up to the McMahon Line. A political officer of the newly raised Frontier Administrative Service was sent to Towang with a strong escort of Assam Riflemen. Tibetan officials were evicted and Towang was thereafter made the seat of an assistant political officer.

Surprisingly the Chinese, who had earlier strongly resented Nehru's critical statements about communist China's military conquest of Tibet, made no protest. Later the same year Chinese Premier Chou En-lai suggested to the Indian Ambassador in Peking that since 'there was no territorial dispute or controversy between India and China, the question of their borders should be settled as early as possible'. Although there was no follow-up to that proposal, the Government of India had good reason to assume that the Chinese, however strongly they might have felt about McMahon's pressure tactics at the Simla Conference of 1913–14, were now willing to accept the McMahon Line as a *de facto* international border.

Thereafter the Indian government decided not to raise the border issue officially with the Chinese government, but to assume that its unilateral delimitation along the whole northern frontier would eventually be recognised by the Chinese. Even during the 1954 trade talks in Lhasa the Indian delegates studiously avoided raising the subject of borders. The Lhasa talks resulted in the famous Panchsheel Agreement, whereby, in an obvious attempt to win communist China's goodwill, India renounced all the rights and privileges in Tibet it had inherited from the British. A brief euphoric period of Sino-Indian amity followed, during which Nehru took advantage of his perceived personal friendship with Chou to raise the question of Chinese maps in which the Assam Himalay was shown as Chinese territory. Chou's casual reply was that they were old maps and his government had not got around to revising them yet. In 1956, when he was visiting New Delhi, the Chinese premier implied that he was willing to accept the McMahon Line as the Indian border, as he had done in the case of Burma (with whom a border agreement had already been signed).

From Chou En-lai's statements about border problems during 1954 and 1956 it appears that the Chinese attitude at that time was moderate and reasonable: although disputes and counter-claims existed, negotiations between two friendly neighbours would eventually result in an agreement acceptable to both; and till then a *status quo* should be maintained. It cannot be assumed, however, that this discreet approach encompassed the western sector also, because, unaccountably, neither prime minister had ever raised the question of Ladakh and the Aksai Chin. The reason Chou did not could be that, unbeknown to India, the Chinese had begun to build a road across the Aksai Chin as early as 1951, soon after their march into Tibet. This was a strategic necessity because western Tibet and even Lhasa were more easily accessible via Sinkiang and the Aksai Chin than over the Khampa-dominated mountains of the east.

India remained unaware of this road-building activity in the Aksai Chin till 1958, although the Intelligence Bureau's patrols had earlier come across signs of Chinese encroachments in the Depsang plain. In 1958 the Indian Embassy in Peking sent a report that a road had been completed connecting Sinkiang with western Tibet through India's Aksai Chin. An army patrol sent out to Haji Langar to investigate the encroachment was taken prisoner by the Chinese and not released for two months (and even this under the most callous circumstances). A Border Police patrol sent to southern Aksai Chin also found evidence of road construction through Indian-claimed territory. The Government of India protested but the protest was summarily rejected by the Chinese, who counter-claimed that it was the Indians who had intruded into Chinese territory.

The dispute over the Aksai Chin had come out into the open at last, and the period of goodwill was over. The Aksai Chin was too vital for the Chinese; as for the Indian government, it also was not prepared to make any compromise over this barren wasteland which had never been visited, let alone inhabited, by Indians.

Till 1956 Chinese claims to territory south of the Kuen Lun range had been vaguely described as 'the southern part of China's Sinkiang Uighur Autonomous Region'. This vagueness could have been a deliberate policy. It gave the Chinese room to make later extravagant claims, unrelated to geographical realities. They progressively advanced their claim lines and set in motion their own brand of forward policy. By the end of 1959 the Chinese had occupied the Lingzhitang plain and advanced beyond the head of the Changchenmo valley, areas clearly within the boundary defined by the 1899 British proposal to the Chinese government – a proposal they had never questioned and which they can therefore be said to have tacitly accepted. In 1960 they pushed their claims even further, to include the Galwan and Chip Chap valleys which clearly formed part of the Shyok-Indus basin.

Chinese repressive measures in Lhasa, culminating in the bombardment of the Norbu Lingka summer palace in March 1959, resulted in the Dalai Lama's flight to India via the Towang route through NEFA. The enthusiastic welcome given to the Lama by the Indian people brought Chinese accusations against Nehru and his government to an hysterical pitch and started a confrontation along the McMahon Line. The cold war between the two great powers of Asia had started.

## NOTES

1. The word 'frontier' is used to indicate not a line but a zone, a tract of territory forming the border region between two countries.

2. There was a curious anomaly here. While Hunza, situated south of the putative border, claimed trans-Karakoram territorial rights in the Yarkand valley, the Chinese (who did not refute the Mir's claims in Taghdumbash and Raskam) in their turn claimed rights over Hunza because of the annual tribute the Mir had traditionally paid to the Manchu emperor through his representative at Kashgar. When the British repudiated the Chinese claim by pointing out that Hunza was part of Kashmir and therefore under British rule, all that the Chinese conceded was that Hunza was 'under the joint protection of the two powers'.

# 3

# WITH 7 BRIGADE IN NEFA

When in March 1959 the Dalai Lama fled to India in order to avoid internment by the Chinese, he decided to make for Towang along the obscure south-eastern route where he could count on the protection of rebel Khampas, rather than risk capture on the traditional passage through Gyantse and Sikkim. The Grand Lama's choice of route inevitably drew Chinese forces southward to the border of Kameng Frontier Division of India's North Eastern Frontier Agency (NEFA). Before long they were operating against Khampa guerrillas in the Khinzemane-Bum-la region, driving many hundreds into NEFA. In the process they began to harass India's outposts on the border; on one occasion they temporarily evicted Assam Rifles personnel from their post at Khinzemane.

Incredible as it may seem, responsibility for the defence of the north-eastern frontier at that time rested not with the Ministry of Defence but with the Ministry of External Affairs, and the force deployed for the role was not the army but the paramilitary Assam Rifles operating under the Foreign Ministry. It was not until late in 1959, after the incidents mentioned above, that the Government of India transferred the responsibility for the security of the north-eastern frontier to the Ministry of Defence. Because there was no field formation available in Assam for this task, Army HQ ordered 4 Infantry Division, then part of XI Corps (and trained for tasks on the Punjab plains) to uproot from Ambala and move across north India to assume a defensive role along the Himalayan borders of Sikkim and NEFA. By the end of November 1959, 4th Division had re-deployed in the north-east, its responsibility stretching from Darjeeling in the west to the India-Burma-Tibet trijunction in the east, covering well over 1,000 km of the border.

The Indo-Tibetan border in eastern India recognised by the Indian government is an arbitrary line drawn by Sir Henry McMahon at the Simla Conference in 1914. He advanced the previously marked administered border some 80 km northward from the Himalayan foothills to the natural, geographical border, the crestline of the range. The McMahon Line purported to follow the line of the watershed, a term in itself something of a misnomer for two reasons. First, the conformation of the frontier here is not so much a mountain range dividing two isobasic regions as a high plateau (Tibet) falling away in a series of ridges and valleys to the plains of Assam. Except for a few famous peaks that reach out to the skies, Assam Himalay in effect represents the southern edge of the Tibetan plateau (as typified, for example, by the terrain at Bum-la, north of Towang, where there is no marked drop northward from the crestline). Secondly, because of this topographical conformation all the major water-courses – the Indus, the Sutlej, the Ganga, the Brahmaputra (Tsang Po in Tibetan), the Subansiri (Tsari-chu), the Manas (Nyamjang-chu) – all flow southward through the so-called watershed of Himalay to the plains of India. There is no river that flows northward from the Himalayan crest into Tibet.

There are two sectors of the north-eastern border through which traditional trade routes (albeit only mule-tracks) connect India and Tibet: Sikkim and Kameng Frontier Division. A brigade was therefore allotted to each of these two sectors, 11 Infantry Brigade to Sikkim (HQ at Darjeeling) and my brigade, 7th, to Kameng (HQ temporarily at Misamari, north of Tezpur). 5 Infantry Brigade was deployed further east, allocated to the vast but relatively secure sector comprising Subansiri, Siang and Lohit Frontier Divisions.

HQ 4 Infantry Division was established at Tezpur, on the north bank of the Brahmaputra. My brigade was responsible for the defence of Kameng FD; a subsidiary task was the defence of Towang.

Local administration in Kameng centred on the political officer located at the recently established settlement of Bomdila (2,800 metres). The political officer, Harmander Singh (formerly of 2nd Punjab Regiment) was a genial and co-operative colleague. He and his wife kept open house for any of us who happened to be passing through Bomdila, and we began a pleasant association. Forward of Bomdila there was a base superintendent at Dhirang two days march away. Thence, across the formidable Se-la massif (another five days march) an assistant political officer was located at Towang, seat of the Buddhist Mompa people. Before the arrival of the army, the security of this stretch of the border had been entrusted to a wing of 5 Battalion, the Assam Rifles, operating under the political officer. The battalion provided a number of small outposts between Towang and the border, some supplemented by elements of Intelligence Bureau personnel from the Home Ministry. The Khinzemane route to Towang was thought to be the most likely approach for an invader because it lay along the valley of the Nyamjang-chu, which crosses the Indo-Tibetan border at the relatively low altitude of less than 2,000 metres. In contrast, the outpost at Bum-la, 30 km north of Towang, was situated at about 5,000 metres. To the west of the Nyamjang-chu, marching with the Indo-Bhutanese border, loomed the high and trackless Thag-la massif.

Road and track communications in Kameng were dismally inadequate for operational purposes. Jeeps or other light vehicles could ply only as far as Bomdila, over a road newly constructed by army and Assam state engineers. Movement farther forward was restricted to hill ponies and footmen. The Border Roads Organisation would soon undertake the building of a motor road through Kameng, but at the time a journey to Towang entailed a seven-day march from Bomdila.

I estimated that it would be a year or more before logistical capability could meet the operational requirement of deploying a brigade in Kameng FD. Accordingly I moved up only one battalion, and that also only to Tenga valley, just south of Bomdila. After installing Brigade HQ at Bomdila I set out on a reconnaissance across Se-la to the western region of my area, the Towang salient, and thence to the Nyamjang valley and finally to the Himalayan crestline at Bum-la.

From the very beginning I was under pressure from Divisional HQ to start pushing troops as far and as quickly as possible towards the high mountainous border. Then, and later as Director of Military Operations at Army HQ, this display of impatience was a recurring leitmotif in most situations of deployment in the mountains. There seemed to be a compulsive urge among commanders and staff located in the plains to push forward troops beyond the reach of normal logistics, without a realistic assessment of their subsequent potential for sustained operations, unmindful that without assured resupply of ammunition, rations, medical cover and other impedimenta of battle, mere numbers of troops count for little. On a map hanging on a wall in an operations room, coloured flags depicting battalions and companies along the border look reassuring; but flags on maps are an abstraction, not a contributing reality towards defensive potential. It is the commander on the spot who knows that unless forward troops can be logistically sustained, they become virtual refugees when ammunition and supplies run out after the first battle.

After my reconnaissance of Dhirang valley and the Towang salient I concluded that the key tactical feature in western Kameng (the 'vital ground' in army jargon) was not Towang but the spine of the commanding range stretching from Bomdila to Manda-la. In contrast, Towang was located on the middle slopes of the Bum-la massif, not on a commanding crestline. Furthermore, there were tracks from Bum-la that by-passed the township and went directly to Jang and Se-la; an invading enemy could easily by-pass Towang. In my opinion these tactical deficiencies made Towang an unsuitable site for the main defensive position.

In contrast, Manda-la and Bomdila passes were tactical bottlenecks on both the routes from the northern border to the Assam plains: the ancient trade route, which went over Manda-la down to Udalguri, and the jeep road under construction which passed over Bomdila. Hence the section of the ridge Bomdila-Manda-la should have been, in my opinion, the vital ground for our defensive layout.

To quote from my subsequent report to Army HQ (*Summary of Events and Policies*):

For the defence of Kameng FD the 'vital ground' . . . was the ridge Bomdila-Manda-la and this was where I intended to dispose the major part of my force. For the defence of Towang (subsidiary task) I was prepared to detach one battalion; but to locate the greater part of my force in the Towang salient, across the Se-la massif, would only invite the Chinese to by-pass my position, occupy central Kameng and move down to the plains. Thus, by concentrating my force in Towang, though I might succeed in my subsidiary task, my main aim -- that is, defence of Kameng FD and thus guarding the routes (through it) to the plains -- would be jeopardised.

I must confess that though my tactical assessment of Towang was correct, I was remiss in overlooking the potential of the Se-la massif as the main defensive sector. Two years later, I was to recommend Se-la rather than the Bomdila range as the vital ground for defence; at the time, unaccountably, I disregarded that pre-eminent tactical feature. Possibly this was because at that stage, when the Indian Army was still unfamiliar with the techniques of high altitude warfare, I dismissed the concept of siting brigade defences at heights of 4,000 metres and over as impracticable.

My appreciation of the terrain did not find favour with the General Officer Commanding 4 Infantry Division, Major General Amrik Singh, MC, who insisted that I locate the greater part of my brigade at Towang. I argued against such a top-heavy deployment both for tactical reasons and because of the absence of adequate logistical facilities, but Amrik would not yield. He countered that Towang could always be maintained by air and that plans for the forward concentration of my brigade must proceed apace. Unfortunately, that was merely a glib evasion of the problem. As became obvious later, our meagre air resources were quite unable to maintain a brigade on those heights. Weather conditions were uncertain, dropping zones limited and there were at that time no helicopters in service in India.

The truth is that we were planning and operating in a doctrinal vacuum. I do not recall receiving any operational guidance except a general warning not to become involved in a skirmish with the Chinese or to approach within three kilometres of the border (except where we had already established posts).

At no time do I recollect receiving an assessment of threat from Divisional HQ. Apart from local briefings by Intelligence Bureau personnel in Towang and Khinzemane, all I had to work on was uninformed conjecture. The result was that I had only a vague perception of the strengths or placements of Chinese forces north of the Kameng border. Even Divisional HQ, as far as I knew, had not received any detailed information on Chinese troop dispositions. Consequently, it based its deployment less on tactical appreciation and more on a gut reaction that all available troops must be pushed quickly up into the mountain reaches. How the defensive positions would be co-ordinated or the troops kept supplied in battle was never made clear. I do not think that any formal study had been made of Chinese army organisations, force structures or methods of warfare; at least, none was ever sent down to HQ 7 Brigade. We were given no policy or guidelines regarding static or mobile defence, harassing roles to be played by stay-behind parties, or the possible employment of tribal manpower for our defence preparations.

Some weeks after we moved into Kameng, an exercise was held at HQ Eastern Command in Lucknow. Amrik attended it and on his return informed us that the GOC-in-C, Lieutenant General S.P.P. Thorat, DSO, had evolved a master plan of defence. Since it was impossible to secure every mile of the Himalayan border, Thorat intended to hold strong-points along a defensive line running more or less parallel to the McMahon Line but between 50 and 60 miles to the south. From this line army patrols or posts could be sent forward to support Assam Rifles detachments on the border. I did not see the Thorat Plan on paper, but from Amrik's account its tactical perception appeared somewhat vague. According to Amrik the tactical points

Thorat had listed on his defence line were obviously chosen from a map; he had not yet carried out a reconnaissance in the mountains. In fact each of these points was separated from the others by many kilometres of high mountain ranges and deep valleys unconnected by lateral routes. The arbitrary alignment of these points – Towang (Kameng FD)-Ziro (Subansari FD)-Along (Siang FD)-Tezu-Hayuliang (Lohit FD)-Jairampur (Tirap FD) – could by no stretch of imagination be viewed as a line of defence.

It was difficult to believe that such an untenable tactical concept could have originated with Thorat, who enjoyed a high reputation in the army not only as a gallant and four-square leader but also as a general officer who had enjoyed vast combat and managerial experience in command and on the higher General Staff (including a tenure as Chief of the General Staff). Nearly thirty years later, after I read his memoirs, *From Reveille to Retreat*, I realised what his actual tactical intent had been. There was at that time so much controversy on the proper approach to border defence that I include a rationale of Thorat's proposed defence plan.

Thorat had indeed made his defence plan from a study of the map and not from personal reconnaissance because, prior to the events of 1959, the government would not consent to his proposal (supported by Army Chief General Thimayya) that responsibility for the defence of NEFA be given to the army. Till the end of 1959 (when 4 Infantry Division was rushed from Ambala to the north-eastern sector) the Government of India had entrusted the defence of NEFA to the Assam Rifles, a paramilitary force under the Ministry of External Affairs, which was neither equipped nor trained for this role. The Prime Minister had made this decision for a socio-political reason. Before the Lhasa revolt of 1959 and the Dalai Lama's flight to India, the government did not consider that there was any danger of Chinese intrusion across the NEFA border. Pandit Nehru had only recently embarked on a new administrative venture in the Frontier Districts according to concepts evolved from the 'Philosophy for NEFA' aimed at protecting the primitive tribal peoples from a precipitate exposure to the commercial and often venal culture of the plainsmen. He did not wish to disrupt this experiment with the sudden influx of large numbers of army troops. The Assam Rifles, essentially a police force operating under the local administration, could be blended in with the tribal experiment, whereas the army would perforce give top priority to defence rather than to administrative requirements.

The Defence Minister's resistance to the army's proposal to take over the defence of NEFA was more egotistical. Krishna Menon had his own self-promoting ideas on the subject, as Thorat records:

A few days later when I met Mr Menon in Delhi I opened the subject with him. In his usual sarcastic style he said that there would be no war between India and China, and in the most unlikely event of there being one, he was quite capable of fighting it himself on the diplomatic level.

Unimpressed by the Minister's bombast, Thorat was sure that when the pressure reached boiling point the responsibility for NEFA would suddenly land on the army. He therefore decided to make paper plans for its defence in anticipation of a sudden emergency:

It must be appreciated that in the early stages of any war the attacker will always have the initial advantage over the defender because he can choose the time and place for the attack and can therefore apply all his strength at any given point. Therefore, he will get into the defender's territory and make penetrations. If this happens the defender must not lose heart because he will have his say when he has located the main thrust and moves his reserves to meet it – very likely on ground of his choosing. There he will give battle, stabilize the situation, and then steadily push the enemy back. This process may take a long time, but there is no other answer to it when one is on the defensive. I make this statement pointedly because I realise that even small-scale penetrations will have great demoralising effect on the country's morale and may embarrass the government. We must therefore condition our minds to expect and accept these inevitable penetrations in the early stages of the war.

Even if I were to disperse my force on a 'thin red line' all along the border, it will serve no useful purpose for I shall be weak everywhere and strong nowhere. Therefore, I do not propose to do so.

As the enemy comes farther away from his bases on the other side of the McMahon Line, his communications will get stretched. He will find it increasingly more difficult to maintain his forces, and the situation will get worse day by day. *A stage will come when his maintenance difficulties will be the same as mine, and it is then that I shall give him the first real fight.* The scene of this battle will be a line running east and west through the middle of NEFA and for purposes of this paper I propose calling it the Defence Line.

The Defence Line will consist of a succession of Vital Points. The choice of these will depend not only on their tactical value but also on our ability to maintain and support them. This presupposes that there should be a roadhead or an airhead at each of these points. Without these the ability of the garrisons to put up a protracted defence will be limited. The Defence Line as I envisage it will be Towang (Kameng division)-Ziro-Daporijo (Subansari division)-Along (Siang division)-Roing-Tezu-Lohitpur-Hayuliang (Lohit division)-Jairampur (Tirap division).

This line shall be the main defensive position beyond which I shall accept no penetration. In other words, it is on this line that I shall stop the enemy and proceed to drive him back across the McMahon Line. I have confidence that given the necessary resources I will not allow the enemy to cross this line. This line will divide NEFA into two halves. The area north of the Defence Line shall be known as the Northern Sector and the area south of it as the Southern Sector. [Emphasis added]

It was not that Thorat was advocating abandoning the McMahon Line. A border loses significance and validity unless it is adequately guarded, that is, manned by forces able to offer initial armed resistance to an invader; but a border is unlikely to be the most suitable locality for the main defensive battle, which is what Thorat was arguing. Paramilitary forces, less heavily armed than the army, can hold a border temporarily, offer initial resistance, but fall back when pressed. The regular army chooses the 'main defensive positions' on the basis of suitable terrain, communications and logistical potential.

The salient point of General Thorat's warcraft was that our main forces must not be stretched thin along the length of the border where every military advantage would lie with the enemy. Instead, the defence plan must allow for an initial enemy penetration, while our main forces prepare to defeat the invader in a depth area, on ground of our own choosing and where we could bring superior resources to bear on the battlefield.

This was no brilliant tactical innovation. It was common military sense, though too often nations at war have fallen into the trap of defending too thinly too far forward, their leaders emotionally unwilling to accept occupation of any part of their country by an enemy. As I later realised, this was why the Thorat Plan was ridiculed, even suppressed, in Delhi (to my knowledge no copy was ever sent to Military Operations Directorate); it ran directly counter to the emotional make-up and half-baked strategic knowledge of well intentioned patriots like the Director of the Intelligence Bureau, B.N. Mullik, who at that time was virtual DMO of the border. As he later wrote in his book *The Chinese Betrayal:*

The main objection by the Army was that the ground was not suitable for fighting by the Indian Army and it must choose its own ground. This was strange logic. *Battles are fought on the borders, be they suitable or not.* One army is always superior to another and on this score no country would meekly allow its frontiers to be overrun by the enemy and choose a battle-ground hundreds of miles to the interior. Defeat at the frontier is always a possibility but the position can be retrieved later but on that account no country gives up the frontier without a fight. [Emphasis added]

Thorat envisaged manning the border with the paramilitary Assam Rifles, whose task it would be to inflict casualties, delay an enemy invasion, give early warning and either harass the enemy's lines of communication as stay-behind guerrillas or fall back to the southern sector to thicken its defences. Regular forces would hold the southern sector which, unlike the northern sector, would be accessible by road and thus logistically feasible.

Even if some of the military terms he used were confusing, there is no doubt about the soundness of the Thorat Plan. Unadorned by emotional attitudes or unrealistic assessments of capabilities, it offered a feasible tactical solution instead of the impracticable posturings that I was to meet even in the highest places in Delhi — the 'fight-for-every-inch-of-our-territory' syndrome.

It was unfortunate that Thorat's map-study had led him

to select Towang as a vital point on the defence line in Kameng. By his own yardstick Towang, only 30 km from the border and more than 180 km (nine days' march) from the plains, did not qualify for this role. Unfortunately, its inclusion on the defence line resulted in increased pressure from Amrik and the divisional staff to expedite the move of my brigade to Towang. It soon became an obsessive urge to push bodies of troops up the hill, and we became so involved in the process that there was little time to spare for the consideration of logistical realities. Nor was there any incentive or opportunity for tactical innovation and training to meet the problems of high altitude deployment – not at Divisional HQ, not in the brigade, not even at unit level. No training directive came from Army HQ to tell us how to prepare to do battle against the People's Liberation Army of communist China.

I made plans for a crash training programme for the brigade to retrain and convert from plains to mountain techniques. Tenga valley, from Rupa to Jamiri, offered good terrain for mountain warfare training and I intended to rotate the three battalions so that each would spend six weeks training on the banks of the Tenga. When I approached Divisional HQ to obtain sanction for the administrative resources for these moves, my plans were vetoed. I was told that the priorities were to send troops up to Towang and to construct defences and *bashas*; our training cycle would have to be postponed till the next year.

This was a disappointment for the whole brigade; even our previous training cycle had been disrupted by Operation *Amar*, the building of troops' accommodation in Ambala using troop labour. Whereas the latter could perhaps be regarded as Defence Minister Krishna Menon's inspired concept to illustrate the use of self-help to mitigate chronic shortages and hardships, a repeat so soon could have disastrous consequences for the morale and fitness of troops.

In retrospect, I think we were remiss in not attempting to involve local communities in our defence preparations. We made no effort to reach out to tap local tribes for their human resources. The incongruity did not strike me then, but I think it is no exaggeration to remark that the Indian Army in Assam behaved much in the manner of an imperial force operating in overseas territory. We established contact with the administrative officials but made no effort to involve Assamese society and tribal organisations in our defence plans and measures. The army lived and worked in a self-constructed cocoon. The officers only emerged from this cocoon to avail themselves of the games and other facilities offered by British planters' clubs in the tea gardens. For the men there was neither incentive nor encouragement for the Sikhs, Dogras, Jats, Gorkhas or other classes of the army to fraternise with the Assamese at any level. We operated in a vacuum, living in but out of touch with our environment.

I think back with both amusement and chagrin to the occasion when I called at Divisional HQ at Tezpur to apply for a week's casual leave. I explained that my wife was coming to visit Assam and I wanted to take her around the north-eastern areas. My announcement was met with gasps of disbelief from the divisional staff. How could I have planned this without the GOC's permission? North bank and NEFA had been declared a non-family field area, did I not realise that? It took me some time to convince them that though declared a field area, north Assam nevertheless remained a part of India and that my wife needed no one's permission to travel in her own country. In the end, of course, the GOC accorded us all the resources at his disposal to facilitate our holiday and the staff went out of their way to ensure that our requirements were met. Nevertheless they continued to discourage family visits when others wanted to follow our example.

The likely consequences of this attitude did not occur to me then. At the time the whole incident seemed more comical than invidious. It was not until two years later, after the agonising debacle at Se-la when a whole division quit its defences and made for the plains without offering battle, that the inherent danger of our segregated culture struck me. Not only was the army out of touch with the peoples and cultures of Assam and NEFA, but by making this region out of bounds to our wives and families we were adding to the feeling of alienation from which both officers and men suffered. In a tribal army such as ours, in which the various castes and regional sub-races are kept segregated in class-composed regiments (a meaningless continuation of Britain's post-Mutiny policy in India) there is always the danger that in dire adversity men will lack the motivation to stand and fight for unfamiliar territory outside their home regions. I feel sure that this was partly the cause of 4th Division's ignominious abandonment of Se-la defences in 1962.

Only in the years following the NEFA debacle, and with some persistence, was I, as Director of Military Operations at Army HQ, able to persuade conservative minds in Delhi that the army's families should be allowed to follow the flag, even to the distant marches, so long as we operated within our own country. As a result, extensive families' barracks were built in NEFA and elsewhere along our frontier zones, in some areas limitrophe with forward deployments. Today troops are unlikely to jettison weapons and equipment and head for the plains, as did the under-motivated men of 4 Infantry Division in 1962. The forward areas are now part of their homes and hearths.

The colonial outlook of the Indian Army in NEFA was nowhere better exemplified than in its unwillingness to enlist the co-operation of friendly tribals, especially the Mompas of Towang. The general tendency in NEFA and north Assam was to treat defence as a reserved subject, not to be shared with the local inhabitants, who were regarded virtually as outsiders. The Mompas are a friendly, gentle and easy-going people of Tibetan stock, with soft wind-etched faces and smiling eyes wrinkled against the glare and dust of the open mountain-sides of Towang. Of Buddhist culture, they are more sophisticated than the Sherdupkens, Appatanis, Daflas, Mishmis and other tribal peoples of NEFA. Their organised lifestyle is based on agriculture, handicrafts and a market economy; above all they are grateful to the new India because, in 1951, we liberated them from the high-handed depredations of Tibetan officials.

When 7 Brigade moved into the mountains of Towang, we found the Mompas helpful and supportive but we used them only as porters on the march or as handy rouseabouts in camp. Here were we, suddenly pitchforked from the plains of the Punjab to the Himalayan heights, groping about trying to overcome local problems and conditions in order to evolve a feasible defensive posture, yet we neglected to seek the assistance of these friendly inhabitants in any meaningful way. The Frontier Administrative Service, which came under the Ministry of External Affairs, was also remiss in this respect. It made no attempt to involve the Mompas or other tribal people of NEFA, many of whom would willingly have stepped forward in a patriotic cause. The political officer and other members of the Frontier Service (in part recruited from the military) were doing a magnificent job in these areas, keeping a discreet balance between extending the government's writ into the remote heights and protecting the aboriginal people from the adverse effects of too sudden an exposure to the sophistication and deviousness of the plainsman. They had created an efficient, close-knit, benevolent cadre and, certainly in Kameng FD, they had established considerable rapport with the tribals; but that relationship was paternal rather than egalitarian.

When the crisis arose it was the Chinese who utilised the Mompas and other tribals. Before and during the invasion of Kameng they pressganged numbers of Mompas for use as guides and informers and for providing safe-houses. Yet in 1959–60, it had occurred neither to the political officer nor to me to enlist the aid of these people to supplement our security measures. The Mompas would have responded enthusiastically because they had every reason to distrust intruders from north of the border. Till only ten years before, Tibetan *dzongpens* had held sway at Towang and Dhirang and had ruthlessly exploited them. Despite Henry McMahon's arbitrary line drawn in 1912, the British had allowed the Tibetans to exercise their sway right down to the Dhirang valley. It was only in 1951 that the government of independent India decided to make good McMahon's claim, push the Tibetans out of Towang and extend its writ to the whole of Kameng FD. The Mompas are not unmindful of the part played by the Indians in the process of their liberation.

In the aftermath of sensation, the urgency of our plight was diverted. The border had been quiet during the spring and summer of 1960; there had been no repetition of incidents such as those at Khinzemane or Longju the previous year. The uproar and the alarms consequent upon the escape of the Dalai Lama to India gradually died down, the influx of fugitive Khampa guerrillas became only a trickle and even the unease and bustle surrounding Mrs Freda Bedi's Tibetan refugee camp in Misamari quietened as increasing numbers of its inmates found work with the many road gangs that accompanied the Border Roads organisation in NEFA. As these visible reminders of the Chinese menace faded, so did the imminence of the threat. Interestingly, the anxiety of the British tea planters, particularly those whose gardens were situated near the foothills, did not abate. I remember visiting a Scottish planter's bungalow in the Paneeri group of gardens near Udalguri. In the course of my reconnaissance along the Inner Line marches I had been told that this particular garden was in a state of panic, its factory shut down, its Santhal tea-pickers preparing to return to their native Bihar and the manager and his family on the verge of decamping. It took a good hour's pep talk to instil a modicum of confidence into the Scotsman and his wife to persuade them to stay and continue with their tea-making. Thereafter I made a point of calling on and reassuring the many British garden managers in remote areas. In general I found them welcoming and co-operative; some even made generous offers of garden labour, transport and other resources to facilitate our tasks.

Meanwhile, a crash programme for road construction in border areas had been launched by the newly created Border Roads Development Board, a high-powered organisation chaired by the Prime Minister. Fortunately for us its Director-General was one of those happy appointments that the bureaucratic process sometimes stumbles upon. Kartar Dubey, a Major General of Engineers, was the ideal man for the job. Indeed, he would have been ideal for any job in the army, technical or generalist. Later, during the lean years of the early 1960s when he was Engineer-in-Chief and I the DMO, we had many dealings together and my admiration for him grew with each encounter. Tall, handsome, secure, he combined an incisive intellect with an open and cheerful disposition that instantly inspired confidence. He frequently visited the outlying marches where his Engineer forces performed miracles of road-building under the most adverse conditions. He was receptive to ideas and gave the impression that any effort to which he committed himself would be in the overall interest; and he was totally free of that insistence on seeing his own view prevail that marks lesser men who need to exercise their egos.

During his first visit to my brigade area we discussed the Board's proposed road plan for Kameng and I expressed my dissatisfaction with the projected alignment from Bomdila to Dhirang. The road was planned to cross over the central ridge at Bomdila, descend into the Dhirang valley to its north and then turn west to Dhirang. This section of the road would thus be dominated by the Poshing-la-Thembang ridge from the north, whence we anticipated a diversionary threat in the event of hostilities. I argued for a change of alignment. In the interest of tactical requirement the road from Foothills Camp should proceed westward along Tenga valley, keeping in the lee of the central (Bomdila) ridge, pass through Rupa and Phudung, and only then cross over the central ridge at Manda-la before descending to Dhirang village directly below. The line of communication to Dhirang would thus be much more secure.

Kartar heard me out, deferred to my tactical argument and promised to persuade the Border Roads Board to alter the alignment. Had he succeeded, I feel sure that the calamity that befell 4th Division in Se-la, Dhirang and Bomdila in 1962 would have been less dire, perhaps less discreditable. (In the event, the Chinese severed the exposed Dhirang-Bomdila section of the road as I had anticipated; and in the ensuing panic, HQ 4th Division and the garrison in Dhirang abandoned their positions and took to the hills.) I learned later that it was the spokesman for the Frontier Administration who vetoed my proposal, on the grounds that it would be more fitting for the main road to pass through the administrative seat at Bomdila.

Meanwhile, we pressed ahead with the logistical programme in Towang – constructing *bashas*, laying out tracks and water-points and creating forward dumps of essential items – although it would be an exaggeration to say that it was carried out on a war footing. Despite the Longju incident the Chinese threat remained an abstraction and, not surprisingly, the tempo of troop deployment remained leisurely. Springtime in the Kameng mountains was beguiling enough and our environment had much to offer. The lush mountains provided exotic game for the sportsman – blood pheasant, bamboo partridge and other game birds; and the mountain streams provided plenty of good mahseer fishing. Down in the plains the British planters' clubs offered tennis, golf, swimming and jolly evening parties. We made long treks to enchanting recesses of NEFA and because they were undertaken on government business we were attended by retinues of camp followers and pack ponies. The journeys were a rare treat for those so inclined. Travel in the high Towang area was a special joy; not only were the Mompas a smiling, hospitable people, the terrain was less severe than in the lower ranges. Sheer ridges of daunting tropical jungle gave place to rolling mountain-sides covered with tall flowering rhododendrons. Winding tracks passed long banks of yellow primroses and every so often, as one clambered breathless over a snow-covered crestline, a vision of peaks.

Those were halcyon days in NEFA, for both the local administration and the army. The political officer and his subordinates, accustomed to an isolated lifestyle in lonely outposts with little or no social activity, found the influx of soldiers stimulating and took pleasure in their company. There was increased activity in their previously sleepy surroundings and greater movement of people and goods up and down their mid-mountain backwaters. Army messes opened, social activities blossomed and life suddenly became more pleasant. Paradoxically, it was the impact of the army's presence that obscured the very urgency and reason for their coming.

I suspect that Frontier Service officers were never fully convinced that the threat of Chinese invasion was real. The Chinese claim on NEFA was seen as a bargaining ploy to induce the Indian government to yield to their claim on the Aksai Chin. After all, they argued, Peking had accepted the principle of the watershed to delimit the border with Nepal and Burma (and, previously, with Sikkim and Bhutan). The Himalayan crestline was the agreed border, so their claim to NEFA and the north Brahmaputra plains could only be a tongue-in-cheek assertion. Who knows? Perhaps they were right, in the context of the time. Who in those days could have predicted a frenzied sabre-rattling across the Namka-chu?

In the summer of 1960, while my staff officers dispersed in different directions to carry out their reconnaissances, I availed myself of three months leave-and-furlough for a stay with my family in Delhi and a visit to England to meet with my publishers and attend to other personal matters. On return to NEFA in August 1960 I decided to resurvey the Towang salient. The motor road was still in the early stages of construction, so our party travelled by foot and pony as before.

My old battalion, 1/9 Gorkha Rifles, which I had commanded only a few years previously and of which I was now Colonel, had by then been inducted into Towang. I was able to spend a Gorkha Dushera with them in their highland location. I stayed with the assistant political officer, Murthi, in his cosy little cottage built of clapboard and turves. He was a kindly host, gave me much of his time and took me round on a tour of his demesne. Together we visited the famous 500-year-old Buddhist monastery, revered as the birthplace of the Great Fifth Dalai Lama. A mile or so to its north, overlooking a remote ravine, was the *anigompa*, whose nuns shyly lined up to greet us.

On this occasion I undertook a more thorough reconnaissance of the approaches to Towang because we had received reports of an incident of Chinese encroachment near Bum-la. I travelled up the Nyamjang valley to Khinzemane and Chutangmu, crossed the 4,800-metre Chamling-la on the way to Bum-la, and called at the lonely Buddhist *gompa* at Taksang, a day's march west of Bum-la. A party of Chinese was reported to have visited this remote shrine a few weeks previously. Ensconced in a bleak and narrow ravine at an altitude of about 3,500 metres, the *gompa* was about halfway between the Nyamjang valley and Bum-la. We found it with some difficulty, a modest edifice consisting of the main shrine and a narrow antechamber adjacent to a long, partly dilapidated stone shed, abode of the humble monk and his lady. (The rules of celibacy are flexible when one ekes out a living in barren, inhospitable regions, days away from one's nearest fellow being.)

Of necessity benighted at the little monastery, we were able to interrogate the lama and his 'wife' at length. We were told that the Chinese interlopers had forcibly thrust themselves upon the *gompa* and its keeper. Their leader had slept in the shrine. (Indeed, I too spent a stifling and near-sleepless night in this room, cloyingly redolent of burning yak's butter.) There had been five in the group. They claimed to have lost their way while searching for bamboo for their *bashas*, but from the lama's account it was apparent that bamboos and *bashas* were mere pretexts for a reconnaissance.

The lama assured me that the Chinese had crossed and recrossed the border at a point just north of the monastery. Although there was no track marked on the map, I found his information entirely credible. Contrary to general belief, parties of footmen can cross the Himalayan watershed at several places along the border. On a map, prominent red lines indicating paths and pony trails create the misleading impression that except along these routes movement is difficult. In the Towang region and, indeed, in much of the area below 6,000 metres, the ground is open and the going good. Barring the snowbound winter months, descent from the high Tibetan plateau to the Towang slopes poses few difficulties.

This is why my remissness in not investigating the terrain west of Nyamjang valley seems to me incomprehensible in retrospect. When I had visited the Assam Rifles posts at Khinzemane and Chutangmu, I had been alarmed at the tactical vulnerability of their location at the bottom of a deep and narrow valley. To the west loomed the dominating Thag-la ridge, which Murthi had told me was, like Khinzemane, disputed territory. The subedar of the Assam Rifles post informed me that tracks of sorts led from Khinzemane up the steep slopes towards Thag-la. I had determined to make a quick reconnaissance of the western heights, and sought advice on finding a good viewpoint. At Zimithang the post commander pointed out the stark silhouette of a long flat spur high above us to the west. This, he said, was known as Lumpu, a summer habitation for semi-nomadic goatherds who visited the region to graze

their animals on the slopes of Thag-la ridge and even across
it on the Tibetan side of the mountain. My first instinct
had been to make a trip to Lumpu, which seemed a good
vantage point from which to assess terrain south of Thag-la.
However, it would have delayed my tour programme by
at least three days, so I allowed myself to be dissuaded
from my resolve by the local commander's assurance that
no great threat was anticipated from that quarter. For the
defence of Towang, the western flank across the Nyamjang
river was indeed at one remove. At the same time, for the
security of the Nyamjang valley and the Assam Rifles posts
strung out along it, the Thag-la heights did constitute a
potential if not an anticipated threat. If a detailed
reconnaissance report of that barren and unsupportable
region had been available in Army HQ in September 1962,
it might possibly have prevented the mindless rush to push
a brigade into that logistical void two years later.

Reports from a touring commander are not always given
due weight at higher headquarters; my views on the
unsuitability of Towang as a defensive locality never found
acceptance. I do not know where the obsession with Towang
had originated, but the GOC would not entertain any
suggestion of an alternative defence plan. Alas only too
often do preconceptions substitute for policy.

After my reconnaissance of the Bum-la region, I was
more than ever convinced that Towang was not suitable
as a defensive locality. Then, for the first time, it occured
to me that the Se-la ridge was a possible alternative. I
resolved to make a more detailed survey of the terrain on
either side of Se-la top, where the map indicated a number
of tracks, many flat stretches suitable for dropping zones
and two small freshwater lakes. Unfortunately on my way
back the weather turned against us. By the time we reached
Nuranang (halfway between Jang and Se-la) we were
engulfed in a raging snowstorm and, to top it all, I had
a sudden and virulent attack of bacillary dysentery. By the
time we had struggled up to the top of the pass, visibility
was down to only a few yards. High fever soon made me
delirious and all I can recall of that nightmare passage
was constantly being forced to dismount from my pony
and made to walk lest I froze to death. So, unfortunately,

no detailed reconnaissance of the Se-la massif was possible on that occasion.

On my return to Bomdila, I discussed with my staff the possibility of siting defences on Se-la. Afterwards I sent Major Raja Fulay, my DAA and QMG (logistical staff officer) to reconnoitre Se-la's surroundings for both tactical and logistical assessments of its defensive potential. I instructed him to return via the circuitous northern track from Towang that by-passes Se-la, skirts the high Mago region and descends to Dhirang valley via Tse-la (pronounced Che-la), Poshing-la and Thembang. This was a possible route for outflanking Se-la and I needed to have a detailed report on it.

While discussing these projects, my staff alerted me to another development which had crept up on us and would soon hamper the brigade's operational capability. An increase in the volume of traffic on our roads and tracks foreboded future administrative difficulties. In NEFA there were few of the facilities taken for granted in an administered society, such as public transport, commodity markets, workshops, hospitals, traffic control police and postal facilities. All arrangements for staging movements of troops, conveyance of rations and supplies, medical services, workshops and numerous other requirements would have to be provided by the army along some 200 km of road and track between Foothills Camp and Towang. Setting up these facilities is the responsibility of a Line-of-Communication Area or Sub-area HQ, not that of a fighting formation, which normally expects to be logistically served right up to its forward location. In our case, since Divisional HQ was making no move to shoulder this burden, it appeared that we would have to provide these services ourselves. That would occupy a large portion of my manpower, leaving all too little for actual defence.

I asked for a meeting with the GOC and his staff to discuss these operational and administrative matters, but before this could be held I received a message from Tezpur informing me that I had been posted to Army HQ as Deputy Military Secretary and was required to report at Delhi as soon as possible. I rang up the Military Secretary, General Bannerjee, at the first opportunity and tried to persuade him to postpone my departure from the brigade by a few months, so that I could complete the process of its deployment. However, the MS was adamant that I join immediately and within days I was packed and on my way.

The Se-la proposal, I learned later, was never considered. Brigadier Ranbir Singh, MC, who took over command from me, was no more successful than I in resisting the unseemly haste to rush troops to the furthermost marches. By mid-1961 two battalions of 7 Brigade had been pushed willy-nilly into the Towang hills; a battery of mountain guns with, predictably, little or no ammunition was later sent up for its support. The garrison had to depend upon air maintenance for a while. After the jeep road crossed Se-la and reached Towang, logistics proved barely adequate, and even then only on a peacetime basis; the management of the long line of communication behind the troops in Towang was never completely undertaken by Divisional HQ. 7 Infantry Brigade was expected to fight the enemy and cope with its own administrative tail simultaneously.

# 4
# DIRECTOR OF MILITARY OPERATIONS

My transfer from NEFA to Army HQ at the end of November 1960 did not occasion the degree of domestic turmoil that a posting to Delhi usually entails. Some years previously, in order to safeguard the continuity of our children's education, my wife and I had decided to establish a family base in Delhi, regardless of my posting. Within the limits of our resources we were lucky to find a small two-bedroom half-house in Prithviraj Road, with its own garden and servant's quarters, a circumstance for which we were to be thankful for many years. After we were allotted a flatlet in Sangli married officers' mess, the family could abide contentedly between our two mini-homes. My wife and I lodged and boarded in mess, her mother ran the house on Prithviraj Road, and the children, particularly my son, formed a floating population between the two.

At Army HQ I moved easily into my chair as Deputy Military Secretary. I had done a two-year stint in MS Branch from 1945 after graduating from Staff College, Quetta, and was familiar with its functions: the management of officer affairs such as commissionings, postings and promotions, confidential reports, honours and awards, releases and retirements.

My boss, Prabhat Bannerjee, innovative, impartial and sensitive, was the ideal MS at a time when a number of prescriptive but not always equitable procedures were in operation in the army, particularly concerning the allotment of senior command and General Staff appointments to the different arms, corps and services. Scrupulously fair and methodical, he made a signal contribution to even-handed career prospects by establishing an unbiased system to replace haphazard and occasionally unjustifiable practices. To cite one example, a disproportionately large number of vacancies for the command of Infantry brigades was being given to officers of the Armoured Corps, Artillery, Engineers, Signals and (in one or two cases) even the Supply Corps. The Infantry itself was the worst served in this respect and, greatly to Bannerjee's credit, he helped restore the balance in its favour even though he himself was an Armoured Corps officer. Other policy aspects that affected the career prospects of officers were tenures of appointment in ranks above lieutenant colonel and allotment of substantive ranks by arms and corps. As far as I knew there had not been a review of these policies since independence, nor had any attempt been made to eradicate arbitrary practices that had crept in during the war years. Bannerjee would hand me files, ask me to digest the subject thoroughly, make a list of possible amendments or suggestions and then discuss them with him, sometimes with senior representatives of arms and corps present. It was interesting and rewarding work, even if it sometimes kept me in office long after work hours.

It was amusing to note that a number of senior generals went in awe of Prabhat Bannerjee. They would telephone me instead of the MS if they wanted a favour – a kinsman to be accommodated conveniently, or an out-of-turn posting for a friend – little acts of nepotism that are basically harmless if the frequency be kept under control. However, even when it was within my power and conscience to concede these favours, I was required to make an entry of the incidents in an unofficial register kept in my office for periodic inspection by the MS. This was his means of keeping nepotism under control and also maintaining a 'crime log' of VIP transgressors. If the demands became too numerous or extravagant, there would be a discreet telephone call from the MS to the general officer concerned and I would hear no more about it – except to receive a dirty glance if I happened to pass the erring general in the corridor!

The winter passed agreeably. This was the first time since had I left command of our regimental centre in Dehra Dun in 1954 that our dispersed family was reunited – myself back from tenures in Kashmir and NEFA; my wife from attending a course on interior design in London, and my daughter home from boarding school in Sanawar. My sister and her husband were also in Delhi and lived in a large house on York Road (since renamed Moti Lal Nehru Marg). We shared common interests and spent many happy weekends out with rod and gun. In particular I recall the long Christmas camp of 1960, spent as guests of Indu, Maharaja of Bharatpur, at his Bayana hunting lodge where fishing in the lake and partridge drives in the surrounding country were a change from the normal (and famous) Bharatpur duck shoots in the Ghana preserve – at which we were, gratefully, permanently on the guest list.

Life in Delhi was exciting. Its society had not yet acquired the fragmented and centrifugal character it took on later. In 1960 it was in essence a large unicentral village. Government officers still controlled the pace of entertainment and recreational activity; the age of big or black money had not arrived.

A few months after I joined MS Branch, Bijji Kaul (my old Divisional Commander, then serving as Quartermaster General) summoned me to his second floor office and told me that he had been selected by the Chief-designate (Thapar) to be the next Chief of the General Staff and that he in turn had nominated me as Director of Military Operations (DMO). He added that he had already obtained the acquiesence of the MS for this transfer, contingent upon my acceptance. I was somewhat taken aback, because I knew from MS Branch gossip that there were at least two senior brigadiers openly aspiring to this most coveted of appointments on the General Staff. One of them was a nominee of General Thapar himself and I had no reason to expect Kaul, whom I had known only for three months in Ambala in 1958, when he was my GOC in 4 Infantry Division, to persist with my nomination as he must have done. Furthermore, by formal standards I was one of the least qualified among my contemporaries for this crucial General Staff appointment. Most of my career, both before and during the Second World War and since, had been spent in command appointments, from a platoon in an Indianised battalion before the war to, just recently, a brigade. (I held the singular distinction of having commanded three different units of my Regiment.) I had never before served in a General Staff appointment in any formation HQ – brigade, division, corps or command. Nor had I attended any army course beyond the unavoidable minimum – the wartime Tactical School at Deccan College in Poona in 1941 (to which I later returned as an instructor); the Quetta Staff College in 1941 (at which I was awarded low grading), and the obligatory senior officers' course in 1953. None of the prestigious overseas courses had come my way.

These self-searching doubts were mitigated by the fact that during the period when Kaul and I had served together in 4th Division I had been much attracted by his ebullient, outgoing personality. Often impulsive and unpredictable, he nevertheless possessed an attribute that I had found in no other general officer I had served with: he was tolerant, not suspicious, of a subordinate with professional curiosity and intellectual pursuits. Despite his lack of combat experience he was professionally competent, resourceful and innovative. Although rumours of his controversial past were freely booted about in the division, to me he remained an army original: there was nobody quite like him in the service. It would be a refreshing challenge to serve with him in the upper reaches of the General Staff.

Kaul gave me time to make a decision and warned me that DMO-ship in the current operational situation would entail exceptionally hard work with little time for personal or domestic pursuits. Having just returned to family life after more than four years of separation I thought it only fair to consult my wife before I made the decision. When I was assured of her approval and support I rang up Kaul to tell him that I would be happy to accept his offer.

The changeover of Army Chiefs was not due to take

place for some three months but I was enjoined by Kaul to make use of the interim period by acquainting myself with the background to the northern border confrontations, which would of course be my main concern as DMO. This was easier said than done. I soon found that a kind of siege mentality had crept into GS Branch. It was obvious to everyone on the staff of the outgoing Chief, General Thimayya, that he was not leaving in the happiest of circumstances. He had suffered undeserved humiliation at Krishna Menon's hands following his sensational but injudicious resignation and subsequent retraction, two years previously. The CGS, DMO, DMI and other members of his General Staff were all being changed; it seemed Thapar and Kaul were determined on a clean sweep before they moved in. This was not conducive to good relations between the old and the new regimes and when I approached the then DMO for friendly guidance all I received for my trouble was a lemon.

There was more to it than just a case of hostility between the old and the new. As I was not *au courant* with Delhi gossip it took me some time to sense an undercurrent of mutual suspicion between groups of senior officers, an outgrowth from the Defence Minister's improper and ill-boding modes of procedure. Krishna Menon had been appointed Defence Minister three years previously. Like many men of intellect, he was a loner by inclination. He had no previous ministerial or administrative experience and found it necessary to disguise this deficiency by affecting a perpetual sneer at officialdom. He also sought to dominate the military bureaucracy by trying to make a dent in the solidarity of its senior ranks. In this he succeeded to the extent that Bijji Kaul – basically loyal by nature but emotional, insecure and ambitious – fell for his blandishments and for a time an unwonted relationship was established between the Minister and the general officer. The result was that the Thapar and Kaul team took over under a cloud of suspicion and resentment.

Thimayya was a popular general. Open, outgoing and with a glowing operational record, he had during his career gained the loyalty and affection of the officer cadre as no other Indian officer before or after him. It was therefore understandable, if not entirely accurate, that his fall from grace was viewed as a Menon machination and that Kaul's name was inevitably linked with Menon. As for Thapar, his choice as 'Timmy's' successor was a disappointment to many senior officers. Upright and conscientious by reputation, professionally well-groomed, Thapar's was nevertheless a lacklustre personality and he did not possess the *réclame* and professional reputation of Thorat who, though a name lower in the army list, was a more charismatic figure and one of a handful of Indian officers who had had operational experience at battalion-command level during the Second World War. Most people had expected that Thorat would be nominated as the next Army Chief. Thus, Thapar's appointment was regarded as another example of the Menon-Kaul conspiracy.

Menon's obtrusive deportment as minister was exaggeratedly portrayed as 'political interference with the army'. A more accurate interpretation of his tendency to short-circuit army procedures would be that it was inspired by self-gratification rather than a deliberate attempt to influence policy through the back door. After the Thimayya episode he had grudgingly to conform to military bureaucratic protocol. In his dealings with senior brass he thereafter observed propriety, albeit with the utmost lack of grace.

It was my experience during the next three years that Menon never actually overrode the professional opinion of his military chiefs, if they were staunch enough to stand firm on their views. He would exercise all the artifices of his make-up − barbed tongue, biting sarcasm or blatant cajolery − to subvert opposition, but if a service chief held his ground he would not overrule him. In subsequent years his directions to the army on operational matters were at times ill-conceived, ill-informed and foolhardy, but they were formal directions, not interference. Recipients at any level were always free to protest against those directions. This clarification is not made to justify Menon's method of operation but to set it in its proper perspective. It is pertinent in assessing the army's share of responsibility in the ensuing debacle in the war against the Chinese.

The second point, a point which should be acknowledged but seems to have been generally misunderstood or deliberately misrepresented, was that it was not Krishna Menon who was primarily culpable for the practice of general officers establishing direct access to politicians. Despite all his airs of self-assurance, Menon was greatly in awe of the Prime Minister and it is unlikely that he would have dared breach military procedure so blatantly had he not had Nehru's precedent before him. It was Nehru who, many years previously, first established this irregularity. He had come across Kaul in the years just before independence and found him a refreshing change from the stereotyped, British-aping and politically uncommitted senior officer of the Indian Army. A strong rapport had sprung up between the two distant kinsmen. It was Nehru who allowed that relationship to grow into an official link after he became Prime Minister. He frequently summoned Kaul for various purposes, some outside the call of army duty, when Kaul was only a colonel. On one occasion he even entrusted to him the task of political troubleshooter in Kashmir. A similar relationship, though not quite as exceptionable, existed between Nehru and Thimayya. The latter was in no way a 'political' general, but Nehru grew fond of him and 'Timmy' did not scruple to exercise his presumed right of access to the PM. Thus, if anyone was to blame for breaches of propriety and procedure that had crept into the Defence Ministry, it was Jawaharlal Nehru. Menon exploited the precedent for his own purposes.

An insidious consequence of the supposed Menon-Kaul intrigue was the barrier of ill-will and suspicion it raised between the many officers professionally loyal to General Thimayya and the few who were close to Kaul. Matters were further aggravated when it became known that one of Kaul's first acts as CGS had been to institute a secret Intelligence Bureau inquiry into Thimayya's alleged treason, citing a number of careless and indiscreet remarks made by him on various occasions, while he was still in service, regarding the army's possible role in a political emergency. I do not know if Menon had a hand in this shabby attempt to persecute Thimayya after his retirement but I doubt it. The *faux pas* was pure Kaul and earned him nothing but calumny for a bungled intrigue.

The reason I have mentioned this unsavoury matter is

that I realised a few months later that in some quarters I had at first been regarded as one of 'Bijji's men', in the pejorative sense, and, I suspect, I never totally escaped the imprint. Be that as it may, I was too busy during my first few months picking up the threads of Military Operations Directorate to be aware of any such insidious undercurrent.

In early June 1961 I moved into the DMO's office. My predecessor had declined to leave behind the customary 'handing over notes' for his successor, so it took me a few days to become acquainted with the general scope of the DMO's charter and to familiarise myself with current operational matters.

My only previous experience on the General Staff had been a makeshift nine-month tenure as GSO-I in the Directorate of Staff Duties in 1948–9, while convalescing from wounds. SD was also a key General Staff function, responsible for the maintenance of, and budgeting for, the army's order of battle and for all staff co-ordination in Army HQ. My brief tenure had provided me only a glimpse of an exciting scope of the professional activities of the General Staff. Now, as I acquainted myself with the DMO's mandate, I was awed by its extent and range.

The prestige and glamour of the DMO arise from his main charge, the preparation of future operational plans and the implementation of existing ones; but his power derives principally from his role as the priorities man at Army HQ. In all matters involving rival demands by the six branches, it is the DMO who arbitrates on priorities. His sway is pervasive and it was to prevent the DMO from acquiring too much power of patronage that his rank was kept deliberately low, at brigadier. (Some years later, in a mindless rush to boost ranks as part of the so-called cadre review, the DMO – together with most other directors at Army HQ – was overly upcast to lieutenant general.)

I was fortunate in my colleagues in the Directorate. They were without exception professionals, well-informed, supportive and diligent. One among them, Lieutenant Colonel Surendra Singh, was a brilliant staff officer, possessed of a degree of practical awareness and professional culture I had not previously met in the army, at any rank. I established an early rapport with them all, collectively and individually, and moved in easily as the new captain of a well-knit team.

I found Bijji Kaul an enigmatic personality but, on the whole, a satisfactory boss. He was a complex being and his role in the escalating crisis in 1962 was so crucial that it would be pertinent to describe his personality, as I perceived it, in some detail.

Personable, even dapper, in appearance, Kaul was a live-wire – quick-thinking, forceful and venturesome. He could also be subjective, capricious and emotional. Once he had taken you into his confidence he gave unstintingly of his personal support and even warmth. There were some among his subordinates, mainly those of mediocre capability, from whom he demanded and obtained a personal and almost feudal commitment, and whom he did not on occasion scruple to use as his confidential henchmen. Yet to those whose professional capability and intellect he recognised, he offered a more egalitarian, though not necessarily close relationship. He could be soft-hearted to a fault, a trait often mistaken for kindness or generosity. However, like many egocentrics, Kaul was not empathic by nature; his way was to dispense his sympathy and support explicitly as largesse rather than as subtle and understanding gifts.

Prominent among his characteristics was hypersensitivity about his lack of regimental and combat service; and he was ever on the lookout for an intended slight in this respect. Yet his *amour propre*, a somewhat lesser thing than ambition, moved him to strive constantly for professional excellence. It is not true to say, as many did, that his primary loyalty was to his own advancement. Although convinced of a great future for himself, even beyond the confines of his service, he did not spend his time accumulating ballast for his career.

His instability was another outstanding characteristic, one exacerbated by his proclivity to be tossed about in a whirlwind of random events. In the midst of an operational crisis one might find him happily spending time and energy on some quite extraneous or irrelevant pursuit. Apart from amateur Hindi dramatics, in which he occasionally dabbled, he appeared to have no personal interests or hobbies and he played no games. After late hours at the office, he would go home and often receive a motley relay of callers, people from all strata of society, not necessarily connected with professional work, and most of them petitioners of some sort. His magpie interest was easily kindled by an emotive approach and these durbar performances became a substitute for social involvement. Only when visiting hour ended would he work at his files, often till midnight or later.

I imagine he made a difficult subordinate. Basically insecure, aware of the hostility and scorn of his seniors, his relationship with Nehru – about which he boasted openly – lent him an air of self-assurance which often bordered on hubris. I think his superiors at Army HQ, Thapar and Wadalia (Deputy Chief of the Army Staff, an appointment later designated Vice-Chief), disliked and distrusted him, although they refrained from open expression of their feelings. At the same time, I think they were both aware that he was an efficient and effective CGS and to my knowledge both had, each on at least one occasion, sought his good offices to resolve some personal problem that required a word in high places. For them Bijji was at once an unruly subordinate and a friend-at-court.

Although I worked closely with him for nearly two years I do not think I completely understood Kaul's chameleon personality, perhaps because, unlike others among his friends, I was never an intimate in his home. In the office he was somewhat punctilious and lacked the light touch; at home he shed his generalship and allowed ceremony to lapse, especially in the company of the very young. He seemed to spend a large part of his life in disguise, even from himself. Indeed, if one were to invent Bijji Kaul as a character in a novel, one might well have difficulty in making him credible.

Kaul may have at first regretted that he had picked a DMO who had numerous recreational interests, who was seemingly easy-going and unhurried and reluctant to sacrifice his domestic and other distractions totally in order to spend long after-office hours at his desk as a matter of routine. On one occasion, during some temporary operational crisis, he remarked somewhat snidely that a DMO in these troubled times must always be available at or near his office. I replied with due deference that I did not believe it either necessary or desirable for me to be at my desk after office hours. Time spent with my family, at games or on outdoor pursuits was, in my opinion, time more wisely spent. I assured him that if an emergency arose, at any hour of the day or night, I would return to my desk at the earliest opportunity. He considered this, apparently accepted it and, to my astonishment (and the delight of my family), instructed the Chief Administrative Officer that the DMO must be granted out-of-turn allotment of a house within walking distance of the operations room in South Block. In less than a week we were out of Sangli mess and installed in an old colonial-style bungalow in Dupleix Lane with a two-acre split-level garden and spacious lawns. It was most agreeable for us — and I was only five minutes from my office, which pleased my boss.

At the time I took over as DMO there was no pressure of operational urgency on the General Staff. Barring trivial incidents such as alleged air violations by both sides or harassment of travellers at checkposts, the northern frontiers had been quiescent for more than a year and the border with Pakistan provided no undue cause for concern. I was therefore able to make a leisurely study of the long-range problems that faced the army at that juncture. This was what the CGS required me to do, leaving day-to-day operational business to be conducted directly with him by Lieutenant Colonels Sanjiva Rao and Pritpal Singh, section officers of MO-1 and MO-2. (Kaul was appointed officiating CGS even before Thapar took over so had already been wo months in the chair.)

Lieutenant Colonel Surendra Singh of MO-4, the section that dealt with future plans, briefed me on the state of the army. There were material shortages in all spheres — arms, ammunition, equipment and General Staff reserve holdings (the maintenance of the latter being one of the DMO's prime responsibilities). In addition, I found that the army's order of battle was not balanced in that there were dangerous gaps in the supporting arms and technical services; even field formations were under strength. Reasons for this deplorable state of affairs were many. Politically, the armed forces had, since independence, been accorded low priority in the allotment of resources. Prime Minister Nehru had displayed marked indifference to the Defence Ministry (as was made evident by his choice of ineffective nonentities as defence ministers before Krishna Menon came on the scene) and was grudging in his allotment of funds to the armed forces. Thus, military procurement programmes were beset by a number of drawbacks, such as shortfalls in production by the ordnance factories, restrictions on imports due to lack of foreign exchange, expansion programmes outstripping procurement and a heavy drain on both manpower and equipment stocks caused by formations and units serving overseas under the United Nations. The CGS directed me to relate these imbalances to the tasks that the army might be required to perform in the foreseeable future in the light of the charter given to us by the government, and to make recommendations on measures the General Staff should take.

Defence policy at that time emanated from the Chiefs of Staff Paper of January 1961, an assessment of the overall requirements of the armed forces. According to this paper, the charter given by the Government of India to the armed forces was 'to be prepared for and to resist external aggression, mainly by Pakistan'. The emphasis implied in the last phrase was curious, to say the least, because it was obvious that the very necessity for a new government directive had arisen from China's hostile activities in 1959. It was almost as a postscript that the Chiefs of Staff Paper recorded: 'We are required by Government to resist to the full *and evict* any further incursions or aggressions by China on our territory.' The paper then made an appraisal of defence requirements to meet both Pakistani and Chinese threats effectively.

As regards the army, the Chiefs of Staff recommended an increase of two infantry divisions and one infantry brigade to meet the threat to the northern border. This would bring the army's order of battle to a total of one armoured division, one independent armoured brigade, eleven infantry divisions, eight independent infantry brigades and one parachute brigade. The paper, however, contained a qualifying statement: 'Should the nature of the war go beyond that of a limited war . . . and develop into a full-scale conflagration amounting to an invasion of our territory, then it would be beyond the capacity of our forces to prosecute war . . . beyond a short period, because of the limitation on size, the paucity of available equipment and the lack of adequate logistical support'.

It seemed a strange approach to the task in hand. The Chiefs of Staff appeared to have conditionally abdicated from their responsibility for the defence of India. Instead of assessing how best we could cope with aggression at various levels (demanding additional resources where necessary) the Chiefs' Paper shirked the issue, lacked strategic content and surrendered to negativism. First, it made the assumption that aggression would be low intensity and asked for only a modest increase in resources. Thereafter, it virtually held up its hands in defeat. I wondered how the cabinet had reacted to its findings.

During a routine discussion with the CGS I raised this matter and asked him if General Thapar would consider pressing for a review of the COS Paper at the next meeting of the Chiefs of Staff Committee (of which I was *ex officio* secretary). I urged that a more positive line be taken regarding the chiefs' strategic responsibilities and that they take note of the charter given them by the government, even if it meant asking for larger force levels. The CGS assured me that I need not be unduly exercised about the COS Paper; General Thimayya's attitude from the earliest stages of the confrontation with the Chinese had been defeatist, he said, and this had undoubtedly influenced the other two chiefs. He added that on one occasion, during a meeting in the Foreign Ministry at which Mullik, Director of the Intelligence Bureau, had been present, Thimayya was reported to have voiced this opinion: 'Against Pak – total war; not against China. I cannot envisage taking on China in open conflict . . . it must be left to the politicians and diplomats to ensure our security.' It was also on record that Thimayya had opined that the Chinese-built Aksai Chin road was of no strategic consequence. He had declined to set up army posts within the Aksai Chin, whereupon the Intelligence Bureau promptly arrogated this responsibility, together with the task of the defence of the border in Ladakh.

This was depressing news because most of us in the army held the former Army Chief in high personal regard.

In the mid-1940s, just after the end of the Second World War, when we were both posted in Delhi (and later when Thimayya returned from Tokyo, where he had been commanding the Indian contingent in the Commonwealth Occupation Force), my wife and I had become close friends with the Thimayyas. Despite the difference in our ranks and seniority, we were on first name terms with 'Timmy' and Neena, and we had shared many mutual friends. During the Kashmir war, as commanding officer (and acting brigade commander) in Poonch, I had for a short while come under Timmy's command when he was GOC Srinagar Division, and thus encountered at first hand his persuasive leadership, his panache and the easy informality with which he addressed himself to the most perilous of operational situations. The only Indian officer to have commanded a brigade in battle in the Second World War, he was seasoned in combat and had been highly decorated. He had the mark of the commander. No other officer of our army was ever so highly regarded or so widely admired. It was difficult for me to believe that he could have adopted such a negative attitude in matters of national security.

The Chiefs of Staff's appraisal of the Chinese threat and their proposals for counter-measures were, in my opinion, perfunctory to the point of being simplistic. In keeping with the general tenor of the paper, the aim seemed to have been to reduce the problem to a statement of figures. The breakdown of threats to the various sectors, from east to west, were: an attack by about two brigades against the NEFA front, mainly at Towang, with a remote possibility of an attack from the east through Burma; about two divisions against Sikkim and Bhutan; a brigade against the Uttar Pradesh (UP) and Himachal Pradesh borders; and, in the west, a divisional threat in the Ladakh sector. To meet these threats the Chiefs of Staff felt that two divisions would be required for NEFA; one for Sikkim and Bhutan; and a brigade each in UP, Himachal and Ladakh. There was no attempt to forecast likely increases in Chinese troop dispositions or other warlike preparations by them. Would they not react with greater troop concentrations when our regular forces began to appear on the border? Would they not begin to build strategic roads, when road-building on their side of the border was so much easier than on ours? What other logistical improvements could they set in motion? None of these questions was either posed or addressed.

It seemed incredible that so grave a matter could have been despatched so heedlessly both by the Chiefs and their staffs. We were planning to meet a possible onslaught by the Chinese People's Liberation Army at altitudes of 5,000 metres and above, hundreds of miles beyond motorable roads – or even mule-tracks in some places. Yet hardly a thought had been given to logistical requirements. At that time we were experiencing difficulty in maintaining even two militia battalions in Ladakh, let alone regular troops; and I had had personal experience of the difficulty of maintaining a battalion at Towang even under non-operational conditions. It would be years before we could build up the capability to maintain battalions and brigades at battle-contact rates in the high ranges. I felt compelled to urge the CGS again to recommend to the COAS that he ask for a new COS Paper, a fresh review of the army's requirements with less emphasis on increased force levels and more on logistical back-up to ensure that even the existing deployment of troops could realistically fulfil the functions planned for them. To quote from my *Summary of Events and Policies:*

*Comment*
After a study of this strategic appraisal I brought the following comments to the attention of the CGS (Lieut General B.M. Kaul):
(*a*) That the Chiefs of Staff Paper of Jan 1961 had not catered for any reserves, either for Army HQ or the Commands;
(*b*) That the Paper had not taken into account the existing imbalances in the Army, which were numerous – particularly, shortages in supporting arms, infantry and logistical elements;
(*c*) That a number of foreseeable strategic developments (whether in India, China or Pakistan) had not been considered, such as a subsequent build-up of forces in Tibet; further development of the Burma-Ledo road as a route of invasion; increasing US military aid to Pakistan; and others;
(*d*) That the existing depleted state of equipment reserves in the Army had not been adequately covered, nor the necessity for a modernization programme projected.

The Paper had not adequately met the requirements given to the armed forces by Government, presumably because it had been written as a short-term appreciation, arising out of the sudden projection of the Chinese threat in 1959–60. What was required, in order to make a planned build-up of the Army, was a long-range appreciation, based on an approved strategic concept to be laid down by the General Staff, within the overall frame-work of which the Army could be methodically built up as a balanced force to meet external threats. I suggested that the planning period covered by such a study be ten years. The CGS obtained the approval of the COAS and we began our study in August 1961.

Thereafter I devoted at least two hours each day, mostly in the late afternoons, with Surendra Singh and others of MO-4, working on what we somewhat pompously called 'A Master Plan for the Army'. Fortunately the Director of Staff Duties, Brigadier J.T. ('Jangu') Sataravala, MBE, MC, was an old friend and proved a willing collaborator. He helped to arrange numerous meetings with staff officers of the QMG and MGO branches, which he chaired if I were absent. It was obvious from the start of our project that our work would be at cross purposes with vested interests that had taken root in certain areas of Army HQ, so we kept our findings to ourselves.

The study would take a few months to complete. (The 'Master Plan' was not presented to the Chief and CGS till February 1962.) Meanwhile, what I termed the army's 'state of unreadiness-for-war' urgently needed rectification. Not only were some formations and units short of component parts on both the Pakistani and northern fronts, there were also crippling shortages in arms, equipment and vehicles. The increase in force levels recommended by the Chiefs of Staff, and already in the process of implementation, would aggravate the situation even further; production levels in the country were low and, due to the scarcity of hard currency, procurement from abroad was restricted.

The first part of the new raisings, two additional brigade groups and sundry units, had started in March-April 1961. The second part, two new divisions, was to begin in December, after completion of the first. I was convinced that a smaller force that was geared for war made better sense than a larger one that was not, so I determined to postpone the second half of the expansion programme till we had formulated a feasible re-equipment policy.

Planning for the replenishment of equipment reserves was complicated by the fact that the army was at that time entering a period of modernisation to replace its Second World War holdings. It would obviously be wasteful to make up shortages in obsolescent items which would have to be discarded as soon as new equipment became available. Yet to accept the existing shortages while waiting for modern replacements meant that the army would remain unprepared for war in the interim – perhaps for two years or more. The choice between the two courses clearly depended on the likelihood of having to fight a war in the near future. I decided to consult the Director of Military Intelligence, Brigadier Bim Batra, but I soon realised, with something of a shock, that MI Directorate was not in fact effective in producing an assessment of threat.

In all armies the Directorship of Military Intelligence is considered a glamorous appointment. In ours, recent incumbents of the office had been eminent, highly decorated officers. I assumed that, as in other distinguished armies, our MI Directorate was responsible for the production of top grade Intelligence, threat assessments and other highly secret and romantically invested activities. Unfortunately, this was not the case. I discovered to my amazement that the responsibilities of MI Directorate (and, presumably, the intelligence directorates of the other two services also) had been drastically curtailed during recent years. The DMI was no longer in the business of gathering Intelligence. He deployed no agent, inside or outside the country; his sources of information were all secondhand. Consequently, he was unable to make threat appreciations based on inside information.

In 1951, the Himmatsingji Committee, unimpressed by the scope and function of Military Intelligence after independence, had recommended that responsibility for gathering internal and external intelligence be taken away from the DMI and vested in the civilian intelligence organisation, the Intelligence Bureau. Thereafter although the DMI retained a sizeable staff and had vast funds at his disposal, he had little to do other than to act as *sirdar* of military attachés or supervise field security tasks within the army. In fact, I found that MO Directorate had more firsthand sources of Intelligence than the DMI, because it was we who received patrol reports and other information from our forward troops deployed on the borders.

I next approached the Joint Intelligence Committee, which was at that time a sub-council of the Chiefs of Staff (as was the Joint Planning Committee, of which I was *ex officio* chairman). The JIC was chaired by a joint secretary of the Ministry of External Affairs, and its members were representatives from the Defence and Home Ministries, the three armed services Directors of Intelligence and a senior officer from the Intelligence Bureau. The latter was, in fact, the only member who could make an original contribution in the way of intelligence. At the next meeting of the JIC, I noticed that the IB had so completely cornered the market in intelligence input that it had taken to presenting its reports as conclusions rather than as items presented for the Committee's assessment. No one challenged this unusual procedure whereby the provider of intelligence had also arrogated the responsibility for collation of information and assessment of threat. The chairman (and other members) appeared to play no part except that of a post office. Most astonishing of all, the representative from the Ministry of External Affairs seldom contributed information regarding diplomatic or international developments, which are as important in helping to form threat perceptions as reinforcements of troops and tanks. I do not recall any mention of the incipient Sino-Russian rift, or of domestic convulsions in China caused by the severe economic crisis in 1961–2 after the failure of the Great Leap Forward and the withdrawal of Soviet economic assistance. Nor, after June 1962, when both the economic crisis and the threat of a Nationalist Chinese invasion had passed, was any indication given that thenceforth Chinese responses to perceived provocations on the Ladakh border were likely to harden and even escalate – as in fact happened.

New to the forms and procedures of the General Staff, I did not then realise the anomaly of this intelligence procedure, but I did suggest to the CGS that we ought to process the IB reports through the DMI before they were sent up to the Chiefs of Staff. The CGS disagreed; he was content to leave the system as it was. He advised me to establish a one-to-one link with Mr Mullik, the Director of the Intelligence Bureau, if I needed firsthand intelligence appreciation.

The IB's figures for Chinese troop deployments along the border were, of course, the same as those quoted in the Chiefs of Staff Paper. As far as I recall, however, there was no clear assessment of China's likely operational intentions, or an assessment of the logistical capability of its forces for operations across the Himalayas. I later realised that a large proportion of IB assessments of Chinese troop locations and strengths (in Tibet) was based on material fed it by the CIA and British Intelligence. Since much of the latter was derived from mechanical surveillance rather than from agents' reports, Chinese aims, intentions and decision-making processes were not easily obtainable; they could only be surmised. I had not yet established a personal rapport with the DIB, Mr Mullik, and so had to be content with whatever assessment his deputy, Mr Dave, gave the JIC.

In the matter of threats from Pakistan, the IB was more precise and confident, because our intelligence network in respect of that country was well-organised. When I consulted the Deputy Director in charge of the Pakistan desk, Balbir Singh, he could offer no assurance about a likely no-war interim period. All that he could guarantee, at best, was a warning period of one month before a possible attack by Pakistan in the Punjab or in Kashmir. This lead time might, under some circumstances, be reduced to ten days; and I had to be content with that.

For our purpose – that is, planning for arms and equipment replacement programmes – we obviously could not risk keeping the army under-armed or ill-equipped for any length of time. Yet, to make up all existing deficiencies with obsolescent items would be a crass wastage at a time of great financial stringency. Accordingly, in early July, I sent a long minute to the CGS, recommending a compromise policy. I suggested that we accept deficiencies in less critical spheres (such as war maintenance stocks and General Staff reserves) but that we keep units in field formations up to strength even if it meant heavy expenditure in local and foreign currencies. The CGS agreed, but felt that the decision should be taken at a higher level. He directed me to arrange a meeting of General Staff directors under the chairmanship of Lieutenant General Wadalia, the Deputy Chief, to review the policy on holding equipment reserves. Only then would he ask the COAS for a decision on the extent of depletion of GS reserves.

I include an account of the proceedings at this meeting for a particular reason. General Wadalia's sophistical pronouncement at the end, in my opinion, revealed an attitude of mind I found prevalent among many senior officers, both military and civilian, and is a commentary on the political logic of the times.

At the meeting we examined in detail the report of the Master-General of Ordnance on the equipment situation. Because of Krishna Menon's determination to make India self-reliant in defence production to the fullest extent possible – his outstanding contribution to national policy – the Controller-General of Defence Production had activated plans for the expansion of ordnance factories. Procurement from abroad was to be kept to a minimum. However, it was evident that in India, where defence equipment is manufactured only by the military and not entrusted to civilian industry or trade, the CGDP would be unable fully to cope with so vast a requirement. The timelag between shortfalls of equipment and their resupply would be considerable. Furthermore, our GS reserve policy of holding six months' stocks was based on the British experience that it takes about that length of time after the start of hostilities for industry to expand to a war footing. I argued that whereas six months might be an acceptable period in an advanced industrial country, in our case it would take considerably longer than that before the CGDP could hope to increase production sufficiently to meet both war requirements and war wastages. Consequently, I argued, holdings of GS reserves should be calculated for a longer period – at least a year and possibly more. I stressed that this was all the more necessary now that we were required to plan for defence against both Pakistan and China.

The aim was to authorise an increase in the General Staff reserve holdings so that we could press the government to sanction foreign and indigenous procurement. We could then use these enlarged reserves as a temporary source from which to equip new raisings while we waited for CGDP to swing into production. In this way the army would be in a state of readiness for war at any given moment, even if it temporarily lost its capability for prolonged operations.

I noticed that the chairman appeared not to be overly impressed by these arguments. When I summed up our recommendations and asked for his endorsement, he declined to give it. He stated that there was no need to plan for increased GS reserves, that if ever we found ourselves at war with China which might predictably be prolonged beyond six months, we could safely assume 'foreign intervention', implying that the United States, Britain and other western powers would rush to our aid with arms, equipment and (perhaps) armed forces. With that we had to be content, for he would not budge from his position.

I was reasonably sure that no such understanding was on record in the Ministry of External Affairs. Apart from being contrary to nationalist sentiment, it would conflict with the central thrust of our foreign policy in which non-alignment and rejection of military alliances were fundamental axioms. At the same time, I knew from personal experience that many in crucial positions in government placed their confidence in a presumed corollary of international accommodation: if it came to a war with communist China, India would not fight alone; the western democracies would intervene on our side. To me this wishful assumption represented an unconscious reversion to the colonial era when national security was not a function of Indian sovereignty but ultimately referable to Whitehall.

I am sure that the younger generation of officers, those not inured to operating within an imperial system, did not share this conviction. It was only the more senior ones, such as Thimayya or Wadalia, whose approach to national security seemed conditioned by an instinctive referral to Britain and the west. This was also the case with senior bureaucrats in the ministries, the ICS clan. In later dealings with Madhav Desai, the Foreign Secretary, I received the same impression. Even Prime Minister Nehru appeared at times to entertain this idea, although he expressed it differently: on more than one occasion he asserted in parliament and elsewhere that in the event of war between India and China, the conflict would inevitably expand to a world war, presumably implying that we would find anti-communist allies fighting on our side. (Indeed when the crisis mounted in NEFA, even the hitherto assertively nationalist Bijji Kaul sent a frantic signal to the government asking it to request 'foreign armed forces to come to our aid' and, *in extremis*, Nehru did just that.)

After the inconclusive meeting under Wadalia, the CGS and I briefed the Army Chief on the arms and equipment shortages. Kaul pointed out that we had reached an impasse: on the one hand the government expected us to raise new units to meet operational requirements; on the other, we were so short of resources that even existing units and formations were being kept under-equipped and could not always be logistically supported. After some discussion, Thapar agreed that we should approach government for *ad hoc* purchases to make up current shortages and equip new raisings, but that the proposal to increase GS reserve holdings should be shelved for the present.

Thereafter the CGS wrote a series of letters to the Defence Secretary emphasising the critical state of our shortages and requesting allocation of funds for the immediate procurement of minimum requirements. This met with no response, so in November 1961 a letter was sent to the Defence Minister over the COAS' signature, with the specific request that it be placed before the Defence Committee of Cabinet. When even that measure failed to evoke a response, Kaul (with Thapar's knowledge) used his personal access to Nehru and took the case directly to him, though on this occasion he was not able to work the oracle. As recorded in Kaul's book, *The Untold Story*, the PM's reply was that 'if we imported the weapons and equipment needed by the armed forces . . . [it] would result in a major economic setback to the country, which he could not accept'. Neither would he countenance acceptance of military aid from any country. The only advice he gave, unreal at that time, was, 'We must mainly rely upon indigenous production.'

This seemingly offhand decree was received in South Block without any great resentment. On the contrary, the bureaucrats in the ministries interpreted the Prime Minister's pronouncement as an indication that we could relax somewhat from the urgency of our task, that India would not actually be required to fight a war against China. At that time Nehru's stature and *réclame* were so considerable that in matters of international policy, and even strategic assessment, his wisdom was seldom questioned. Consequently the feeling ran that if the PM were content to allow the army to remain under-armed and ill-balanced for a period of years, he did not foresee the possibility of a war against a major power. This in itself did not lead to a change in border policy but it did contribute to the climate of opinion in government which began to regard General Staff urgencies as alarmist and, that, in its own way, affected policy. Furthermore, this downgrading of operational anxiety in South Block would eventually cause a rift within the army's command levels. The General Staff at Army HQ would continue to hustle field commanders, urging them to expedite a forward policy, whereas the field commanders, short of resources and faced with the realities of unequal confrontation on Himalayan heights, would receive our goadings and blandishments with suspicion and even distrust.

At this point it is necessary to outline briefly the border policies the government had hitherto followed, the more so because there were circumstantial differences between the eastern and western sectors. In NEFA it was we who were in occupation of disputed territory (territory claimed by both India and China). There had been indications that the Chinese would observe the McMahon Line as the *de facto* boundary and even retract their claim if we made similar concessions in the Ladakh sector. In NEFA, therefore, it was clearly expedient for us to preserve the *status quo* and not to provoke the Chinese in any way. (Accordingly, when 4 Infantry Division moved into NEFA in November 1959, orders had been issued to the troops not to approach closer than three kilometres from the McMahon Line, except, of course, where the administration had already established Assam Rifle posts on the border, as at Khinzemane and Bum-la.)

In the central sector (Uttar Pradesh and Himachal Pradesh) India regarded the line of the main passes as the border, though at places such as Bara Hoti the Chinese claimed pastoral stretches on our side of the watershed. In general, the principle of the high watershed was being tacitly observed throughout the central sector, from the border with Nepal to Demchok in Ladakh. There was no big dispute involved.

In the Aksai Chin the situation was the opposite of that in NEFA. There it was the Chinese who occupied disputed territory. Part of this area had never been inhabited, administered or even properly surveyed by either country, a totally sterile stretch of territory visited only by transient pasturers during the brief summer months. Neither side could base its claim on traditional occupation. Only after the invasion of Tibet, when the Chinese perceived the area's strategic value as a route of access from Sinkiang to Lhasa, did they surreptitiously start a road-construction programme through it. A few years later they began to lay formal claims to the area and to establish posts within it. By 1959 they had moved well inside the Aksai Chin, at places even up to their claim line, as at Kongka-la and Fort Khurnak.

Our operational policy in Ladakh was at first purely defensive. In September 1959 the PM had laid down:

The Aksai Chin area has to be left more or less as it is as we have no check posts there and practically little of access. Any questions in relation to it can only be considered when the time arises, in the context of the larger question of the Chinese border. For the present we have to put up with the Chinese occupation of this north-eastern sector and their road across it.

At that stage the keystone of Nehru's policy was crisis management, with repeated insistence on negotiations. (At the same time he was unyielding about India's claim to the general line of the boundary as defined by the British during the days of Empire and which, in 1950, had been incorporated in the Indian Constitution.) However, after the failure of the Chou-Nehru talks of April 1960, when Opposition leaders in parliament became more vociferous against any kind of compromise, there was a noticeable change in the government's policy and its directives to the army. Previous orders were modified in that the army was required to send patrols into 'disputed' areas of the Aksai

Chin which were unoccupied by the Chinese, but without becoming involved in clashes if they encountered a Chinese post or patrol. Thimayya, still the Army Chief, demurred on grounds of lack of logistical resources, a problem seldom clearly understood by civilians (bureaucrats and politicians alike). In passing on government's orders he toned down the operational instructions to Western Command: 'to maintain our positions firmly on *our side* of the international border . . . *status quo* to be maintained . . . prevent any further infiltration into our territory . . . [by] establishing additional posts ahead of our present defensive positions.' (Emphasis added.) Thus, despite the change in government policy, Army HQ continued with its purely defensive stance. The actual task given by Thimayya to Western Command was: 'to deny the main approaches to Ladakh and to defend Leh'. No mention was made of patrols to the Aksai Chin.

Even for this limited defensive role the troops and logistical resources were hopelessly inadequate. Against an estimated threat of more than a brigade, we could deploy only one militia battalion (later increased to two). Without a road link with the rest of India, and in view of shortages in aircraft and para-dropping equipment, regular troops could not then be sent to Ladakh. (The requirement of forces was estimated at a brigade of five regular battalions supported by artillery, besides the two militia battalions already there.) In the circumstances the only concession that Army HQ made to increasing pressures from the government to patrol forward into claimed territory, was to leave the decision to the local commander – that is, to *permit* him to patrol if he felt he could do so.

In April 1961, when the Ministry pressed upon Thimayya the necessity of opening a post near the Karakoram Pass, he agreed to establish Daulet Beg Oldi, west of the Chip Chap valley and well on our side of the Chinese claim line. Shortly after that Kaul, as officiating CGS to Thimayya, minuted to the Ministry in a MO file that the logistical situation in Ladakh was so precarious that should the Chinese mount strong incursions into our territory 'the Army would not be in a position to prevent them from doing so'.

At the time when I took over as DMO the Chinese were not as aggressive as they became a year later. I remember discussing with Kaul his minute quoted in the previous paragraph. It has always been my understanding of military observance that when a commander is given a task for which he feels he has inadequate resources, he should make an assessment of how much he can do, rather than issue a negative statement of what he cannot do. Even more emphatically, in a case involving defence against external aggression, he must react – even though his range of options is limited by lack of resources. I suggested tactfully to the CGS that his minute to the government should have followed through to a conclusion; if we could not prevent the enemy from crossing our border, we must nevertheless prepare to stop them at some point within our territory. I suggested that we ask Western Command to inform us of their plans in the event of a strong incursion into Ladakh by the Chinese: Was the main battle to be fought at Leh? If so, was a close defence of Leh feasible in the circumstances? At the same time, I added, Army HQ should study the possibility of taking offensive action on some other front (such as the Chumbi valley east of Sikkim) where logistics would be in our favour.

The CGS directed that before we proceeded any further in the matter I obtain from Western Command a forecast of its logistical build-up during the coming year, in particular air supply tonnages. Based on that estimate I should suggest a provisional induction programme for at least one complete regular infantry battalion to join the two militia battalions and one regular infantry company already in Ladakh. (There was still no road link with the rest of India, but four airfields were in operation.) Only after that could we ask HQ Western Command for its contingent plans.

While on the subject of logistics, and mindful of the unseemly haste to push troops into forward areas without ensuring adequate logistical cover – as I had experienced in 7 Brigade – I urged the CGS to issue firm instructions to discourage this approach. He agreed as far as NEFA was concerned and I conveyed the message to Eastern Command with a degree of personal satisfaction; but he was reluctant to issue any such cautionary note to Western Command where, he said, there was already a tendency inherited from the Thimayya era to drag its feet about forward deployment. He explained that in Ladakh, where we were not in occupation of territory we claimed, it was imperative to demonstrate a presence in the empty spaces, even if such forward moves temporarily outran maintenance capability at war rates. When I pointed out the risk involved in carrying out flag-waving operations in a logistical vacuum, he cited our policy in NEFA, where we had taken the risk and extended physical possession right up to the border, and had got away with it. He was convinced that we must do the same on the Ladakh front. There was, of course, an obvious flaw in that argument: in NEFA we had forestalled the Chinese in disputed territory and arrived first – a *fait accompli* that the Chinese appeared to have accepted; in the Aksai Chin it was the Chinese who had forestalled us. Any incursion we made now would be viewed as aggression, just as a Chinese incursion in Towang would appear to us. Therefore, I argued, we must be prepared to meet resistance if we went forward with regular troops into Chinese-claimed Aksai Chin. In that case we could undertake the task only when we were reasonably capable of supporting the troops in action, logistically as well as tactically. However, the CGS was adamant that we must not remain passive while the Chinese nibbled away at our territory. The DIB's assessment, he said, was that the Chinese were unlikely to resort to large-scale military action, particularly at a time when political negotiations between India and China were under way. When I pointed out that only four months previously we had cautioned Western Command (in our Operation Instruction No. 26 of February 1960) about the possibility of 'an armed invasion with superior forces through the major passes', Kaul replied that our intelligence appreciation had been revised since then. The Chinese had displayed no sign of taking offensive action and we could assume that they would not initiate a war against India. The CGS had clearly decided on a more aggressive posture in Ladakh and for that it was convenient, it appears in retrospect, to make an assumption of Chinese good will. In time this kind of wishful projection would have its effect on many of us in Army HQ.

I had not yet become accustomed to the political culture that prevailed in South Block in the aftermath of the border confrontation. There was a propensity to ignore military reality and adopt an emotional attitude that pandered to patriotic urges while shrugging away inter-related problems with optimistic assumptions. After the failure of the Nehru-Chou talks parliament and government resorted to slogans that, once adopted, forced us inexorably into channels of action from which there was no drawing back. Mullik, for example, was one of those who firmly believed that we should not yield 'one inch of our territory', a slogan quickly taken up in those heady days. This meant, of course, that we must defend the whole length of the border. He strongly refuted the argument that the army should give battle only on ground of its own choosing, where its tactical and logistical resources could be optimally mustered. The way Mullik saw it, we had to fight at the border, whatever the consequences; voluntary surrender of any part of our motherland would disgrace the nation. It was a deathwish attitude, a visionary outlook that overshadowed military logic.

In September 1961 the post at Daulet Beg Oldi reported that one of its patrols had found a strong Chinese picket established in the Chip Chap valley, barely 15 km from DBO. Vehicular traffic had also been observed, indicating the existence of a motor road to the post. When he sent out a second patrol for further reconnaissance Chinese troops attempted to encircle and capture it.

The Foreign Secretary, Madhav Desai, asked for a meeting with Army HQ. Thapar and Kaul were both in England at the time, so the senior officer present in General Staff Branch, Major General D.N. ('Danny') Misra, MC, Director of Military Training, attended the meeting in the Foreign Secretary's office. Unfortunately I was not able to brief him on the operational situation before we went to meet Desai. Danny returned from the meeting with the alarming information that the Foreign Secretary was 'up in arms' about the incident in the Chip Chap valley and wanted us to take more aggressive action should any of our patrols again be confronted by the Chinese. As for the Galwan valley (to the south of DBO post) Desai wanted us to send a 'fairly strong and well-equipped party so that it could deal with any Chinese it met during its reconnaissance'.

I told Danny that Desai's instructions were downright

unrealistic. I explained the logistical difficulties in Ladakh and in particular on our Aksai Chin border, where we were in no position to support even the smallest-scale hostilities. In any event, I pointed out, these instructions were contrary to the PM's directive that we were to avoid conflict not only in a big way but even in a small way. Danny agreed to refer the matter back to the Foreign Secretary. Accordingly we sent a note to the Ministry of External Affairs, pointing out that

. . . a reference was also made to the aggressive action that was to be taken by our own patrols on encountering the Chinese in this region. It was suggested that one of the most effective methods of stemming the Chinese policy of gradually creeping westwards across our borders in Ladakh would be to give them an occasional knock during these chance encounters within our own territory – particularly in the areas east of the 1954 claim lines. For instance, if we found one of their patrols in a setting tactically favourable to us, it would be worth our while to engage them in a short offensive action aimed at inflicting casualties and/or taking prisoners.

Before orders are issued to local commanders to implement the above, a formal approval is requested. This is necessary because our existing operational policy on the border is in accordance with the note recorded by the Prime Minister on 13 Sep 59. . .

The next day the Foreign Secretary asked for another meeting with the officiating CGS. This time I accompanied him. At the meeting I once again outlined our logistical difficulties and stated quite definitely that we could not support our troops anywhere forward of the vicinity of Leh or Chushul if they became involved even in a minor skirmish. Desai countered by saying that according to intelligence appreciation the Chinese would not engage in hostilities against us. I pointed out that that appraisal was made about six months previously; since then the Chinese had acted more aggressively than ever before. I suggested that we obtain from the DIB a second assessment of probable Chinese reactions before we issue any instructions to Western Command that might provoke a confrontation in the Aksai Chin. The Foreign Secretary reluctantly agreed.

I wondered whether senior ICS bureaucrats prosecuted the confrontation with the Chinese as a continuum of the imperial posturings of their British predecessors – never mind that the emperor now had no clothes. Did Madhav Desai (or Nehru himself, for that matter) imagine himself vicariously in the chair as a latter-day Henry McMahon, laying down terms to the orientals and authoritatively drawing lines across maps? Or did their smugness stem from a subconscious reliance on Whitehall and Washington to rush to their rescue if things got out of hand?

On 26 September 1961 we received a reply from the IB in the form of a long and comprehensive paper describing the whole background of Chinese activities along the northern border since June 1959, when they had first demonstrated their intention to push forward up to their claim line. After a detailed list of Chinese encroachments it continued:

(a) In north Ladakh they had come up to their 1960 claim line, thus incorporating about 1400–1800 square miles of territory; in the south they had not yet come right up to their 1960 claim but they commanded most of the unoccupied areas by occupying about 400 square miles of territory between the Chang Chenmo valley and Fort Khurnak.

(b) Elsewhere also there had been a gradual move forward of their forces – for instance in north Punjab (south of Ladakh) and in the Pemako region of NEFA.

The paper drew the following conclusions about Chinese tactics:

(a) The Chinese would like to come right up to their claim of 1960 wherever we ourselves are not in occupation. *But where even a dozen men of ours are present, the Chinese have kept away.* [Emphasis added]

(b) They would invariably protest when we try to go forward and occupy areas which are distinctly ours but have not been occupied by us yet.

(c) By putting in their protests first, they would like to stop us from protesting. They would also like our border forces to become extremely cautious and to condition them to ignore Chinese intrusions or advance.

Mr Dave, under whose signature the paper had been

sent, then went on to suggest certain courses of action:

*Recommendations*

As the Chinese have been found to have violated the agreement not to send forward patrols and have even occupied new areas which were not in their occupation in 1959 or even in 1960, and as they are unlikely to withdraw from these positions even if diplomatic protests are made, it is for consideration whether Indian Army should not fill up the vacuum which still exists at certain places as, otherwise, the Chinese are bound to move into these areas within a few months. Patrolling on the frontiers also has to be intensified to find out signs of new Chinese encroachments.

In Ladakh itself, the Army have already opened a post at Daulet Beg Oldi and another at a point about 8 miles south-east of it. They have also decided to open new posts at Chang-la (about 20 miles north of Demchok) and at Charding-la (16 miles south of Demchok where they are in occupation of a commanding position. It seems necessary to consider following further steps in Ladakh:

— To reconnoitre the Galwan river valley and to open a post as far forward along it as possible.
— To reconnoitre the yet unoccupied area north of Pangong Lake and the area between Pangong and Spanggur lakes for establishing new posts, if possible. It seems desirable to prevent the Chinese from consolidating their hold in the area north of Rezang-la and south of Spanggur lake because by doing so the Chinese post at Spanggur may well become militarily untenable.
— To continue to send patrols forward from the new post 10 miles south-east of Demchok to the limit of our frontier and, if possible, even to consider having a small post right at the edge of our border.
— To open a post at Chumar in southern Ladakh so as to bar entrance to the Chinese.

It is also necessary to examine the disposition of outposts in the disputed areas of Uttar Pradesh with the object of preventing the Chinese from occupying the disputed areas surreptitiously. The existing outposts should stay on during the winter months as far as possible.

It is essential to give over-riding priority to the airdropping of supplies for all these outposts.

Similarly, in NEFA we should immediately try and go forward to establish outposts on the McMahon Line wherever there is a gap. As many reconnaissance expeditions as are necessary should be organised so as to occupy territory right up to the border.

Many years later, in an article I wrote as Military Correspondent of the *Hindustan Times* (11 April 1971), I made the following comment on this IB paper:

Looking back on it now, it seems to me that this formed the turning point in our border policy. From a simple statement of fact – that the Chinese have so far kept away from our posts – it was but a short step to the assumption that they would always keep away; but that short step crossed a dividing line and none was able to see it.

Furthermore, now the IB was laying down tactical policy. From then onward, Army HQ was always made to feel as if it was dragging its steps – not deploying far enough forward or in sufficient strength. A General Staff paper of 21st October pointed out again to the Defence Minister that the Army's existing force levels, as also shortages in air lift resources, prevented us from both manning and maintaining the scale of border outposts suggested in the IB's recommendations – but the DM continued to express concern, both to the Army Chief and to the CGS, that 'the Army appeared to be doing nothing' to protect our borders.

Now, as I write this memoir nearly thirty years after the event, it seems inconceivable that a civilian Intelligence organisation should have made recommendations concerning military operations. The information provided was, in parts, tendentious, and the advice to the government reads like an operational directive from a super-DMO That such a directive from an intelligence chief was not regarded as exceptionable is in itself a commentary on the regimen of the time. The procedure had obviously been established by custom over the years since partition. It was not until much later that I discovered how this usage came to be established. When I was writing my *Summary of Events* paper after the operations against the Chinese, I sought out old files and documents from Home and Foreign Ministries, consulted old IB reports and cross-checked with other General Staff directorates – clearly something I should have done when I first took over as DMO. It was then that I learned for the first time how closely the DIB had been associated with northern border operations. Before the border had been handed over to the army in October 1959, the DIB had been in charge not only of intelligence but also of 'operations' along the whole frontier extending from the Burma–India–Tibet trijunction to the Karakoram pass in Ladakh.

The Himmatsinghji Committee had given the IB this role, independent of Army HQ and the Ministry of Defence; and once the procedure had become formal the DIB became the *de facto* DMO for the northern border, siting checkposts along the whole length of the watershed and sending reconnaissance patrols into disputed territory. Although technically under the Home Minister, in fact the Director reported directly to the PM and, since in those days anyone operating within the reaches of that aura enjoyed automatic prestige and authority, B.N. Mullik became a sort of *eminence grise* within a small and *ad hoc* decision-making cell. By 1958 he had deployed over sixty posts in Ladakh, twenty-two in NEFA and a total of about thirty along the borders of UP, Sikkim and Himachal Pradesh. He had also set up an effective pattern of sending long-range summer patrols into the extreme north-west territories where permanent posts were logistically impossible to maintain. Even after he handed over border responsibility in Ladakh to the army (in October 1959) Mullik insisted on retaining direct control of all intelligence posts deployed on the border – and thus his prescriptive role as adviser to the PM on border strategy.

Mullik, like other IB officers of the post-independence era, hailed from the old Indian Police cadre. Under the British, the IB was responsible, apart from its routine police duties, for internal intelligence, both political and criminal. External intelligence was primarily directed by the government in London, which, to a degree, delegated authority for sub-continental matters (such as those concerning Iran, Afghanistan and Tibet) to the Political Department of the government of India. For this purpose the department recruited personnel from the army to an extent not appreciated by the Himmatsinghji Committee. Army officers were posted to the IB offices at Peshawar and Quetta for intelligence-gathering roles. Others recruited for the IB came from the Survey of India or were explorers and traders, people with a generally outbound orientation.

At the time of independence the British quite understandably dismantled their intelligence system and burned most of its files, leaving only those that dealt with petty crimes and criminals. Of external intelligence not a vestige remained, not one file in either the IB or in the DMI's office. When Nehru formed his interim government, as he was unaccustomed to handling intelligence matters he assigned the task to the Home Minister who, in turn, according to the only precedent of which he was aware, chose a police officer to co-ordinate intelligence matters – a Mr Anwar Ahmad, if memory serves. On partition Ahmad went to Pakistan; the new Home Minister of independent India appointed his successor, Sanjivi, also from the police and made him responsible for both internal and external intelligence. (Sanjivi left after only a short time in office, making way for Mullik, whose tenure eventually lasted for nearly twenty years.)

In post-independence India, the Military Intelligence Directorate was even more of a non-starter in the pursuit of external intelligence. The British had not allowed Indians to serve in Army HQ before the war, the Indianisation scheme being applied only to a few selected units, mainly of infantry and cavalry regiments. During the latter half of the Second World War, a trickle of Indians were at last posted to Army HQ but were not placed in the sensitive directorates of Military Operations (MO) or Military Intelligence (MI). After the end of the war, one or two Indian officers did find their way to MO; none to MI. After independence, when Indian officers were first appointed to the MI Directorate, they took over in a complete vacuum as far as external secret service activities were concerned. The Kashmir war started soon afterwards, and intelligence efforts were confined to matters concerning field security and other routine chores. The DMI never got off the ground as regards the acquisition of intelligence, in or out of India. Thus it came about that when the Himmatsinghji Committee began its investigations it found that Military Intelligence had not even begun to collect external information from across our northern borders. Somewhat hastily, I feel, it handed the whole responsibility over to the police.

One consequence of this unqualified transfer of intelligence operations to the police was that intelligence-gathering in India acquired an introverted security emphasis rather than a quality of outbound quest and adventure usually associated with foreign agents. This shortcoming was exacerbated by the fact that there seems to have been no established procedure whereby requirements or tasks could be assigned to the IB, or, when information had been acquired, for a central agency or committee to collate and assess it. These functions are usually the responsibility of a Foreign Ministry, but since India had inherited no Foreign Ministry from the British, a formal system of gathering and managing intelligence had never been effectively established. The IB subsumed all these roles and thus became an end in itself, without adequate regard for those whom it should serve – for instance, the General Staff. Although its Director was a discerning and dedicated man, he was unable to avoid the pitfalls that such an autocratic mandate inevitably creates. The intelligence-gatherer, willy-nilly, became part of the policy-making élite, a situation that inevitably compromises the quality of intelligence.

Another important factor was that our intelligence system was launched when the developed nations of the world were switching from personal to mechanical means of information-gathering. Aerial photography, wireless surveillance and (soon afterwards) satellite cover, not cloak-and-dagger methods, were to be the tools of the future – and the Indian police had neither the training nor the equipment to adopt them. Nor did the ministries concerned have the comprehension or foresight to harness the signals resources of the army or the aerial reconnaissance capability of the air force in a joint intelligence enterprise. Only after the war with China was the Signals Intelligence Organisation created and the DMI at last made responsible for intelligence responsibilities such as area studies of our border regions.

When the CGS returned from abroad I briefed him on the development in the Aksai Chin and Desai's reaction to it. I told him about Desai's combative posturings during his meeting with Misra and myself, and I suggested that in order to dispel some of the illusions that civilians appeared to harbour about our operational capability, we should take steps to educate the key bureaucrats on the realities. My idea was to invite them to the DMO's Ops Room, where we could brief them on the map and tell them about problems of supply and maintenance in NEFA and Ladakh. The CGS disagreed; he felt that the briefings might appear presumptuous and therefore be counterproductive. Instead, on 21 October he sent a long note to the Ministry describing our logistical inadequacies in statistical terms. He pointed out that we had been unable to deploy the requisite forces in Ladakh because of the lack of a road to Leh and the shortage of airlift resources and air supply equipment. The situation was so desperate, he emphasised, that not only had we been unable to effect our defence plans, but even the patrolling programme had been curtailed, since 'all long-range patrols must of necessity be maintained by air. . . . At present, the reinforcement of any particular area or the setting up of a new outpost can only be done if a comparable withdrawal or abandonment of some other post in Ladakh is carried out.'

If we expected that this elucidation would produce a clearer understanding of our practical difficulties and, therefore, an end to unrealistic demands, we were soon disappointed. The truth is that our politicians and bureaucrats had little knowledge of military matters. Unlike western societies where experience of wartime enlistment or peacetime national service give many politicians firsthand knowledge of military matters, no one in our government had ever served in the armed forces. Nor had they (politicians or civil servants) been even remotely concerned with operational matters before independence. Proudly aware of the martial *réclame* the army had acquired during two world wars, they were apt to endow it with a mystique that made them insensible to its many post-partition difficulties and shortages. Thus Nehru, alluding to the security of our northern borders, could glibly misinform parliament in November 1959: '. . . at no time since our Independence, and of course before it, were our defence forces in better condition, in finer fettle. . . I am quite confident that our defence forces are well capable of looking after our security.'

As recently as April 1961 Krishna Menon, also speaking in parliament, stated that the morale of the services had 'never been higher', and that the Indian defence services had 'vastly improved their logistic capacity . . . There had been a great improvement in training, provisioning and manufacture of arms . . . Our equipment are (*sic*) of a better character: our troops are in advanced positions.' He blithely misinformed the House that a 'new Corps had been raised' to cope with the situation in the eastern and northern frontier regions. In fact, all that had been raised was a new headquarters – HQ XXXIII Corps – as a controlling HQ in Shillong.

It is difficult to reconcile these pronouncements in parliament with what Army HQ had been telling the government during the past year. Kaul had personally apprised the PM of the shortages in our order of battle, in arms and equipment and in our logistical potential. There could have been no room for a misunderstanding.

It is true that at that time Nehru was under great pressure from a hostile parliament. We were passing through a divisive period in internal politics. Many members from both sides of the House were deeply suspicious of Menon and greatly concerned about his ability to safeguard the security of India from Chinese machinations. Furthermore, parliament had been kept in the dark about border encroachments until mid-1959. When the full extent of Chinese aggressive moves were at last revealed to the House, many members were greatly alarmed. With Acharya Kripalani and others openly demanding Menon's dismissal, Nehru found himself on the defensive. The sad truth, of course, is that in order to stifle criticism of his China policy – and, perhaps, in a gesture of support for Krishna Menon – Nehru did not scruple to mislead parliament about the operational situation in the north. That is a tactic that can create its own problems. If the army were so well-prepared, why did we tolerate Chinese aggression? asked the Opposition. Member after member demanded that government take steps to 'push out the intruders from Indian soil' or 'take action to recover such territory as is in their possession'. They criticised Nehru for being over-cautious in ordering the army 'not to fire till they were fired upon'. A Congress member was moved to urge government to 'throw out the aggressor', remarking that the PM should be bold and fearless, not timid.

During October, presumably unnerved by attacks on him in parliament, Menon held a number of meetings with the Army Chief and his General Staff advisers, the main purpose of which was to heckle Thapar about the army's 'inactivity' on the borders. It was galling to witness this undeserved hectoring. Only a few months previously we had sent several urgent appeals to the Minister, asking him to make up the serious shortfalls in our resources. All of these appeals had either been ignored or turned down. Surprisingly, in countering Menon's harangues neither Thapar nor Kaul referred to those documents, even though I had prepared an *aide memoire* for them.

On 2 November a meeting was called in the Prime Minister's office to discuss Chinese incursions along the Chip Chap valley. Besides the PM and the Defence Minister, present at the meeting were the Army Chief, the CGS, the Foreign Secretary, Harish Sarin (Joint Secretary Defence) the DIB and his Joint Director, Dave, the DMO and the DMI. Decisions were taken at this meeting that eventually led us past the point of no return. I shall describe it in some detail.

Krishna Menon opened the proceedings with a review of border developments during 1961, stressing that in NEFA there had been no Chinese incursion into our territory but that in Ladakh army patrols had recently stumbled on a new Chinese post in the Chip Chap valley (in the Aksai Chin) about 15 km east of Daulet Beg Oldi. According to IB reports this post had not existed in 1959 and had not been sighted during aerial reconnaissances in 1960 and early 1961. Dave asserted that this move was part of a systematic pattern of infiltration westward by the Chinese, but Mullik intervened to reassure us on that score. He said that once an Indian presence was established – 'by even a dozen soldiers' – the Chinese would refrain from any action to contest it physically. The worst we need anticipate on the Ladakh front, he added, were patrol clashes, not war. By that time, I think most of us had been conditioned to accept this speculative prognosis, even though that is all it was. It occurred to none of us, not even to the Foreign Secretary, that only the Foreign Ministry, not the Intelligence Bureau, was competent to arrive at a political determination of this nature.

There was some discussion on measures to forestall or prevent further Chinese encroachments. A number of places were chosen from the map as likely sites for new army deployments, but Thapar pointed out that the army had already overextended itself in setting up new posts at Daulet Beg Oldi, Sultan Chushku and Jara-La (north of Demchok). He declined to make firm commitments for further ventures until he could support these posts both tactically and logistically.

The PM had listened to the discussions in a detached manner. I think he had already made up his mind about what steps needed to be taken. At one stage he asked what the term tactical support implied, and it fell to me to explain. I said that should the soldiers in a post became involved in an exchange of fire with a Chinese force of superior numbers and firepower, it would be necessary to send them not only logistical items, such as supplies and munitions, but also reserve troops and reinforcements, to restore the balance. I said that as matters stood at the time, we could not perform this role anywhere forward of Leh and Chushul airfields because of lack of roads, mules and even porters. Air-drops were the only method of resupply – and even this alternative was restricted by weather conditions, insufficient aircraft and air-dropping equipment.

Nehru heard me out, then somewhat impatiently remarked that he did not envisage a battle with the Chinese. After some more discussion he gave his directions in a rambling manner not untypical of him. These were to the effect that we must go forward into our claimed territories and establish a presence. Where we were already in occupation, as in NEFA, we must 'plug the holes' through which the Chinese might attempt to infiltrate.

Before the meeting I had primed Kaul that in case it were suggested that the army move forward in strength to the line of the border, we must emphasise our logistical inadequacies. At this stage of the proceedings I pointedly looked at the CGS, but he took no notice of my visual prodding. By the time I could write down 'logistical inadequacies' as an *aide memoire* on a piece of paper, the PM had begun to give his instructions. These were later issued in the form of minutes of the meeting under the signature of the Secretary General, R.K. Nehru (who, as I recall, had not been present at the meeting). The PM's directions, as recorded in the minutes, were:

(a) So far as Ladakh is concerned, we are to patrol as far forward as possible from our present positions towards the international border. This will be done with a view to establishing our posts which should prevent the Chinese from advancing further and also dominating any posts which they may have already established in our territory. This must be done without getting involved in a clash with the Chinese, unless this becomes necessary in self-defence.

(b) As regards UP and other northern areas, there are not the same difficulties as in Ladakh. We should, therefore, as far as practicable, go forward and be in effective occupation of the whole frontier. Where there are any gaps, they must be covered either by patrolling or by posts.

The unusual part of the directive was the inclusion of a third sub-para (c) which read:

(c) In view of numerous operational and administrative difficulties, efforts should be made to position major concentrations of forces along our borders in places conveniently situated behind the forward posts from where they could be maintained logistically and from where they can restore a border situation at short notice.

I noticed that the instructions forwarded to us in the Foreign Ministry's directive were more specific and more high-pressured than the PM's verbal directions at the meeting, and that sub-para (c) was clearly a bureaucratic afterthought; the Prime Minister had not mentioned it. Nevertheless, it was obvious that the PM's policy for Ladakh had radically changed from crisis control to confrontation. The passive stances of September 1959 ('the Aksai Chin has to be left more or less as it is . . . for the present we have to put up with the Chinese occupation') had now burgeoned into combativeness. Although the move was to be made within what we claimed was our own territory, it pointedly ignored the army's misgivings on the subject of 'logistical and tactical support for operations in outer Ladakh'. Whatever the IB's assurances about the unlikelihood of an outbreak of hostilities – and we had accepted that assessment – the General Staff would still have to cater for the worst case. In order to do this in a systematic manner we were even then working on a 'Master Plan' in MO Directorate which, if implemented in some measure, would, in three or four years time, give us adequate defensive potential against a possible Chinese aggression. Till then, as we had repeatedly informed the government, we would have little operational capability forward of the main airfields, and we could not with any justification upgrade the task given to Western Command from the defence of Leh to an advance into enemy-dominated territory.

Even the NEFA–Tibet border, quiescent since the incidents of 1958–9 and not explicitly under threat, was not excluded from the new activism of the forward policy. The former self-imposed restraint of prohibiting troop activity in the vicinity of the border (a 3-km zone) was lifted and a systematic advance to the McMahon Line was ordered in order to 'plug the gaps' – Operation Onkar, as it came to be codenamed.

It was the third sub-para of the directive which struck me as a piece of jobbery. It was a brazen ploy at alibi-making by the bureaucrats of the Foreign Ministry, in effect turning our own guns against us. At the meeting I had explained the significance of our lack of tactical support for the forward posts. Before that we had repeatedly brought to the notice of government our inability to support border operations should hostilities break out, precisely because we could not, without a road link, send reinforcements or supplies to Ladakh except by air. Furthermore, at the meeting Nehru had made no reference to 'positioning of major concentrations of forces along our borders'. This entirely gratuitous insertion was an afterthought by the bureaucrats seeking, presumably, to hedge their bets. Apparently the Foreign Ministry officials were determined to proceed with their plans on the assumption that the Chinese would not go to war on the border issue and, at the same time, they wished to create an escape-hole for themselves in case they did.

I took these points to the CGS, determined that we should dispute parts of the minutes issued by Ratan Nehru.

Kaul agreed with my comments but somewhat sheepishly confessed that he had been shown a draft of the Foreign Ministry minutes before their issue and, without reading between the lines, had already accorded his approval. He said that he could not now go back on his endorsement. I argued that these points were too crucial to ignore and tried to persuade him that, without appearing to renege on his approval of the draft, we should nevertheless reiterate our doubts about the feasibility of the forward policy (as the move forward came to be called). I also asserted that if sub-para (c) were to stand it must logically be renumbered sub-para (a) and given priority over the other two. In other words, the forward policy should be implemented only after the completion of an operational and logistical build-up. Kaul, however, was reluctant to agree even to that. He was convinced that the forward policy must be implemented as soon after the winter as possible.

Perceiving that Kaul, on the defensive because of the cursory manner in which he had dealt with Ratan Nehru's tendentious minute, was becoming brusque and peevish under pressure, I changed tack. I suggested an alternative that I had previously discussed with my staff: instead of a move forward with regular troops, which could provoke border clashes, why did we not hand the borders back to the DIB? Mullik could then carry out an 'administrative move forward' with police posts. This would require less logistical support, was less likely to result in open hostilities and would leave the army free to concentrate on organising a credible defensive position around Leh.

Kaul did not accept this suggestion either. He said that apart from the fact that such a course would cause loss of face for the army, it was quite unnecessary. The danger of the Chinese reacting militarily to our forward policy was minimal. He was in agreement with the PM, whose appreciation of the international situation (as related to him, Kaul) was that the Chinese were going through a very bad patch. They faced a threat of invasion from the Nationalist Chinese in Taiwan, supported by the United States; their economic policies had failed for two consecutive years, and the Soviets had recently withdrawn economic aid. As a result of all these crises the morale of the Chinese people in general and the People's Liberation Army (PLA) in particular was very low. They could not afford to undertake armed hostilities on the Himalayan front.

This was news to me. The JIC, as far as I was aware, had never projected this picture at its briefings and neither had the Foreign Ministry. In any event, the crisis of the Taiwan straits, as I recalled, had passed more than two years previously. However, I did not persist with my recommendation about handing back the border to the IB.

Kaul felt that with the whole winter to plan in, we could use our airlift capacity to build up sufficient logistical potential in Ladakh to provide adequate support for the projected forward posts. He thought we were wrong to assume that in six months' time we would still lack operational capacity in Ladakh. He would not budge from that stand and directed me to issue instructions to the Commands based on the Foreign Ministry directive. His only concession was that he agreed not to relay the contents of sub-para (c) to Command HQs. It was for us to provide back-up troops in Ladakh, not to advise Western Command to organise resources it did not possess.

Thapar wrote to the GOsC-in-C Eastern and Western Command to the effect that we were to patrol as far forward as possible towards the line we recognised as the border. The Commands were to establish posts blocking further Chinese advances and to dominate any Chinese posts already established, 'without getting involved in a clash with the Chinese unless it becomes necessary in self-defence'. The letter then asked for a fresh appraisal of logistical requirements.

The letter was drafted at the CGS and COAS level and I saw the office copy only when it came down for filing in MO Directorate. I drew Kaul's attention to the fact that the Chief's letter appeared to be making deployments first and asking for logistical requirements as an afterthought. I suggested that we order the forward movement only after linking it with such matters as scales of ammunition to be carried, supply requirements and the availability of ponies and porters. The CGS thought me over-cautious; he said the posts were being sent out not so much to fight as to establish a presence. He would brook no further argument on the subject.

# 5

# 'OPERATION VIJAY':
# GOA NATIONALISED

A colleague in Army HQ once described the Goa episode as light relief from the gloom and foreboding of the general strategic scene. In a way the comment was apt; the involvement in the south did indeed offer respite from the continuing crisis in the north. Activities set in motion by the decision to liberate Goa, however hectic and pressing, were untainted by concern about national security. The strength of the Portuguese forces was negligible; at no time had they posed a military threat to India. Indeed the entire course of the operation amounted to little more than large-scale military manoeuvres and it provided incidents of theatrics that would have kept a cynic well amused.

Yet, in its consequences, this episode was not just comic relief. Operation Vijay eventually took on greater significance; the easy conquest was taken too seriously in many official quarters. The euphoria of success inflated a passing interlude of secondary military consequence into 'a famous victory'. Rather than being alarmed by the military inadequacies displayed by the operation (such as the plethora of shortages that came to light – the best part of one battalion marched to battle in canvas PT shoes because our Ordnance depots were out of army boots!) the powers-that-be preened themselves as though they had struck a stunning blow at

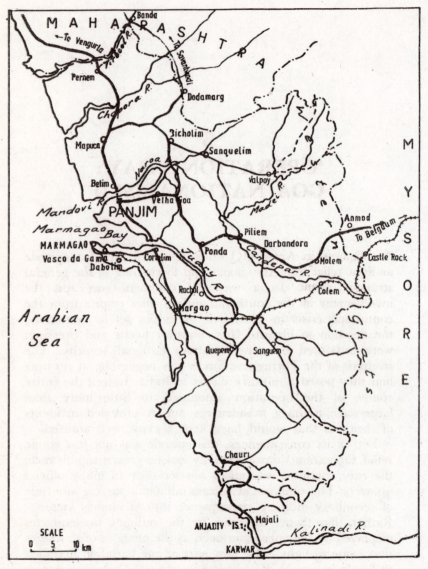

Goa

a major enemy; that in turn led to false confidence in our military dynamic. The last thing required at that phase of growing rashness in our northern border policy was a mood of combative smugness. Yet I suspect that, after Goa, that is exactly what ensued. Although the army itself did not indulge in a prolonged aftermath of self-delusion, policy-makers in government continued to view our martial potential in a rosy light. *The Hindu* (Madras) quoted Home Minister Shastri as asserting, in February 1962: 'If the Chinese will not vacate the areas occupied by her (*sic*), India will have to repeat what she did in Goa. She will certainly drive out the Chinese forces.'

The Goa webwork first surfaced at the end of August 1961, in a setting reminiscent of a comic opera. Thapar and Kaul were away on a prolonged visit to the UK, attending Exercise Unison run by Admiral Mountbatten, the British Chief of Defence Staff. 'Muchu' Chaudhuri, GOC-in-C Southern Command, was in Delhi on one of his periodic visits as officiating COAS. In normal circumstances I did not see much of him during his visits because he was not required to concern himself with operational matters, as Danny Misra or I discussed these directly with the Defence Ministry. So it was with some curiosity that I received an urgent summons from him one morning. When I arrived at the office of the Chief's Military Assistant, I found Brigadier Jangu Satarawala (DSD) and Brigadier Bim Batra (DMI) also waiting to see the officiating Chief, neither any better informed than I about the reason for our call.

After the Military Assistant had ushered us into the presence and had sat us down, Chaudhuri dismissed him, adding that he did not wish to be disturbed for the next half-hour, 'unless, there is a call from the Prime Minister, of course,' he added grandiloquently, glancing meaningfully in our direction. After the colonel had left the room he subjected each of us in turn to a few seconds' close scrutiny. Presumably satisfied with what he saw, he began by warning us that he was going to entrust us with a matter of the greatest import and the highest security grading. 'So far only the Defence Minister, Harish Sarin and I are privy to this secret,' he said. 'I don't want you to discuss this matter with anyone else. I am taking you into my confidence only because I shall require you to produce a document for my signature; but you will not consult anyone else, not even your own staff. The document will be handwritten if you can't use a typewriter. Is that absolutely clear?'

We assured him that it was, whereupon Muchu Chaudhuri let us into his secret: according to Krishna Menon, the Prime Minister was of the opinion that the situation in Goa had deteriorated so alarmingly that it had reached a stage where armed action against the Portuguese administration had become unavoidable. He said that the Defence Minister wanted him to produce a provisional plan of operation for the liberation of all Portuguese territories in India. He then turned to me and said that I was to prepare a directive to Southern Command requiring it to submit an appreciation of the situation and an outline plan for the liberation of the three enclaves of Goa, Daman and Diu. He wanted the directive within twenty-four hours and added that as officiating Chief he would sign it himself.

He then filled us in on some news from Goa, describing atrocities the Portuguese had supposedly committed. I was unaware of any recent press reports on this issue, nor had Southern Command brought anything unusual to our notice. I was a little sceptical, but I let it go. When we were leaving his office, Chaudhuri told me to stay behind. He asked how long it would take to draft the directive, adding that when he was DMO a thing like this would have taken him not more than ten minutes. I murmured that I would see him after lunch and give him an answer.

The others came back with me to my office. I told them what I had begun to suspect – that Muchu was trying to stage a *coup* of sorts while he was in the Chief's chair: he was taking advantage of his presence as officiating Chief to try to corner the 'operational market' and to present Thapar and Kaul with a *fait accompli* on Goa. I suggested that because of the widely known antagonism between Kaul and Chaudhuri we would have to tread carefully if we were to avoid a major pother. Since no action was required of either the DSD or the DMI at this stage, they agreed to let me handle the matter.

Muchu Chaudhuri was a particular type of well-born, urban, bicultural Bengali, suave, quick-witted and articulate.

One of his obvious traits was his affectation of anglicised modes and mannerisms, something which, if over-indulged, often generates a sense of racial inadequacy. Despite his glamorous personality, Muchu's outstanding characteristic was his insecurity, which he attempted to dissemble under an exterior of flippant drollery and a constant striving to be brilliant. I had come into contact with him in the early 1950s when he was Adjutant-General and I the Commandant at the 9th Gorkha Regimental Centre in Dehra Dun. He had deputed me, the senior Centre Commander of Gorkhas, to arrange a conference of Gorkha Centre Commanders and do the lobbying and spadework for an AG Branch plan to amalgamate some of the centres. During the course of a succession of formal and informal meetings I had become well-acquainted with him. A few years later, when I commanded our First Battalion in Kashmir, he had been the Corps Commander. Again, I had had occasion to interact with him, socially on a friendly basis but adversely on the few official occasions when we had had a direct exchange. As on the previous occasion, I found not only that his *armour propre* was easily threatened, but that he was also intellectually irresponsible. It could be that a succession of high positions in his early career had acquainted him with the glamour of decision-making, but not its substance. Muchu jumped to conclusions too quickly, although he could also respond to reason and reverse a decision if the process did not threaten his ego.

Aware of the personal animosity and the mutual mistrust between Kaul and Chaudhuri, I felt that I must at all cost prevent the latter from dragging their feud into the operational precinct of Army HQ. Muchu was sensitive to the fact that as Southern Army Commander he was not directly concerned in the operational aspects of the western and northern borders, and Bijji had kept him as uninformed on these subjects as hierarchical propriety allowed. Muchu was now obviously only too eager to seize the opportunity of putting his imprimatur on the Goa operation, not only for the sake of one-upmanship with Kaul but also, perhaps, to sanction for himself, as the Army Commander who would be responsible for any military task in Goa, greater latitude and resources than Army HQ might normally have conceded.

During the lunch-break I pondered the matter and discussed it with my wife, without of course mentioning Goa. We were both firmly of the opinion that I must stall Muchu and, at the same time, avoid tripping over his ego. The difficulty was that Kaul was not due to return before the end of the month and even Thapar was not expected back for another ten days or so.

When I went to see Chaudhuri in the afternoon I began with a suggestion that his informal directions to us on Goa be recorded in writing; also, I added, I should be authorised to show it to the officiating CGS. His first reaction was to brush the suggestion aside: the more people that knew, the less the security, he said. I told him that if he had consulted me first I would have advised him that neither the DSD nor the DMI were concerned at this stage and need not have been called in, but to keep the officiating CGS out of the picture would be an impropriety on his part and would put me in an invidious position. Without giving him a chance to reply I placed before him a manuscript memorandum for his signature, recording the gist of what he had told us about Goa. I commented, perhaps somewhat unctuously, that so momentous an occasion should go on record for future historians, and to ensure its security I would keep it in my personal possession for the time being.

Chaudhuri asked me when the directive to Southern Command would be ready. Why had I not brought it with me? Could the DMO not produce such a simple document without a lot of fuss? I assured him that there would be no fuss. The directive would be ready within the deadline he had set. He then acknowledged that perhaps I was right about recording his instructions in an official note and said that he would have one typed and sent to me which indeed he did a day or two later (4 September):

On the afternoon of 30 Aug 61, while travelling back from the NDC in a car with the Defence Minister, the DM mentioned GOA. He said that the PM had now agreed that a plan for the use of troops in or against Portuguese possessions in India, might be committed to paper. Later that afternoon in his office, with the JS(G) and myself present, the DM again said that a plan as above could be prepared but it should be kept at a very high and top secret level. He was categorical in stating that the number of people to be informed of the existence of this plan was to be limited, while at this stage the other Service Chiefs were not to be consulted. In the preparation of a plan, however, reasonable assumptions of air and naval cooperation could be made.

2. Based on the above, which has been checked back with the JS(G), suitable directions have been given by me verbally to the Offg CGS, DMO, DMI and DSD to prepare a draft directive to GOC-in-C Southern Command.

*sd/-*   JN Chaudhuri
Lt Gen
Offg COAS
4th Sep 61

I considered this enough of an achievement for one day and, somewhat pusillanimously, shirked from tackling Muchu on the propriety of his signing an Army HQ directive to himself as Southern Commander. This would certainly raise his hackles; another day would do.

The next morning I took him the handwritten directive I had drafted. He played about with the wording of the preamble and seemed generally to be enjoying himself. It was when he came to the allotment of troops that he showed some annoyance. I had provisionally allotted (in addition to all troops within his own Command) HQ 17 Infantry Division with one infantry brigade and the Parachute Brigade, both of which were Army HQ reserves. He struck out the infantry element and substituted 'HQ 1 Armoured Division and the Lorried Brigade'. He also increased the allotment of unbrigaded armour, commenting that he was an Armoured Corps general and fought best with tanks. This was a typical Muchu remark — flamboyant and unthinking. I remarked courteously that as a former CGS he must know that the Armoured Division had been permanently allotted to Western Command for a key role in our plans for the Pakistan front. He would have to consult the Western Army Commander, General Daulet Singh, and even if the latter agreed for a temporary loan of the Armoured Division, I did not think the government would allow it to be diverted elsewhere even for a few weeks. I advised him not to try. Furthermore, I added, I had studied the map of Goa. Neither the *ghat* approaches nor the riverscape foreland seemed like suitable tank country, and the numerous bridges over the water courses were almost certainly of too low a classification to take the weight of medium tanks. Sheepishly, he gave in; I pressed home the advantage by pointing out that it did not befit him to sign the directive himself – that should be left to the CGS. Before he could run riot on this I opened a file on Operation Polo that I had brought with me and showed him that the directive to Southern Command for the Hyderabad Police Action of 1948 had been signed not by the then Chief but by himself as officiating CGS. I could see that he was not pleased with my strictures but he gave in with good grace.

The next morning Chaudhuri called me in again. This time he was exercised about his command function. He asked me to insert a clause in the directive to define his overall command of the operation to ensure that all naval and air elements would be subordinate to him. I told him that such a command arrangement could be determined only by the Chiefs of Staff Committee or by the Defence Minister. In any case, the Naval and Air Chiefs had not yet been alerted on the Goa issue. He would have to wait till a more formal stage of the proceedings. He knew I was right, yet he resented the fact. 'I am not going to share my responsibility with anyone,' he said. 'If I am not to be in charge, I'm not going to take it on,' he added, with an attempt at bravado.

Chaudhuri returned to Poona soon afterwards. I remained busy with the Chip Chap river episode and, unable to delegate the Goa file to anyone else because of its 'for your eyes only' security, I shelved it for a few days, and no one else raised the issue. It was not till Thapar returned from England in the middle of September that I sent him Muchu's noting of 4 September together with a short manuscript account of what had transpired. Two days later, when I was giving him a briefing on other operational developments since his departure, he asked to see the Goa file again. He made a few corrections to my draft directive, instructed me to process it as a special security document for his signature and to send it by hand of an officer to Southern Command by 20 September. When I pointed out that the CGS was expected back in a few days and that it might be better to await his return, he ignored my remark.

After I had taken over as DMO I had observed a noticeable lack of warmth in Thapar's attitude to me, which was uncharacteristic of him because he was by nature affectionate and affable. I had known him well since 1945 when, after the end of the war, I was posted to MS Branch in Delhi and he had been my immediate boss as Assistant Military Secretary. Many years my senior in age and service, he unhesitatingly offered his friendship. He and his wife Bimla warmly welcomed my wife and myself to their home and, without a trace of patronage, introduced us to what still was, in 1945, the restricted Indian social circle of official Delhi. It was a spontaneous and freehearted kindness. His recent attitude towards me had therefore been puzzling me. Perhaps the reason was Bijji's insistence on appointing me as DMO in preference to Thapar's own nominee. If that were so his resentment, though unjust, was understandable.

Be that as it may, I knew that Thapar would himself regret the decision if he sent out this important operational directive without waiting for Kaul's return. Why he had suddenly changed his mind, I could not gauge; certainly, it was not for self-glorification, because that was not in his nature. He could of course have been under pressure of urgency from Krishna Menon, but I doubted it. Anyway, I sent a note to Danny Misra urging him to have a word with the Chief and to persuade him to await Kaul's arrival. This he succeeded in doing and I was grateful. The behind-the-scenes theatrics were over, for the time being anyway, and there the matter rested till Kaul returned from abroad a week later.

My own feelings about the proposal to liberate Portuguese territory by armed action were ambivalent. On the one hand, as a key member of the General Staff I was excited by the prospect of mounting a decisive yet cut-and-dried military operation – a planner's dream, no less. After all the fumbling and uncertainty on the northern borders, it would be a stimulating change to be able to direct what was virtually a predestined, no-risk military campaign. Yet a sense of unease about the project kept stabbing at my conscience. Like many thinking Indians I had become conditioned by the moral tone set by the Nehru government after independence, particularly in international affairs, and I regarded the proposed military aggression in Goa as a breach of profession, however justified it might appear from the nationalistic point of view.

After I apprised Bijji Kaul of the developments concerning Goa, I had a long and informal discussion with him. I told him about my reservations on the subject and my doubts on the sensational items about Portuguese atrocities which were being put out by our intelligence sources. Bijji reacted strongly to this, firmly asserting that there was no doubt about Portuguese brutality and suppression. He knew that to be true because his good friend Gopi Handu was the Inspector-General of police in charge of the Goa border and Handu had often spoken of the arrogance and ruthlessness of the colonial administration. For the past fifteen years they had consistently ignored India's overtures and refused even to discuss the Goa problem. Instead, they had suppressed Goan nationalism with savagery. The only alternative was to settle the matter by armed action; either that or we must be prepared to tolerate for ever the existence of a foreign enclave within our territory. I asked him why we could not engineer a liberation movement similar to those so successfully carried out in Nagar Haveli and Dadra, the two Portuguese enclaves north of Bombay where we had encouraged the local inhabitants to rise up and liberate themselves. We could arm the Goans, I added, and even provide the military leadership to lead an uprising in the main colony. After all, the Portuguese had only three battalions of second class infantry and some two thousand armed police to guard a fairly extensive enclave. I argued that we would besmirch our international image if we used our armed forces to liberate Goa, however valid our political claim.

Kaul was opposed to any form of moderation in carrying out the task of liberation. He felt that unless firm action were taken we would get bogged down in delays caused by UN intervention and perhaps interference by some of the Christian – particularly Romanist – powers of Europe and the Americans. No, to be successful it would have to be a quick, surgical strike. With that I had to be content — more than halfway convinced that he was probably right.

We finalised the directive on Goa and sent it to Lieutenant General Chaudhuri, by name, on 7 October. The troops allotted for the task remained the same as I had originally proposed. The directive asked for Chudhuri's operational plan, including his requirements of naval and air support, by 15 November, and cautioned him that he was not to convey the contents of the directive to any one except his Chief of Staff, BGS and Brigadier in Charge of Administration.

Towards the end of the month the Prime Minister for the first time in a public speech made a reference to possible armed action in Goa. Although he qualified the statement by saying that he would again attempt to open negotiations with the government of Portugal, he implied that this attempt would be the last. I had a lurking suspicion that the inspiration behind the mounting momentum for military action in Goa had come from Krishna Menon, who was to contest a parliamentary seat in Bombay in early 1962; a takeover in Goa would effectively promote his election image. Politicians do not always scruple to exploit military operations for their own benefit, as indeed was demonstrated at the start of the Goa operations. (The official history of the Goa operations, *Operation Vijay: The Liberation of Goa and other Portuguese Colonies: 1961*, records that a number of 'minor politicians' descended on the scene at Advanced Tactical HQ 'who, with the calmest disregard for security and secrecy, were anxious to get as much out of the situation as they could. One politician in fact hired a car and set off towards the border, determined to precede the troops.')

I hoped that once Southern Command had been alerted, I would be given security permission to expand my planning base in order to set in motion activities and commissions essential for sudden mobilisation. This was all the more urgent because Army HQ was not conversant with mobilisation schemes in Southern Command, its operational interests having till then focused mainly on the northern and western borders. Even a hasty perusal of the 'War Book' we maintained in MO Directorate indicated that I would have to activate a creaking machinery that controlled such unfamiliar measures as the Fortress Defence Scheme of Bombay, the Southern Command Anti-Aircraft Defence Scheme, the Embodiment of Coastal Batteries Plan and similar precautionary measures, some with inter-service complexities – and all unrehearsed for years. The sooner I took my JPC colleagues into my confidence the more smoothly this machinery could be coaxed into operation. As for the concentration of troops and stores for the invasion force, this would require a finely co-ordinated rail movement plan for which the QMG's staff and the Railway Board needed to be alerted as early as possible. I explained these points to Kaul and asked to be allowed to start making the first moves, but he was unwilling to lift the security ban. He argued that government had yet to confirm its intention in writing: we must not 'go off at half-cock'. When I explained that the mobilisation and movement phases could well stretch to three or four weeks, whereas a certain amount of preliminary action might cut this period by half, he relented somewhat. On his own responsibility he allowed me to expand my consultation base to include the staff in MO Directorate and the General Staff in QMG (Movement and Operations), but that was as far as he would go. He could not include my JPC colleagues because, he argued, the Defence Minister had till then kept even their Chiefs out of the secret.

I could not fault Kaul for his logic but I did seize the opportunity to point out to him – and not for the first time – the need to rectify the *ad hoc* way that operational policies seemed to be formulated, and higher direction exercised, in the Defence Ministry. I urged that the three Service HQs should plan and operate within a formal integrated framework rather than in their current isolation. As an example of the exclusion of other services from strategic deliberations, I cited the PM's border conference of 2 November. The Air Chief had not been invited, despite the fact that air logistics was still the cardinal factor in all Ladakhi operations. In the present instance, exclusion of the navy and the air force was undermining the army's planning and preparation from the outset. I suggested setting up a functioning joint-services staff cell under the Chiefs of Staff Committee to synergise planning and operations. Bijji heard me out and, in general, seemed to accept my views, but he did not promise to promote them.

I recall that after I had taken over as DMO it was with some consternation that I experienced the considerable extent to which both political and military decisions seemed to be made in an *ad hoc* way. On the political side, the PM's border conference on 2 November clearly demonstrated the Nehru style of functioning: the abandoning of a formal consultation procedure and its replacement by an arbitrary decision-making process. The obvious danger in this, of course, is that the different issues raised by a decision – the various component parts that make up the whole, such as intelligence, communication, logistics – are likely to be pursued singly or wrongly, or even neglected. Furthermore, limiting discussion to the top people precludes detailed staff study. In time it becomes convenient to view things in outline without a clutter of details, but it is detail that gives substance to an outline.

I confess that at the time I had no explicit idea of the organisational form a high command system should take within the Ministry; I lacked previous personal experience of policy-making at governmental level. However, extensive study of military history had given me sufficient insight to perceive that the present system was haphazard and inadequate. Some years later I recorded my comments on this system when I was Military Correspondent of the *Hindustan Times* (11 April 1971):

The decision-making system that was established during the years of the India-China confrontation of 1959–62 was starkly *ad hoc* and designed primarily to suit the personality of the Prime Minister. Alone among the leaders of post-Independence India Nehru possessed an insight into the deeper aspects of national and international strategy and defence policy. No other colleague in the Cabinet, not even Mr Krishna Menon, could make a significant contribution in these fields; and therefore the Prime Minister preferred to deal with these matters personally – or directly with those concerned. Mr Krishna Menon as Defence Minister, whose brilliant intellect in any case drew him to the PM, was of course in the direct chain – though, uncharacteristically, he seldom took a stand on any point or even made any great contribution when the Prime Minister was in the Chair.

Of all the officials in the Government, Nehru had the greatest confidence in Mr Mullik, Director of the Intelligence Bureau. And in Army Headquarters, it was General Kaul (both as Quarter Master General and later as Chief of the General Staff) who had caught the PM's eye. Thus, the 'War Council' of the 'China days', the body that evaluated all the strategic (and often tactical) factors and took all the decisions, consisted of the Prime Minister (and certain members of his External Affairs Secretariat), the Defence Minister (and members of the Defence Secretariat), Mr Mullik (as an individual), the Army Chief and the CGS (and key members of the General Staff). No one else was privy to its proceedings and I doubt if even members of the Cabinet were kept informed of the major decisions taken by this *ad hoc* body – except incidentally.

The great drawback of this system was not that the *ad hoc* 'War Council' was too restricted – because expansion would not necessarily have gained it any expertise – but that the marked dividing line that should separate intelligence from advice and opinion tended to become blurred. Intelligence is fact – or should be; action on it must be based on logical deductions (or on reasonable assumptions). When the same authority is permitted to provide the one and also advise on the other, both fact and deduction tend to become compromised. This is what gradually happened between 1959 and 1962 – and eventually none was quite able to see where the dividing line actually lay.

Misapplication of intelligence was not the only catastrophe. The risk at *ad hoc* meetings of decision-makers is that they are liable to become involved in policy decisions without the supportive analyses of their staffs; thus crisis management becomes an unruly affair in which wrong decisions are made, or errant priorities set, based on unexamined assumptions. This was certainly true of the Indian government's decision-making process regarding the Chinese confrontation.

On the military side also, I found that high command procedures lacked organic integration and format. Although the Indian military high command system is supposedly based on the British wartime practice of the Chiefs of Staff Committee, this is a fallacy. The Indian system is basically different from the British: our Indian Chiefs of Staff lack the weight and authority of their British counterparts, mainly because the interface between government and the armed forces is differently structured in India. In the British system service Chiefs function as part of government (they are part of the Ministry of Defence) while the Indian system keeps the two separated. Indian service Chiefs are not part of the Ministry and do not function as such; they are mere heads of department outside the Ministry and therefore do not share governmental power and authority. The irony is that this state of powerlessness was self-inflicted.

In the early 1950s when Prime Minister Nehru set about replacing the old British-Indian colonial organisation of commanders-in-chief with a system more in conformity with a democratic form of government, he offered to substitute the colonial hierarchial concept with a system modelled on the Whitehall type of Army Council. At that time the person whose opinion on this was decisive was of course the then Army Chief, General Rajendrasinhji, but his confidant and chief adviser was (successively as AG and CGS) none other than the high-flying Muchu Chaudhuri. As the latter says in his book, *Arms, Aims and Aspects*, it was he who persuaded his Chief to reject the Army Council system because, he explained, in that scenario the Chief would relinquish personal command of the army to become one of four principal staff officers in the Ministry – though *primus inter pares*. On Muchu's advice Rajendrasinhji rejected the offer and chose to remain in command of his service, preferring the trappings of power to its substance. And that is how in India the authority and standing of the service Chiefs have remained limited to this day. According to Harish Sarin (then Joint Secretary, Defence) a move was made in 1957 by Thimayya, when he was COAS, to introduce the British Army Council system, but in the end he too opted for local rather than real power. When he realised that under the Army Council system each PSO would have an independent voice on the council, he turned his back on the reform.

Today in India a service Chief's function remains restricted to the affairs of his service alone, with only lip service paid to the committee system of consultation. As secretary to the Chiefs of Staff Committee, I found that our Chiefs seldom deliberated or acted in conclave on matters of strategy or operational policy. Except when required to meet a specific demand by the government, such as the preparation of the Chiefs of Staff Paper of January 1961 referred to above, the Chiefs-in-Committee appeared to deal mainly with service routine such as pay and allowances, niceties of dress, service customs, co-ordination of inter-service courses of instruction and similar minutiae. In matters of importance, even including instructions for warlike operations, they were constrained to deal with the Ministry of Defence, separately and individually, and so the Ministry became inured to issuing directions through each service separately. Service HQs processed them in the same manner, with only occasional inter-service synergy, and even that based more often on personalities than on usage. Furthermore, this single-service processing has crystallised into an unwritten governmental convention wherein the defence bureaucracy plays the role of co-ordinator. The inevitable result was that with the passage of time the Defence Secretariat virtually became a supreme HQ between the Minister and individual Service HQs. No Service HQ or its Chief has, in the past, done much to mitigate each other's mutual isolation.

Except for an occasional visit by Gopi Handu to Army HQ, Goa ceased to be a distraction for a few days and I was able to revert to the more urgent compulsions on the northern border. We were engrossed in handling the aftermath of the PM's decisions about forward moves when, on 10 November, we received Southern Command's 'Appreciation'.

Muchu and his Chief of Staff Pat Dunn (an old regimental colleague) had obviously laboured to compose a textbook document. The authors had precisely evaluated many factors of import such as the general nature of the terrain, roads and rivers, bridges (or lack of them), strengths and dispositions of Portuguese armed and police forces and the political climate in the colony. Collating them, they had framed an outline plan, but for all their pedantry they overlooked the paramount requirement. From the beginning it must have been obvious that the time factor would be crucial. Gopi Handu had assured us that the Portuguese forces were demoralised and would offer no more than token resistance (a forecast that was largely borne out by the event); thus the outcome of the campaign was a foregone conclusion. The main prerequisite for success would be to forestall international interference. For this it would be essential to catapult a small, hard-hitting force into the capital, Panjim, within a day or so of the start of the main invasion, so that it would be in a position to accept a surrender before the UN or western powers could intervene. The Southern Command plan laid no such stress on urgency and timing. It envisaged a formalised three-pronged advance from the north, east and south – a set piece attack that would take, by its own reckoning, three or four days to reach Panjim.

I discussed the provisional plan with the CGS, pointing out that we needed to establish a presence in Panjim in a matter of hours, not days. I also suggested that the invading forces should not be dispersed. The attack should be launched along two axes only: the main body could invade from the east (Belgaum), with a brigade thrust by the Paras from the north (Savantwadi). The main goal of the overall commander, however, would be to launch a mobile force from either column to break into the Velha-Goa-Panjim peninsula as quickly as possible. I also suggested that there was no need to mount simultaneous operations against Diu and Daman, as the Command plan recommended. Neither enclave could hold out for long once Goa was occupied; they could be liberated subsequently. All resources must initially be made available for the main operation.

The CGS agreed with my comments but thought I was being too optimistic about the timing: he felt that even if the Portuguese did nothing more than demolish a few of the more important bridges and crater the main roads they would still be able to delay our advance for more than a day or two. I then told him about the idea that had been growing at the back of my mind – the use of part of the Para Brigade in an air-dropped role. If they could capture and hold the two key bridges on the northern route, there should be no reason why the northern column could not be in Panjim by nightfall on the first day. However, as we had never carried out an air-dropped operation before, I would have to consult my air force colleague before I could confirm its feasibility; but, I added, in any event we must impress on HQ Southern Command the necessity of getting to Panjim within twenty-four hours. The CGS accepted my comments and I endorsed them to Poona.

Weeks passed without any further development and I began to think, not without some relief, that perhaps the Goa project had died a natural death. I had begun to suspect that there was something phony in the build-up of information about Portuguese provocations; the bizarre incident involving the *Sabarmathi*, an Indian merchant ship, did nothing to allay my suspicions.

It was put about that on 18 November the small Portuguese garrison on Anjadiv, an island lying off the coast of southern Goa, had fired at the *Sabarmathi* as she was passing through the narrow channel between the island and the Karwar coast, wounding one of the ship's engineers. A day or two later the Portuguese were reported to have shot at and killed an Indian fisherman while he was about his business in the same channel. The Portuguese denied these allegations and said that, on the contrary, there had been an attempt by unidentified armed personnel to land on the island. They had repulsed this attempt by fire.

It is difficult to believe that the Portuguese would deliberately have chosen such an obviously self-destructive course, though Bijji Kaul in his book *The Untold Story* provided a plausible explanation. He suggested that the Portuguese could well have staged the incident to take advantage of the presence of warships from Britain, the United States, Pakistan and other CENTO powers then taking part in a naval exercise in the Arabian Sea. Their aim could have been to provoke an incident which would force India to display her hand prematurely and thus give sufficient time to test the western powers, or for the UN to react.

Whatever the true story, the incident very nearly succeeded in inciting just the reaction that the Portuguese reportedly desired. On the morning of 27 November Krishna Menon sent for the three service Chiefs, their deputies and the CGS. Gopi Handu, who was also present at the meeting, opened the proceedings with an account of the *Sabarmathi* incident. Menon then announced that as a consequence of these aggressive acts by the colonists the government had decided to send a naval force to capture Anjadiv island, even if that resulted in a clash with Portuguese warships, two of which were reported to be present in those waters. He went on to say that if the Portuguese subsequently 'took retaliatory action against our nationals in Goa, Diu or Daman, we would have to concentrate forces in the requisite areas to meet with this situation' – a roundabout way of saying that the government had decided to invade Goa. He asked the service Chiefs to consider the implications of the operation and to let him have their views the following day.

Bijji Kaul sent for me after lunch and told me about the Defence Minister's meeting and his resolve. He said that in the course of the discussion the Minister had asked Thapar how long it would take him to get an invasion force ready. The Army Chief had estimated that it would take about fourteen days. Kaul now wanted an exact figure from his DMO, but I was warned that I would have to work on it by myself: I was no longer permitted to consult even my own staff. Menon had clamped an absolute need-to-know security restriction which only he could lift.

Fortunately I had already discussed rail plans with QMG's Branch and had prepared a provisional timetable for the move of a force of 20,000 troops from Ambala, Agra and elsewhere to Belgaum. I showed this to Kaul later in the evening, quoting an estimate of twelve days for its completion, to which the CGS added one extra day as contingency to cater for unforeseen hitches. However, when he told me that I could start putting the machine in motion at once, I thought it about time to make a stand against Menon's absurd security clampdown. I protested that the General Staff could not be expected to plan for war and put those plans into operation without recourse to normal staff procedures, and pointed out that the countdown of thirteen days would start only after the DM lifted his security restriction. I also cautioned that we should not take any major steps towards implementing the Goa plan until we received formal orders from government. Kaul thought that over and finally suggested that we walk over to Thapar's house, only a short distance from South Block, to put these matters to the Chief.

On the way to the Chief's residence I also expressed misgivings about showing our hand at Anjadiv a fortnight

before we were ready to take action against the main colony.
The lead time would afford the UN or western powers
ample opportunity to intervene and frustrate our purpose.
Why not wait till the main force had been assembled and
then mount a combined army and navy attack on Goa?
Was the charade of Anjadiv necessary as an excuse for our
subsequent invasion?

Kaul replied that he had also had doubts about the
Anjadiv plan and, in fact, had discussed the matter with
Handu. He added that he intended to consult Vice-Admiral
Katari, the Naval Chief (who was also currently the chairman
of the Chiefs of Staff Committee). I was rather surprised
when he cautioned me not to raise the point in Thapar's
presence. He indicated obliquely that the Army and Naval
Chiefs were not on the most co-operative of terms, implying
that were Thapar to suggest the cancellation of the preliminary
capture of Anjadiv, Katari would be sure to take the
opposite line. It would be better, Bijji added, if *he* could
persuade Katari to make the suggestion himself.

This was ominous news for the 'private enterprise' I had
in mind – the promotion of a joint-service approach to
planning and operations. At the risk of being considered a
crank, I used the opportunity again to urge the CGS to
try to establish an inter-service routine for staff procedures.
I told him about my discussions with my JPC colleagues
and added that the present crisis was a providential
opportunity to make a start on inter-service integration and
form a small joint-services cell at the level of operational
staffs. Should we succeed, we might influence the three
service Chiefs to establish a joint operations staff cell at a
higher level. I added that we should aim to establish an
integrated joint-service 'theatre' command at Poona for the
conduct of the Goa campaign. It could well become a
model on which to build future plans.

Kaul heard me out but made no comment except that
the staff cell we planned would have to be improvised
because he saw no hope of obtaining government sanction
for its establishment without a recommendation from the
Chiefs themselves. We soon arrived at White Gates, the
Army Chief's residence, so the conversation was perforce
curtailed but at least I had obtained an approval of sorts

from the boss.

Our discussion with Thapar determined the order of battle for the task force and though it was more lavish than I had proposed, I was content that the matter had been decided. As for my advice on obtaining formal government orders before taking any action, Thapar told me (though not in so many words) that that was none of my business: I was to proceed with getting the task force going. He did, however, agree to my request for relaxation of the security restrictions, to widen the need-to-know confines laid down by the Minister. Thapar telephoned Menon to ask for an immediate appointment. When we were about to leave, he told me that I could assume that normal security procedures would be restored from the next day, at least as far as the movement of troops was concerned. The nature of the operation, however, was not to be divulged to anyone. I made no comment; in view of the sensational reports in the press, what other interpretation could be put on a division of troops being rushed down from the Punjab to Poona I could not imagine.

Leaving Kaul to have a word with Thapar about the command organisation in Delhi, I sped back to my office to write out a manuscript note to GOC 17 Infantry Division by name, informing him of the provisional movement plans for his force but not its task. I instructed him to report to the DMO on the morning of 29 November, after he had issued his own warning orders for the projected moves. I arranged for an officer to take the despatch by staff car to Ambala that night, to be delivered to the GOC by eight o'clock next morning. As for the Para Brigade, I telephoned the Brigade Commander, my old friend Sagat Singh, and told him to meet me in my office on the 29th 'on an urgent operational matter'.

Meanwhile, at my request the CGS had undertaken to tackle the Army Chief about an integrated 'theatre command' system for the projected Goa operation. Just before I sat down to a late dinner, I telephoned Kaul to inquire how his discussion with Thapar had progressed. I was disappointed to hear that Thapar was against any such idea. He had decreed that for the present the conduct of land operations would be the responsibility of the task force commander.

The task force was to be placed under HQ Southern Command and Command HQ in its turn would receive orders from Army HQ. According to Bijji, Thapar did not envisage any difficulty in allotting 'supporting roles to the navy and air force'.

At an early morning meeting with the CGS next day I informed him of the actions I had taken to alert GOC 17th Division and the Commander of the Parachute Brigade and I added that we must issue formal Warning Orders soon. We also discussed various operational measures it would be wise to take in order to safeguard our strategic interests on other fronts while we were preoccupied in Goa. We agreed that the Armoured Division should be moved from its normal peace station at Jhansi to the Punjab; this would require careful co-ordination to make optimum use of rolling stock during the major rail moves southwards. Another important requirement was the formation of an *ad hoc* Army HQ reserve while 17th Division and the Paras were committed in the south. However, I stressed that we should not act on any of these plans before the government issued formal orders on Goa. Kaul agreed and, as Thapar had gone on tour to Dehra Dun for the day, went off to tackle Krishna Menon himself. On his return he told me that Menon was reluctant to commit anything to formal communication. At Kaul's insistence they had gone off to see the PM. That interview, judging by Kaul's account, was an arm-twisting session to convince an unwilling PM to authorise military aggression against Goa. However, they were only partially successful: the only commitment the PM made was that he would decide 'in favour of armed action if the situation deteriorated'.

Late that afternoon, while the CGS and I were discussing the results of the visit to Nehru, Air Chief Aspy Engineer telephoned to say that he had some startling information he would like to discuss with the CGS. The two of us decided to walk over to Air HQ.

The information Engineer gave us was indeed startling. That morning one of our Canberra bombers on a photo-reconnaissance mission over Goa had been tailed by two unknown fighters even before it had crossed the Goa border. Warning of the presence of the fighters was received on both the audio-warning system and radar. Preliminary evasive action had failed to shake them off, and as the Canberra began its photo run the fighters began to close in. When they had approached to within 1,500 metres the Canberra broke away and escaped, but not before its radar had indicated a burst of fire from one of the fighters. Engineer said that in his opinion, based on the rate of close-in, the fighters were probably F-86 Sabre jets, and so could have been from either the Portuguese or the Pakistani air force. The results of the photo-recce mission indicated that Dabolim, Goa's only airfield, had recently built two hangars that could possibly have sheltered fighter aircraft; it was, however, later ascertained that the Portuguese had at no time stationed fighter aircraft at Dabolim. (The mystery was never solved, but in all likelihood fighters from Pakistan had temporarily operated from Dabolim.)

From Air HQ we went on to the residence of the Army Chief, who had just returned from Dehra Dun. The two Chiefs agreed that we should mount a dummy run with a Canberra, lure the mystery fighters out over our territory and then pounce on them with our own fighters. To obtain the Defence Minister's approval we drove to 17 Roberts Road (Teen Murti Road now), Menon's residence. The DM, however, forbade any such venture. He said that for the time being the IAF was to restrict its operations to radar listening watches. An attempt to lure hostile aircraft over Indian territory could be made at a subsequent stage.

Krishna Menon then asked Bijji whether the word 'go' had been given for the move of the task force. Bijji replied that he was still waiting for formal government direction. Menon, in some agitation, said that he had made it clear that we were not to wait for written orders. We were to go ahead immediately with the move of the task force.

Although not suspicious by nature, I was not convinced that we should take this step without formal orders or even recorded minutes. I felt we ought to get something down in writing as a record of the government's direction.

The Air Chief offered to drop me back at my house, as it was located near Air HQ. On the way I gently suggested to him that the three Chiefs would be wise to send a joint note to the Defence Minister recording the latter's decision to go ahead with the Goa operation. Aspy gave me a conspiratorial smile and said that I was not to worry: the Chiefs of Staff had already thought about this and taken appropriate action. He took me back to his office and showed me a joint minute they had sent to Krishna Menon the previous day:

In a meeting held this morning in your office in which the Chiefs of Staff along with the CGS, DCNS and DCAS were present, you stated that, as a result of recent hostile Portuguese actions against our nationals, Government propose taking certain steps in area Anjadev [sic] Island and that, as the Portuguese were likely to take certain retaliatory measures, we may be compelled to take armed action against their territories in India.
2 For this purpose you directed us to concentrate forces as soon as possible with a view to operating in the areas Anjadiv Island and the Portuguese territories of Goa and, if necessary, Diu and Daman. You have accepted the time of 14 days which we will take to concentrate our forces in various areas for our operational tasks. Necessary orders have been issued to all concerned accordingly. This is for your formal approval.

(*Signed by the three Chiefs and endorsed to the Minister for Defence*)

As far as I know, Menon did not respond. This was the only record, however one-sided and indirect, of the government's direction to the armed forces for the Goa operation.

Only late that evening was I able to invite my JPC colleagues to my office and give them all the information I had on developments on Goa. I discussed with them the possibility of establishing a Joint Operations Room somewhere in South Block. We agreed that in the absence of formal sanction for the project, the only staff we could use for this purpose would be the members of the small Joint Planning Staff in the Cabinet Secretariat's sub-office for the Deputy Secretary (Military). They could be reinforced with Operations Officers from our own Ops Rooms. A small beginning, but we hoped to pioneer a reform effectively. In the event we did succeed in setting up a Joint Ops Room under Lieutenant Colonel 'Jimmy' Sircar with other members of the JPS staff kindly loaned by Air Commodore Mehta, Deputy Secretary (Military) to the Cabinet, but the 'reform' did not survive the Goa operation by more than a fortnight.

I look back on the events of the next three weeks with a mixture of wonder and satisfaction, always tinged with a feeling of anti-climax. It was an experience that uplifted our professionalism in many ways, even if the effect was transient. The military achievement was not a memorable feat of arms, but the process was enlightening. I recall with admiration Bijji Kaul's infectious dynamism and drive, especially his effectual interaction with that mammoth but spirited organisation, the Indian Railways, which unhesitatingly gave of its best. The quality of its staff effort came as a surprise, and not only to me. I also remember Bijji's central role, a one-man co-ordination system between government and the three Chiefs, between the Chiefs and their HQs, down to the level of PSOs and directors. There were periods of stress and high drama and moments of light comedy. There were gratifying responses from many quarters and there were grotesque reactions from others, such as from the appointed task force commander. I also recall, even if only at second hand, the behind-the-scenes attempts to obtain from a reluctant Prime Minister consent to a course of action which he must have felt in his bones was greatly against his conscience.

The countdown started on 29 December 1961. The morning began with a flurry of activity. The principal task was to link up the railway movement-table with 17th Division's loading schedule. After GOC 17th Division arrived at my office, I sent for the Director of Movements so that I could brief them jointly and thus make certain that they co-ordinated their efforts to get the troop-trains moving on time. Rolling stock would start arriving at the marshalling yard in Ambala on 1 December; the first fifteen trains were to leave by the morning of the 3rd. I wanted to be sure the army didn't drag its feet, now that the railways had responded so magnificently. Furthermore, there was a personal challenge to be met: Muchu Chaudhuri had openly scoffed at our movement timetable and declared it impossible to achieve. Kaul had heatedly retorted: 'The GS Branch is under new management now: you need have no doubts about the Task Force getting there in time.' We *had* to live up to that.

Having obtained permission from Kaul to disclose the operational task, I was able to discuss with Sagat Singh the role I wanted his northern column to play. I was sure that the ponderous advance by the main body from the east was not going to meet the deadline. The *coup de main* would have to be delivered by the Para Brigade.

I had known Sagat for some years. He was an unorthodox, rough-cut and practical soldier, always happier with troops than behind a desk, and with a field operative's disdain for the systematist. He was just the man to make a cross-country dash from Sawantwadi with his brigade, and he revelled in the challenge. I told him that the possibility of a para-drop would be discussed at the CGS conference that afternoon, but in any case he must make alternative plans to have a part of his force in the Goan capital within twenty-four hours.

At one o'clock GOC 17th Division returned to my office to share a snack lunch. Unlike Sagat, he was my senior in age and service, and he was not known for establishing an easy camaraderie with juniors. A down-to-earth professional, somewhat unimaginative and humourless, his main fault was that he took himself too seriously. Two years later when I was posted to his corps as a divisional commander I never lacked for personal kindnesses from him, but at the time I went in awe of him. Even so I was not prepared for the vehemence of his tirade as he sat down at my table. He railed at me for having done him 'a great injury' by naming him task force commander. Why could I not have chosen some other infantry division? Did I not know that he had been selected for the Imperial Defence College course in London and was due to leave for England within a few weeks? By holding him back from the IDC I had, he accused, marred his chances of future advancement.

Taken aback by the unexpected (and undeserved) invective, it took a moment to recover. I politely, but firmly, told the general that he would do better to make his protests to the CGS, or even to the Chief. He brushed this aside and continued with his harangue. I could see that he was highly upset, to the point of paranoia. I understood but could not sympathise with his agitation. The prestigious IDC course was regarded as a stepping-stone to the highest ranks. It also offered an occasion for a year's sojourn in the western world with all the material and cross-cultural advantages that entailed, a rare opportunity for someone from a country under tight foreign exchange controls.

I tried to explain to the general officer that there was no question of his missing his course. The Goa operation would be over in three or four days – *we* would see to that – and he could proceed abroad before the end of December. I tried to persuade him that with a Goan victory behind him and the initials 'idc' next to his name in the Army List, nothing could stop him from reaching army commander's rank. Unfortunately, I failed to convince him and he remained unplacated. In the end I went in search of my boss, leaving the general to his sandwiches.

I tracked Kaul down in QMG's Branch and told him the story, suggesting that rather than have a dispirited task force commander we would be wiser to replace him immediately, if possible that very day. Kaul said he would have to consult Thapar, but for the time being the GOC had better continue to attend to the business of readying his troops and stores for entrainment.

That afternoon the CGS held an inter-service co-ordinating conference on Goa at which operational tasks for the air force were agreed and air transport allocations made. Thereafter, to my delight, Kaul raised the question of command at the 'theatre' level, suggesting that a joint command HQ under the Chiefs of Staff be established at Poona or Bombay. Contrary to my expectation, there was little enthusiasm for discussion of this vital subject. Unexpectedly, it was the Deputy Naval and Air Chiefs, whose services most stood to benefit by such an arrangement, who vetoed the proposal, arguing that 'in the present extraordinary circumstances and in view of the security restrictions imposed by the Defence Minister, no elaborate High Command structure could be organised. The three Chiefs of Staff should be separately responsible for the operation ("Op Vijay") and should issue orders to their own Services which would then be executed through Service channels'. I recorded this decision with great disappointment.

The air force agreed to make available a fleet of Dakota C-47s to drop a parachute battalion, but had only sufficient aircraft to do so in two waves, one half at last light on D-day and the other at first light next morning (they possessed neither the equipment nor the training for a night drop). I suggested that the only likely time for a drop would be the early morning of D-Day and added that half a battalion would suffice.

Next day the Chief appointed Major General 'Unni' Candeth, Director of Artillery at Army HQ, to the command of 17th Division and the task force. I rang up to congratulate Unni and suggested that he walk over to my office to be put into the operational picture. At the same time, meeting Muchu Chaudhuri in the corridor I told him of the change in command and invited him also to my office to meet the new GOC. After a short briefing in the Ops Room we went to the CGS' office. Chaudhuri again voiced his doubts about the movement timetable but Kaul cut him short, saying that if there was to be any change in the plan it would be only to improve on the timings, not retard it (and in the event that is what we did).

When I mentioned the possibility of a limited air-drop for the Para Brigade, Chaudhuri rejected the suggestion without pausing to give the matter even a moment's thought. He gave no reason for his veto, but I later surmised that he did not want the Para Brigade to get to Panjim before the main body (he even refused the offer of a mule company for the Para Brigade's use on the northern route). Chaudhuri was planning to stake everything on the main column getting there first, so that he could helicopter in, join the leading elements of the column and accept the surrender himself.

Thapar sent for me in the evening and instructed me to arrange a meeting of the Chiefs of Staff at 10 o'clock next morning (2 December) and to officiate as secretary at the meeting. When I began to raise a point, he anticipated me by adding, 'You can tell Admiral Katari that *I* want this meeting and that *I* shall prepare the agenda.' The implication, presumably, was that while he was aware of normal procedure (that it was the chairman's prerogative to call a meeting) in this emergency he was going to do things *his* way. This placed me in an awkward position. Katari was the chairman of the Chiefs of Staff and I could not ignore that fact, even though it was patently obvious that the capture of Goa would be mainly an army operation with lesser contributions by the navy and the air force.

Vice-Admiral Ramdas Katari was the only one among the Chiefs whom I had not known well previously. In June 1961 he had taken over from Thimayya as chairman of the COS Committee, (an appointment that, on the retirement of the last incumbent, passes to the next senior in terms of tenure in office, regardless of rank). Not only was Katari many years Thapar's junior in age and service, he was also outranked by him. It could not have been wholly agreeable for him to preside over the Chiefs' Committee during those critical times, particularly because in the years since independence the navy had not been in the mainstream of national security concerns. His asset, however, was his personality. Always friendly and polite, he was too sensitive and sophisticated to exult over his chance eminence as chairman. As his committee secretary I had found him easily approachable, helpful and consistent, and he did not talk down to his juniors.

When I went to him with Thapar's message he fortunately raised no objection to holding a meeting the next morning, and in the event he gladly allowed Thapar to conduct the business as he wished. The Deputy Chiefs of the navy (Rear Admiral Chatterjee) and the air force (Air Vice-Marshal Nanda), GOC-in-C Southern Command, Flag Officer Commanding Indian Fleet (Rear Admiral Soman), AOC-in-C Operational Command (Air Vice-Marshal Pinto) and the task force commander were in attendance.

Thapar's main purpose at the meeting was to set the pattern for the Goa operation: a land invasion, with minimum use of force but with utmost speed. In order to minimise damage to life and property, the roles of the navy and air force were to be limited. The navy was to patrol the waters off Goa before and after the commencement of hostilities (outside a 13 km territorial zone) and was to effect a landing on Anjadiv after H-Hour. It was not to bombard shore batteries or engage the *Alfonso de Albuquerque*, a Portuguese warship in Goa that kept vigil between Marmagoa harbour and Anjadiv island.

The tasks for the air force were to be prepared to support the surface forces if required, and to carry out photo-reconnaissance. The only targets to be bombed were Dabolim airfield and its wireless installations.

Soman was appointed the naval task force commander and would function from his Bombay HQ under the orders of the Naval Chief. Pinto would be the task force commander for the air, operating from Poona but under Air HQ. The Air Chief undertook to position a Tactical Air Command alongside HQ Southern Command and air liaison officers at the Maritime Operation Room in Bombay and on board the cruisers *Mysore* and *Delhi*.

It was provisionally decided that D-Day would be 14 December. It was also decided that as there were sufficient troops available in Southern Command, Daman and Diu could be taken on D-Day instead of subsequently. An infantry battalion supported by a battery of field guns was allotted for the capture of Daman, and an infantry battalion for Diu.

Later, while drafting the minutes of the meeting, I mused over Thapar's design for the command system and realised that in the circumstances of scrambled urgency and improvisation he was right to keep it simple and the command chain direct. With the Anjadiv assault downgraded in importance and with naval and air roles necessarily restricted, it was going to be an almost exclusively army operation. It would add to the confusion at this stage to innovate joint-staff procedures or introduce an unfamiliar theatre command system. I conceded this with some disappointment; the chance – a three-service combined operations – would not come again for many years.

The next two days kept the DMO busy almost round the clock with a number of high priority tasks: the preparation of a detailed operational instruction for Southern Command and messages to Western Command ordering the move of the Armoured Division to the Punjab and other security measures on the Pakistan border. I had to brief the key directors at Army HQ about measures they would be expected to take to ensure that the troops who had so suddenly been pitchforked into active service would, when they arrived at Belgaum for pre-battle assembly, have all their deficiencies of clothing, equipment, arms and ammunition made up. This was a pressing need because in many items 17th Division, being a reserve formation, had been kept short in order to meet the needs of those stationed nearer the Pakistan border. Another urgent requirement was to ensure that the task force was given sufficient bridging equipment, Handu having warned us that the Portuguese were busily preparing most of the bridges for destruction. All these chores had to be undertaken by me personally, because I had sent my senior staff officers to call on other directorates in turn to ensure that follow-up actions were being pursued as relentlessly as we demanded.

There were constant visits to the 'Railway Counter' in my Ops Room in order to ensure the rapid progress of troop specials and goods trains in their journey southward and of empty rolling stock rushing back for a second loading. The chairman of the Railway Board had fortunately attached a helpful Joint Director (Milrail) to QMG's Branch, whom I had given free access to my office and Ops Room. We had obtained government permission to delay, halt or even cancel mail, express, passenger and goods traffic on the Delhi-Bombay-Poona line; this responsibility required decisions to be taken several times a day – at the beginning, anyway. When the moves first started, Mr Shiv Kishore of the railways kept a twenty-four hour vigil on the state of the traffic so that he could advise us on priorities. The first fifteen trains steamed out of Ambala at mid-morning of 3 December. By the next day, a total of fifty-six were on their way. By the early morning of 5 December troops were detraining at four points in Poona and preparing to change trains to the narrow gauge. It was not long before the first set of rolling stock was on its way back for a second carry.

On 4 December the two Commands were to be given their formal operation instructions. Lieutenant General Daulet Singh came down from Simla and I briefed him on the measures to be taken by Western Command. As for Southern Command, the Chief asked for a detailed presentation of the Operation Vijay plan on the map before the despatch of formal orders to Poona. I took him to the Joint Ops Room (newly set up under 'Jimmy' Sircar in the gallery of the Defence Department's central conference room) and ran over the details of the operational plan for the capture of Goa. Thapar made a few changes, which I incorporated into the document, and despatched it by air to Poona by hand of Lieutenant Colonel 'Tappy' Raina of MS Branch.

After 5 December a new vexation arose to complicate an already highly charged atmosphere. The morning papers carried the story of heavy troop movements to the south. In order to prevent undue speculation in the press and public, the government followed this up with a communiqué in the evening's news broadcast. All India Radio quoted an official spokesman from the Foreign Ministry confirming that 'the Government of India had issued orders for the move of troops to the Goa border as a precautionary measure'. These disclosures opened floodgates of inquiry from many quarters – the press, diplomatic missions, other government departments and, of course, friends and acquaintances. I had to quarantine myself from incoming calls for a day or two, using only the internal secrophones. A number of British and American diplomats of my acquaintance sought me out at home and I had difficulty fending them off. I recall one in particular, a Polish-American shooting companion, who insisted on seeing me in the small hours one morning to register his anguish at what we were proposing to do to 'a peaceful Catholic people'.

Not all inquiries could be so conveniently fielded. Reports in the press led to a number of parliamentary questions on the situation in Goa and on the build-up of Portuguese forces in the three territories. When questions began to be referred to MO Directorate I protested, arguing that Goa was still territory occupied and governed by a foreign country and it was the Ministry of External Affairs' responsibility to answer parliamentary questions on its affairs. No one was persuaded by this red-tape argument and in the end MO Directorate had to undertake the chore – though, mercifully, the CGS had by then attached a number of officers from other directorates to carry out the less prescriptive MO chores.

The CGS kept me informed about the pressures that were being put on the Prime Minister by western powers, either advising restraint or offering mediation. Nehru sent for Kaul on the morning of 5 December to tell him that he wanted D-Day to be put forward to 7 or 8 December in order to forestall any move by the United Nations to prevent the occupation. Kaul firmly resisted this, saying that the date of invasion could be advanced by perhaps one or two days, but not by a week; furthermore, he would have to consult the GOC-in-C Southern Command and the task force commander before he could agree to an earlier date. Nehru withdrew his request and we heard no more about it. (There is an insert in the DMO's daily record for that period: 'The morning's newspapers on 7th December gave an indication that the United States would not interfere unduly in the Goa impasse should India decide to take firm action.' Perhaps this is what took the pressure off the Prime Minister.)

At a meeting of the Joint Planning Committee on the morning of 6 December the members decided that although there was no longer scope for a joint planning staff such as we had envisaged, we ought to set up a staff cell to co-ordinate those operational measures ordered by the three services which might otherwise be mutually incompatible. My colleagues proposed that we reform the JPC and its Joint Planning staff into a Joint Operations cell for the duration.

The first problem we faced was the plan for the assault on Anjadiv. Neither the cruiser *Mysore* nor the *Trishul* was able to provide a landing party; nor did the navy have the time or the resources to train such a force. As the obvious answer was for the army to provide an assault landing party, I agreed to make available a trained platoon of Gorkhas. Since the *Mysore* was due to sail from Bombay on 11 December, I sent for Captain Partho Choudhuri of my Directorate (and my Regiment) who was on duty in the Ops Room. I explained the requirement to him and ordered him to commandeer a staff car, proceed to 39 Gorkha Training Centre in Dehra Dun that evening and, armed with an authority from me, select an *ad hoc* platoon from among the personnel of our Fourth Battalion then in the process of raising at the Training Centre. He was to assume command of the platoon, arm and equip it on his own initiative, take the Bombay express from Dehra Dun on the evening of the 7th and proceed to Bombay with his party. Harold Claudius, our naval JPC colleague, undertook to have them met at Victoria Terminus and conducted to the *Mysore*. As Colonel of the 9th Gorkhas I presumed to take this liberty.

Unfortunately, the attempted initiative came to nothing, much to the regret of young Choudhuri and the men he had pressganged. Bijji Kaul, when I told him of the enterprise, felt that he must keep Thapar informed. Katari had accepted my offer gratefully, but Thapar's reaction was different. He decreed that the navy must carry out its tasks with its own resources and ordered the cancellation of my project. Pettiness is not confined to smaller people; and the postscript to the pettiness accentuated its unworthiness. In the event the navy had hastily to improvise an assault landing party for D-Day (without any previous training in infantry tactics and equipment) and, inevitably, met with difficulties while skirmishing inland after the landing. According to the Defence Ministry's official history, *Operation Vijay*, by far the highest casualties of the Goa campaign – seven killed and nineteen wounded, including two officers – occurred in this action, one of the hardest fought but least consequential of the invasion skirmishes.

The Joint Ops cell met again the next day to continue with its self-imposed task of integrating the projected operations of the three task forces. There was some debate about H-Hour. The army's preference was to cross the Goa border well before first light and this view would probably prevail, though Pinto, the air commander, pointed out that if the northern column found themselves in need of air support in the open country through which they were to operate, he would require good light conditions to carry out his task. Since the Chiefs were not inclined to confer with each other, we decided to co-ordinate this and other matters (such as air priorities for support for the various phases of the operation) at our level, take our recommendations to the Deputy Chiefs and hope for decisions. By and large, we managed to muddle through. H-Hour was appointed as 0400 hours on D-Day.

When we received a copy of General Chaudhuri's operation instruction to the task force command, I noticed that, unlike his Appreciation, this was far from being a meticulously drafted document. There were numerous discrepancies and omissions. The most serious was that the air force role had been virtually omitted, despite the detailed arrangements for air support that Thapar had sent him. I inscribed my comments and sent the file to the CGS, suggesting that this would be a good occasion for me to pay a visit to the three task forces to ensure that they fully understood Thapar's plan. Kaul agreed and I rang up my naval and air colleagues, Keki Gocal and Harold Claudius, to warn them to obtain permission from their Chiefs for a visit to Bombay and Belgaum as members of the Joint Operations Committee.

We flew to Bombay by the evening Viscount service on 9 December. We agreed that as we would be taking off for Poona early next morning, we would set out after a quick dinner and visit the Maritime Operations Room, located in the Naval Signal Centre near the Naval Dockyard. Arriving there at 11.30 p.m., we found that it had become fully operational, manned by navy and air components as well as a detachment from Fortress Defence, Bombay, representing the army. An interesting item of information given us was that on 7 December our anti-submarine frigate had reported positive identification of a submarine off Goa and had fired a depth charge at the target. Afterwards, Naval HQ had authorised FOCIF to attack and destroy any submarine located in those (international) waters. The astonishing aspect was that other Service HQs had not till then been informed of the incident; it came as news even to Claudius. (Years later I learned that when some of our naval ships made a courtesy call at Singapore some time in 1963–4, they picked up dock gossip that a damaged British submarine had limped into port at Christmas-time for repairs to what appeared to be bomb damage.)

Early next morning we flew to Poona in an Otter aircraft, transferred to an Illyushin and flew on to Belgaum. Handu joined us in Bombay and, during the flight, gave us the latest intelligence on Portuguese activities. It appeared that Portuguese nationals had been withdrawn from the forward outposts and replaced by Goan personnel. His main warning was that although we need expect only token resistance, the Portuguese intended to carry out a scorched earth policy along the expected routes of invasion. They were preparing bridges, the famous Goan iron mines, petrol stations, public buildings and all utility services for demolition, while roads were being mined.

I called on the task force commander for a private briefing on his plan. Unni Candeth was an agreeable and approachable colleague with whom I had become well acquainted during many meetings of the Master-Plan-for-the-Army Committee. As Director of Artillery his advice on many aspects of artillery reorganisation had been useful; although he sometimes shied away from new ideas he always presented both sides of an argument meticulously. Like most Gunners he was professionally qualified and competent.

I realised, as he unfolded his plan on a wall map, that he was intending to carry out a copybook advance, not the dash-and-scurry spurt that would see his forward elements into Panjim within twenty-four hours. Needlessly cautious and deliberate, he planned to move forward in formal stages (or bounds) at infantry pace, with many of his bridging vehicles cluttered up forward on the line of march. He himself would march with his Divisional HQ, well behind the leading brigade. My tactful suggestion that he should place himself up with the leading brigade, so that he could expedite the movement of forward elements with on-the-spot decisions, did not convince him. Unni suffered from the occupational hazard of many Gunners — the tendency to view an operational problem at one remove from the front, which is of course where the guns are normally deployed. I also realised that Army HQ had over-insured by providing too much bridging equipment. Since it was already there, and since Handu had warned us of potential widespread blowing up of bridges, I could not blame the task force commander for planning to use it all, but he had unfortunately placed some of the equipment too far forward on his order of march, a placement which I felt would clog up road space and slow the column down.

An amusing piece of information from Unni was that Muchu had tried to use pressure to obtain direct control of the northern column (50 Para), arguing that it was somewhat detached from the area of the main thrust and might require closer supervision than Unni could provide from his location. Unni had remained firm and vetoed the Army Commander's plea for meddling. The latter then suggested that perhaps he could 'control' the infantry company that was to march north from Karwar. Unni, much amused, realised that Muchu was desperate for a personal share in the operation and agreed to this request.

I borrowed a jeep from Unni and made a hurried trip to Sagat at his Para Brigade HQ near Sawantvadi, where he gave me a run-down of his plan of advance on a map. In order to get his battalion columns off to a quick start, he intended to send strong patrols into Goan territory the night before D-Day to secure essential bridges (or, if they had already been blown, to establish sites for the launching of Bailey bridges). Thereafter he intended to advance on two axes, the eastern column heading for a conjunction with the main force at Ponda and the other rushing forward and attempting to reach the Madavi estuary despite blown bridges. He convinced me that his leading elements would be in Panjim by nightfall on the first day.

Back at Belgaum I had a hurried lunch with the Air Force Commander, Shivdev Singh, before flying to Poona, where Muchu joined us on the flight to Bombay. At Santa Cruz airport Muchu, who was also going on to Delhi, invited me to sit with him during the flight and join him in a drink. The companionable offer from so senior an officer was gratifying, but I was somewhat wary. Muchu, I suspected, had a plethora of problems to solve and demands to make at Army HQ. What better way to attempt suborning the DMO than over a glass of whisky?

My suspicions could not have been more unfounded nor, indeed, more uncharitable. Apart from a few general comments, Muchu did not even mention the Goa operation, or any other form of 'shop'. He was entirely relaxed, informal and friendly, and good entertainment. Sophisticated, articulate and amusing, he spoke engagingly on a number of topics varying from the merits of French wine (on which he affected to be an expert) to the poetry of Tagore (about which he knew a little and I not much more). Blessed with catholic tastes, he welcomed almost any topic as a subject for conversation. We discussed books, and particularly those by military commanders during the Second World War. He pleased me greatly by asking if he might, during his stay in Delhi, visit my library and collection of militaria, of which, he said, he had heard much. Agreeable and interesting, he drew me to him with a hypnotic charm – a vastly different personality from the opportunist army commander who had tried to browbeat a DMO three months previously.

Early the next morning I went to see Bijji Kaul at his house. He filled me in on the latest news on the diplomatic and political fronts. It appeared that there was much dithering in government, with the Foreign Ministry blowing hot and cold between the need for urgent action before the UN compromised our resolve and a drift towards deferment in the hope that a convincing offer of mediation would avert the necessity for armed aggression. Bijji added a tidbit of information – the Chargé d'Affaires of the Mexican Embassy had tried to pull off a coup of his own by offering his government's good offices for mediation between India and Portugal; when New Delhi approached the government of Mexico it denied having given the Chargé any authority to offer mediation or take any other steps.

Kaul said that till then Pakistan had not reacted to our troop movements to the Punjab, and although the DIB had reported that an armoured brigade had been sent up from Kharian to Sheikhupura on 25 November, that had been well before we had begun our Goa preliminaries. At the same time, the political officer in Sikkim had reported that 'major fresh Chinese reinforcements of men and material' were arriving in the Chumbi valley and the Chinese were apparently strengthening their positions in the Nathu-la, Jelep-la and Kongra-la (north Sikkim) sectors. It was unlikely that they would exploit the Goa situation to an alarming extent but, to be on the safe side, I suggested to the CGS that we alert Eastern Command to the necessity of building an Eastern Command reserve around 23 Infantry Division in Nagaland, using forces deployed either in the

Naga insurgency operations or on the border with East Pakistan.

An unexpected contretemps came to light at this stage. There was disaffection among certain Goan officers (presumably those whose homes were actually within the Portuguese territory) who found themselves included in the task force. One case was that of a commanding officer of an armoured regiment who had expressed misgivings about the invasion; more importantly, a battery commander in a heavy mortar unit had to be put under arrest by the GOC. I recalled that even during the earlier days of planning Kaul had surmised that some among the Goan officers and JCOs serving in Army HQ were passing information to embassies in Delhi. As early as 12 December, Portugal's Permanent Representative at the UN had alerted the Security Council regarding India's aggressive moves. He had correctly named General Chaudhuri as the overall commander and fairly accurately listed the Indian order of battle at Belgaum.

By 13 December work pressure at Army HQ had eased. Not much more needed to be done than to inform Southern Command of the date for D-Day. This was decided at a meeting of the Defence Minister's Committee that afternoon. The CGS summoned me to his office at 5 p.m. and directed me to bring with me a letter addressed to GOC-in-C Southern Command ready for the Chief's signature, but with the date of D-Day left blank. Thapar was waiting with Bijji in the latter's office. With uncharacteristic melodrama he took the message from me without saying a word and in his own hand inscribed the date: '18th December'. He cautioned me that it was not to be inscribed in the office copy; in Delhi none but the three of us were to know about the date until the event. I wanted to ask whether the navy and the air force were to be let into the secret but thought better of it. My concern was genuine, but the question might have sounded frivolous.

I returned to my office and despatched the letter to Poona by hand of an officer. Later in the evening Kaul sent for me again. Thapar was still closeted with him. They had decided to prepare various government despatches such as warnings and ultimatums that would be necessary before and after the commencement of armed action. By rights these should have been issued by the government but since neither the Foreign nor the Defence Ministry was taking the initiative in the matter, the General Staff assumed the responsibility. Thapar instructed us to restrict such communiqués to the bilateral setting and not address the general international community; it was not 'war' we were undertaking but 'action to reoccupy our own territory as a matter of right'. He added that a note to emphasise this point was being circulated in the Security Council by our Permanent Delegate to the UN, so it would be unnecessary, for instance, to issue a general warning for all shipping to avoid Goan waters during the expected period of hostilities. The DMO was directed to draw up a list of such despatches and prepare drafts which the Chief would approve the following day when he returned from his visit to the task force.

When Thapar left, Bijji sent for coffee and sandwiches for both of us. I could tell that there was something on his mind. Hesitantly he confided that he had made plans to fly to Belgaum on the eve of D-Day, stay the night in the Assembly Area and set out with the leading brigade of the main invading column next morning. I was not to publicise this fact, but I was required to make all the necessary arrangements.

I should not have been surprised at this piece of peacockery by Bijji Kaul – but I was. How could he be so insensitive to the incongruity of his proposed venture? I tried to dissuade him but lacked the courage to tell him bluntly that his gesture would be held up to ridicule and not, as he perhaps hoped, be taken as proof of personal courage and operational management. Although he was sensitive about his lack of battle experience and therefore over-eager to get into the act, I would have expected him to have enough subtlety to discern the touch of burlesque in the idea of a CGS marching into battle with the vanguard. I attempted a more tactful line and argued that in view of his antagonistic relationship with the GOC-in-C his presence at Anmod would cause unnecessary provocation. In any case, without the GOC-in-C's permission, his presence there would be regarded as an unwarranted presumption. My words were all wasted and, aware of his growing resentment at my arguments, I let it go. Later, discussing arrangements for his trip, I advised him that if he wanted to be in at the kill the troops to accompany would be the Para Brigade and not the main divisional column. He brusquely rejected this attempt my suggestion. Perhaps he thought that I was attempting to sidetrack him from a too-obvious presence at the main front. As it turned out, the pace of Unni Candeth's column on D-Day was so leisurely that the Portuguese commander's surrender to the Para Brigade took place long before the main column reached the scene.

15 and 16 December saw increased diplomatic activity in Delhi. The US government urged India not to lower its prestige and moral standing by using military force in Goa, though it added that due to its anti-colonial outlook it held no brief on behalf of Portugal. This token protest, however, was accompanied by pressure on Nehru from the US Ambassador in Delhi, Kenneth Galbraith, to postpone any contemplated action in Goa till the matter could be discussed at the United Nations. British Prime Minister Harold Macmillan also advised restraint.

On the 15th Nehru sent for Kaul to discuss a possible deferment of the operation. The cabinet had not been consulted; in this instance even Krishna Menon seems to have been short-circuited by the extraordinary procedure of a PM-CGS consultation on a matter of high diplomatic policy. Kaul told me after returning from the Prime Minister's office that it had taken him a good half-hour to convince Nehru that with troops poised for action 'no other course was open to us now' – unless, of course, Portugal were to undertake to evacuate Goa within an acceptable time-limit.

The stage was thus set for the liberation march. Ever alert for such an opportunity, Pakistan promptly put in a claim that after the government of India took possession of the Portuguese territories, Pakistan as the inheritor of one-third of the former foreign possessions would be entitled to a one-third share of the newly acquired real estate!

According to Candeth's plan the leading (63) brigade of 17 Infantry Division was to capture Ponda in the first phase; in the second, 48 Brigade would pass through Ponda, making for Panjim. The Para Brigade's role was to move down from the north on a wide front, with its left flank making contact with 63 Brigade at Ponda where it would establish a firm base from which 63 Brigade would deliver the *coup de grâce* at Marmagao.

It was 17th Division's tardiness that prevented this plan from being realised. 63 Brigade, in an unopposed but laboured advance from Anmod, reached the area of Darbandora only on the evening of 18 December. The bridges forward of Darbandora and Pillem were reported blown, so the brigade decided to spend the night there and wait for 48 Brigade to pass through next morning. Throughout the night, HQ 17th Division remained out of wireless touch with both Command HQ and the Para Brigade and was thus unaware that Ponda had in fact been captured by the latter hours previously. In any case 48 Brigade was impossibly positioned to play its role in the plan. Its place in the order of march was behind a long column of the Engineer bridging fleet, whose ancient vehicles repeatedly broke down and held up movement on the narrow one-way road. By 9 o'clock on the morning of 19 December 48 Brigade was still at Mollem, only a few kilometres inside Goa's border.

Para Brigade's three battalions progressed far more rapidly despite a number of skirmishes, including encounters with Portuguese armoured cars. They suffered a few casualties but by mid-day all opposition had dissolved. Although the major bridges at Sanquelim, Bicholim, Assanora, Banastarim and others had been destroyed, the Paras pushed forward, making skilful use of their meagre allotment of Engineer equipment and using local resources such as country boats and rafts. An hour after mid-day 2nd Para Battalion captured Ponda.

In the middle sector 1st Para Battalion captured Banastarim by evening and began to prepare for a night river crossing. At about eight o'clock a mysterious message was received saying that the Army Commander would visit them at Banastarim at 9.30 next morning. That put a stop to their advance across the river.

The third battalion of 50 Para Brigade, 2nd Sikh Light Infantry, was on the right flank, nearest the sea. It led off with a squadron of light tanks and took Assanora by mid-morning. Finding the bridge destroyed, the leading companies hastily built a causeway across the river and reached Mapuca in mid-afternoon. The battalion then made a dash for Aguada Bay and reached Betim at six o'clock. The commanding officer initially intended to cross the bay during the night and thus be the first in Panjim. On reconsideration, however, he felt he ought to obtain the Brigade Commander's permission, as the capture of Panjim had not been included in his task. Unfortunately he was unable to establish wireless contact with Brigade HQ and unenterprisingly decided to go into harbour for the night.

By the morning of 19 December, the main 17th Division column had still not progressed beyond Darbandora. Candeth's headquarters, like 48 Brigade, was still at Mollem, also stuck behind a bridging column. Out of touch with the battle and with no wireless contact with Command HQ, Candeth could only send a message confirming his previous day's orders – that Para Brigade would hold firm at Ponda waiting for 48 and 63 Brigades to pass through for the kill. Fortunately, Muchu Chaudhuri, more aware of the unfolding opportunity at the front, countermanded that message and issued orders directly to 50 Para Brigade to exploit its success and make for Panjim.

50 Para Brigade had in effect made a half-circle round Panjim by last light on 18 December. 1st Para had halted at Banastanim but an alert commanding officer, anticipating a possible change of orders next morning, sent patrols up and down the river to procure country boats. None had been found by the time orders to go for Panjim came from Command HQ in the early morning, so the CO promptly lined up two rifle companies on the river bank, ordered his men to strip, use their packs to make rafts for their weapons and swim across the river. On the far bank they were met by a truckload of cheering Goans. Soon a couple of cars joined the group, all willing to lend their vehicles to the Indian Army. As soon as the men were dressed and had checked the actions of their weapons, the colonel piled as many as he could into the waiting vehicles and himself led the ragtag assault team in one of the cars.

Early on 19 December the Sikh Light Infantry at Betim had at last been able to make contact with Brigade HQ and received permission to enter Panjim. At 7.30 a.m. the CO loaded two companies into the boats he had collected during the night and ferried them across the estuary, while his tanks, artillery and mortars were lined up menacingly on the near embankment, in full view of any possible enemy on the far bank. In the event there was only sporadic firing and soon the main objectives were taken – the Governor General's House, the Secretariat and military and police headquarters.

By 8.30 a.m. the CO of 1st Para entered Panjim from the east and the two battalions met in the middle of what was by then a gala festival, the people of Panjim pouring out into the streets in their thousands to welcome the Indians. With some difficulty the CO of 1st Para made his way to the Portuguese officers barracks, where the senior commander agreed to the surrender of the Portuguese armed forces.

The GOC-in-C helicoptered in from Belgaum, accompanied by Air Vice-Marshal Pinto. He landed in a field just outside Panjim and was met by a Para Brigade jeep. By the time he reached the capital, however, the surrender had already taken place.

On 20 December, the day after the Portuguese surrender, I received a message from Sagat reminding me of our date to meet for a drink at the Mandvi Hotel (as the name was then spelt) if Para Brigade succeeded in beating the main column to Panjim. Keki Gocal was kind enough to arrange an aircraft to fly me down to Dabolim airport, where Sagat had me collected. He gave me a Cook's tour of the Velhagoa, Marmagao and other settlements before taking me to his own HQ.

I recall meeting the general officer of the Portuguese forces at the prisoners-of-war camp. On hearing that I was from Army HQ he requested that his officers be returned their swords, taken from them at the surrender. Through an interpreter I promised that I would certainly convey his request to the Military Governor (to which post Unni Candeth had been elevated), but I also added, only half jokingly, a crass and totally unnecessary aside in English which unfortunately the commandant understood – a remark that I was to recall with chagrin and shame almost exactly ten months later in the aftermath of Se-la.

# 6
# THE SUMMER OF 1962

Following the Prime Minister's directive of November 1961, Army HQ held a number of meetings with representatives from the Commands to determine the minimum additional resources in men and material required to enforce the forward policy. As MO Directorate was then heavily involved in the preliminaries to the Goa operation the CGS undertook to handle the NEFA sector himself, leaving the DMO to deal with Ladakh.

Before taking any decision on reinforcing the western sector we asked Western Command to make two assessments: first, a review of force requirements for the main task (that is, for the defence of Leh) and, second, an estimate of resources required for the deployment of new posts in pursuance of the forward policy.

In 1960 Army HQ had estimated that the minimum force requirement for the defence of Leh would be a brigade of five infantry battalions (three regular and two militia), but even by January 1962 this target had not been achieved; it was still short of one regular battalion. The Srinagar–Leh road was not expected to be open for normal traffic till the late summer of 1962, so we were unlikely to be able to make up the requisite strength before then.

The implications of reinforcing and maintaining Ladakh by air in terms of aircraft and supply-dropping equipment were immense. Also, we had no artillery or heavy mortar support for the infantry, while Chinese forces in the Aksai Chin (previously estimated at about one brigade and since reinforced by at least another) were provided with artillery and, reportedly, even some light tanks. These forces were logistically maintained from Sinkiang and the construction of a number of feeder roads east of the Karakoram range had considerably increased their operational potential. In view of these developments, Western Command revised its force requirements in Ladakh upwards, to a full division, complete with artillery and other supporting arms. Thereafter the logistical prospect became a nightmare.

We were still negotiating these matters with HQ Western Command when a series of directives came down from the CGS ordering the establishment of new posts at localities across the Karakorum range, forward of our line of control. I learned later that it was Mullik who, now that he had the Prime Minister's ear on border strategy, had been goading Kaul to specify precise localities for new posts.

Western Command HQ expressed alarm at having to take on these additional commitments without a corresponding increase in supply and maintenance resources. Its representatives at our meetings kept stressing their difficulties, particularly in the barren marches of the Karakoram range, where the altitude at which our posts were located averaged between 4,000 and 5,000 metres, the temperatures in winter often fell several degrees below zero and the air was so rarefied that movement was laborious under the best conditions. In the absence of ponies and porters, forward posts had to be supplied by air, but the inability to backload used parachutes was causing an acute shortage of this imported item (a shortage that we had not yet been able to circumvent with the use of jute parachutes manufactured in our own private sector). In the circumstances, Command and Corps HQ justifiably protested against Army HQ orders to set up new posts in the unwelcoming void of the Aksai Chin.

MO Directorate was only too acutely conscious that Army HQ lacked the capability both to reinforce the garrison at Leh and to provide support for the move into the Aksai Chin, but we were unable to convince the CGS. The fact was that whereas at the staff level my counterparts in Command HQ (Major General Jogindar Singh) and HQ XV Corps (Brigadier John Dalvi) would often attack me for issuing such impracticable instructions, their commanders hesitated to thump the table in the CGS's office. Both Daulet Singh (Western Army Commander) and Bikram Singh (XV Corps Commander) were often in Delhi and both were on good terms with Kaul, but although they discussed the logistical difficulty with him, neither, to my knowledge, ever made an issue of it. The truth is that they (like most senior officers at the time) were reluctant boldly to oppose Kaul's policies and orders. Neither had a sufficiently forceful personality and both allowed themselves to be wheedled into a resigned acceptance of operational impracticabilities.

This was also partly true of Umrao, the corps Commander in the east. He was friendly, even intimate, with Kaul, having been his immediate superior when they had served together as subalterns in the Rajputana Rifles, but he did not take advantage of this special relationship to protest about the setting up of the many new posts the CGS had recently ordered to be located at the extreme reaches of NEFA. In general, I think it would be true to say that although there were written protests from the lower formations highlighting the difficulties involved, no determined, articulate protest against the forward policy was expressed personally by the senior commanders.

So far I have omitted mention of HQ Eastern Command in our dealings with NEFA; this is because it was not a particularly effectual organisation. The GOC-in-C who succeeded Thorat was Lieutenant General L.P. ('Bogey') Sen, DSO who, after a very promising early career, had allowed himself to lapse into stagnation when he reached the higher ranks, possibly because of a desolating domestic setback in his life. A quiet, gentle and non-controversial personality, he was content to allow Army HQ to deal directly with HQ XXXIII Corps. Nor was his senior General Staff sufficiently caring, aware or authoritative to take exception to this impropriety.

My own relationship with Kaul was such that although he would give a hearing to my views, he would resent them if they were offered in the form of gratuitous advice; since it was not in his nature to seek counsel, it was difficult for a subordinate to express criticism. The best approach to make was an intellectual one, because he was quick of comprehension and did not lack mental vision. As long as one let the proposition appeal to him by its own logic, he was likely to be open to persuasion – always assuming that there was no emotional block in his mind.

In the matter of implementing the forward policy, Bijji Kaul did appear to suffer from such a mental block. My own appraisal was that he firmly believed that his live-wire personality and drive could help overcome logistical problems to establish forward posts and pickets, even if these were only established on a tenuous basis. If the bureaucrats in the ministries were willing to take the risk, it would not be he who would cry halt. Central to his inhibitions was the fear of being regarded as operationally unenterprising. I suspect that he hoped, however irrationally, that forceful pursuit of the forward policy would establish an operational reputation for him despite his lack of combat experience.

In early January 1962 I held a meeting with my staff to determine how to impress upon the CGS the extent of the logistical impasse without antagonising him. We decided that the way to get the runaway *ad hoc* nature of decision-making under control would be to project an overall staff study of detailed force requirements measured against threats and logistical realities. As we were already working on our 'Master Plan' (re-entitled 'The Army of the Foreseeable Future') what could be more appropriate than to link it with the immediate strategic commitment on the northern borders? I obtained the CGS' approval to present such a paper, arguing that 'only by adopting a pre-planned policy could equipment provisioning be progressed effectively on a long-term basis . . . [and thus avoid] acute shortages of arms, equipment and accommodation'.

Our aim was to project, for the first time, a long-term assessment of operational and logistical requirements for conducting a policy of confrontation along the northern borders. Based on threat perceptions and a concept of war which the Chief had approved, we recommended the raising of (or conversion to) an eventual total of twelve mountain divisions,[1] besides an additional armoured and some infantry divisions. Half the field force was to be earmarked for the Pakistani front and half for the northern, besides four divisions in Army HQ reserve. The new divisions were to be raised in 'priority bricks'. We stressed that the operational and logistical requirements must be matched within each 'brick'.

We presented our paper to the Chief and the principal staff officers in early February. There was some debate but eventually most of our recommendations were accepted. However, the intention to link it up with immediate tasks and deployments was undermined. The Chief decided to send our recommendations to the Army Commanders for their comments and, in the process, unfortunately decreed that we were to detach the logistical aspects of the paper (including equipment and foreign procurement programmes) from the strategic elements, to avoid unnecessary delay in presenting our force requirements to government. After the meeting I tried to persuade the CGS to have this decision reversed, arguing that the unwisdom of de-linking operational moves from logistical capabilities was precisely what we were trying to rectify. I also stressed that it was imperative that we postpone forward policy moves till we had built up a modicum of maintenance backing in Ladakh, but Kaul would not agree. It was not that he was unconvinced by my arguments – they were too self-evident to be refuted – but he had turned Operation Onkar (the establishment of new high altitude posts in NEFA) into a personal challenge and wanted to push it through to completion before the monsoon season (which in fact he did, except in the case of one or two near-inaccessible heights). In common with most of our senior officers, inexperienced in battle, he too could readily de-link logistics from operations without a qualm. The last thing he wanted at that stage was a delay in the execution of Op Onkar.

In retrospect I am sure that I should have been more insistent. A DMO does not serve his CGS by subduing his objections; clearly, I did not measure up to my responsibility. However, under pressure from me Kaul undertook to expedite the process of logistical reinforcement by hastening the completion of the two main roads then under construction (to Towang and Leh). With Kaul as the executive member of the Prime Minister's Border Roads Development Board and with Kartar Dubey as the Director General, this was eminently feasible. Kaul also began to work on a sub-plot to form an unofficial pressure committee with the three key Secretaries to government – Finance, Home and Defence – whose task would be to lobby in the government's powerhouses for an increased allocation of foreign exchange for the army to procure its requirements of trucks, parachutes and other maintenance items. What he was determined not to do was to subordinate the forward policy to logistical priorities. To be fair to him, he did not believe that there was any great operational risk, having unreservedly accepted the DIB's assurance that the Chinese would not go to war on the border issue.

Thus was the essence of the 'Master Plan', on which we had worked so hard to ensure a systematic approach to operational planning, virtually cast aside. We continued, willy-nilly, to establish new posts forward, without further increasing our operational or logistical capabilities. A number of new posts were established forward of Daulet Beg Oldi in the Depsang plains, with the aim of containing Chinese infiltration into the Chip Chap valley. These activities on the ground involved a considerable increase in supply dropping by air, which the Chinese must have viewed with some alarm because they of course had no air suppport of any sort. It was not long before they sent strong protest notes about the intrusion of 'Indian aircraft . . . into Chinese air space again and again to carry out wilful reconnaissance and harassments'.

I must reiterate that it was not only Kaul who fell victim to the DIB's mistake about Chinese intentions; by then most of us had accepted his assurance that China would not go to war with India. Intelligence estimates at that time, reinforced by international news sources, indicated that China was beset by both internal and external crises. Although there was insufficient realisation in India of the growing Sino-Soviet confrontation, our Intelligence Bureau had been kept up to date in this respect through its CIA connection. The withholding of Soviet economic aid and technical assistance during 1958–9 was having a disastrous

effect on the Chinese economy. The failure of the Great
Leap Forward of the previous years, and unprecedented
floods in the northern provinces, had led to countrywide
food shortages and widespread famine. At the same time
there had been a real threat of invasion from Taiwan,
where official proclamations, military preparations and actual
rehearsals for an assault on the mainland had been actively
encouraged by the American defence establishment.
Consequently, a large part of the People's Liberation Army
had had to be deployed in the south-eastern provinces
facing Taiwan. Furthermore, the flare-up in Laos in May
1962 had resulted in the despatch of US bombers to
Thailand. Each of these threats overshadowed the minor
Indian build-up in the Himalayas. For all these reasons,
it was not difficult to be persuaded that the Chinese would
not resort to open warfare on the Aksai Chin front. As
Kaul later wrote in his book *The Untold Story*, the PM was
firmly convinced that owing to internal disorders 'the morale
of the Chinese people and their Armed Forces was cracking
up; and that if we dealt with them strongly, we should
have the better of them. . .'

At the same time, we in Army HQ were certain that
there could be a strong reaction – but not war – to our
advance into disputed territory, and we were only too well
aware that in this regard their range of options was greater
than ours. Even if the Chinese restricted themselves to
tactics similar to ours (that is, playing at chessboard moves
with border posts without actually resorting to hostilities),
they would have the better of us at the game because they
had more troops and more resources, and their roads and
vehicles reached right up to their forward posts.

When the weather improved in April 1962 there was a
marked increase in the air force's allotment of supply
dropping sorties on the Ladakh front. Although this did
not add substantially to the total maintenance tonnage for
Leh and Ladakh, it did signify a quantum leap in logistical
capability up at the front – at Daulet Beg Oldi and the
Chip Chap river. Western Command reported the
establishment of several new Chinese posts in the Aksai
Chin salient north-east and south-east of Daulet Beg Oldi,
the farthest being about 30 km beyond the Chinese (1960)

claim line.

A Chinese government note at the end of February, protesting about India's increased activity on the Aksai Chin front, carried an implicit indication of what one of their options could be. Contrasting the aggressiveness of our forward policy in Ladakh with the restraint they claimed they had displayed on the McMahon Line in NEFA, the note went on to state:

. . . Yet it [the Chinese Government] has strictly restrained all its military and administrative personnel from crossing this [McMahon] Line. If, like the Indian Government, the Chinese Government had also taken unilateral action to violate the status quo of the boundary, what would the relations between the two countries have been?

This was clearly a warning that they might start aggressive moves in NEFA, but the Chinese also suggested an alternative. The note went on to express the hope that India would 'translate into action' its 'previously indicated desire . . . to settle the border through peaceful means and not create an everlasting enmity with China'.

Strange to relate, this was the first time that I had seen the text of a Chinese communication to our government (or *vice versa*), and I saw this one only because I happened to be paying a visit to the office of N.B. Menon, who occupied the China Desk at the Ministry of External Affairs, when the document arrived on his table. There was no arrangement whereby either the DIB or the DMI circulated these inter-governmental communications (or even a resumé) to MO Directorate. When I complained to the CGS about this remissness, he shrugged it off by saying that these were political matters and as a Director of Military Operations I need not concern myself with them. I pointed out that this particular note clearly indicated possible Chinese military action in NEFA and was therefore of great interest to a DMO. Kaul then advised me that my best bet would be to establish personal rapport with Mullik, as indeed he had suggested once before. He said that he would speak to Mullik and ask him to arrange periodic meetings with the DMO.

Thus started a period of close association between Mullik and myself. The Intelligence Bureau offices, ensconced behind sturdy iron grilles and relays of police sentries, were only a few yards down the passage from my office and I soon became a regular visitor. From the day I first called on Mullik I fell under his spell. Previously I had met him only at meetings in the ministries or in the office of the Chief or the CGS. On such occasions Mullik would affect a forbidding, uncommunicative and lowering countenance. Except in the presence of Nehru, where he would be deferential and compliant, he exuded an aura of self-command and authority. Recently widowed, he had become reclusive in his habits and spent long after-office hours at his desk. He had few friends and seldom attended any social or even official functions. I also knew that his attitude towards the army was antithetical, reflecting the policeman's customary mixed feelings of envy, suspicion and cynicism. It was therefore somewhat of a surprise to be received by a smiling, mellow personality. He welcomed me with a warmth I did not suspect he possessed and he at once put our relationship on an informal level by insisting on speaking to me in Bengali. When I explained my purpose he willingly agreed to keep me abreast of behind-the-scenes diplomatic exchanges as well as other similar happenings not reported in the press. He urged me to visit him as often as I pleased, an invitation which I gladly accepted because I realised that there was much that was happening on the international scene about which, in the absence of a functioning Military Intelligence routine, I had remained largely uninformed till then. For example, Mullik told me about the sequel to the Chinese note mentioned previously: the Government of India, it appeared, had replied to it (predictably) by rejecting the allegation of 'aggression' and by reasserting its standard position that before any negotiation could be held China must withdraw from the Aksai Chin (a demand to which, the government surely knew, the Chinese would never agree).

It seemed extraordinary to me, to say the least, that bureaucracy should deal so perfunctorily with a matter that contained an explicit military threat and that also without consulting the General Staff, but I did not on that occasion take it up with Mullik because, frankly, I had a lurking suspicion that Kaul might well have been consulted and had then neglected to keep the DMO informed. It was not long, however, before another such occasion would arise when I was unable and unwilling to conceal my misgivings.

A few days later it was the CGS who showed me a note from the Chinese, dated 30 April, protesting strongly against one of our new sitings north-east of Daulet Beg Oldi (in the direction of Chungtash). This militia post had intentionally been located close to, and dominating, an existent Chinese one. The setting up of these posts was usually attended by supply drops by the IAF and, presumably, reconnaisance flights over adjacent areas, all of which could well have alarmed the Chinese. For this reason, perhaps, the Chinese for the first time used terms such as 'aggressive posts' and referred to (possible) 'incidents of bloodshed'. The note threatened that unless the Government of India withdrew that particular post, or if it continued to carry out provocative actions, the 'Chinese frontier guards *will be forced to defend themselves*' [emphasis added]. More ominously, it mentioned a specific retaliatory measure:

. . . In these circumstances the Chinese Government, exercising its sacred right to defend China's territory and maintain the tranquillity on the border, has ordered Chinese frontier guards to resume border patrols in the sector from Karakoram Pass to Konga Pass, where recently the Indian side has made repeated intrusions. . . . If India continues to invade and occupy China's territory . . . the Chinese Government will be compelled to consider the further step of resuming border patrols along the entire Sino-Indian boundary'.

The CGS and I discussed the implications of the two recent protest notes and we agreed that the Chinese reactions clearly indicated a major change of posture that we could not ignore. The threat to resume patrolling 'the entire Sino-Indian boundary' explicitly contradicted the unilateral decision of the Chinese in 1960 to suspend patrols 'within twenty kilometres on its side of the boundary' in NEFA, as suggested by Chou-En-lai during the Nehru-Chou talks in April of that year. However, there was no actual agreement, verbal or written, and the Indian government had not felt bound by what Mr Chou had termed his 'six points of proximity'. The Chinese had observed their self-imposed restriction as far as the McMahon Line was concerned but in Ladakh they had not been quite so meticulous; their movements in Chip Chap valley and their establishment of posts in the area could be regarded as violations of their undertaking.

Although we could not foretell exactly how strongly the Chinese might react to further forward policy moves, we obviously could take no chances. We felt that we must expect an attempt by them to push back or even overrun our posts, and this would pose a serious problem because we had not planned our deployment with a view to conducting armed resistance. The total strength of the six posts in the Daulet Beg Oldi area was sixty militia personnel! That was how thin we were on the ground. Although provisioned for about forty-five days, these 'penny packets' had no reserve ammunition and obviously could not withstand a determined onslaught by the Chinese. Army HQ did not expect them to stand and fight, but even to offer token resistance they would need to be given tactical and logistical support and, possibly, reinforcement by regular infantry. Fortunately a regular battalion of Gorkhas was even then being assembled at Srinagar for despatch to Ladakh.

Kaul was at that period preoccupied with arrangements in connection with the marriage of his younger daughter, Chitralekha. As the ceremony was being held at his house (and not in the anonymity of a five-star hotel, which became all the rage in a later *nouveau-riche* era) he had taken a week off from work to attend to the domestic chores. He left it to me to prepare a detailed operational review for the Chief in which I was to emphasise the threats implicit in the Chinese protest notes and recommend measures we should take in case of possible aggression on the Aksai Chin front.

On 2 May MO Directorate sent a detailed note to the Chief. Our appreciation was that the most likely course the Chinese would take would be to 'surround, isolate and generally harass our forward posts' and, at the same time, 'establish more posts themselves, perhaps even beyond the 1960 claim'. An open attack against the posts, we felt, was unlikely but we would have to be prepared for such a course. In my paper (MO3/15458/H/TS of 2 May) I recommended the following courses of action:

In case of the Chinese adopting course (a), our troops should be ordered to stand firm and open hostilities only in self-defence. But, if the Chinese attempt fresh incursions into our territory as a retaliatory measure, we should prevent them even if it means a clash.

In case the Chinese attempt to overrun a forward post, the latter will defend it at all cost. You may also consider recommending to Government that, in such an eventuality of blatant aggression, *we should take offensive air action*, as is normal in an operational situation like this, against the exposed Chinese posts at Chip Chap (Point 16820) and Sumdo [i.e. limited to the Aksai Chin area]. [Emphasis added]

Thereafter, highlighting the disparity between the Chinese strength and ours, the paper recommended that the total personnel in the Daulet Beg Oldi sector should be brought up to 150 immediately, and to a full militia battalion supported by a company of regular infantry after we had built up maintenance stocks. We also recommended reinforcement of the Sumdo and Sultan Chushku sectors (immediately south of the Chip Chap valley in west-central Aksai Chin). At the same time, the paper warned that if these recommendations were to be put into effect we would have to divert aircraft and supply-dropping equipment from other crucial tasks such as the construction of the Chushul airfield; we might even have to withdraw some of the DIB's Indo-Tibetan border posts at Murgo and other localities. (These were posts manned by the paramilitary police under the control of the DIB but logistically maintained by the army.)

The suggestion to the Chief about the use of offensive air power was neither an impetuous afterthought nor a last-minute inspiration. I had discussed the matter previously and at length with the CGS. At that time there were two schools of thought on the question of the use of tactical air support in case of hostilities on the northern border. The General Staff was strongly in favour of it because we felt that it was the most effective way of restoring the imbalance of forces at the front, particularly in Ladakh.

Furthermore, air force officers at squadron and wing level considered it an eminently feasible task. I recall the occasion during my command of 7 Brigade when I was taken up in a Vampire fighter for an air reconnaissance of western Kameng. Although the pilot had kept the aircraft well within our airspace, when flying over the Towang area it was possible to obtain a distant panoramic view of the generally flat and featureless plateau north of the Bum-la divide. I had discussed the possibility of air strikes in that area with the pilot and he had agreed that identification and destruction of ground targets would be much easier on that high and open expanse than in the rugged, heavily forested and weather-driven terrain on our side of the border. Later, in informal discussions with other officers of the squadron the consensus was that strikes on targets north of the border were a feasible task. (In Kameng the frontier zone was close to the airfield at Tezpur, a factor that would allow our fighters enough time-over-target to be effective. In Ladakh the circumstances would be more adverse but the task could still be worthwhile.)

Professional opinion in Air HQ was divided, but for a different reason. I do not recollect whether it was the Defence Ministry or the Air Chief who led the counter-argument: that India would be the loser should hostilities escalate to the use of air forces, because cities in north India were vulnerable to Chinese bombers based in Tibet, whereas Chinese cities were clearly beyond the range of our aircraft. Whoever offered this argument, it was an unthought-out piece of timidity that caused immense harm to India's defence response mechanism.[2]

The CGS had discussed this point with me during a brief session in the Ops Room when we were preparing the note to the Chief. My staff and I had argued that there was little reason to fear strategic bombing by the Chinese. First, we had no positive intelligence of a bomber base anywhere in Tibet. Second, if hostilities broke out over border claims, all indications till then were that fighting was unlikely to spread beyond the border regions. Third, even if the Chinese action did escalate to air bombing of civilian targets, our air defence potential, although not sufficiently well equipped at that stage, could still meet the challenge. The most the enemy could hope to do would be to mount occasional raids over northern India which, while causing some damage, would have little effect on the border war. We had convinced the CGS and he said that he would be able to persuade the Chief. However, I do not remember any follow-up action being taken at the time.

The Chief did not approach the Minister for permission to use tactical air strikes because operational developments a few days later defused anxieties sufficiently to allow the matter to lapse. This was a pity because I am sure that if it had been pursued then there would have been a more deliberate examination of the problem than there was later. (When the Chinese finally attacked, in October, a hasty decision was taken under a counsel of fears and with no homework done by the Air Force. It was decided that it would be best not to escalate the intensity of operations in case the Chinese retaliated in like measure. This was a grave misjudgment because, as Deputy Air Chief Arjun Singh admitted to me a year later, the Chinese could not have launched bombers and fighters from Tibet at that time. Airfields located at heights of 4,000 metres or more require protracted and costly preparations, such as extended runways and other facilities. This was a gross failure of air intelligence.)

I well remember my call at Mullik's office the next day. We fell to discussing the significance of the Chinese threat to resume 'patrolling' on the Ladakh border. At one stage I recall remarking that the Foreign Ministry appeared not to have taken note of the recent major change of posture on the part of the Chinese, especially the implied threat to retaliate in NEFA. Mullik smiled knowingly and said that indeed the Foreign Ministry had taken note of it. Had I not read the statement of the Foreign Minister in parliament? Only the day before, he informed me, Nehru had, in the Lok Sabha, referred to the Chinese note in question and said, 'There is nothing to be alarmed at, although the [Chinese] note threatens all kinds of steps they might take. If they do take those steps we shall be ready for them.'

I was quite taken aback, both because the head of government had issued what seemed to me to be a public challenge to the Chinese, and because his Intelligence Chief appeared to be gloating over this piece of verbal derring-do on the floor of the House. Mullik smirked amusedly at my dismay and when I said that the Prime Minister's statement was in contradiction of what Army HQ had informed him on the subject of the army's lack of operational potential on the northern border, he continued to smile in a knowing way. He gently chided me for lack of enterprise on the border issue. He suggested that the army was understimating its own capability. That was what, according to him, Thimayya had been guilty of; the present military leadership must not commit the same error.

· Like most politicians and many bureaucrats (and even some senior general officers for that matter) Mullik had only a shadowy notion of the restrictive characteristic of long-range logistics. To him, as to many others, the main index of defensive potential on the Himalayan fronts was represented by the numbers and strengths of border posts – the clusters of paper flags pinned on the map. Although hazily aware that troops and weapons at the front had to be kept supplied through a tenuous line of maintenance, he did not fully comprehend either the extent of the dependence of the former on the latter, or the exponential degree to which the dependence of high-altitude border posts increased according to their remoteness from bases in the plains.

I thought it was time that the Director of the Intelligence Bureau received some instruction on these matters from the DMO. I gave him facts and figures of land and air tonnages required in Ladakh and of the crippling shortfalls in targets during the past winter's air-stocking effort. Even the completion of the Srinagar–Leh highway would not greatly mitigate the situation because the army's vehicle fleet, which then comprised mostly overused trucks of Second World War vintage, was grinding to a halt on the steep gradients and rugged terrain of NEFA and Kashmir. Until these ancient transports could be replaced from the newly erected Tata-Benz and Shaktiman factories, or by imports, the logistical build-up would continue to lag well behind operational requirements. It was for these reasons, I explained, that the General Staff advised against being too venturesome on the Aksai Chin front before a semblance of maintenance potential was established.

Mullik heard me out patiently, but I could see that he was not overly impressed. He said that I was being too rigidly professional. He then proceeded to construe for my benefit the underlying purpose of the forward policy. (I do not recollect whether he purported to give it as his own interpretation or whether he was quoting the Prime Minister.) He said that although the Aksai Chin was indubitably Indian territory, no Indians actually lived there and few visited it; consequently there was no evidence of Indian administration there. It was the Chinese who, by building their roads and tracks, could claim to have an administrative presence and subsequently use that argument to press their claim on the territory. It was therefore vital for us to establish an administrative presence as soon as possible. He said that since the army had taken over responsibility for the border from the DIB, and anyway was better organised and equipped for the task than police forces, it was now up to the General Staff to fill the vacuum in Aksai Chin. He implied that the new posts, while established and manned by the army, would in fact play mainly a civilian administrative role – that is, affirm a presence. He did not think that the Chinese, preoccupied as they were by their own grave internal problems, would react forcibly over this issue; at the most, they would play the same game as us – push forward new posts while avoiding open clashes.

Given the fact that we had become inured to the presupposition of Chinese non-belligerence, Mullik's explication seemed to contain some merit. I confess that at the time I was persuaded by it when I should not have been. I do not possess a controversialist's mind; my thought processes are deductive and deliberate and therefore not best suited to discourse or debate. My obvious rejoinder should have been that even if we were justified in the *a priori* assumption that the Chinese would not resort to open war under existing circumstances, we should nevertheless prepare for an *a posteriori* change of circumstance that might alter the strategic situation. We had not, in our diplomatic exchanges, explicitly declared that the army posts in the

Aksai Chin would be primarily an 'administrative measure'; to the Chinese they were obviously a military provocation. To provoke an enemy without making preparations for a possible warlike reaction amounts to playing a game of bluff, and in war bluff is only permissible if one has already allowed for the possibility of its being called.

By the time I had thought it out there was no opportunity to go back to Mullik with some such rebuttal of his arguments, and it so happened that events moved swiftly to give further credence to his line of polemic.

I have mentioned this episode at some length because of what Mullik later recorded about the official attitude to border policy at the time; and it is pertinent to refer to it here. He asserted in his book *The Chinese Betrayal* (published in 1971) that the aim of the forward policy was to fill the gaps on the border, because it was

fully realised that the Chinese had to be fought at the frontier [border]. So there was complete ideological [sic] acceptance of this policy by the Army. . . . We had frequent meetings with the CGS to devise ways to fill the gaps . . . there was no question of the Prime Minister or the Defence Minister forcing the Army to go to any particular place. . . .

In the circumstances, when the enemy was set on a particular line of action, which was to grab as much of the neighbour's territory as possible, and was prepared to use every possible method . . . even outright invasion, what other alternative was there than to confront him all along the frontier . . .? This was exactly the policy Pandit Nehru had decided to follow, and there could have been no other policy at this time. . . .

To do justice to our Army leaders it must be stated that they were in complete tune with this policy and proceeded to implement it in right earnest.

Mullik was quite mistaken in asserting that the General Staff had accepted his concept of border strategy — that is, to meet a possible Chinese invasion by deploying the army along the whole length of the Himalayan border. This was not our strategy in either NEFA or Ladakh. I cannot conceive what caused this aberration in Mullik's memory. I have too great a regard for his integrity to believe that he deliberately fudged his memoirs in order to play down the government's share of the responsibility for the subsequent debacle. At the same time he was clearly suggestible. Writing his memoirs ten years after the event, his memory could well have been led astray by a subconscious desire to substitute a convenient reconstruction for the harsh reality. This is of course the main hazard in recording events with the benefit of hindsight. Just as it can rescue some events from obscurity while casting others into oblivion, it can also ascribe rationality to actions that had in fact been mainly a series of random measures and counter-measures.

As far as the defence of Ladakh was concerned, Thapar, Daulet Singh and Kaul had each in turn explicitly stated (either verbally at meetings in the presence of Mullik or in recorded minutes) that because of the crippling shortages in arms and equipment and in road and air transportation, the army could not hope successfully to conduct even small-scale operations at the border and that in the event of an invasion our main aim would be to fall back for the defence of Leh.

The army's acceptance of the forward policy did not amount to a reversal of this opinion. Eventually, by an unwritten understanding, the advance into unoccupied territory in the Aksai Chin came to be regarded as a political requirement of government – and that also under an intelligence assurance that the Chinese were not likely to go to war over this issue. That we had no business to accept such an assurance is another matter; the fact is that we did and were, to that extent, at fault.

Incidentally, when Mullik began writing his memoirs I was out of the army and had launched myself on a literary career which included starting my own publishing firm. At his request I undertook the publication of his first two books, which dealt with aspects of his early career in the police. He then sent me the first volume of a projected trilogy to be entitled *My Years with Nehru* (subtitled *The Chinese Betrayal*), purporting to be an authoritative account of the Chinese episode of 1959–62. Having read the manuscript I spent long hours with him discussing certain discrepancies in his record, some of them amounting to factual misstatements of crucial importance. He took note

of my objections, and at times he would be doubtful about
his own remembrance, but in the end his innate egotism
and obstinacy always prevailed. I urged him to allow me
to edit his narrative, but he refused. Reluctantly I had to
withdraw from my agreement and dropped the project to
see his book through to publication.

I well remember that 6 May 1962 was a holiday. In the
morning many of us had gathered at Bijji's York Road
residence for the concluding ceremonies connected with
Chitralekha's nuptials. Towards mid-morning I received a
message from the Ops Room conveying the gist of a report
from HQ Western Command that one of our posts north
of Daulet Beg Oldi was about to be attacked by a Chinese
force. I hurried to South Block, leaving a scribbled note
for Bijji that I would inform him if his presence were necessary.

The duty officer in the Ops Room gave me the details
of the telephone message from Simla. It appeared that
earlier in the morning about 100 Chinese troops 'in assault
formation' had advanced right up to one of our new posts
(the one north-east of Daulet Beg Oldi, located at an
altitude of over 5,000 metres). The post commander, a
jemadar of the Jammu and Kashmir militia, expected an
attack at any moment but had remained steadfast under threat.

When I telephoned the Army Chief at his residence, he
said that he had spoken on the telephone to the GOC-in-C,
Daulet Singh, and the Army Commander had urged for
permission to withdraw the post. I told the Chief that I
would be at his house in five minutes to discuss the matter
with him.

When I arrived at White Gates (4 King George's Avenue)
I found Thapar speaking on the line to Simla. Covering
the mouthpiece with his hand, he said, 'Daulet is again
on the line and he is getting jittery. He strongly advises
withdrawal of the post.' I advised the Chief that the Army
Commander should be told to order the post to hold out
for the time being. I suggested that we discuss the situation
before he came to a decision.

I was subsequently criticised for taking a hard-line attitude
and for giving the Army Chief the wrong advice. In order

174 / WAR IN HIGH HIMALAYA

to indicate the reasons why I did so perhaps it would be best if I quote from my official report, *Summary of Events and Policies:*

I advised COAS that since we had embarked upon the Forward Policy on the appreciation that the Chinese would not actually use armed force, to withdraw the first post to be threatened would lead to a repetition of the same tactics by the Chinese and our eventually having to withdraw all the posts we had set up. I advised that the Prime Minister's approval be obtained . . before we could take this decision.

I informed the COAS that we had (two days previously) instructed Western Command to reinforce the whole of this sector. The Chief thereupon directed GOC-in-C Western Command to hold out and not to withdraw.

A meeting was arranged shortly thereafter in the Foreign Secretary's room, which the Prime Minister, Defence Minister and COAS attended (later joined by the CGS). I was present throughout. After some discussion, it was decided by the Prime Minister that the post should stand firm and reinforcements be sent up immediately. The Prime Minister stated that this step was necessary to study the 'behaviour pattern' of Chinese aggression. He felt that this was only a show of force.

Daulet Singh was not too pleased with the decision when Thapar conveyed it to him. The Chief reassured him, explaining that it was necessary to stand up to the Chinese threat in order to see what their reaction would be. It was his (Thapar's) assessment that the Chinese would back down from their offensive posture.

The Chief was proved right: the Chinese eventually withdrew without firing a shot. Our stand had been vindicated, but I was glad that I had dissuaded Thapar from having a dig at Daulet Singh for his irresolution. I think Daulet, as the general officer ultimately responsible for the Ladakh front, had every cause for alarm. We were lucky to have got away with our bluff. If the Chinese had decided to attack our post it could have done little more than extract a price in Chinese lives before being overrun. Our posts in the Aksai Chin had neither the numbers nor the reserves of ammunition to hold out for anything more than a short, sharp action – against an enemy whose supply lines ran right up to the front.

The obvious lesson to be drawn from this contretemps should have been that future moves into the Aksai Chin should be made less provocative. A bluff that has worked once should not become a precedent and used to formulate permanent stratagy.

Clearly that was not how the Intelligence Bureau interpreted the event. Directly after the incident of 6 May the DIB put up a fresh review of the border security situation, making renewed demands. Although confirmed reports indicated that the Chinese were continuing to build up their military strength along the whole length of their borders with India and Nepal, the DIB insisted on more and more forward policy posts being positioned in disputed territory, both in Ladakh and in NEFA. To quote from the DMO's official *Summary*:

*DIB Assessment*

In an assessment entitled 'Frontier Security Situation' dated 8 May 62, the Director, Intelligence. Bureau, argued that since forward patrolling by the Chinese had in the past generally been followed by the establishment of posts in Indian territory we should now fill in the gaps which still existed in our coverage of our borders. 'It is necessary', he recommended, 'to physically occupy all these areas in order to checkmate any Chinese moves.' The gaps listed were: the Galwan Valley and Panggong Lake in Ladakh; several existing gaps in NEFA, even after the virtual completion of *Operation Onkar*.

The General Staff, in their comments to the Ministry, agreed with the DIB's assessment but drew attention to a previous note (1960) in which we had pointed out: 'It may, however, be mentioned that any intensification of patrolling in these disputed areas, as also establishment of posts in such areas, is likely to produce reaction from the Chinese. In fact, the likelihood of the international border, which is dormant at this present moment, becoming active again, cannot be ruled out.'

The General Staff also listed the measures that were being taken in each sector. It was pointed out that 'in view of our limited logistical resources, particularly air maintenance and supply dropping equipment, it is not possible to deploy troops on all possible routes and passes.'

After the Chip Chap valley episode both Thapar and Kaul felt that we would be safe to pursue forward policy moves without anticipating violent reaction from the Chinese. I was not so optimistic. If formal intelligence procedures had been operative in South Block I would at this juncture have asked the Joint Intelligence Committee for a fresh examination of Chinese behaviour patterns, particularly in view of the recent announcement of a Sino-Pak agreement to negotiate and delimit their common border in Kashmir. Unfortunately, the JIC had virtually ceased functioning and I had long since given up on it, so I could do nothing about this. In retrospect, I realise that I should have raised the issue informally with Mullik; had I done so he would probably have told me about a warning he had conveyed to the government and the Chief, about which I remained in ignorance not only then but for many years afterwards.

It was not until nearly ten years later, when I was reading through the draft of Mullik's book with a view to undertaking its publication, that I came to learn about the extraordinary incident of this warning. Mullik wrote in his book that sometime in May or June 1962 he had come into possession of two very important pieces of intelligence which gave a clear indication that the Chinese were planning to go to war against India. (It appears that the Chinese Consul in Calcutta had secretly forewarned Indian communists about possible armed action against India because of India's alleged border aggressions, and had suggested to the Communists the role they were to play in the event of this action.) The reports were so authentic that he immediately circulated a note to the Defence Minister, Joint Secretary Sarin, the Army Chief and the CGS, sending them this information and sounding the warning that the Chinese were planning military action in the coming autumn.

I had at first doubted the veracity of Mullik's reminiscence, thinking that hindsight must again have played tricks with his memory. It was K. Subrahmanyam of the Institute for Defence Studies and Analyses who, a few years later, revealed to me that he had in fact seen the note Mullik had circulated in June 1962, and he confirmed that it had been initialled by Menon, Thapar and Kaul. Clearly not one of them had reacted to the alarm raised by the head of intelligence in any practical way, not even to the extent of passing the warning on to the DMO. The note had been initialled by each, passed on to the next name on the list and, I suppose, eventually filed in Defence Ministry records. The warning certainly did nothing to restrain the thrust of forward policy moves. On the contrary, it seems to have been totally ignored, because the top political leaders, including Nehru, Menon and Finance Minister Desai, made no adjustments to their plans to leave the country for prolonged foreign tours during the autumn. Nor did Mullik in any way moderate his combative incitements to push eastwards in Ladakh in a succession of provocative moves.

In retrospect what seems surprising is that neither the DIB nor the Foreign Ministry appear to have been aware at the time that the internal situation in China had changed considerably for the better during the late summer of 1962. We know now that the threat from Taiwan had all but disappeared because the deterrent posture of the PLA in south-east China had proved convincing. Furthermore, at the end of June President Kennedy had given an assurance that the United States would not support an invasion of the mainland by Nationalist China. The Laos crisis had been defused at Geneva, and the best harvest in five years promised an improvement in the economic situation. If our intelligence community were aware of these radical improvements in the internal situation of communist China, they gave no indication of it to the General Staff, as far as I was aware. We continued in the complacent belief that the Chinese were too preoccupied with internal problems to mount a trans-Himalayan invasion.

By the end of June Western Command had deployed a number of posts well forward of the Chinese claim line of 1960. Both shores of Panggong lake had been occupied and in the central region our troops had established themselves east of the Thratsang-la watershed. The military potential of these posts was, of course, virtually nil and it would have behoved us at that stage to soft-pedal these forward policy thrusts. No such restraint was displayed by either the government or the press. The Foreign Ministry put it about that by the end of June we had 'brought under physical control more than 2,000 square miles of Chinese claimed area', while an article in one of the leading dailies clamorously exaggerated Nehru's forward policy as 'Napoleonic planning'. The press in general portrayed a totally false picture of the situation, asserting that our forces were installed in great strength and faced only second-grade Chinese troops, whereas the truth was of course just the reverse.

The Chinese found no difficulty in setting up a chain of strong-points to confront our posts, or in forestalling us in areas previously unoccupied by either. The race for one-upmanship in this game of leap-frogging of posts came to be referred to as 'chessboard tactics', but the metaphor was only relatively apposite, because one side fought with pawns whereas the other deployed knights and castles, as the Galwan episode soon demonstrated.

The Galwan valley (only approximately surveyed and mapped at the time) was located between the Chip Chap and Sumdo regions and the Hot Springs salient further south. The DIB had long been clamouring for us to set up a post in this valley, which he felt was a possible approach to Leh through the Nubra basin. Daulet Singh had objected to this proposal because he felt that the Chinese would interpret it as a deliberate measure to cut off the lines of communication of their post at Samzungling, but he was overruled and the post was ordered to be established.

Western Command had previously sent two patrols to the western end of the valley but the terrain was so rugged that they had failed to get through. In the summer of 1962 it planned to try again, this time from the south. This attempt was successful and on 4 July a platoon of 4/8 Gorkha Rifles was installed as a post in the upper reaches of the Galwan. As Daulet had foreseen, the Chinese were not amused.

My *Summary of Events and Policies* records:

The Chinese reaction was immediate and violent . . . by 10 July they had deployed approximately a battalion in the area, not only surrounding our post in its immediate vicinity but also cutting off all its possible routes back to base. Attempts by our reinforcement and supply columns to break through this ring of Chinese were opposed by a show of force on each axis of approach.

Our post was thus completely isolated and even out of wireless touch. Maintenance had to be carried out entirely by air-drop and, later, by helicopters. On several occasions the Chinese threatened our post with attack and also aimed a propaganda offensive against the Gorkha personnel. Our troops withstood all such measures and continued to hold firm in their precarious position. By early October, the personnel of the post were relieved by half a company from 5 Jats; the latter were still holding out when the main hostilities started, after which they were presumably attacked and overrun.

At one stage in the Galwan crisis the Chinese troops surrounding our post had closed to within 100 metres of our positions. The Foreign Ministry summoned the Chinese Ambassador and warned him that if the Chinese troops came any closer we would regard the move as an act of aggression and open fire. This had the desired effect, because the Chinese did pull back. As was to be expected, when the news broke in the press, another series of articles appeared hailing the forward policy as a military success.

We in MO Directorate shared Western Command's alarm at the swift build-up of Chinese troops and in no way contributed to the bravado being displayed by politicians and civilian bureaucrats. I remember addressing an operational meeting on the Galwan situation in Menon's office one afternoon. The Prime Minister, the Foreign Secretary, the DIB and, of course, Thapar and Kaul were present. After I had finished explaining the situation on the map I added that the Chinese had deployed a whole battalion for this task, wishing to imply that the odds were heavily against us in the race for a local build-up. Menon, usually word-bound in Nehru's presence, intervened for once, to suggest that we should also expand our force by sending in a few more platoons. I looked dubiously at Kaul, who raised an objection on the grounds of shortage of air-dropping equipment. It was then that the decision was taken to use helicopters to augment air supply. While the Defence Minister, Thapar and the CGS were playing at moving platoons and helicopters on the Galwan 'chessboard', I scribbled a note hastily and passed it to the CGS. In it I suggested that this was a good opportunity to wring a decision from government permitting us to use the air force in an offensive ground support role in case a shooting war started in the Aksai Chin. I saw Kaul glance at my note and pass it to Thapar. I waited in suspense, but neither broached the subject. However, Thapar did make a stand on the proposal to reinforce our post. Voicing a firm veto to the idea, he argued with convincing logic that since it had been the intention that our posts would be established merely to study the Chinese reaction, we could as well do that with one platoon as with five. There was more argument, for it takes time even for the obvious to sink in, but in the end his wiser counsel prevailed.

When we returned to Thapar's office after the meeting, the Chief invited me to stay for a few minutes to discuss the developments in Ladakh. This was the first time he had included me in such a discussion and I took advantage of it to express my concern at the manner in which the government was reacting to the Chip Chap and Galwan episodes. I said that there was a danger that the PM and the Defence Minister might lose sight of the premise under which the army had agreed to move forward into the Aksai Chin – that is, as an 'administrative measure'. In their present euphoric mood they could well begin to regard these posts as the leading elements of a general advance by our forces; if that happened we must firmly disillusion them. I also added that we ought to write to Western Command to emphasise that the PM had ordered the new posts to be established in order to study the 'behaviour pattern' of the Chinese. Hence these posts were, in everyday tactical terms, reconnaissance patrols rather than defensive posts. And since we could not support them in operations either with land or air forces they should, after offering token resistance, be empowered to make a tactical withdrawal in the face of a large-scale Chinese attack. It would be professionally immoral, I argued, to order them to stand and fight it out if we ourselves were unable to support them in battle.

Kaul looked not at all pleased at my comment, but Thapar appeared to be giving it some thought. Leastways, he did not dispute my argument and, when the crisis finally came upon us three months later, he accepted my urgent advice in this respect, as I will later record.

The Galwan confrontation served to increase the tension between the opposing forces on the Aksai Chin front. The Chinese moved vigorously to outsmart us in 'chessboard' manoeuvres, positioning their own posts in a manner designed to winkle out ours. For instance, if one of our posts was located at some distance from the dropping zone, the Chinese would be sure to attempt to cut it off from the latter by interposing a series of pickets between them or even by physically occupying the dropping zone, as they did in Sirijap on the north shore of Lake Panggong. Such manoeuvres were doubly profitable for them in that they in effect reversed the roles between aggressor and defender; when our troops tried to break through the cordon or to evict Chinese soldiers from the dropping zone, it was we who then became the perceived aggressors – and this gave the Chinese the excuse to open fire. I suspect that this was what happened in the incident in the Depsang plain area on 21 July when an exchange of fire took place and two Indian soldiers were wounded.

Fortunately there was a softening in political tension at this stage. On 21 July, the Chinese government, in a note to the Ministry of External Affairs, asserted that they were not willing to fight India and that the Sino-Indian boundary question could only be settled through routine negotiations. The Government of India responded with a proposal to open negotiations on the basis of the officials' talks of 1960. After a further exchange of notes, the Chinese government suggested that the talks should start at Peking in mid-October. Unfortunately, Opposition members in parliament and even some of the leading newspapers vehemently decried these overtures as indications of political accommodation. A motion tabled by the Opposition demanded the breaking off of diplomatic relations with China. Soon after that the Thag-la confrontation erupted in NEFA, eventually resulting in a heavy build-up of troops on the Chinese side. The detente collapsed and the Indian government decided not to negotiate 'under duress or continuing threat of force'.

It is pertinent to mention here that throughout this period Daulet Singh remained unconvinced that the forward policy was a workable plan. In a letter dated 17 August 1962, he expressed his apprehensions: 'Our forward posts in

Ladakh are nowhere tactically sited, whereas the Chinese everywhere are . . . our general deployment has been dictated by . . . political requirement . . . I would be failing in my duty if I did not draw attention to the size and shape of the potential threat.' Army Headquarters replied to the effect that 'whereas the GOC-in-C's contention was partly correct, . . . in that the forward policy was undertaken without military back-up, (owing to lack of logistical capability), subsequent events have justified the policy adopted.'

I must record that most of us in South Block were by then convinced that the forward policy was, despite the contretemps, achieving its purpose. During August and September there were several more incidents of exchange of fire in the Chip Chap and other areas, but none of them resulted in casualties to either side or in any serious follow-up action. As I recorded in my *Summary of Events and Policies:*

The reaction of the Chinese to these were as we had appreciated – first a show of force (as on May 6) and when that failed, to try and contain our forward movement by setting up a chain of posts facing our new posts and also forestalling us in areas yet unoccupied.

There was one point in Daulet's letter that I felt needed investigation. If the Chinese could site their posts tactically, why couldn't we? Even if what we were engaged in was an administrative move by the army, there was no reason why normal military precautions should not be taken. I wondered what instructions HQ Western Command had issued in this respect. To clear these and other doubts I rang up the Chief of Staff of Western Command, Major General Jogindar Singh. He too was not fully aware of the local arrangements in the Aksai Chin and suggested that we should visit the front together to learn at first hand what was going on.

To most of us western Ladakh and the Aksai Chin were unknown reaches of a mystery land. There were no air photographs available then and the existing maps were inaccurate, sometimes drawn by guess-work as much as by survey – or so it seemed. Years previously, in 1956, I had gone to Ladakh on a fortnight's shooting expedition, chasing mountain game such as ibex, markhor and shapoo between Baltistan and Leh, but I had not gone much further west than Khardung-la, the 5,600 metre pass just beyond Leh. Jogi's suggestion was therefore more than welcome. If we could arrange for helicopters to fly us out of Leh, we could be back in three or four days.

When I sought Kaul's permission to make the trip, I found him unaccountably reluctant to let me go. He argued that Army HQ should not become embroiled in the setting up of 'observation posts' on the ground – which, of course, was not the point. I argued that we must take note of the GOC-in-C's point that our posts were not being tactically sited; if this statement were true we must remedy the position. However, Kaul said that he would speak to Daulet about it himself and find out the exact position. I never got to visit the Aksai Chin.

The summer had passed more quietly in the eastern sector but, as in Ladakh, the passage of time did not witness an improvement in the relative strategic situation. As I later recorded in the *Summary:*

*NEFA-Sikkim*
In the eastern sector, Chinese forces had moved closer to the McMahon Line during the past year. They had developed their road system in the area south of the Tsang Po and by the summer of 1962 had deployed an estimated total of three divisions between the Tsang Po and NEFA. It was reported that the Chinese forces deployed opposite Kameng Frontier Division had been issued with automatic rifles and a large number of artillery pieces during June–July (IB Report). They had also undergone a period of intensive collective training.

On the other hand, their immediate reaction to *Operation Onkar* (that is, the occupation of some 45 new forward posts by our troops) was not marked – except, perhaps, in the Pemako and Migythun areas, where about two battalions were pushed up close to the border.

Our forces, in the meanwhile, had not increased in strength. *Operation Onkar* had pushed our physical control of territory to the border, but catered for no major concentrations behind the outer line of posts. 4 Infantry Division still had only two brigades in NEFA – one in Kameng (with a brigade headquarters and two battalions in Towang) and one spread out in Subansiri, Siang and Lohit Frontier Divisions. (The third brigade had meanwhile been sent to Manipur, under command of 23 Div.)

The road to Towang had still not been completed, though limited jeep and one-ton traffic could be sustained. The brigade in Towang was largely air maintained and thus had not yet been able to induct normal allotments of supporting arms and reserves of ammunition.

In Sikkim, we still had only one infantry brigade. The (new) division, which was planned for this area, had not as yet started raising. The Chinese, as far as we knew, had about a division in the Chumbi-Valley-Khamba-Dzong area.

This was generally the situation when the Thag-la dispute came into focus.

Meanwhile, the General Staff drive to improve the state of the army's preparedness for war had made some headway, although this was of a long-term nature. Because higher priority had been accorded to the restoration of existing imbalances than to new raisings, the divisions which were to be earmarked for Ladakh and Sikkim had not even started raising.

To quote from the *Summary* again:

As a result of the temporary brake applied to the expansion programme, unit holdings of arms, equipment and vehicles were in the region of about 85 per cent, except for certain items in short supply, such as 106 mm recoilless rifles, one-ton vehicles and certain types of armour ammunition. This position could have been accepted as reasonably satisfactory were it not for the fact that General Staff reserves of arms and equipment had been almost completely exhausted in making units up to 85 per cent strength. Also, new raisings under Phase-I were being given only 66 per cent of their entitlements of equipment. (In a note to the Defence Minister, the COAS had projected an estimate of 459 crores[3] – including 108 crores in foreign exchange – merely to make up existing deficiencies. This figure did not include requirements for fresh raisings or for the modernization programme.)

I have included this excerpt in order to refute the criticism made in later years, by a new generation of journalists and latterday defence analysts, that the responsibility for the debacle lay mainly with the military, which did not take adequate steps to prepare for the Chinese aggression. The army can be blamed for certain command lapses and for amateurishness and naivety in its unquestioning acceptance of political and intelligence assessments, but not for failing to prepare for war. The General Staff did take steps to increase the state of readiness of the field formations and to make up deficiencies in arms and equipment. What it could not do in the existing circumstances was to plan to meet the enemy at the border and stop him there. Indeed our main culpability lay in the fact that we failed to convince the government of this basic truth.

## NOTES

1. Mountain divisions would be based largely on animal transport and therefore would not be as road-bound as the normal infantry division.
2. In his book *Ambassador's Journal*, Professor J.K. Galbraith, US Ambassador in Delhi, claims that it was he who dissuaded Nehru from committing the IAF to air strikes.
3. A crore is 10 million rupees.

# 7
# PAPER TIGERS ON THE PROWL

During the hurly-burly of the Goa campaign in 1959 Bijji Kaul had assumed direct supervision of border operations in NEFA in order to ease the workload of an overworked DMO. Once he became involved with Operation Onkar (the establishment of Assam Rifles posts along the McMahon Line) he came to regard his control of this area as a personal commitment and continued to deal with it personally, even after the end of operations in Goa. When he finally handed it all back to me in May 1962, I was somewhat out of touch with affairs on the north-eastern frontier where a new GOC, Niranjar Prasad, had taken over command of 4 Infantry Division. Clearly, it was time for me to pay a visit to Tezpur and Kameng FD. The Chip Chap and Galwan river episodes in Ladakh kept me at my desk during most of the summer and it was not till early August that I managed to get away from Delhi for a few days.

When I called at HQ 4th Division in Tezpur, I found the atmosphere gloomy, in some ways almost hostile. Niranjan Prasad received me with a studied coolness, but he was too old a friend and too extrovert a character to continue with that for long. It was obvious that he was nursing a grievance and I persuaded him to come out with it.

Once he had started, the floodgates opened. He virtually accused the General Staff of cravenness for meekly accepting from the government so impracticable and tactically pointless a task as Operation Onkar. He said that the establishment of thirty-five posts on the McMahon Line, some of them many days march even from the nearest mule-track, would strain his resources to such a degree that stocking programmes for his two infantry brigades would in all probability have to be cancelled.[1]

Niranjan pointed out that although the forces to be deployed on Operation Onkar consisted of Assam Rifles personnel, it was his division that had been made responsible for establishing the posts and, despite disclaimers to the contrary, it would be from his quota of airlift that the Assam Rifles' maintenance requirements would be met, thus hindering the logistical build-up at crucial places such as Towang and Walong. Furthermore, he saw no sense in locating a whole platoon at each of these remote border sites where, in any case, their potential for defence was virtually nil. A section at each site, he felt, would be sufficient to offer initial and temporary resistance. In his opinion some of the less critical approaches could be covered by periodic patrolling from bases in the rear. He added that when he had tried to offer these suggestions to the CGS during the latter's visit a month or so before, all he had received for his trouble was a blast of invective and threats, even though his own Corps Commander, Umrao Singh, had supported his arguments. The CGS had peremptorily asserted that since it was the Prime Minister himself who had ordered the posts to be set up, no counter-proposals would be entertained.

Niranjan asked me why Army HQ had accepted such operationally absurd directions from the politicians. Was the General Staff merely acting as a post office? he gibed.

Niranjan's tirade placed me in an awkward situation because essentially I sympathised with the greater part of his complaint. Not so long ago it was I who had railed against the mindless rush to hustle troops up to the McMahon Line without giving them the potential to offer battle; now, as a representative of Army HQ, it was my role to defend that policy; it was I who would now have to act the would-be hustler. I felt that it might help clear the air if I gave a talk to the brigade commanders and the divisional staff to explain the General Staff's border options. I suggested as much to Niranjan and he willingly agreed.

In my talk to the officers of 4th Division I reiterated the Intelligence Bureau's appraisal that while the Chinese might actively demonstrate against our posts, as they had done in the Chip Chap and Galwan valleys, they were unlikely to go to war on the border issue – and certainly not in NEFA, where they had tacitly agreed not to press their claims. This estimate, I said, was accepted by the government and by Army HQ and I added that in case we were proved wrong and the Chinese did launch a cross-border attack, the Army HQ plan was not to fight the main battle at the border; the Assam Rifles, after offering token resistance, would fall back to join the army, who would plan the main defences at selected and prepared positions such as Towang, Bomdila or Walong. I emphasised that that had been the concept of battle when I had commanded 7 Brigade; no orders from Army HQ had suggested a change from that concept.

I had expected a barrage of complaints about inadequate logistical cover but, curiously, no one raised that issue, and I assumed that the maintenance arrangements at Towang and other forward areas had improved as a result of the progress of road-building activities. (The road to Towang had reached Dhirang and beyond. Over Se-la it was still only a jeep track, expected to reach Towang within a month of the end of the monsoon season.)

Later, almost as an afterthought, Niranjan told me about the incident of the Dhola post and about his doubts regarding the alignment of the McMahon Line in the area west of the Nyamjang-chu. He said that whereas all the way from the Burma border to the Nyamjang valley the McMahon Line, as marked on the quarter-inch scale Survey of India map sheet, coincided with the Himalayan crestline, westwards from Khinzemane the Line was marked as lying well to the south of the main Thag-la ridge. (The extent of the area between the Thag-la crestline and the McMahon Line marked on the map was about 60 sq km.)

A patrol had set out across the Nyamjang river in mid-July to establish an Assam Rifles post near the Bhutan border. The political officer's representative accompanying the patrol had insisted that the Thag-la ridge itself was the watershed border and that was where our post should be. The patrol leader, a regular army officer, disregarded this advice because his map clearly showed the McMahon Line as passing well south of the ridge. Accordingly, he established a post on the southern bank of the Namka-chu, a stream flowing along the lower slopes of Thag-la ridge. He called it Dhola post, though in actual fact the site was known as Tsedong. Actually Dho-la was a pass on the ridge 3 km to the south.

HQ 4th Division had referred the doubt about Thag-la ridge to HQ XXXIII Corps, asking for clarification on the exact alignment of the McMahon Line west of Nyamjang-chu.[2] Niranjan had also suggested in his letter that if indeed the border lay along Thag-la ridge, he would like to establish his post tactically on the crest of the ridge, rather than in the valley below. In the month that had since passed he had received no reply and now, he added, the Chinese had beaten him to it because they had occupied Thag-la ridge. He told me that he would still like a clarification of the correct alignment of the border and asked me to have the reply expedited from Army HQ.

I had wanted to make a flying visit to Towang to see my old brigade, then commanded by Brigadier John Dalvi, but since the CGS had allowed me no more than five days off from Delhi for this tour, the only way I could have managed the visit would have been by helicopter. Unfortunately, the air force was unable to lend me one and I had to forego my visit to 7 Brigade in Towang.

Earlier in the year Dalvi, on his way to NEFA to take up his appointment, had called at my office and asked me for any personal information that I could pass on to him about the brigade and its area. I had recounted for him, among other things, my experience of continuously having to resist pressure from the division to push more and more troops up to the McMahon Line. I had warned him, informally, to resist such pressures if he could, because of the logistical difficulties. As he records in his book, *Himalayan Blunder*, I had also told him about my uneasiness regarding the dominating heights of the Thag-la ridge overlooking

Khinzemane, and my own remissness in not having undertaken a reconnaissance of that area two years previously. I had suggested that he might do that as soon as possible, especially now that his Brigade HQ had moved up to Towang. I would greatly have liked to have discussed these matters again with Dalvi, especially as his brigade's operational jurisdiction had by then been extended to the Bhutan border (with the establishment of Dhola post). Unfortunately I never got even as far as speaking to the Brigade Commander because the telephone lines were down.

On my return to Delhi I referred the Thag-la dilemma to the Director of Military Survey. The latter commented that as the existing maps of the area were 'sketchy and inaccurate, having been compiled from unreliable sources', the map co-ordinates of the new post quoted by the patrol leader were of doubtful accuracy. He confirmed that the recognised border was the watershed, but qualified this statement by adding 'the exact alignment of [this] will depend on accurate survey'. This, he added, would take two to three years to complete.

That was not greatly enlightening so I sent the file to the Ministry of External Affairs. The Historical Section of which replied: 'We may permit the Army to extend the jurisdiction, if they have not already done so, up to the line suggested by them.' Since the Chinese had already occupied Thag-la, I went to see Dr S. Gopal, Director of the Historical Section (and, incidentally, son of the then President of India) in order to double-check before I passed on this decision to HQ 4th Division. Gopal explained that at the time of the boundary talks with the Chinese, the government of India had been aware that the actual terrain in the area of the trijunction was different from that depicted on the quarter-inch scale map sheet. The Chinese were therefore given the reference in northings and southings (91° 40' East, 27° 40' North). He noted on the file: 'This point was further north of the tri-junction shown on our maps and nearer the point now suggested by Army Headquarters. Furthermore, the Chinese had been told that the alignment (of the McMahon Line) followed Thag-la ridge, which is also the ridge shown by Army Headquarters in the sketch.' What Gopal had not told me – and I found out only later – was that the Chinese had not accepted our arguments and had counter-claimed Thag-la ridge, as well as the valley at Khinzemane, as Chinese territory.

I passed on Gopal's remarks to HQ Eastern Command for onward transmission to 4 Infantry Division, but by then it was mid-September and events in that remote region on the border of Bhutan and Tibet had already reached a critical stage.

Although the post at Dhola had been established as early as June, for three months the Chinese had made no protest about its siting. This was probably in conformity with the relatively soft diplomatic approaches by both Delhi and Peking during July and August. This short spell of detente ended in early September, when there was a sudden increase in the severity and frequency of Chinese protests.

As a mark of appreciation for my work during the Goa crisis as his COS Committee Secretary, Admiral Katari had promised that he would send me on a cruise on the aircraft carrier *Vikrant* whenever he found a suitable opportunity. This soon presented itself. The Ministry of Defence invited a group of members of parliament to attend a naval exercise off the coast of Goa in September 1962. Lieutenant General Muchu Chaudhuri was to accompany them as conducting officer and, true to his word, Katari suggested my name as Liaison Officer (or some such sinecure role). I was to leave Delhi on the morning of 9 September, meet the rest of the party at Cochin the next day, board the *Vikrant* and attend routine naval manoeuvres in the Arabian Sea off the coast of Goa. We were to be landed at Bombay on 15 September.

The proposal for the cruise had been made during the period of the detente, so Kaul had raised no objection to my joining it. However, since then Krishna Menon and Kaul had fallen out. This was a periodic occurrence in their relationship, but this time Kaul had insisted on taking a month's leave and going off to Kashmir on holiday, an added reason being an illness in the family. After Kaul's abrupt departure on leave I should, in all conscience, have voluntarily withdrawn my name from the naval junket, but I was able to justify the excursion to myself. It happened to be a quiet period in the Sino-Indian confrontation; the

PM was about to take off for Europe for a prolonged visit, and the Defence Minister was shortly due to go to the UN General Assembly session. It was reasonable to conclude that the government did not expect any crisis to develop in the near future.

It did, and at the eleventh hour when I could not extricate myself from the cruise. On the evening of 8 September, just as I was sitting down to dinner, I received a message from the Ops Room conveying the alarming news that a large body of Chinese troops had come down the Thag-la slopes and surrounded Dhola post (Tsedong). They had destroyed one of the several log bridges over the Namka-chu in order to isolate the Assam Rifles detachment; the JCO in command had asked for urgent reinforcements.

It was then that a personality problem that must have been long brewing suddenly projected itself on the General Staff tableau; it concerned Major-General Jogindar Singh Dhillon, the officiating CGS.

When Kaul had been putting his team together, picking the best and the brightest for his staff, he had nominated Jogi Dhillon as his Deputy CGS. Originally an Engineer officer, Jogi had been specially selected for command of an infantry brigade. Thereafter, having come to the notice of higher authorities (including, it is said, the Prime Minister) he progressed along the command and General Staff chain. His last appointment before being posted at Army HQ had been that of Chief of Staff to Lieutenant General Kulwant Singh, GOC-in-C Western Command, whence he had been sent to attend a course at the Imperial Defence College, London. He possessed all the qualifications for assured advancement.

Kaul was unwise in selecting so high-powered an officer for a job that was one of the least glamorous or challenging in General Staff Branch. The Deputy CGS did not figure in the chain of interaction in sensitive matters such as Operations and Intelligence. By tradition and usage these key functions, as well as policy matters on Staff Duties and Military Training, were dealt with between the directors and the CGS. The Deputy CGS supervised the more routine directorates such as those of Armour, Artillery, Signals, Infantry, the Territorial Army and the Security Corps.

Furthermore, even in the absence of the CGS he was not admitted into the mainstream of events; it was the DMO who dealt with the Army Chief on operational matters, as did the DMI on intelligence. The DCGS was not even routinely kept informed on these matters; by definition he was not a member of the inner circle.

It would have been unusual for someone as high-profile as Jogi not to have resented relegation to a sidestream while a junior colleague conducted the main flow of crucial operational transactions. I had sensed this resentment, though to be fair to Jogi he had never allowed it to surface or to affect our formal relationship. Nor had he ever explicitly expressed his dissatisfaction with the system. Despite his well-built and impressive physique, and a seemingly strong and fearsome mien, he was by nature too compliant a subordinate to say or do anything that Kaul might construe as criticism.

When I tried to ring up Thapar on the evening of 8 September to convey the news about Dhola post I was told that he was busy entertaining dinner guests, so I telephoned Jogi instead, mainly to inform him that I intended to cancel my cruise on the *Vikrant* just in case the Dhola incident led to graver consequences. Jogi reacted forcibly; he expressly forbade me to do this, saying that he could handle the situation adequately and that I was to fulfil my obligation to the parliamentary delegation. When I suggested that we consult Thapar about my departure, he said that I need not worry, he would see to that himself.

When I told my wife what had transpired on the telephone, she at once suspected Jogi's injunction as a manoeuvre to pack me off and get into the act himself. She strongly urged me to go and see Thapar, the rear gate of whose residence was not a hundred yards down Dupleix Lane from our house. My wife had had occasion to experience Jogi's brusque and captious nature and enjoined me not to be too complaisant in the matter. She argued that I would be letting Bijji Kaul down if a crisis developed in his absence and Thapar were left without either adviser.

Even if it were in my nature to disobey a direct and lawful order from a superior officer, I would have been constrained by doubts about whether Thapar would in fact have asked me to cancel my tour in order to stay at my post. During the past two years he had not drawn me into his confidence. On the few occasions I had gone to him directly to discuss operational matters he had been distant and matter-of-fact, as though wishing to make it clear that there was to be no return to our former closeness of association. In the circumstances I decided that I had no option but to go on to Cochin to join the cruise and hope that a *démarche* would not develop during the next week.

The cruise on the *Vikrant* was enjoyable even if the so-called naval exercise was little more than a demonstration of naval gunnery, resupply at sea and other routine functions. My one great thrill was the experience of being catapulted up on an *Alisée* aircraft and then violently jerked to a landing on a deck that seemed no larger than a postage stamp from the air.

I put Delhi out of my mind and threw myself into discovering something about the navy and, of course, its aircraft carrier. During after-dinner walks on the flight deck I met and had long talks with many naval ratings, and I came to realise that in our navy a great gulf existed between the men and their officers. Unlike in the army, man-management did not appear to be part of the value system of the navy. I never saw an officer take a walk on the long flight deck — only the ratings did this — and the latter's obvious pleasure in seeing a senior army officer (and an occasional member of parliament) mingle and talk with them informally was almost embarassing. I recall an occasion when I asked the captain if I might dine with the ratings some night; my request was regarded with total amazement, even disbelief. Although it might be an unconscious exaggeration, my recollection is that he replied that he didn't even know on which deck in that multi-level ship the men's dining-room was located. I never got my dinner.

I remember wondering at the time if the same culture prevailed in the British Navy, of which (at that time) the Indian Navy seemed to be an offshoot — at least, it deported itself as though it were. Whereas we in the army had merely retained anglicised ways in speech, dress, professional procedures and messing customs, the Indian Navy virtually operated as part of the 'parent' arm in Britain. Its ships regularly attended the Royal Navy's exercises and training courses, visited their home and overseas bases and (unless, again, I am unconsciously exaggerating in retrospect) shared common training systems and even codes and ciphers. It was not until the drastic switchover to Russian equipment in the late 1960s that this imperial subservience at last faded.

During the voyage I received no news about the NEFA incident, because on the few occasions I could persuade a naval officer to tune in his set to the AIR news bulletin, there was nothing on border incidents. Also, of course, we received no newspapers, not even when we put in for a few hours at Marmagao harbour in Goa. It would be only a slight exaggeration to say that officers of the Indian Navy seemed to be unaware that there was a crisis along our northern borders.

The *Vikrant* berthed at the naval docks in Bombay on the morning of 15 September and I caught the next plane to Delhi. As soon as I arrived home I rang up Kaul's house, to be informed that he was still on leave in Srinagar. This was somewhat reassuring. If he were still on long leave, no critical steps could have been taken by Army HQ – or so I consoled myself. Just how wrong I was I found out when I went to my office early next morning.

Military Operations Directorate was in a state of confusion, its normally confident and cool deportment clearly ruffled. From what I could gather it had suddenly found itself relegated from its normal dynamic functioning to a role of silent proxy. The directorate was now merely relaying orders on behalf of the officiating CGS, or handling telephone and signal messages from Command and lower HQs to the CGS secretariat. Lieutenant Colonel Pritpal Singh of MO-I section told me that as a result of the Dhola crisis 7 Infantry Brigade had been peremptorily ordered to move from Towang and concentrate post-haste at the bottom of Thag-la ridge, with the task of chasing the Chinese up the mountain and across the watershed. He could not show me any minuting, records of meetings or other documents to indicate how or by whom such an incredible decision had come to be taken. MO Directorate had merely been ordered to issue the necessary signals; it was not consulted in the process. I clearly remember being shown an operational signal authorised by the COAS, addressed to all formations down the chain, ordering the capture of Thag-la by 19 September! I could scarcely believe my eyes.

Pritpal told me that the decision to mount an attack on the Thag-la ridge appeared to have been taken at the Defence Minister's conference three or four days previously, on the advice of Lieutenant General Sen, GOC-in-C East. I could only presume that 'Bogey' Sen had given this advice after consulting Umrao Singh, the Corps Commander in Shillong, but there was nothing on record in MO files. After 8 September we had simply dropped out of the running.

It was difficult for me to believe that Niranjan, with all the logistical difficulties he had encountered in maintaining one weak brigade in a defensive role in Towang, could have agreed to 7 Brigade moving into the attack in the uninhabited desolation of the Bhutan frontier – where even footpaths were difficult to find – against a stronger and better armed enemy. How could an infantry brigade with all its impedimenta of battle move out on a man-pack basis to mount an attack across an unknown, mountainous tract? And what of Towang? Who would take over its defence – which was 7 Brigade's main task?

These questions and a number of dire doubts and anxieties kept crowding into my mind. Pritpal could not enlighten me about any of them, and Jogi was at the Minister's conference all morning. I do not recollect how I whiled away the hours. My thoughts were in turmoil, reflecting on the desperate unreality of the task that had been given to 7 Brigade. I tried to conjure up, from memory of the air reconnaissance over Towang plateau, a mental picture of the bleak and forsaken heights that towered above the Nyamjang-chu on the west. I even remember consulting Lieutenant Colonel Bailey's old book, *No Passport to Tibet*, to see if the author had included a reference to the area of Thag-la or the Namka valley. He had, but it was of no help. Captain Morshead's sketch showed Thag-la ridge, and also the Namka-chu, running roughly north to south, whereas our small-scale map showed them going north-east to south-west!

It was not until the early afternoon that I was at last

able to catch Jogi in his office. My memory of that meeting
could well be biased, as much by retrospective recrimination
as by emotional distortion. (I had at last realised, not
without both chagrin and alarm, that Jogi had done exactly
what my wife had suspected he would do: set about
eliminating the DMQ from the General Staff chain in order
to consolidate his seizure of the operational network.)
Therefore, in order to preserve objectivity in my recollection
of that meeting with Jogi, I shall begin the account by
first quoting from a report written nearer the time, my
*Summary of Events and Policies*:

I arrived back at Headquarters on 16 September 1962. Broadly,
the situation at that time was as follows: According to the reports
of Intelligence Bureau personnel deployed on the Towang border,
there were only 50–60 Chinese located in the vicinity of Tsedong
[Dhola] and about two companies between the Namka-chu and
Thag-la. Having destroyed the bridges in the vicinity of Tsedong,
the Chinese had withdrawn to the north bank of the river. As
for our own forces, 9 Punjab was moving up to Tsedong, with
orders (emanating from Army Headquarters) to capture the
Chinese post north of Tsedong, contain the Chinese south of
Thag-la and, if possible, establish posts on the watershed heights
west of the Thag-la Pass. At the same time, the rest of 7 Infantry
Brigade had begun its forward concentration in the Lumpu area
while three (newly arrived) Infantry battalions were on the move
from Misamari to Towang. 62 Infantry Brigade was on its way
from Ramgarh to join 4 Infantry Division. Stocking for the
Tsedong operations was to be undertaken by Headquarters Eastern
Air Command, commencing on 28 September and to be completed
by 5 October.
   The pattern of operational policy and high command decisions
evolved during these days was that the Defence Minister held a
meeting every day which was attended, from the Army side, by
the Chief of the Army Staff, the Officiating CGS (the CGS being
on leave) and GOC-in-C Eastern Command whenever he visited
Army Headquarters. I was informed by the Officiating CGS that
minutes of such meetings were maintained by the Joint Secretary,
Ministry of Defence, though they were first seen in draft form
by himself. He also stated that he had access to these records
at all times and therefore I was not required to maintain separate
records in Army Headquarters.
   As I did not attend any meetings held by the Defence Minister,
or any meetings that may have been held at PSO level at Army

Headquarters, I am unable to comment `on the various considerations or discussions that led to policy decisions during this period. Action to be taken on them, however, was conveyed to me by the Officiating CGS or COAS and recorded in my files.

As for command and control of the operations, although the responsibility was entirely that of XXXIII Corps, Headquarters Eastern Command exercised close supervision and also consulted Army Headquarters at each step. Army Headquarters' involvement in the day-to-day operations was necessitated because of the need to direct the build-up of the necessary logistical support, which at that time was beyond the capacity of Eastern Command. . . .

The criticism implicit in these paragraphs is a restrained expression of my feelings at that first meeting with Jogi in the CGS' office, the remembrance of which has not dimmed with the years. After summarising developments in the Towang sector, he told me that my responsibility as DMO would now be to ensure that the concentration of troops at Lumpu and in the Dhola area was proceeding at an adequate pace. He added that since it had been confirmed that there were only about sixty Chinese at Dhola, one battalion (9 Punjab) was considered adequate for the task of evicting them.

Ignoring the implied dimunition of the DMO's function, I tried to explain to Jogi the constraints imposed on troop movements, even on foot, by the terrain, weather and lack of mule-tracks and footpaths forward of Towang, and I expressed doubt that adequate logistical support could ever be built up at Lumpu, let alone within the time stipulated. When he glibly remarked that Army and Air HQ would ensure sufficient air supply sorties to fulfil 9 Punjab's requirements, I countered by pointing out that the high Lumpu spur had never been tried out as a dropping zone, that the weather at that time was most uncertain and that the collection and retrieval of loads in the mountains was a major problem. Jogi remained unimpressed. He assured me that the Army Commander was confident about the task being carried out successfully. I told him that I knew the terrain at Lumpu, whereas Bogey Sen had never visited the mountains of NEFA; nor had Umrao, to the best of my knowledge. I urged Jogi to obtain the views of the Divisional and Brigade Commanders before the Army Chief took a final decision but he rejected this suggestion as

improper and quite contrary to procedure. He told me that
I could best serve the army by ensuring that Lumpu base
was developed and stocked as early as possible.

Jogi remained equally adamant when I changed tack to
discuss operational matters. When I raised a point about
possible reprisals by Chinese forces north of Thag-la, he
assured me that there would be no major Chinese attack
across the watershed. As for my concern about the defence
of the divisional vital ground at Towang after the move
out of 7 Brigade, he said that a brigade from Ranchi was
being sent there for the purpose.

It was obvious that Jogi was not open to persuasion. I
suspected that he had been so fascinated by his chance
involvement at the summit of the decision-making process
that he was not going to allow it to be threatened by
doubts cast on what should have been his main purpose:
the ordering of priorities. He focused on the political decision
– the attack to clear the Chinese from Thag-la ridge –
rather than on the logistical and tactical factors that clearly
denied the feasibility of that option. His mind-set was so
rigid that further discussion could only become banal and
defeatist and, in the final analysis, irrelevant.

Before I left I broached the subject of formal staff
procedure. I said that I had found no papers in MO
Directorate recording the various decisions taken at the
Defence Minister's conferences and that I would like to
have all such documents to start maintaining proper records
of decisions taken and orders issued. Jogi glared at me;
and the otherwise informal conversation changed to a formal
tone. Sternly the officiating CGS instructed his DMO that
he, the DCGS, was in full control. The records were being
maintained, he said, by Joint Secretary Sarin in the Ministry.
He, the DCGS, was satisfied with that procedure, because
he had access to those records at all times and I was not
to concern myself with them. He emphasised that I had a
full job on my hands and I was to get on with it.

Back at my desk, I called a meeting of MO-I staff to
improvise a system of maintaining *aide memoires*, in the
absence of formal records, on Operation Leghorn (as the
Namka-chu operation had been codenamed). In addition,
I directed Pritpal to maintain a day-to-day situation report

on the build-up of ammunition and stores at Lumpu. He was to try to obtain figures of air-drops directly from 4th Division (whose main HQ was still at Tejpur) and not rest content with information provided by the air force because the latter could indicate only tonnages dropped, not quantities retrieved by the troops.

Although not too familiar with the lie of the land beyond Lumpu, I nevertheless realised that little of what was dropped there, even if retrieved, could in fact be sent forward to the troops deployed along the Namka-chu. This was because only porters could negotiate the 4,600 metre pass at Hathung-la, and each porter, after carrying his own blankets and rations for the four-day turn-round to Dhola, had an effective load capacity at those heights of only 5–6 kg, as against a battalion's estimated battle requirement of 2–2,500 kg per day even when fighting with small arms only. Also, the number of porters to be found in that sparsely populated region was limited (and even they soon melted away, so that the troops meant to fight the Chinese eventually had to do their own porterage).

It seemed a time out of reality. I spent the rest of the afternoon brooding in my office, uncertain what action to take to reverse the potentially disastrous process that had been set in motion. I shirked the obvious but openly defiant course of going to see Thapar over Jogi's head, although I think I might have done just that had I not felt convinced that Thapar would spurn my protests, making my position as DMO untenable.

The surprising fact was that Thapar knew the terrain, at least as far as the Towang plateau. I had earlier persuaded him to visit 7 Brigade, and although he had done the trip by helicopter, I had sent a bright young MO-I staff officer, Major Sant Singh, to accompany him and to brief him on the terrain, communications and logistics of the Towang commitment. (I had hoped, in good time, to persuade Thapar to order a rethink on the defence of Kameng so that the main defensive position could be pulled back from Towang, to Se-la or Bomdila-Manda-la.)

My surmise was that Thapar was being arm-twisted by Menon to accept the impossible operational commitment of Operation Leghorn, and that Jogi had failed to advise

caution and deliberation. Summarily, orders for an offensive
had been passed down the line. Bijji Kaul – I felt sure –
would have been more deliberate and consultative. I began
to perceive the wisdom of Thimayya, whose happy-go-lucky
solution to the problem – as I have recorded – was to
wink at implausible directives from the PM or the Defence
Minister and merely pass down to Command HQ what
he, Timmy, thought was a feasible plan. But then only a
Thimayya could have done that and got away with it!

I decided to seek out Bogey Sen who, I learned, had
come to Delhi for the Defence Minister's conference. Although
Bogey and I had not been closely associated for some years,
we had served together on familiar terms in the past. When
I had joined the Indialised 5th/10th Baluch Regiment on
my first commission, he had been the hero of all the
subalterns, a popular and much admired adjutant. His
wife's family and mine had known each other on an intimate
footing at one time, so that his house and table soon
became a young bachelor's occasional refuge from the
rigidity of British-Indian mess life. During the war Bogey
was second-in-command and I the senior company
commander of a battalion of Baluchis on the Burma front.
In November 1947, when suddenly ordered to proceed to
Srinagar to command a newly raised brigade against the
Pakistani raiders, Bogey (then Deputy DMI) had walked
into my office in Army HQ and asked me to take a few
days leave and fly up to Kashmir with him to set up his
Brigade HQ for him – an arrangement to which (then)
Brigadier Thorat, my boss, had reluctantly agreed.

Bogey's senior general staff officer was also an old Baluch
colleague as well as a friend and kinsman. I think that
had I at that stage been able to meet them both personally
and impress upon them the realities on the ground at the
Thag-la front, I might have been able to moderate Eastern
Command's headlong meddling in 4th Division's operations,
especially in view of the fact that Bogey had, till the Dhola
affair, been content to play a low-key role on the operational
scene. Unfortunately, when I called at the house where he
had been staying with friends, he had already left for the
airport. An opportunity for personal persuasion did not
come till a fortnight later, and by then it was no longer

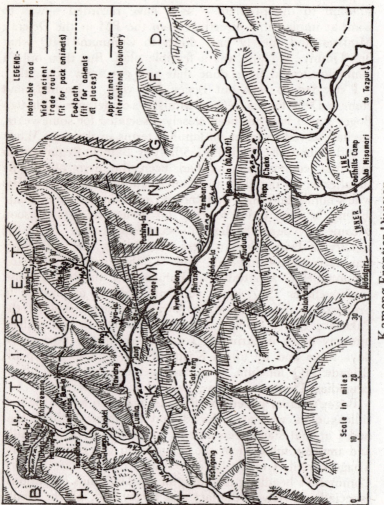

Kameng Frontier Division

within HQ Eastern Command's power to alter the decision on Operation Leghorn.

Either that day or the next I wrote a personal letter to Bijji Kaul in Kashmir, urging him to return to duty. I informed him that there had been gross 'over-reaction' to the Dhola incident on the part of all concerned and that his presence at Army HQ was now indispensable. I hoped that he might rejoin duty almost at once.

It then occurred to me that the best person whose support I should attempt to enlist was Mullik; I knew he held me in high regard and had confidence in my professional judgment. I called at his office late in the evening and told him about my anxiety and alarm at the runaway operational extravaganza unfolding on the Namka-chu. Knowing that he had visited many remote Himalayan regions, I assumed that he would be aware of the difficulties of movement and maintenance in the mountains but my expectations were disappointed. Mullik shrugged off my remonstrances. He roundly asserted that it was the army – that is, General Sen – that had quite definitely assured the government of the feasibility of the operation. To my protest that it did not matter who had given that advice, it was still wrong advice, he paid no heed.

It was soon obvious that Mullik had himself become one of the 'hawks' on Operation Leghorn, and if a seasoned general like Sen could be so oblivious to logistical realities, it would clearly be impossible to impress Mullik with my arguments. I therefore changed tack and asked him why we had suddenly revised operational policy by going on to the offensive in NEFA. Why were we not following the same policy as in Ladakh – that of 'chessboard' tactics to outmanoeuvre, and thus try to forestall, Chinese encroachments? Mullik would not have that either; he countered that unlike the Aksai Chin, where the Chinese were trying to creep forward into territory *claimed by them*, in the Thag-la region they had been blatantly provocative by intruding into territory *held by us* and which they had tacitly conceded as being Indian. He said that the Indian people would not stand for that and the government might fall if we did not take steps to evict the aggressors. He advised me not to create obstacles but to assist Command

and Corps HQ to prepare for the operation against the Chinese.

I asked Mullik if there had been any signs of a recent Chinese troop build-up south of Tsona Dzong. He replied that there had; the Chinese had massed nearly two brigades between Tsona Dzong and Le (4 km north of Thag-la), which were well stocked with rations and ammunition. I was taken aback at this information. As I have recorded, there was a period of a few months during which I had become out of touch with affairs in NEFA; the last I had heard, there had been only a battalion or so forward of Tsona Dzong. Mullik went on to explain that the build-up had been continuing over a long time, but the move forward of the Chinese forces as far south as Le was a recent development. At the same time, he assured me that they would be unlikely to cross into Indian territory in large numbers. I do not remember if we argued about the validity of this assumption, but I was able to get him to agree to raise at next morning's conference the issue of tactical air support for our troops in case a large Chinese force did march into Indian territory across the Thag-la ridge. I convinced him that 7 Brigade, under-strength, under-provisioned and lacking artillery and heavy mortars, would not be able to stand up to even one fully equipped Chinese battalion unless it were given air support. I stipulated that once Chinese troops crossed into Indian territory in strength, the IAF should be permitted to strike at targets in Tibet, especially at Le and Tsona Dzong. I also urged that permission to use air strikes should include Ladakh, by arguing that the Chinese might react to our NEFA operations by mounting an offensive to overrun or push back our posts in the Chip Chap and Galwan valleys. I convinced Mullik of the urgent need to do this and he agreed to do as I asked. If I remember correctly, he told me that General Daulet Singh was in Delhi just then and had also raised the question of a possible attack by the Chinese in the Chip Chap and Galwan regions. Mullik said that he would talk to Daulet and suggest that he also ask for offensive air support.

Before leaving Mullik's office I made one final request. I urged him to intervene in the matter of the missing CGS and to get Kaul back from Kashmir. I did not, of course, tell him about Jogi's *démarche* in GS Branch, but I convinced him that Kaul's presence at Army HQ had become both essential and urgent. Mullik, who had long established a close rapport with Kaul, readily agreed and said that he would put in a word with both Menon and Thapar.

I returned from my visit to Mullik with mixed feelings. I had reason to be elated by my success in getting him to agree to argue a case for air support. His standing with Menon, as with Nehru, was high and his counsel was always respected. I felt certain that he would succeed with both the proposals he had agreed to take up at the meeting. Where I had not achieved my purpose was in persuading him to ask for a relaxation of the operational pressure on the Namka-chu front, the main purpose of my visit.

In order to be even-handed in reporting these events, I must in all fairness make one thing quite clear, lest I be accused of laying claim to greater percipience and keener judgment than others. I have to acknowledge that my misgivings about the developments on the Namka-chu arose not so much because I foresaw a massive Chinese reprisal. That would not be the truth; like all the others in the 'kitchen cabinet', I also had come to accept the DIB's assessment on 'Chinese goodwill' – that in the final analysis they would hold back from attacking Indian-held territory in pursuance of border claims. My anxiety and resentment stemmed from another source – that is, the gross mismanagement of troops by uncaring generals and politicians. I strongly felt that, from a man-management point of view, the ill-considered and hasty despatch of a brigade of under-equipped troops on an *ad hoc* man-pack basis to the freezing heights beyond Lumpu was a thoughtless, callous and futile act amounting to outrage. I could not condone the extreme folly of sending troops to live and fight at heights of 4,000 metres and more without adequate clothing and rations, and with only fifty rounds of ammunition per man with which to wage war. Perhaps I felt it all the more deeply because it was my former command – 7 Brigade – that was being so monstrously misused. I am sure that most officers reared in the culture of the Indian Army would have felt the same about such ill-use of the uncomplaining and dutiful Indian *jawan*. Knowing Niranjan

Prasad and Dalvi as well as I did, I could not believe that it was either of them who could have advised the move of 7 Brigade to the Namka-chu. I suspected that Umrao and Sen, more senior in service (both had been commissioned from Sandhurst in the early 1930s) had possibly grown out of touch with the troops following their rapid promotion to high rank after independence and, in my mind, I blamed this move on them, as also I blamed Thapar and Jogi for being so lacking in vision as to countenance this absurd deployment under political pressure. (It would have added greatly to my disquiet had I then known that a battalion of my regiment, 1/9 Gorkha Rifles, only recently sent down to the Assam plains after a three-year tenure in Towang, had been virtually pulled out of railway carriages on their way to the Punjab and summarily ordered to march back all the 250 miles to Towang, still in their summer uniforms. Thence, without a re-issue of warm clothing or bedding, they were hustled to Lumpu and beyond, where several men would soon die of pneumonia, oedema and other pulmonic afflictions.)

It was not until much later in the Namka-chu episode that I foresaw a major attack across the Thag-la ridge; earlier, as I have acknowledged, I too had accepted the DIB's persuasion that this would not happen. Mullik's revelation of the forward build-up at Le had given me cause for alarm but I was still beguiled by his main assurance. I also drew some consolation from my conviction that 7 Infantry Brigade could not be made ready for an offensive on Thag-la before the winter set in.

I must also add, however, that although we had come under the DIB's spell, it was by no means a total capitulation – not by the General Staff, anyway. MO Directorate had been alive to the responsibility of preparing contingency plans in case the Chinese did mount an offensive, either local or general. We had undertaken a revision of long-range strategic and logistical preparation based on the Chiefs of Staff appreciation; and, in the short term, the Commands concerned had done their best to draw up plans to meet possible threats from the Chinese. In Ladakh, Western Command's strategy was to fight a delaying action back to Shyok valley and then hold the enemy offensive at Leh.

In NEFA, the strategic planning had been less well developed, mainly thanks to Menon's egotistical response to Thorat's proposals in 1959 and his risible solution to counter a possible Chinese threat. Only in Kameng had there evolved a feasible defensive posture, based on the defence of Towang; not the best tactical solution perhaps, but a sound enough basis for operations. In the last few days Bogey Sen had willy-nilly abandoned that plan for a blind gamble in the unknown reaches of the Thag-la nexus; and Jogi, entranced with his newly acquired eminence, would not heed the danger. Even if fresh battalions were rushed up to Towang they could not, unacclimatised, unrehearsed and under-provisioned, effectively conduct a defensive battle against a determined thrust from Khinzemane or Bum-la – and certainly not from both.

It took me some time, and then only in retrospect, to descry what appeared to be a fundamental limitation in the thought processes of our senior generals. Strategic planning seemed to focus on short-term solutions, too often concerned with producing a blueprint for battle rather than a plan for sustained campaigning. Whether it was Thimayya propounding a policy for the Aksai Chin, Daulet Singh planning the defence of Leh, or Thapar precipitately ordering 7 Brigade up the Thag-la slopes, there was no evidence of a long-term agenda of follow-through forecasts, or of any planning for requirements beyond the immediate. Thorat was the only one among the top commanders who had produced a policy (and a style) that aimed at an eventual solution rather than a stop-gap gambit. Even Kaul, who could think things through a little more persistently than others, was too inclined to be bewitched by the spell that surrounds an immediate venture rather than thinking objectively in the long-term. I remember that even at the time when I had argued the case for a long-term army 'Master Plan', an overview placed in a ten-years time frame, it was the novelty of the project and not the need for it that had caught his fancy. I suspect that intrinsically many of our generals thought like Mullik: it was the emotive and immediate gesture that appealed.

During the next three or four days most of my time was occupied in progressing the stocking programme for Lumpu (and, later, Tsangdhar). Since Eastern Command could not undertake the logistical effort with its own resources, Jogi took charge. He held a co-ordinating conference every afternoon at which representatives from the air force, the railways, QMG's Branch, Eastern Command and others would report progress and discuss means of further expediting the build-up. Air Vice-Marshal Jaswant Singh from Shillong, AOC-in-C East, himself attended one or two meetings. Jogi excelled at these performances and did his utmost to ensure that there was no shortfall in the despatch programme; if it had been physically possible to receive and distribute most of the loads Army HQ arranged to be dropped, there might have been some chance of equipping 7 Brigade for a limited operational role. As I commented in my *Summary*:

The Officiating CGS himself coordinated the combined effort of all branches at this Headquarters to ensure that all possible efforts were being made to support Eastern Command for *Operation Leghorn*. As a result of this, forward movement of stocks to Gauhati was begun almost immediately and the position had improved considerably by the time hostilities had started. The process of delivering these stocks to formations deployed in the mountains, however, continued to pose serious difficulties.

With the cooperation of Air Headquarters, the airlift capacity was raised from 20–30 tons per day at Gauhati to 60–70 tons by the beginning of October; and to 150–200 tons per day by the middle of October. As for the road lift capacity, 80 one-ton vehicles from the Ordnance Depot at Jabalpur were sent forward to increase the Corps resources in NEFA. (Some 225 others were later ordered forward from the Armoured Division and XI Corps, but arrived too late to influence the operations.)

As for porters, one pioneer company from DGBR (Border Roads) resources in Kameng was moved up to Lumpu.

Witnessing this truly impressive scale of air effort, some of my gloom lifted and my concern for the plight of the troops deployed at the Namka-chu was temporarily allayed. It was not till many days later that we heard the full tale of the fiasco at the dropping zones. A large proportion (nearly 50 percent by some accounts) of the (recycled) parachutes failed to open; of those that did a goodly number were wafted over the precipices to the steep valleys below; of those among the latter that were eventually located, many loads were found to be too heavy to be manhandled up the steep slopes. Little wonder that my *Summary* ruefully recorded:

However, in spite of all efforts, the build-up achieved by 17/18 October was still far short of minimum targets for the sustenance of operations. Against a target of 5 first lines of ammunition and 15 days supplies only the following reached the forward troops:

    (*a*) *Tsang Dhar*
| | | |
|---|---|---|
| | (i) Supplies | 8 days |
| | (ii) SAA (small arms and ammunition) | 1/16 first line |
| | (iii) 4.2 in mortar | 3/4 first line |
| | (iv) 75 mm | 0.5 first line |

    (*b*) *Lumpu*
| | | |
|---|---|---|
| | (i) Small arms and ammunition | about 0.5 first line |
| | (ii) Supplies | about 5 days |

    (*c*) *Towang*
| | | |
|---|---|---|
| | (i) Small arms and ammunition | 2 first lines |
| | (ii) 4.2 in mortar | 1 first line |
| | (iii) 3.7 in | 1.5 first lines |
| | (iv) 25 pdr | 2 first lines |

For the benefit of readers unacquainted with military terms, the definition of a first line scale is the amount of ammunition required for just one day's fighting when in contact with the enemy. Thus, all that had been dropped at Lumpu and Tsangdhar by the time the Chinese attacked at Namka-chu was barely sufficient for about an hour's battle – and that only if all air-dropped items were located, retrieved and transported to the troops, which would have been impossible, as neither mules nor porters were available. However, all that knowledge belonged to the future. For the moment if appeared to us in Delhi that the maintenance system might have a chance to catch up with the troops deployed on the riverline.

In mid-September Jogi informed me that Bogey Sen had revised his plan and decided, after all, to use the whole of 7 Brigade for the attack. He had, therefore, postponed the date of attack, estimating that the operation could not be launched before early October. I rejoiced at this because it meant that Kaul would in all probability be back at his post as CGS before the operation started and I was confident that I could persuade him to have some of the bizarre decisions reversed. I knew that no amount of air effort at Lumpu could enable logistics to catch up with the requirements for a whole brigade. (MO-I had calculated that the tonnage required for a brigade attack including an air-drop of four pack artillery pieces and a minimum stockpile of ammunition would by themselves amount to 560 tons.) Kaul, I felt sure, would appreciate the unreality of these figures.

During the next two or three days only tidbits of information came my way, either garnered from messages passing through MO Directorate or from Jogi's briefing sessions. It was from him I learned that 7 Brigade was not expected to sit idle during the period of preparation for the attack; it had been ordered to infiltrate small groups forward to occupy tactical points on the main ridge or on its flanks – for instance at Tsangle, or at minor passes such as Karpo-la or Yumso-la (lesser passes to the west of Thag-la). I could not locate Tsangle on the map. According to Jogi it was a herders' shelter a couple of miles to the west, near a group of small lakes that formed the headwaters of the Namka-chu. It later turned out to be two days' march to the west of Dhola! In retrospect it appears incredible that senior officers with no knowledge of the terrain could sit around a table with politicians and bureaucrats and conduct chessboard strategy as a kind of blind-man's buff. Tactically Tsangle was irrelevant to the Tsedong deployment; yet, inexplicably, the urge to occupy it remained an obsession with Menon and Thapar.

The Chinese facing our troops on the Namka-chu had been generally quiet after the first encounter on 8 September, but busy improving their defences with the help of barbed wire, digging tools, power saws and sandbags – all of which our troops lacked. (During those earlier days there had even been a degree of fraternisation between troops of the opposing forces – exchanges of cigarettes and greetings and the like – till orders were issued to put a stop to any such display of camaraderie.) On the night of 20 September they made their first attempt to infiltrate forward and harass our posts by throwing grenades. This led to exchanges of fire, which continued intermittently thereafter both by day and night, with both sides suffering casualties.

On the 20th, HQ XXXIII Corps informed 4 Infantry Division of its operational task: to evict the Chinese from our territory. The division was ordered to send its operational plan for approval. At the same time 5 Infantry Brigade in eastern NEFA was ordered to reinforce its forward positions at Limeking, Taksing, Mechuka, Tuting and Walong.

I saw this signal at about the time that I learned from Mullik that he had failed in his efforts to persuade either Menon or Thapar to recall Bijji Kaul. Mullik explained that Menon and Kaul had earlier fallen out; as for Thapar, he was adamant that he could deal with the crisis without his CGS. Mullik told me that his suggestion for air support had also been turned down. Aspy Engineer had been enthusiastic about bombing targets in Ladakh and Tibet, but the Defence Ministry decided not to risk air action over Chinese territory for fear of retaliation against Indian cities.

I think it was then that my mind was first troubled by forebodings of disaster. I had banked on Kaul's early return from leave, certain that he would be able to restrain Menon's reckless gambits. Unlike Thapar, Kaul could not be browbeaten into acquiescence in some operational misadventure, or so I thought at the time. News of the refusal to recall him struck me like a physical blow.

Soon after this, Umrao's BGS at HQ XXXIII Corps, 'Jaggi' Aurora, rang up from Shillong with a long list of complaints and reproofs about the order to evict the Chinese, which he assumed had issued from my office. (I should explain that he could take the liberty of berating me because seniority in the General Staff chain in Eastern Command was exactly topsy-turvy. Jaggi in Corps HQ was a year and more senior in service to Krishen Sibal BGS at HQ Eastern Command who, in turn, was six months senior to me; whereas, of course the placements should have been precisely the opposite.)

It was Jaggi Aurora who first informed me that both
Corps and Divisional HQ had consistently and emphatically
advised against any offensive across the Namka-chu. The
riverline, he added, had become the *de facto* border between
the opposing troops; the Chinese would react strongly *to*
any crossing of it by our troops. He expressed surprise that
a former commander of 7 Brigade, familiar with the terrain
in that forbidding region of NEFA, should have sent out
orders for an attack on Thag-la. I mumbled some excuses
over the line, none of which could have improved my
standing with Jaggi. I could not, of course, explain my
dilemma about Jogi's 'cornering of the market', or the
communication gap in GS Branch created by Kaul's absence.
I told him that I had been away from Delhi for nearly a
fortnight but would do what I could to project his views
in the right quarters. I felt somewhat of a sham but I
could think of nothing else to say.

During my afternoon session with Jogi Dhillon – I think
it was on the same day (21 September) or perhaps the
next – I told him about Jaggi Aurora's *cri de coeur* from
Shillong and that according to him Corps HQ opposed
any operational commitment forward of Lumpu. We argued
about the contradictions in the situation but Jogi felt that
Bogey Sen was a much more seasoned soldier and his
assessment must be given greater weight than that of
Umrao, who had little operational experience. My own
advice seemed to count for little.

I did succeed in one area. I persuaded him that we
should start maintaining our own documents on these
momentous decisions in case things went disastrously awry.
Later in the day, or perhaps on the day after, Jogi handed
me a record of a meeting held in the Ministry the previous
day and said, 'There you are. Now you can keep that in
your files.'

Checking back on dates I find that by 22 September
Menon had left for New York so it must have been the
Minister of State in charge of Defence Production, Raghu
Ramaiah, who presided at the meeting of which Jogi Dhillon
handed me the record which follows:

RECORD OF A MEETING IN THE DEFENCE MINISTER'S ROOM
ON SATURDAY 22 SEP 62

After giving the uptodate position in the Bhutan-Tibet-NEFA trijunction area, the COAS gave his appreciation of the Chinese reactions to our operations in the Dhola area.

He stated that the Chinese could do any or all of the following:

(a) Send more reinforcements against Dhola
(b) Retaliate elsewhere in NEFA
(c) Retaliate in Ladakh

He considered that it was most likely that the Chinese would attack our posts in Ladakh in the area of the uncharted Chip Chap and Galwan rivers, as by so doing they would be achieving their aim of reaching their 1960 claim line. They were only about 8 to 10 miles from the claim line and we were comparatively much weaker to resist any determined attempt on their part to achieve their aim.

The Foreign Secretary then explained the PM's instructions on the subject of our posts in Ladakh and elsewhere. He further stated that the Government's view·was that we must not accept any infringement of our border in NEFA. He was of the opinion that as we built up strength in the Dhola area we should evict the Chinese from our territory even at the cost of Chinese reaction in Ladakh, where owing to our weakness, we may lose further territory. He felt that in Ladakh the Chinese would probably NOT react strongly but may try and capture one or two posts.

The COAS then asked for written instructions of the Government to evict the Chinese in the Dhola area. After some discussion the MMD [Minister, Ministry of Defence] decided to issue instructions as drafted in the meeting.

The instructions issued are at 1-A.

Sd/- (JS Dhillon)
Maj Gen
Officiating CGS
24 Sep 62

## Annexure 1-A

### MINISTRY OF DEFENCE

At a meeting in MMD's room, this morning COAS raised the specific question whether action to evict the Chinese can be taken as soon as the Brigade has concentrated. The decision throughout has been, as discussed at previous meetings, that the Army should prepare and throw the Chinese out as soon as possible. The COAS was accordingly directed to take action for the eviction of the Chinese in the Kameng Division of NEFA as soon as he was ready.

*11987/JS(G)/62*
*COAS of 22-9-62*

*Sd/-* (HC Sarin)
Joint Secretary
22-9-62

If the instructions at '1-A' had not been attached in the original, I would have had difficulty in believing that orders to launch an offensive against the armed forces of a great power had been issued by a middle-ranking civil servant, endorsing the decision of a minister who did not have cabinet rank and who, into the bargain, had till then not been connected with operational matters. Furthermore, in retrospect it seemed incredible that it was the Ministry of Defence and not the Foreign Ministry that had ordered the army to commit an act of war.

I could not understand Thapar's thought processes. The very fact that he had asked for a written order from the Minister indicated that he was not wholly in agreement with the content of the verbal one. Despite the DIB's and the Foreign Secretary's optimistic speculations about Chinese reactions, clearly he was alarmed about a possible riposte in both Ladakh and NEFA, and he must have known that in either event our forward posts stood no chance of withstanding a co-ordinated attack. Furthermore, since Menon was away he would not have to face any browbeating; so why did he not resist the pressure on him to amount a reckless offensive at Thag-la?

I do not recall whether I discussed these oppressive misgivings with Jogi on that occasion. Perhaps not, because by then I had rather given up on him, but I do recall his telling me that he would himself draft the signal to the Commands conveying government's orders, an uncalled for arrogation that did not, as it turned out, serve him well.

At home later in the evening I received a message from Thapar's ADC summoning me to the Chief's residence. I

walked over to White Gates and found the Chief and Jogi
Dhillon busily discussing the text of Jogi's draft signal to
the Commands. Thapar showed it to me and asked for my
views.

Not expecting this sudden readmission to the insiders'
circle, I was perhaps somewhat wary, uncertain how far
to press my views. The signal to Eastern Command was
brief and to the point: Chinese troops who had entered
Kameng FD were to be evicted as soon as preparations
had been completed. When I began to discuss the feasibility
of such an operation Thapar cut me short and told me
that I had not been called to question the government's
directive but to suggest ways of implementing it, especially
in regard to Western Command. Irresolutely, I gave way
and did not pursue the matter. I glanced at the sub-paragraph
in Jogi's draft addressed to Western Command:

(b) To Western Command
Since it was likely that the Chinese might react to the above by
attacking some of our forward posts in Ladakh, all posts will be
alerted, their defences strengthened and, if attacked, would fight
it out. No withdrawal would be permitted.

When I had finished reading I found Thapar looking at
me questioningly, as though he expected me to raise an
objection. I did. To quote from the *Summary*:

On being asked to give my comments . . ., I pointed out that
the deployment of forward posts in Ladakh had been based on
an administrative rather than a tactical plan. . . . These posts
were therefore deployed in 'penny packets', not mutually supporting
and could neither be reinforced nor logistically maintained in
case of open hostilities. In these circumstances, it would be wrong
to lay down from this Headquarters that there would be no
withdrawals. This flexibility should be left in the hands of the
local commanders. The COAS agreed and the signal was amended.

I gathered that there had been some argument between
the two on this point and Thapar seemed gratified at my
response. He at once amended Jogi's draft, but he did not
want to leave it entirely 'in the hands of the local commanders'
as I had suggested, because (he said) Daulet Singh had
recently asked permission to withdraw all his border posts

as a precautionary measure – and his intention had been to pull in all his resources to Leh for its defence. This had not been permitted. Thapar felt that if he were given a completely free hand now he might do just that.

The signal approved by the COAS read:

*Firstly(.)* personal from CAOS for GOC in C Eastcom (.) govt has decided that the Chinese troops who have entered the Kameng Frontier Division of NEFA will be evicted as soon as you are ready (.) all necessary arrangements required to achieve this aim will be made at top speed (.)
*Secondly(.)* for GOC-in-C Westcom and GOC XV Corps (.) the above action is likely to have repercussions in Ladakh to the extent that Chinese may attack some of our forward posts (.) all posts will therefore be alerted and their defences strengthened as far as possible (.) if attacked posts will fight it out and inflict maximum casualties on the Chinese (.) any adjustments which may be considered necessary to strengthen our present positions may be carried out.

By 25 September our casualties at Namka-chu had risen to eleven and Chinese losses were reported to be even higher. On one occasion our troops opened fire on the Chinese with 3-inch mortars, inflicting a number of casualties whom they could see being carried away on stretchers. Protests from Peking were not long in arriving, proclaiming 'the most serious and strongest protest . . . [against] the frenzied criminal provocations of the intruding Indian troops in the Tsedong area . . . [where] the flames of war may break out any time'. At the same time Peking issued a notification to New Delhi that active patrolling had been ordered along the McMahon border – as if to betoken that not all its threats were empty.

More than these diplomatic developments, it was the skirmishing on the Namka-chu that I found ominous. Since no one in Delhi had any idea of the exact lie of the land, or how the troops were tactically disposed on the ground, we could not understand the reason for these constant exchanges of fire despite strict injunctions to avoid them. It is an indication of the irrationality of the situation that although Army HQ was attempting to direct 7 Brigade's operations, none of us had any idea about what was actually going on at the front. That the two forces were strung out along a riverline, facing each other across a narrow mountain stream in eyeball-to-eyeball hostility, would have seemed the least likely probability.

I tried to ring up Niranjan Prasad at Tezpur to find out more about the situation, but was told that he was not available; he too had been prodded up the mountain by HQ Eastern Command and was on his way to Lumpu, out of communication with both 7 Brigade and his own HQ, temporarily *hors de combat*; HQ 7 Brigade, by then located at Lumpu *en route* to Namka-chu, had not yet established wireless communication with Tezpur. Almost on the eve of battle everyone appeared to be out of touch with everyone else. If one could have retained one's sense of humour in these trying times, it all would have seemed quite comical, like an act in a vaudeville show.

On 26 September HQ Eastern Command ordered XXXIII Corps to establish a company post at Tsangle. Having been briefed earlier by Jogi I assumed that the order had originated at the Minister's conference. Umrao, however, mistook it for undue interference by Sen and it was then that I received the first inkling of strained relations between Sen and Umrao – and, indeed, between Command and Corps HQ. On 28 September BGS Eastern Command forwarded a copy of a XXXIII Corps signal to me, in which the Corps Commander had given vent to what appeared to me to be a justifiable grievance: '. . . submit humbly while I welcome any suggestions advice and guidance from you I would be failing in my duty if I were not to point out the undesirability of higher headquarters giving orders on the deployment of platoons and companies.' The BGS requested that I bring his signal to the notice of the COAS. I sent the file to Jogi without adding any comment from the DMO

The next day, on learning that the Army Commander was to visit Delhi on 1 October, I rang up Krishen Sibal, the BGS, to invite them both for breakfast at my house after their early morning flight from Lucknow. What I planned to do was, first, to determine who exactly had inspired and counselled the unfortunate Namka-chu venture; and, thereafter, to try to subdue the enthusiasm with which

7 Brigade was being urged into an offensive, hoping to convince them by using my firsthand knowledge of the difficulties of the terrain and weather and their impact on logistics forward of road-head or dropping zone. I knew Bogey well enough to do this without being thought presumptuous, and I knew I could count on moral support from Krishen.

Unfortunately Bogey arrived in a dour mood, which not even the banter that usually passed between him and my wife could dispel. Breakfast over, we repaired to my study to discuss the Namka-chu operation. It was not long before I began to realise, with something of a shock, that it was Bogey who was mainly responsible for promoting the idea of an offensive at Namka-chu. It also become obvious that he had little knowledge of the terrain but, uncharacteristically, he would not back down from his commitment. He told me that he had just returned from a visit to Tezpur. Niranjan and Dalvi, who knew the terrain, had between them drawn up a plan of attack: a sweep across the Thag-la slope from west to east to clear it of the Chinese presence. The plan had his approval; he added that the opposition to it came mainly from Umrao, who 'was not exerting himself fully to ensure that the build-up in the Tsedong area was being carried out with maximum speed and capacity.'

I tried to probe into Bogey's mind, only to come up against a doggedness that, instead, had the effect of undermining my own conviction in the matter. Although I knew him to be somewhat unimaginative by nature, he nevertheless had wide (and successful) experience of battle – more than any other general officer still in service. It would not have occurred to me to suspect that he and his staff would commit forces to a crucial operation without having considered all its logistical and tactical aspects (although, indeed, that is exactly what this general officer and his staff did in fact do).

Before the meeting broke up, Bogey said that he would appreciate any help I could give him in replacing his Corps Commander. My *Summary* records:

I advised the GOC-in-C to bring this matter to the notice of COAS. I also advised him that so far as Army Headquarters was concerned, we would hold HQ Eastern Command responsible for the success of the operation; if he felt dissatisfied with his subordinate commanders, it was always open to him, at this operationally vital juncture, to assume personal command at Corps Headquarters to ensure that the operation did not fail by default. I suggested to him that in this national emergency if he were dissatisfied with the conduct of operations in a lower formation, he could not leave it at that. The GOC-in-C stated that he was not willing to act according to this advice.

When I went to the Ops Room after breakfast I was told that Mullik had been asking for me on the telephone. I walked over to his office and found him greatly troubled about the command crisis in NEFA. He had been told about the Sen-Umrao clash by Krishna Menon on the latter's return from the UN the previous day and felt that a new corps commander should be appointed: Umrao, Menon suspected, was obstructing the execution of Army HQ orders. I countered that this was not the time to introduce a new man into the chain of command. It would be much more effectual and appropriate if Sen took over direct command of the corps. I told him about my morning meeting with Sen and my advice to him to assume command in Tezpur – and his rejection of this advice. Mullik said that he would have a word with Thapar and recommend the course I had suggested.

I had been sickening for a bout of 'flu for the past day or so and, as luck would have it, I had to take to bed that afternoon with a sudden high temperature. Bogey Sen was to have stayed over in Delhi till the next day but I was in no condition to meet him for a further discussion.

On the morning of 3 October Pritpal Singh rang up to say that Bijji Kaul was back at his deck, news which cheered me enormously but not enough to want to leave my bed to go and meet him. I instructed Pritpal to call at the CGS's office, or telephone him on my behalf, and pass him a message that I was ill and would be much obliged if he could drop in at my house on his way back from the office. However, I waited in vain all evening; late at night Pritpal rang up to say that the CGS had been closeted with Thapar most of the evening and had then gone on to see the Prime Minister (who had returned from abroad the day before).

I was up early next morning and felt considerably better. Knowing that Bijji was an early riser, I telephoned him at home. He asked me to go to his house immediately and he startled me by adding that I had better hurry because within the next few minutes he would be leaving for the airport 'to take up a new assignment'.

Mind and body galvanised by turmoil, it took me less than ten minutes to shave, pull on shirt and trousers and drive to Bijji's house in York Road. I found him in the little bedsitter den where he usually worked when at home. I was startled to see, sitting beside him on the divan, Prem Bhatia, editor of the *Times of India*, looking like the proverbial cat who has just swallowed a large yellow songbird. He got up as I arrived, wished Bijji good luck and left, still with a greatly pleased smirk on his face.

Before I could blurt out all my questions (and also my pent-up resentments of the past fortnight) Bijji got in the first word, with the information that he was leaving for Tezpur in half-an-hour to take command of a new corps, which he had decided to designate IV Corps (resurrecting the formation that had fought at Imphal in the war against the Japanese). I was as surprised as aghast at the news. What new corps? Why him? Who would do the CGS's job when he left? When was all this decided? Would he not reconsider his decision? The questions came tumbling out of my mouth after the first shock had passed, as Bijji moved about the room, hastily packing his grip or shouting instructions to Dhanno, his wife, who was obviously busy in the next room getting his travelling kit ready. 'Put these in the staff car,' Bijji said, handing me a briefcase and some odds and end. Very soon I had joined the domestic workforce, helping Bijji get organised for his journey into battle. A hurried cup of tea for me, a few last minute instructions to his wife and daughter that took the place of leave-taking – and we were soon being driven at a smart pace towards Palam airport.

In the car he at last began to take notice of his erstwhile DMO. He explained that on his return to Delhi the day before he had gone to his office – even though still on leave – to be briefed on the Namka-chu incidents. In the evening Thapar had sent for him and told him about the impasse created by Umrao's 'stubborness'. The Chief then asked him whether he would accept command of a new corps to replace XXXIII Corps in NEFA. Thereafter, Thapar had sent him on to Menon and finally to Nehru. Nehru, he said, had more or less ordered him to take command in NEFA – not that his own decision would have been any different. So here he was, on his way to his new command.

Still puzzled by this unexpected and startling development, I expressed doubt about the so-called new corps he was to command. Where was it to come from? Was Umrao being sacked? If so, why wasn't Bijji merely taking over XXXIII Corps with its established staff? Why send in a new corps on the eve of a campaign?

Under my cross-questioning Bijji confessed to the details and a clearer picture of the Menon-Thapar fake solution began to emerge. Bijji reluctantly admitted that he was, in fact, merely going to raise an *ad hoc* Corps HQ to command the NEFA sector. He had been told that Umrao had failed to deliver the goods but was not, for the time being, to be sacked; he would continue in command of XXXIII Corps, but would be responsible only for Sikkim, Nagaland and the East Pakistan front, leaving Bijji to get on with operations in the Frontier Divisions of NEFA.

I digested this for a moment and, incredulous, asked whether he felt justified in vacating the CGS's chair just to go and 'take command of a couple of brigades?' Bijji was somewhat taken aback at this artless, though not inaccurate, description of his role. He replied, somewhat defensively, that he would soon be given more troops as other divisions would be sent to him and that eventually his corps would command the whole frontier from the Uttar Pradesh Himalayas to the Burma border. But yes, he agreed, for the time being his only scope for exercising command would be to supervise brigade battles in Kameng. It was a crucial responsibility, he added, given him by the Prime Minister himself. When I expressed my doubts about the feasibility of mounting an offensive in that terrain, Bijji assured me that, according to Thapar, both 7 Brigade and 4th Division had produced workable plans for the attack; it was only Umrao who (he had been told) was being obstructionist.

By this time I had become quite intrigued about this supposed divisional plan of attack that Sen and now Kaul had mentioned, but I refrained from making a remark. I could see that Bijji was greatly pleased with himself and I could imagine why. He was going to war at last, and at the top level. Here was his chance to make up for the past, to fill in the blanks in his credentials and to give the lie to his detractors. There would be no holding him back.

I was amused to observe the motley collection of individuals gathered near the aircraft waiting to accompany Kaul as his corps staff. Apart from a few officers handpicked by the Military Secretary, there were those whom I recognised as belonging to Kaul's 'private squad' of strong-arm men, whose personal loyalties were pledged to Bijji Kaul. I was sad to see among them one of my own GSO-1s, who appeared to have been snatched from MO Directorate without a by-your-leave. (He did, I am glad to report, find his way back to MO Directorate after a brief sojourn at HQ IV Corps.)

I discovered next morning why Prem Bhatia had looked so pleased with himself when I had seen him: The *Times of India* carried its scoop on the front page. Bold headlines announced the creation of a 'Special Task Force under General Kaul . . . to oust the Chinese'. I realised of course that Kaul was responsible for this glaring breach of security. The DMI was subsequently ordered to conduct an inquiry to trace the source of the leak. It was a farcical ritual; it must have been obvious who had informed the *Times of India*. Nevertheless, the DMI professed to be 'totally stumped by the mystery'! The DMO was neither asked for nor volunteered evidence.

After 4 October, though I was still being quarantined from high-level conferences both in the Ministry and at Army HQ, at least I was able to keep myself in touch with developments on 4th Division's front because Bijji Kaul established the practice of sending a stream of detailed, chatty reports – sometimes two or three long signal messages a day – addressed to Eastern Command but with a copy direct to Army HQ. For the purposes of maintaining records this was an improvement on the Bogey-Thapar-Jogi regimen of undocumented messages and decisions. (With Kaul at the far end of the link, Bogey Sen found himself temporarily by-passed, his HQ reverting to its previous role of acting as a post-office.)

Kaul's intrusion into the NEFA scene transformed the hitherto delusory reportage into a more realistic depiction of the operational picture. Not content to depend on secondhand information, the new Corps Commander flew up to Lumpu on the very first day after his arrival and trekked to the Namka-chu, the first general officer to have done so. Once there, he was able clearly to discern the tactical absurdity of the project and the almost total absence of logistics to support it, should it ever be undertaken. He issued a succession of top priority signals from the forward position which had a sobering, not to mention dismaying, effect in the army and the Ministry. He had it in his power then to defuse the whole situation and, perhaps, gradually to unravel the tensions of the deadly drama that was developing along the river front. He had the ear of the Prime Minister, and the *réclame*, to do these things – but he did not do them. Some inhibition in his personality would prevent him from offering any counsel that might be interpreted as fainthearted or non-combative. He would describe at length the futility of the situation, predict the dire consequences of continued confrontation and then, in a total *non sequitur*, make a rash personal commitment to warlike action. Overawed by what he saw of the terrain and the enemy, and sensitive to the helplessness and the vulnerability of our troops in Namka-chu valley, he still could not bring himself to recommend the slightest retraction from the government's belligerent stance. According to my *Summary:*

In his first signal sent on 5 October, the Corps Commander reported that there were a number of logistical difficulties along the administrative pipe-line, which had received his prior attention. In the Tsedong area, he was planning to send forward 1/9 GR, which was still held up at Lumpu. Apprehending that the concentration of our forces in the Tsedong area had laid bare the defences of Towang, he was taking steps to ensure that a minimum of two battalions, with increased supporting arms, would be kept in that area. As for D Day, he stated that he would give his appreciation on 6 October, though he felt that D Day would be before 10 October.

On the next day, when the Corps Commander had had an opportunity of reconnoitring the terrain, he was able to make a more detailed assessment of the task. He felt that the enemy strength facing him was a battalion in the forward positions, backed by a brigade in the Thag-la ridge, supported by artillery, heavy mortars, machine guns and recoilless guns. The enemy infantry were armed with automatic rifles.

In spite of this, the Corps Commander undertook the acceleration of the process of forward concentration and was still confident of commencing the eviction operation by 10 October. He, however, pointed out the possibility of the enemy overwhelming our own force, 'which would lead to a national disaster'. He therefore recommended that offensive air support be planned and made available, if necessary, at shortest notice.

At the same time, GOC IV Corps pointed out the tremendous difficulties being experienced in the collection of air dropped arms, ammunition and equipment at Tsangdhar where 70 per cent of the loads were being lost on the mountain slopes. . . .

By 7 October, the Corps Commander had completed his reconnaissance along the length of the Namka-chu positions. He reported that the Chinese were in the process of deploying their second battalion forward, thus confronting 7 Brigade with an equally matched force in superior defensive positions. He again pointed out the extremely unfavourable logistical situation. The forward battalions had only 50 rounds of ammunition per man, some still in summer clothing (at heights of 16,000 feet); and there was an acute shortage of porters. He also pointed out that he had no reserves to meet a possible Chinese counter-attack.

On 9 October, IV Corps reported commencement of its 'preliminary operations', that is, occupation of Sing Jang position (north of the Namka-chu) to forestall its capture by the Chinese. Also, in view of the Chinese strength in the area, the Corps Commander had ordered forward a fourth battalion to the Tsedong area. . . .

## Sing Jang attack

On 10 October, the situation on the Namka-chu front took a grave turn. The Corps Commander reported that the Chinese had concentrated a battalion against the Sing Jang position overnight and, using heavy mortars and medium machine guns for support, launched an attack against our post. He had also observed two other battalions moving in to positions along the north bank of the river. Thus, the enemy had four battalions deployed. 'This has raised a serious situation which is raising grave issues when judged in the context of enemy threat which is developing against Towang Sector.' He sought approval to fly to Delhi at once to put before Army Headquarters and Government of India 'the grave aspects of the new and sudden development'.

We lost the Sing Jang position, with 6 killed, 11 wounded and 14 missing out of a strength of two platoons. The enemy, in the meanwhile, 'were pouring out of Thag-la like ants. . . .'

(Sing Jang, we discovered subsequently, was the name given to a herder's hut on a prominent ridge some way up the Thag-la slope, north-west of Dhola. It possessed no marked tactical merit.)

I could write a whole chapter on the operational risks that were taken (and the decisions that were not) during Kaul's five days on the Namka-chu, but it would be an exercise undertaken with hindsight, not a contemporary comment. At the time, and even long afterwards, the sequence of events that culminated in the battle at Sing Jang and Kaul's headlong scamper to Delhi were not fully known at Army HQ or, for that matter, at corps and command. Even when Kaul arrived in Delhi in 11 October, attention did not focus on the causes of the Sing Jang battle but on its aftermath. The main characters – Kaul, Prasad, Dalvi – have since published accounts of those crucial days in their memoirs. There are striking inconsistencies; each had his own wicket to defend. It is clear that the occupation of a feature partway up the Thag-la slope was a precipitate move, and one not taken lightly by the Chinese. I remembered Jaggi Aurora's statement of a few days previously, that the Namka-chu had become, for both sides, the *de facto* boundary: its crossing in strength had almost certainly been regarded by the Chinese as an overt act of war, and they had retaliated with a bludgeoning display of military superiority.

I had been shown the messages that Kaul sent from the Namka-chu. For the first time someone on the spot was reporting directly to Army HQ the hard facts of the situation: the hopeless logistical predicament, the desperate ammunition situation (only fifty rounds per man) and the overwhelming Chinese build-up on the dominating heights of Thag-la; yet, characteristically, Kaul could not forbear from ending his long, self-boosting and chattily descriptive messages with some dramatic bombast, such as declaring that he was 'taking every possible step to evict the Chinese from our territory (despite many difficulties) as ordered' (Kaul's *Untold Story*, p. 377). Bombast or not, I was concerned about the effect his hollow histrionics would have on those in South Block eagerly waiting for the great offensive to begin. When, therefore, I learned in the afternoon of 11 October that the Corps Commander was flying in to Delhi, I was both puzzled at this sudden *démarche* and considerably relieved that the reckless operation to cross the river in strength would not be repeated.

A meeting had been arranged in the Prime Minister's house late in the evening. I went to see Jogi and suggested that he might require me to be present at the meeting to take notes, but the ploy did not work: my presence, he said, was not at all necessary. Thus frustrated, but determined to have a word with Kaul before he went to the meeting, I went to his house after dinner to await his arrival from Tezpur, but there also I was to be disappointed because he had arrived early and had already left for the PM's residence.

I had hoped that the next morning I would, on seeing the signal messages which normally issued from MO Directorate, be able to learn what decisions had been taken at the previous night's meeting. To my disappointment I discovered that neither the COAS nor the officiating CGS had sent any messages through the Ops Room. Nor did the acting CGS in the course of the morning deign to inform the DMO about developments on the operational front. It was not till Bijji Kaul paid a surprise but welcome visit to my office during the lunch-break that I first learned, albeit informally and unofficially, of the travesty of misunderstandings and make-belief that resulted in the issue of gross misdirections to brigade and division on the Namka-chu.

Bijji gave me an informal account of the PM's meetings the night before. He assured me that he had unambiguously stated at the PM's conference that the Chinese were in such overwhelming strength and in such dominating positions on Thag-la ridge that there was no possibility of 7 Brigade being able to launch a clearing operation up the Thag-la slopes; on the contrary, the brigade was unlikely even to withstand an onslaught by the Chinese should they decide to mount one. He had recommended not only that the offensive be called off but also that 7 Brigade be withdrawn from its defenceless posts on the riverline to positions further back on Hathung-la and Tsangdhar ridge. Bijji said that only the PM had seemed to accept his assessment without demur. Menon had made no comment, but most of the others, including Desai, Thapar, Dhillon and Sen, could hardly conceal their incredulity; they might even have suspected him of faintheartedness, Bijji added bitterly. Sen, of all people, vehemently protested against Bijji's assessment. Perhaps because he felt that his previous judgment was being discredited, he insisted that the Namka-chu position was strong enough to hold out against a Chinese attack and Thapar agreed with him − although neither had the slightest knowledge of the terrain or the layout of the brigade's posts! That is how, Bijji added, the decision came to be taken: that while 7 Brigade was no longer required to mount an offensive, it must continue to hold the line of the Namka-chu. A withdrawal from the riverline was ruled out.

Bijji stayed for over an hour in my office, sharing my sandwich lunch. In his inimitable way he gave me a blow-by-blow account of his hazardous voyage to the Thag-la region and of the hardships he had endured. Always quick to perceive the ridiculous, even when it related to himself, he described the unceremonious manner of his crossing of the Hathung-la, pick-a-back on a sturdy but strongly malodorous Mompa porter. His account became a mixture of absurd exaggeration, comic understatement and, occasionally, obvious dissembling. With his gift for diminishing the distance between the sublime and the ridiculous without losing credibility, he made a fascinating raconteur. At the same time, his tragi-comic account bespoke a sensitive and acute perception and was a vivid sketch of the escalating drama being acted out in that forlorn outpost. For the first time I learned of the strong and determined attack the Chinese had launched on the company post established at Sing Jang. I was appalled that Sen and Thapar had, despite the evidence of Sing Jang, offered reckless opinions that had resulted in 7 Brigade being made to remain in an exposed and vulnerable riverline position dominated by the enemy on the higher slopes. I pleaded with Bijji to use his personal influence with the PM to have the decision reversed. I urged that, knowing how defenceless the line of the Namka-chu was, he must not leave our troops in that trap. Unfortunately, he would not be persuaded. There was nothing he could do, he said, except to issue orders to HQ 4th Division when he got back to relocate the Namka-chu positions in a more tactical deployment. He promised to do that as soon as he returned to Tezpur, but from the evasive manner in which he said it I doubted whether he would adhere to the commitment.

I could see that Kaul, despite his facade of light-hearted raillery, was uncharacteristically diffident and uncertain. He was very obviously a sick man, having caught a severe chill during the night-crossing of the Hathung-la on his return journey. In fact I had never known him to be so down and I felt a mixture of respect and pity, for his ebullient personality and for his present limitations. I sensed that the transfer from Delhi to Tezpur – the physical move from centre stage to a job in the wings – had had the effect of diminishing his self-image. A month ago he would not have allowed himself to be overruled by Sen or Thapar; yet, at that moment, knowing that the decision taken at the PM's conference was tactically insupportable and potentially disastrous, he lacked the self-assurance to use his influence to have it reversed.

It was after the meeting with Kaul that I first began to suspect that the Chinese were preparing to launch a major attack against our forces in Kameng, whatever Mullik might say. The Chinese troop build-up, as reported by the IB and by Niranjan's forward HQ at Zimithang, had been ominous. As the *Summary* recorded:

During this period, Chinese build-up activity had been considerable. The southern slopes of the Thag-la feature were reported to be criss-crossed with tunnels and trenches, barbed wire obstacles and other fieldworks. Anti-aircraft guns and mortars had been seen arriving and the troop build-up continued to increase daily. An alarming feature was that the Chinese had also begun to concentrate forces in front of Khinzemane, where they were reported to be digging in within a few hundred yards of our post.

Corps Headquarters estimated that the Chinese had probably built up one division each in the Thag-la and Bum-la sectors. It recommended that the strength of Towang garrison be made up to a brigade group, supported by a squadron of AMX tanks and a field regiment.

Even allowing for a degree of exaggeration of enemy strengths not unusual in reports from troops in actual contact, Chinese concentrations at Thag-la and Bum-la were clearly formidable and, together with their mortar and artillery reinforcements, could by no stretch of reasoning be regarded as merely a defensive precaution against what they must have known was India's token offensive posture by a weak infantry brigade, with neither artillery support nor logistical backing. At the same time, Chinese official protests had resumed their threatening tone: they 'would not stand idly by while their frontier guards are being mercilessly killed' (presumably alluding to the Sing Jang incident). On 14 October the *People's Daily* (the semi-official organ of Chinese government propaganda) called upon the PLA to 'defend our territory . . . and . . . deal resolute counterblows to any invaders.'

I had become increasingly aware of my own ineffectuality since Jogi Dhillon had sidetracked me from my normal functions as DMO. By blocking my access to Thapar and to the Ministry of Defence he had reduced me to the role of a ghost walking the corridors of Army HQ. The few clandestine attempts I had made on my own initiative to influence decisions – with Mullik and Bogey Sen, for example – had failed to achieve anything. When I examined my position critically, I felt that my authority and influence were slipping away from me because of the difficulty of my circumstances.

After Kaul's visit to my office on 12 October, this sense of helplessness intensified. It was not that my self-esteem had suffered, although there must have been an element of that too, but that I could in no way, and to no one who mattered, convey my certainty that in keeping 7 Brigade where it was we were heading for disaster. I felt sure that could I but take a sketch map to Thapar and describe the hazards and restrictions of the terrain (without the dissenting presence of Jogi Dhillon) I might persuade him to relent on his decision to keep 7 Brigade pinned down at the bottom of the valley.

The opportunity did come a few days later, but I failed to grasp it in time.

On 13 October several newspapers headlined a sensational statement allegedly made by Pandit Nehru at the airport the previous day, just before taking off for Colombo on some trivial, unofficial mission. It was reported that the Prime Minister had told press correspondents that he had ordered the army to 'throw the Chinese out'. In fact the Prime Minister had not been quite that blatant. When answering questions he made a general and qualified statement confirming the government's determination to force the Chinese to cease their encroachment upon Indian territory. He went on to clarify this: 'Our instructions are to free our territory . . . I cannot fix a date, that is entirely for the Army to decide', pointing out the difficulties of terrain and enemy superiority at that time. Unfortunately, All India Radio and some newspapers conveyed the impression in their bulletins that the PM had issued instructions to the army to 'throw the Chinese out' immediately. That was irresponsible reporting. Nevertheless, it was an impetuous and unnecessary disclosure on Nehru's part, particularly in view of the fact that he had revoked that specific instruction only the night before.

There has been much argument whether the PM's statement, in its original or reported version, precipitated the Chinese attack a week later. This is a difficult matter to comment upon. The Chinese had been building up their forces behind Thag-la for some weeks, so an attack on Kameng FD must have been one of their options. Furthermore, subsequent analyses suggested that a number of national and international developments indicated mid-October as an opportune time to strike. Among these were the incipient Sino-Soviet rift (of which few of us were then aware); the lately concluded Indo-Soviet MiG-21 deal (a sore point with the Chinese because they had not been thus favoured), and the emerging Cuban missile crisis (which would keep the Soviet and United States governments preoccupied during the third week of October). After all these years it is difficult to say how greatly Nehru's airport speech influenced the precipitation of the Chinese offensive. Hindsight tends to lend rationality to events that in fact are innocent of coherence or logical sequence.

What is astonishing is that despite all the alarums and excursions at home and abroad, Indian intelligence was unable to warn Nehru about the possibility of imminent attack across our borders, both in Ladakh and in NEFA. The DIB's intelligence summaries on Chinese movements and their arms build-up, their road-construction activities and forward stockpiling of supplies and munitions were accurate and timely, but that was not enough. Ultimately, the only intelligence that matters is that which reads the political intentions of one's opponents; in this Indian intelligence failed. One of the reasons for the failure could be that too much was left in the hands of the Director of the Intelligence Bureau, Mullik. Political intelligence must be assessed by statesmen and generalists, not by systematists, yet India's Joint Intelligence Bureau had not even met for more than a year. All gathering, collation, assessment and interpretation of information had been carried out by the Intelligence Directorate.

My opportunity to see Thapar came on 16 October. I cannot recall where Jogi Dhillon was that day, but it fell to me take to the Chief a long and alarming signal from HQ IV Corps.

Kaul had been sending dispiriting reports since his return to Tezpur. The latest message highlighted his apprehension about holding Tsangle, because of a considerable enemy build-up reported in that area. He recommended that 'we give preference to discretion over prestige and pull back our isolated company from Tsangle . . . .' He also expressed concern about lack of logistical support for Operation Onkar posts along the border and added that if the supply situation in these posts continued to be so precarious it might result in 'starvation and desertion of Assam Rifles personnel'.

Thapar became quite agitated on reading the Corps Commander's forthright phrases and remarked that Bijji had lost 'his nerve' after his Namka-chu experience. When I observed that it was also possible that for the first time someone was reading the situation correctly, Thapar was unconvinced. I suggested that he keep an open mind on the subject. It would be best, I added, for him to make a personal air reconnaissance of the Lumpu-Dhola area the next day and then judge for himself. I said that Bogey Sen, not having visited the forward areas, might have been over-optimistic about the potential of the Namka-chu defences. Thapar brightened a little at my suggestion and agreed to make the journey. He sent me off to his Military Assistant to arrange for an aircraft to take us both over NEFA the next day. When I returned about ten minutes later, Thapar had drafted a reply to Kaul's signal. I despaired at what I read; I quote from my *Summary*:

Reference discussions COAS, GOC-in-C and Corps Commander during last visit to Delhi STOP firstly STOP reinforce Tsangle if possible up to a battalion and carry out aggressive patrolling in this area STOP secondly STOP also consider harassing fire on enemy movement particularly across Thag-la STOP thirdly STOP forward earliest your recommendations regarding commencement of operations to evict Chinese from area south and south-west of Thag-la including your requirements of any additional troops, administrative cover and airlift.

Thapar was now going one better than the ministers. Despite the PM's temporary reprieve (and the Corps Commander's dire warnings) here was the Army Chief giving every indication of proceeding willy-nilly with the doomed offensive. Thapar had not discussed operational matters with me for over a month; I was unsure how to tackle him since his mind appeared to be made up, and so I decided to wait till the next morning when I would have an opportunity to discuss things with him during the flight. I would persuade him with facts and figures on the Namka-chu situation by preparing a topographical brief on information such as the rugged terrain, the steep slopes and the lack of tracks and paths, and by giving him a table of figures depicting the degree of failure of the air-drops at Tsangdhar. I felt certain that I could dissuade him from a blind rush into disaster.

I spent the rest of the day preparing a brief for Thapar. I also decided to take with me a copy of Colonel Bailey's book with its heavily hachured sketches that emphasised the steep slopes of Thag-la ridge. Late in the evening as I was preparing to leave my office the telephone rang. The Chief's MA was on the line to inform me that the flight to NEFA had been brought forward: the Chief, accompanied by the Defence Minister, the DIB and Sarin, was leaving for Tezpur that very night, in fact within half-an-hour. I would not be required to accompany him. Instead, the Chief was going to pick up General Sen at Lucknow.

In postponing my attempt to bear upon Thapar that morning I lost an opportunity; I should have tackled him then and there. Opportunities are fleeting and once lost are seldom recovered. Thapar could not have had worse company for his trip than that assemblage of high-powered hawks. It was obvious that Menon and Mullik would constitute the sledgehammer with which to batter down Kaul's resistance. There was to be no air reconnaissance by Thapar, no attempt to review the situation from the point of view of those on the ground, no change of position.

I never learned at first hand exactly what transpired at the meeting in Tezpur but I gathered that Kaul had been persuaded to continue to hold the line of the Namka-chu and to reinforce Tsangle. Mullik in his book, *The Chinese Betrayal*, has contrived to establish that the decision was a purely military one. Whatever his reasons for this sidestepping of the responsibility borne by Krishna Menon, it is clear from his own narrative (and from Kaul's account of the conference in *The Untold Story*) that the Defence Minister insisted that we yield no more territory, emphasising that it was politically necessary to hold Tsangle. Kaul had no chance. The civilians did in fact retire to the mess after a while, to enable the military to come to a decision by themselves, but that was a charade. The damage had been done. Neither Thapar nor Sen had the grit to challenge Menon's political overstatement and Kaul, who did, was a confused and desperately ill man (he had to be evacuated to Delhi the next evening suffering from pulmonary oedema).

Meanwhile, MO Directorate had received instructions from the COAS to reinforce the Kameng front. Accordingly, we ordered the move of the Army HQ reserve, 65 Infantry Brigade, to Misamari. For the next lot of reinforcements,

I rang up GOC 17 Infantry Division in Ambala to warn him that he should be prepared to send an infantry brigade to IV Corps (48 Brigade moved on 20 October). I was not clear in my own mind about the exact roles these two brigades would be given but I determined to ensure that they would not be rushed up to the mountain-tops with just fifty rounds of ammunition in their pockets. (In the event, this was exactly what happened: 65 Brigade was sent to reinforce Towang and barely managed to escape being trapped there by the enemy; 48 Brigade was sent to Bomdila, where their innings lasted a little longer, but not by much.)

On the evening of 17 October Sanjiva Rao (the officer from MO-I who had gone with HQ IV Corps to Tezpur) rang me up with the news that Kaul's illness had taken a turn for the worse. His temperature was high, he was finding great difficulty breathing and the medical officer at Corps HQ had recommended immediate evacuation to Delhi. Rao himself was in an agitated state and pleaded with me to act at once as he feared for Kaul's life. He stressed that he was telephoning on his own initiative and had not informed the patient who was, according to him, barely conscious.

I at once rang up Thapar, who had only just returned from Tezpur. I asked whether I should arrange for an aircraft to be sent to Tezpur but he replied that he would handle it himself. I learned the next morning that after consulting Menon, Thapar had sent Colonel Lal, the medical officer at the Army HQ medical facility, in a special aircraft to Tezpur to examine Kaul. Lal decided to bring him to Delhi.

On 19 October I learned that although the illness had been diagnosed as pulmonary oedema in acute form, Kaul had been allowed to remain at home, on the condition that a sentry be posted at his bedroom door to keep out all visitors. I did not, therefore, call at his residence during the lunch-break, as I had intended. Meanwhile, we received messages from HQ IV Corps bearing the ominous news that the Chinese had reinforced their positions on Thag-la ridge with another battalion. Chinese troops had also been observed for the first time at points on the ridge far to the west of Thag-la (at Karpo-la and Dum-Dum-la, north of Tsangle). These moves were clearly visible from Tsangdhar and from the positions occupied by 1/9 Gorkhas, halfway up the Tsangdhar ridge.

A few days previously there had been an exchange of fire in the Tsangle area and the Chinese had suffered casualties. I surmised that the Chinese were now preparing to mount an attack against Tsangle – as they had done at Sing Jang – to throw our troops back south of the riverline.

In the afternoon, restless, vaguely apprehensive and with not much to do, I drove to No. 5 York Road to inquire after Bijji Kaul. To my surprise there were two or three staff cars parked in the forecourt. On inquiring, I was told that the Defence Minister, the Chief and the DIB were all sitting around the sickbed. So much for doctor's orders!

I was about to leave when Thapar came out of the house and, catching sight of me, handed me a draft signal to HQ IV Corps to be despatched at the highest priority. He said that the Divisional and Brigade Commanders at Namka-chu 'appeared to be in a panic', so the Corps Commander had made some suggestions. I read the draft; as far as I recollect, it was a hotch-potch of instructions to move companies and platoons to Tsangle and other locations, and advice on how to fight a brigade battle in Namka-chu valley. It was another embittering anti-climax; by then I should have grown accustomed to them.

Perhaps it was the strain I was under that gave me the courage to force my views on the Army Chief. I told him firmly that the most important requirement at that time was to order a pull-back from the riverline to Tsangdhar and Hathung-la. I explained that this would not constitute a withdrawal in the military sense of the term, only a redisposition of defences from an untactical to a tactical deployment. I told Thapar that according to Kaul the riverline was at the bottom of a narrow valley, overlooked by Chinese positions on Thag-la ridge; furthermore, our positions lacked depth. Now that the Chinese were building up for an attack, the brigade should be allowed to redispose its defences tactically, in depth, and on ground of its own choosing.

Even as I spoke I could sense Thapar's growing irritation. Before I was to told to shut up I hastily added that it was also necessary for him to appoint a new Corps Commander without delay. In normal circumstances command of the corps would devolve on Niranjan Prasad, but he was still up forward with 7 Infantry Brigade and could not possibly be expected to take command of IV Corps during Kaul's illness. The alternative, I added, would be to direct GOC-in-C Eastern Command to take over the IV Corps temporarily.

'There is no need for that,' said Thapar, taking up my second point first. 'General Kaul will continue in command.'

'What, from his sickbed in Delhi?' I asked, scarcely able to conceal my disbelief. To be fair to him, Thapar himself looked somewhat abashed at what he had just said. He was essentially a fair man and knew that there could be little excuse for such a bizarre parody of military practice. He did not rebuff my unasked for intrusion, not even by gesture; he merely said that the Defence Minister had so ordered.

He walked to his car and got in. I remember making a sign to the driver not to start the car yet. Having sensed a temporary advantage, I asked Thapar if I could modify the signal somewhat to enable at least part of the brigade to pull back to tactical heights, leaving listening posts and patrols on the riverline. Thapar thought about it for a minute and said: 'It's too late. The message has in fact already been sent, informally by telephone, a half-hour ago!'

I did not return to my office, so I did not bother to despatch Thapar's signal that evening; by next morning it was too late.

## NOTES

1. The third brigade of 4 Infantry Division (11 Infantry Brigade) had been loaned to 23 Infantry Division for operations in Nagaland.
2. Till then this region had not been reconnoitered except, perhaps, by the two Royal Engineer officers, Bailey and Morshead, whom Henry McMahon had sent to the north-eastern frontier in 1912 for a reconnaissance (as narrated in Bailey's book *No Passport to Tibet*) and on whose report he had based the drawing of his famous Line on the map.

# 8

# DRAGONNADE AT NAMKA-CHU: 'THE VALLEY OF THE SHADOW OF DEATH'

During my first year as DMO, the government's policy in Ladakh consisted largely of empty defiance, but it would be misleading to suggest that the General Staff was always disregarded or overruled on operational matters. Although the politicians took to long-range bluffing, the army also played a part in the charade, even if not as zealously as the hawks in the ministries. The civilians set the pace but the army went along, beguiled by the conviction that the Chinese would not call our bluff – that is, believing that they would not resort to force of arms. Even if they did, the field commanders and the General Staff possessed reasonably accurate estimates of the army's potential for defence at Leh and Chushul: there would be a setback at the border, but the war would not culminate in national disaster.

The tragedy unfolded differently in NEFA because the roles acted out were different. There the senior commanders were ignorant of both the terrain and logistical difficulties in the forward areas. They could only guess at the operational potential at the crestline of the Himalayas, and their guesses turned out to be wild. There was no Daulet Singh to give us factual and sobering (if at times over-cautious) assessments, and Thorat's solid advice had been replaced by feckless and irresponsible speculation by his successor. Even at Army HQ, the Chief remained largely unaware of operational inhibitions in NEFA and, consequently, was unable to withstand Nehru and Menon's pressures for bellicose action. Inexorably the Indian Army was pushed over the edge to disaster.

The eminence of military leaders derives from professional authority and from their moral courage to uphold it. It is not necessary, even in a democratic system, to subordinate that eminence to blind obedience to politicians. The concept of the supremacy of civilian government does not embrace surrender by the military of its right to dissent. A military mind must develop the art of prevailing; but if it cannot prevail, it must not abdicate from its professional position. Furthermore, even when the government's decisions stand firm, if those decisions have not been made collectively by the cabinet but at the whim of individuals, a statutory alternative to abject compliance is always open to a service Chief – if he feels strongly enough. Thapar seemed to lack the will to contemplate that choice; he allowed himself to be browbeaten into a war he didn't foresee and was powerless to wage. Even Bijji Kaul, with all his seeming self-assurance, did not succeed in upholding his own conviction on any major issue, either as CGS or as Corps Commander, against the government's wishes. He too allowed himself to be caught up in the drift toward disaster. Neither possessed the resolve to resign his post while such a display of protest might still have acted as a check on government obduracy.

The standing of the military in India reached an all-time low during Krishna Menon's tenure as Defence Minister, but nothing that Menon did to undermine the prestige of the generals served that purpose as effectively as their own failure to resist political pressure and uphold military precepts. Nor did the stature of the generals grow as the debacle in NEFA gradually unfolded. In time of war soldiers gain political and moral strength from the tendency of civilians to be deferential before the brisk military figure. There was no sign of that in the weeks that followed the

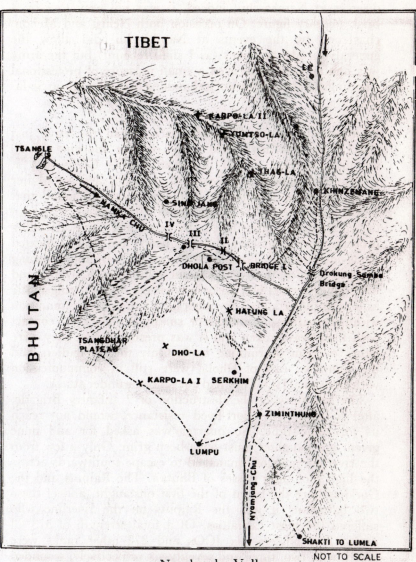

TIBET

LE

KARPO-LA II

YUMTSO-LA

TSANGLE

THAG-LA

KINNZEMANG

SINGJANG

NAMKA CHU

IV
III
II

DHOLA POST
BRIDGE I

Drokung-Samba
Bridge

HATUNG LA

TSANGDHAR
PLATEAU

DHO-LA

KARPO-LA I
SERKHIM

ZIMINTHUNG

LUMPU

Nyamjang-Chu

SHAKTI TO LUMLA

NOT TO SCALE

Namka-chu Valley

disaster at Namka-chu; indeed, it was not easy to espy a brisk military figure. On occasion both Nehru and Menon, chastened by the events at Namka-chu, did allow the generals to take decisions (as I shall recount) but the army was unable to retrieve even a small measure of professional standing after the manner of its handling of the debacle at Se-la.

First reports of the Chinese attack began to arrive just after I reached my office early on the morning of 20 October, but for several hours afterwards Corps HQ at Tezpur was unable to give us a coherent account. Later in the morning I called at Mullik's office and found that it was better served with information than mine. His man in Zimithang, unburdened by encoding and decoding procedures, was quicker with the news, and he was located alongside Niranjan Prasad's Advance HQ. By mid-morning we had learned that the posts in Khinzemane, Dhola and Tsangdhar sectors had all been silenced, after offering battle as best as they could. They must have run out of ammunition within a matter of an hour or so. By 8 o'clock all contact with them was broken and it was presumed that they were either overrun or running back. Only the Grenadiers and the Punjabis, east of Dhola, were still in communication with Divisional HQ. They had not yet come under attack.

The full story of the destruction of 7 Infantry Brigade, after a heroic but short-lived resistance, would not reach us for some time. No quarter was asked for and none given; the slaughter must have been grim. Only a few from the riverline positions managed to escape southwards across the high mountain passes of Bhutan. The Rajputs and the Gorkhas bore the brunt of the first onslaught, and of these two battalions it was the Rajputs on the riverline who suffered the most casualties. Of a total strength of 513 all ranks, four officers, six JCOs and 272 other ranks were killed, with two, three and seventy-six respectively, wounded and three, two and eighty-five captured. Only one officer and sixty other ranks (mostly from rear parties) managed to escape.

Niranjan Prasad decided to remain at Zimithang that night. This was what any conscientious commander would have done; but it caused me some concern. In my opinion, once the Chinese attack had started, the Divisional Commander should have made straight back for Towang — if not even further to the rear — in order to co-ordinate and conduct the defence of Kameng, his main responsibility. Furthermore, despite the fact that Sir Oracle had announced that battle-command could best be exercised from a sickbed in Delhi, I was sure that military commonsense would soon prevail, in which case Niranjan would probably be appointed officiating Corps Commander (which is what happened, although unceremoniously and too late). What I did not know then was that Niranjan was blissfully unaware that his Corps Commander had even been evacuated. The staff at Corps HQ, either at their own initiative or under orders from above, had kept the Divisional Commander in the dark about Kaul's illness and evacuation to Delhi. When the disaster at Namka-chu became known, command of the corps was hastily and gracelessly dumped on Niranjan Prasad while he was still at Zimithang, where it was impossible for him to exercise that command because of his total lack of staff and communication facilities.

My concern deepened as we received news that the Chinese had either launched attacks or were massing forces all along our Himalayan frontier, from Kibithu in NEFA (near the Indo-Burma border) to the Chip Chap river in Ladakh. It was obvious that they had mounted a major offensive and I felt certain that a concerted attack on Towang would not be long deferred.

My views on the tactical unimportance of Towang had not changed. There was only one battalion (1 Sikh) left for the defence of that whole salient, with another (4 Garhwal) arriving piecemeal. I was convinced that the township and its defences would be by-passed by the enemy after they captured Bum-la; if they did that, our troops at Towang would be caught in a trap. To prevent this Niranjan Prasad needed to withdraw his forces from Towang at his discretion. Should the irresolution of the Namka-chu episode be repeated here, the enemy would find himself on an open road to the Brahmaputra plains.

I had intended to confront Jogi Dhillon and ask to be allowed to convey these views to the Chief, but he was away from the office during most of the afternoon and messages were coming in so thick and fast in the Ops Room that I did not get an opportunity to see him. By the evening we knew that the Namka-chu line had been overrun. Remnants of the Rajputs, 1/9 Gorkhas and Brigade HQ were escaping to the mountains behind. In the eastern half of the line 9 Punjab and 4 Grenadiers, still not under attack, were ordered by Niranjan to pull back to the high ground of Hathung-la ridge and to defend the approaches to Zimithang and Lumpu respectively (although by the time they complied with that order it was already too late; the Chinese had by-passed them and got there first).

On my own initiative I rang up HQ 17 Indian Division at Ambala and ordered the immediate move of 48 Infantry Brigade to Misamari, to pass under command of HQ IV Corps. I also rang up the Secretary to the Border Roads Development Board, obtained his approval to place all the Board's resources under the army's command and so informed HQ IV Corps. One other thing I did was to leave a message at the office of the Deputy Air Chief, Arjun Singh, asking him whether he would consider sending up an aircraft over the Tsangdhar-Karpo-la mountains at first light next morning to see if it could discern the routes along which our troops were escaping southwards to eastern Bhutan. Arjun, kindly and decisive as always, did just that; even if the aircraft failed to locate any of the fleeing troops, on the ground some of them may have gained heart from seeing evidence of their air force overhead.

On the morning of 21 October Niranjan Prasad at last decided to move back to Towang. By then 7 Infantry Brigade had virtually ceased to exist; even the two battalions on the eastern flank of the Namka-chu line found themselves encircled and cut off. Many were killed in the running battles that ensued. Those who managed to slip out of the noose scattered over the inhospitable ranges of Bhutan Himalay. Thus, the whole of the Nyamjang valley and the western approach to Towang fell under enemy control, presaging a two-pronged attack on Towang within a day or two. It was high time that the Divisional Commander took control at Towang.

With Niranjan was Brigadier Kalyan Singh, Commander

of the Artillery Brigade of 4th Division, who had been appointed commander of Towang Brigade. (He had gone forward on 19 October to consult his divisional commander and been caught up in the fighting.) Since the laborious plod from Zimithang to Towang would take the best part of two days, this meant that the acting Corps Commander, the GOC 4 Infantry Division and the local Brigade Commander would all be temporarily *hors de combat* and out of communication with everyone till they reached Towang. There would be no one available to co-ordinate the defence of Kameng during the next two crucial days.

I went in search of Jogi again and finally ran him to earth in Joint Secretary John Lall's office in the Defence Ministry. He was clearly pleased to see me, I noted with some pleasure. Walking back with him I unburdened my many concerns, stressing the fact that for the time being there was no one between Lucknow and the battlefields of NEFA to take charge of operations against the enemy. I expressed the hope that Thapar could be persuaded to order Bogey Sen to move to Tezpur and assume temporary command of IV Corps till Niranjan resurfaced. Jogi, in a receptive and co-operative frame of mind, readily fell in with my suggestion. He said he would see Thapar immediately.

I had instructed the duty officer in the Ops Room to maintain hourly contact with Tezpur. I do not remember the exact sequence of events, but I think it was on the morning of 22 October that I was shown a signal message from IV Corps, issuing orders for the despatch of all newly arriving battalions of 62 and 48 Infantry Brigades to Towang. I had to move quickly to have this countermanded because, besides ending in possible disaster, these moves would only clog up the road forward of Dhirang and further aggravate logistical holdups. Again I went to Jogi. I expounded my tactical views, stressed that Towang was not a sound defensive locality and suggested that we withdraw our fores to prepare new defences on Se-la. He accepted my arguments but when I suggested that we see Thapar together he said that these was no need for both of us to go; he would see to it himself. Although I knew that he would not be able to put the case to Thapar as authoritatively, I could not budge him from that position.

After leaving the office that evening I went to Bijji's house for a friendly visit, but was again unable to see him because, as on the previous occasion, I found a galaxy of VIPs around his bed when I peeped into his room. Thapar, Menon, Mullik and Sarin were sitting around in funereal silence. I discreetly withdrew and waited outside, in my car. After a while Thapar came out, caught sight of me and walked over to my car. He looked careworn and depressed. I asked after the Corps Commander but he appeared not to have heard me. Instead he mused, almost in soliloquy, that there were problems regarding command arrangements for NEFA. Apparently Menon and Sarin still held different views from him. Krishna Menon, he said, wanted Kaul to remain in command because he did not wish to add to the latter's embarassments at a time when some newspaper reports had insinuated that the Corps Commander was feigning illness in order to avoid having to return to the front. Thapar said that Kaul himself had reacted strongly against the suggestion of a replacement, even as a temporary measure, confident that he could continue to command IV Corps from Delhi.

I must have appeared open-mouthed with amazement. The Chinese had resorted to armed action and in the middle of a crucial battle here was the high command ordaining that a desperately ill man conduct the war from his sickbed a thousand miles away! Before I could think of an appropriate comment, Thapar went on to say that in his opinion Bogey Sen should hold the fort for Kaul till the latter recovered sufficiently to report back for duty. I ventured to dissent: Sen was not the right man to command the Kameng battle. He had never seen the ground and, I added in the mildest phrases I could muster, his judgment of the operational potential on the Namka-chu had proved dangerously unsound. Sen, I suggested, should be allowed to take control only till Niranjan Prasad reached Towang. Thereafter, Niranjan should assume responsibility for the defence of Kameng as acting GOC IV Corps, without interference from either Bijji Kaul or Bogey Sen.

Thapar made no response; there was a glazed look in his eyes as he got into his car and was driven away. It suddenly struck me that perhaps Jogi had not been able to persuade him about my views on Towang. On an impulse I went back to South Block and to Jogi's office, to find out − which was just as well because, as I had feared, he had indeed been unsuccessful in persuading Thapar to permit a withdrawal from Towang. Thapar had argued that the government would never countenance the abandonment of such an important administrative and religious centre as Towang.

I told Jogi firmly that we would have to persuade Thapar. The defence of Kameng Frontier Division, and perhaps of northern Assam, depended on this crucial decision being taken in time. If he did not wish to pursue the case, I would go to Thapar's residence myself and put the case to him again. I fully expected Jogi to blow up at this, but he did not. Instead, to my surprise, he said that that might be a good idea and that he would accompany me.

Thapar was about to go in to dinner when we arrived, but he straightaway led us into his study. I had taken a map of Towang with me and on it I explained in detail, and as forcefully as I could, my views on its tactical drawbacks. I said that to continue to hold it could lead to the annihilation or capture of the only troops then available for the defence of Kameng. I urged Thapar to take the decision, then and there, to allow a withdrawal to Se-la so that the troops would have a chance to prepare a defensive position before they were attacked, but the most I could get him to agree to was to 'think it over' and to consult the Defence Minister the next morning.

Early on the morning of 23 October Thapar rang me up from his residence to say that he was meeting the Prime Minister in Menon's office at 10 o'clock, to discuss Towang, and he wanted me to be present at the meeting. I hurriedly prepared a written analysis of the tactical alternatives, in case the PM or the Defence Minister asked for it, collected my map and presented myself at Menon's office to await the Chief.

When we went in we found Nehru seated at the head of the table, Menon on his right and beyond him, Desai the Foreign Secretary. Nehru indicated that Thapar should sit on his left with me beside Thapar. However, before I could sit down Thapar told the PM that his DMO had some important points to make on the Kameng situation, explaining that I had previously held brigade command in the Towang area and was well acquainted with the terrain.

The PM looked pale and subdued. He motioned to me to bring the map to him. I unrolled it, placed it before him and began to describe the tactical environments of Towang, in particular pointing out the tracks from Bum-la that by-passed Towang.

'What is it you wish to convey?' Nehru asked, looking up at me.

'Towang is not a suitable area in which to site the main defences,' I answered. 'The Chinese could entrap the garrison and move into central Kameng without attacking Towang. What the army desires is permission to withdraw from the Towang salient and to hold a defensive position further back, because if we continue to hold on to Towang with the only troops we have available, the Chinese would before long be making for the Brahmaputra plains via the undefended Manda-la.' I stressed that the decision to evacuate Towang needed to be taken without delay.

It took the PM only a moment to make up his mind. As I recorded at the time (I quote from my *Summary*):

When the Prime Minister had been briefed on the situation in Towang, he unhesitatingly left the decision to his Army Chief. 'It is a matter now for the military to decide – where and how they should fight,' he said. 'I have no doubt in my mind that what we lose, you shall eventually win back for us. I cannot lay down conditions about Towang or any other place on grounds other than military.'

Inwardly I heaved a sigh of relief, and I expect Thapar did the same, at this spontaneous and generous response from the PM. I had come determined, if necessary, to argue the case – not an enviable prospect when confronting a giant personality like Nehru – but for once the PM had seemed trustful of the military and took a decision based on a professional evaluation rather than the shibboleths of the times.

Menon sat through the meeting with a half-scowl on his countenance; his gloom must have related to some other cause because he had not displayed any interest in the proceedings. Fearing that the Foreign Secretary might raise some political objection, I quickly rolled up the map, clicked my heels at the PM and, without waiting for permission, left the meeting. Proceeding directly to the Ops Room, I instructed the duty officer to get through to Lucknow and Tezpur on the telephone and issue orders, later to be confirmed by signal, to stop all forward moves of units of 62 and 48 Infantry Brigades beyond Dhirang. I would have liked to add that Towang was to be evacuated and a defensive position prepared on Se-la top, but that order would best be given personally by Thapar to Sen. I had begun to draft a message to this effect for the Chief's approval when his MA rang me up on the in-house telephone to say that the Chief wanted to see me immediately.

Thapar greeted me with a smile, a rare enough indulgence those days.

'Well done, Monty,' he said, 'you handled that well.' The approbation was spontaneous and warm, and the use of the nickname after a gap of years was like the bestowal of an accolade.

I showed him the draft signal to Eastern Command about the occupation of a defensive position at Se-la. He read through it, thought for a moment and then said, more decisive than I had ever known him, that it would be best if he went to Tezpur in person to issue the necessary orders. I said that that was an excellent idea.

'I want you to come with me,' he added. 'You are the only one who knows the terrain. I will inform the DCGS; you go ahead and make arrangements for our flight.'

I realised that I was back in business.

After making arrangements for the journey I called a conference of MO and QMG (Ops) staff to alert them on priorities for the stocking of Se-la. Fortunately the officiating Master General of Ordnance, Major General A.C. Iyappa, whom I had invited to sit in at my conference, agreed to attend. A helpful, practical and no-nonsense general officer, A.C.I. was the ablest and most accommodating among the PSOs at Army HQ and I did well to get him to sit in with us. I told them about the proposal to pull out from Towang and establish a new defensive position on Se-la consisting of four or five battalions supported by a field regiment. I said that road and air transport would be used on top priority to stock the new defences with ammunition and supplies for fourteen days; loads were to be ready for despatch within twenty-four hours. I read out a list of items required and the quantities needed, and I asked my staff to add to it after they had had time to consider the problem in greater detail. A.C.I. readily agreed to keep in touch with MO staff in my absence and to do everything in his power to collect the requirements and expedite the stocking. (I had taken the precaution to enlist his help because I planned, if necessary, to stay on at Tezpur for a day or two in order to hasten procedures at HQ IV Corps and I needed the MGO's 'weight' at this end to ensure a rapid build-up of stocks at Se-la.)

I informed Jogi of the steps I had taken and asked him to keep an eye on airlift priorities for the stocking programme. He agreed and at once walked over to MO Directorate to discuss figures with my staff. When I was on my way out, he walked down the back stairs with me to the canteen gate to see me off. His manner was friendly and supportive; he said that he was very glad Thapar was taking me with him, and wished me luck. Then he told me about Bogey Sen's move to sack the Divisional Commander.

'Sen telephoned the Chief a few minutes ago to tell him that Niranjan Prasad had run away from the front and that he had lost all confidence in him,' Jogi said. 'He wants Niranjan replaced. I think this is grossly unfair and a calumny, because Niranjan obviously had no option but to withdraw from Zimithang. He saw 7 Brigade disintegrate in front of him, and he has now to command both the division and the corps in the battle for Towang. What else could he do? He *had* to come back to take command of the rest of his division. It is most unfair to sack him for that, but I know that the Chief is carrying the name of his replacement – Anant Pathania – with him in his pocket. He wishes to discuss this with Sen before finally issuing orders. You are not supposed to know this officially, so you can't speak to the Chief, but perhaps you could have a word with Bogey Sen. He should at least give Niranjan a hearing before sacking him.'

I was appalled to hear that Bogey Sen had so precipitately

demanded to be rid of Niranjan Prasad. Not only did I know the latter to be a stout-hearted and level-headed soldier, his dismissal would mean that both IV Corps and 4th Division would be left without a commander acquainted with the topography of the battle zone, and that would leave Bogey Sen in control of operations. From what I had seen of his performance in the past few weeks, the result could only be further disaster. I told Jogi as much.

'If Bogey is left in command of the battle,' Jogi said, 'I suggest that you persuade the Chief to let you remain behind as his personal representative. I will handle things this end for you – you need not worry; but you must ensure that there is no bungling about the tactical and logistical build-up at Se-la.'

As I was getting into the waiting staff car he shook my hand and wished me luck. 'A lot will depend on you now, Monty,' were his parting words. He was convincingly sincere and straightforward and I warmed to him; clearly the crisis had served to smother his need for self-projection.

I went home to collect the grip my wife had packed for me, then walked to the Chief's residence. On the way to the airport Thapar informed me that he had invited Mullik to accompany him to Tezpur, a prospect I did not particularly welcome. Knowing the latter's views about defending 'every inch of the motherland', I feared that he might set about dissuading Thapar from his resolve to withdraw from Towang. Fortunately, when we boarded the plane Thapar asked me to sit beside him to discuss some General Staff points. I took care to prolong the discussion till we were nearing Tezpur, so that Mullik had no chance to get at the Chief.

Thapar sought my views on his proposal to reorganise command arrangements in NEFA. He wanted to allot separate brigades to Walong, Siang and Subansiri Frontier Divisions and, to ease the load on a newly raised HQ IV Corps, raise a new divisional HQ under IV Corps to command the eastern NEFA brigades. I told him that it had always been our plan to use the division in Nagaland as a reserve in case of war in the north and suggested that we take a risk with the Nagas and move HQ 23 Division to NEFA, leaving an *ad hoc* HQ in Kohima under a major general. He agreed and said he would issue orders after consultation with the Army Commander in Tezpur.

When I told Thapar about the procedures I had set in motion to expedite the stocking of Se-la, he was displeased and remarked that I should rightly have waited till he had discussed the matter with the GOC-in-C and obtained his approval. I replied that I could always change the site for the stocking operation, but since it would take twenty-four or forty-eight hours to get things moving I had initiated staff procedures in anticipation of approval. It would take seven to ten days for the stocking to be completed and we might not have that long before the Chinese followed up from Towang. I quickly went on to impress upon him the strategic importance of the pass; there was no alternative to Se-la. I added that he must not leave the final choice to a GOC-in-C who was not really acquainted with the geography of Kameng. I pointed out on the map that Se-la controlled all movement from Towang to central Kameng. Only small bodies of troops could by-pass it (to the east, by the high and difficult Mago route) whereas if we withdrew east of Se-la we would have to organise two widely dispersed defensive positions: one at Manda-la, to cover the old bridle trade-route from Towang to Udalgiri, and one at Bomdila, to cover the motor road to Tezpur. This would weaken our forces, whereas a single defensive position in the Se-la-Senge area would not only guard both routes but also constitute a sufficient barrier to any foreseeable Chinese offensive. Thapar had himself journeyed over the pass. I recalled for him some of its numerous natural advantages: extensive dropping zones on Se-la top, with clear run-ins for aircraft; availability of fresh water from the two lakes just west of the top of the pass, and several delaying positions on the long approach from Jang. From memory I drew a rough enlargement of the Jang-Se-la-Senge area and left it with him to brood over.

At Tezpur we were met by the GOC-in-C, Bogey Sen, who had been directed by the Chief the day before to proceed to Tezpur to assume temporary command of IV Corps. He informed us that he had paid an overnight visit to Towang the previous day, whereupon Mullik questioned him about the strength of its defences. Sen replied that in his opinion Towang's defences were adequate to hold out against an attack, but the Divisional Commander, he added, had thought otherwise and had decided to withdraw his forces to a more suitable defensive position in the rear. Sen said that he had not interfered with the Divisional Commander's plans because by then Bum-la was under attack and the battle for Towang had virtually started. Mullik was dismayed by this news but before he could begin an argument, I unobtrusively pulled him to one side and whispered that the Prime Minister had agreed to a withdrawal from Towang should the military so decide. He looked dispirited but forbore from joining issue in the matter.

We travelled in different vehicles for the journey to Corps HQ. I went with Sen's BGS, Krishen Sibal, and took the opportunity to discuss Bogey Sen's proposal to sack Niranjan Prasad. (Sibal belonged to the same regiment as Niranjan and I knew that they were close friends.) I told him that the Army Commander was being unnecessarily hasty about sacking Niranjan. I argued that he owed Niranjan a fair hearing on the Namka-chu and Khinzemane battles before making a decision. Sibal said that Sen was quite convinced that Niranjan had 'lost his nerve' and was determined to replace him, but he undertook to have a go at dissuading him. What he did not tell me was that he and Sen had met Niranjan that morning in Towang in circumstances not entirely creditable to the Army Commander. Sen, I was later told by others who had been present, had only fortuitously landed in Towang and then been held up there. Dismayed by this contretemps, he had not left the vicinity of the helipad nor visited the defences of Towang. As a consequence of his apparent lack of interest, there had been a heated exchange between him and Niranjan. The opinion Sen had expressed in answer to Mullik's question was thus an uncalled for dissemblance which, fortunately, had failed to convince the Chief.

Arrived at HQ IV Corps Thapar asked to be taken to the Ops Room to be briefed on operational plans. Sen searched for a face among the Corps staff that might indicate a willingness to take on the job. As no one volunteered he was obliged to conduct the business himself, but it soon became obvious that he was familiar neither with the terrain nor with IV Corps' operational plans. His depiction of the threats to Towang and Bomdila was perfunctory and misleading, but it was when he started on future courses of action that I could no longer contain myself. Bogey Sen, waving the pointer staff vaguely over the sand model, said that he had directed 4 Infantry Division 'to hold the line of defence Jang-Dhirang-Bomdila'.

I interrupted to protest that what he had just described was not a line of defence but a line of withdrawal. Going up to the sand model I delineated the road from Towang to the Assam plains. On it, successively in depth, lay Jang, Dhirang and Bomdila. I forbore from stressing the obvious; instead I pointed out that Se-la was the only geographical feature between Towang and Bomdila that could constitute a defensive locality. I described in some detail the environment of the pass. I knew the terrain, I said, because I had walked all over it before motor roads ever came to Kameng. I described the main tracks over and around Se-la top, not all of which were correctly marked on the IV Corps sand model.

I could sense hostility from the Corps staff, resenting outside interference on tactical matters, but Thapar gave me a look of encouragement and so also, surprisingly, did Sen. He seemed almost relieved that I had taken over. I pressed home the advantage. As the *Summary* records:

I strongly advocated holding the Se-la massif. I suggested that a brigade sector, later to be built up to two brigades, be established forthwith at Se-la-Senge. As more troops arrived and logistics permitted, a brigade sector could also be established at Bomdila to guard the approach from the north via the Lap valley and Poshing-la. . . . After some discussion on the map, COAS and GOC-in-C agreed to my recommendations and the latter telephoned GOC 4 Division, who had reached Dhirang by then, and ordered him to return to Se-la and organise a defensive position on that feature. The COAS desired that I go up to Se-la next morning and, because of my intimate knowledge of the terrain, advise the GOC regarding the lay out of the defences. The GOC-in-C Eastern Command readily agreed to this suggestion.

Night falls early in those eastern longitudes. When we had finished our discussion in the Ops Room it was only

late afternoon but already quite dark. Although Thapar
was anxious to leave early for Delhi, I found an opportunity
to speak with him alone and urged him to hold another
discussion with the Army Commander about plans for the
proper deployment of reinforcements as and when we sent
them. I said that neither the Army Commander nor his
staff officer appeared knowledgeable about operational
matters in NEFA, and the corps staff were new to their
jobs. It would be wise for us, I added, to hold a full
operational discussion in order to put the GOC-in-C in the
picture regarding Army HQ policy on reserves and
reinforcements for NEFA. Thapar was persuaded, and after
a hurried cup of tea back we went to the Ops Room.
Thapar let me conduct the briefing. I recorded in the *Summary:*

The COAS had a long discussion with the GOC-in-C about
further reinforcements for Eastern Command. . . . The only
reserves available' to Army Headquarters were 50 Para Brigade
and 65 Infantry Brigade Group in Secunderabad, the latter newly
raised and not yet complete [it had only two battalions]. I
advised against the premature commitment of 50 Para Brigade,
because of its potential para role, to which the COAS agreed.

I also advised that if a risk could be accepted against Pakistan
in the Punjab, 17 Division in Ambala, less one brigade, could
be regarded as an Army Headquarters reserve for commitment
in Eastern Command, leaving behind one brigade in Ambala.
As for 23 Infantry Division, it had always been our plan that
this Division or parts of it would be available to Headquarters
Eastern Command as a reserve division in case of operations
against the Chinese.

The COAS had already accepted these recommendations. Prior
to the commencement of hostilities 62 Brigade (from Ramgarh)
had been sent to reinforce 4 Infantry Division; and 65 Infantry
Brigade had been moved north to be readily available in case
of hostilities. . . .

The various threats that arose in Eastern Command were
considered:
(a) Threat of the Siliguri corridor being cut by a thrust from
the Chumbi Valley through Sikkim or Bhutan;
(b) Threat of an attack from Towang area, through East Bhutan
to the plains (Daranga area);
(c) The threat to Bomdila and eastern Kameng;
(d) The threat to Walong and an encircling move to
Hayuliang-Lohitpur;

(e) A minor threat in Central NEFA.

The GOC-in-C Eastern Command was unwilling to move any troops out of Nagaland, but the COAS decided that the time had come to relax the intensification of operations against the Nagas and spare some of 23rd Division's forces to reinforce the Chinese-front. As far as I recollect, he took the following provisional decisions:

(a) Move of one brigade from 17 Division to the Siliguri area to be followed by the rest of the Division;

(b) Move of one brigade from Nagaland to the Daranga area (south of east Bhutan);

(c) Move of one brigade from Nagaland as Corps reserve to Tezpur area;

(d) Move of HQ 11 Brigade from Manipur to the Walong area, where it would relieve 5 Brigade, which could then confine its responsibility to Central NEFA;

(e) Set up a new divisional headquarters in the Digboi-Tinsukhia area to control central and eastern NEFA;

(f) Move of an AMX (light tank) regiment to IV Corps and a Sherman (medium tank) regiment to Siliguri corridor area.

The COAS directed me to issue a signal immediately on his behalf to move one brigade group from 17 Division to Siliguri area. Action on the remainder was to be taken upon his return to Army Headquarters. . . .

Although I had not intended to stage-manage this operational discussion, a considerable side benefit from it was that I was able to obtain the Chief's decisions on a number of operational points which I had not had the opportunity of discussing with him before. In Delhi it was not always easy to get a conclusive resolve from Thapar. By nature he was not at his best in the ambience of office or meetings, never really secure. It was my experience that his decisiveness increased in direct proportion to his distance from Delhi. In bureaucratic precincts, sandwiched between Menon as Defence Minister and Kaul as subordinate, it took time and effort for him to leap the psychological hurdle to decision.

After the Sing Jang fiasco earlier in October, when I first began to be apprehensive of a possible Chinese reprisal, we in MO had made tentative plans for the security of the Siliguri corridor, the narrow neck of territory between Tibet and East Pakistan, because we discerned a likely threat of a southward thrust from the Chumbi valley to sever the land link between Assam and the rest of India. A second possible target was the north Brahmaputra plains near Tezpur. Nowhere else did the Chinese possess the logistical capability for a strategic move into the Indian plains. To safeguard against these threats MO Directorate had calculated that we would need about a division in each area, each supported by an armoured regiment. One of these required divisions was available in Nagaland, the other would have to come from the order-of-battle of Western Command – that is, from the forces earmarked for the western border with Pakistan. We had provisionally planned to switch 17 Infantry Division (Western Command reserve) to the eastern front.

The Army Chief had the constitutional right to order the move of the rest of the division but it was improbable that Thapar would take this decision without seeking the approval of the Minister – and that was most unlikely to succeed because one of Krishna Menon's pet theories was that the only threat to India was from Pakistan. It was almost an article of faith with him that China would never go to war with India and, clearly, he had influenced Nehru to a like conviction.[1] For these reasons I felt pleased with myself for having dragged the Chief to the Corps Ops Room for an operational review. In order to ensure that follow-through actions were taken at Army HQ, I drew up a rough *aide memoire* in pencil for him to take back to Delhi.

I stayed behind at Corps HQ when the Chief and the DIB left for Delhi late that night. Early in the morning of 24 October I accompanied the local Air Force Commander in a helicopter reconnaissance flight over the Senge-Se-la area and pointed out to him the likely dropping zones, particularly the long spur of Senge, an area less prone to weather interference than Se-la top. When we returned to Corps HQ, I was informed that Major General Anant Singh Pathania, MVC, MC, till then Director of the National Cadet Corps, had arrived at Tezpur and had already left by road for Dhirang to take over command of 4th Division from Niranjan Prasad. I also learned that Major General Harbaksh Singh VrC had been appointed officiating GOC IV Corps in Kaul's place and would be arriving soon.

That day I made a second helicopter trip to Dhirang with Harbaksh. Major General Mohinder Pathania, an old friend from the Baluch Regiment (and a cousin of Anant Pathania) happened to be in Corps HQ and temporarily at a loose end. He asked if he could accompany me to Se-la and I gladly agreed.

At Dhirang, Niranjan and Anant met us at the helipad, the former dispirited and obviously in ill humour. On the way to the Border Roads mess where we were to stay, I had a brief talk alone with Niranjan. He complained bitterly about Bogey Sen's ineptitude and indecision at Towang the previous day. He said that he had clearly told Sen of his intention to pull back to Se-la, yet later in the day Sen had ordered all troops and Border Roads personnel to withdraw to Bomdila. Niranjan added that he had to countermand these orders on his own responsibility. He turned everyone around and sent them back again to Se-la, which in his opinion was the only suitable location for divisional defences — a decision he had arrived at independently. I was a little surprised to hear about the orders regarding Bomdila; nothing in what Bogey told me indicated that he had ordered 4th Division to fall back on Bomdila. I wondered if someone at Corps HQ had, consciously or otherwise, meddled with the GOC-in-C's verbal directives. The incident remained a mystery that was to have a bearing on the eventual fate of Se-la.

There has been so much uninformed comment and afterthought regarding the choice of Se-la as a defensive position that I digress briefly from the narrative in order to clarify doubts that may still exist.

The staff at HQ IV Corps preferred Bomdila as the divisional defence locality on the grounds that it was 'the farthest point to the north where the Indians could have built up more quickly than the Chinese' (as Neville Maxwell writes in his book *India's China War*). Presumably influenced by opinion at Corps HQ, Maxwell goes on to comment, 'the DMO Brigadier Palit (who had commanded 7 Brigade in NEFA) was urging . . . to hold Se-la. . . . That view, urged by the forceful and articulate Palit, was disastrous . . . a trap for the Indians. Se-la was too far from the plains to be quickly built up as the main defence position.' The

Corps evaluation, however, was bad strategy and faulty judgment: if Bomdila had been chosen as the defensive position the Manda-la route would have been left unguarded and the Chinese could have used that track to reach the north Assam plains without having to fire a shot. (The centuries-old caravan route from central Tibet passed through Towang, Dhirang, over the 2,900 metre Manda-la, to Udalguri in Assam.)

Additionally, in the event, using both road and airlifts, Se-la was in fact made ready for battle before the Chinese could build up for an attack. Bomdila would have taken longer to prepare logistically because there was no dropping zone nearer than Tenga valley, and although that was only a 25-km haul from Bomdila, the state of the road and the shortage of trucks would have prevented an adequate stocking programme relying solely on surface transport.

Lastly, the implication that we lost the battle for Se-la because its logistical preparation was inadequate is, of course, totally misleading. The stark truth is that the defences were never tested: a battle for the pass was never fought. In the event, the men of the reconstructed 4th Division abandoned their positions and fled well before a Chinese offensive was launched.

Se-la was the unhesitating choice of the only two local commanders who had had an opportunity to tramp over the ground: Niranjan Prasad and myself. Not only that; after the war, when a deliberate defensive position for 5 Mountain Division had to be reconnoitred and selected, Se-la was again the final choice for a IV Corps bastion in western NEFA, as, indeed, it is to this day.

Harbaksh held an operational discussion with Niranjan and Anant (at which, it was made clear, I was not welcome). Mohinder and I spent the evening speaking to stragglers from Towang who had taken refuge at the camp. Some belonged to the Sikh company that had defended Bum-la and from their account it appeared that they had offered strong resistance and the Chinese had suffered considerable casualties at that battle. Most of them had brought their weapons back with them.

Next morning, 25 October, Harbaksh and Anant went by helicopter to Se-la while Mohinder and I drove up in a jeep, climbing some 2,000 metres to the pass. After we met up with the others I spent the day indicating landmarks, tracks and other ground features to the new Corps and Divisional Commanders. I recorded in the *Summary*:

The situation on the Se-la front had considerably stabilised. On the previous day, HQ 4 Artillery Brigade had established a 'rallying point' at Jang, where gradually, the Towang garrison began to concentrate. By the evening of 24 October, 1 Sikh and 4 Garhwal, with six mountain guns and four heavy mortars, had come through – though the field guns, some vehicles and nearly all heavy baggage had had to be left behind in Towang.

Jang was shelled by mortar fire in the evening and Commander 4 Artillery Brigade decided to withdraw to Se-la. This move took place on the night 24/25 October.

When we reached Se-la on the morning of 25 October, 1 Sikh had reorganised on Se-la top, and were starting to build their defences. A battalion of Sikh LI was also in the process of arriving (from Tezpur). Headquarters 62 Brigade had arrived and was in the process of taking over command from Headquarters 4 Artillery Brigade. . . .

4 Garhwal had left behind much heavy equipment, including four mortars, at Jang. They were still acting as rearguard and had established a post just south of Nuranang, a little more than half-way down the Se-la gorge towards Jang.

I conferred with GOC 4 Division and pointed out the features on the ground and map. I also advised him that as contact with the enemy had been broken because of a premature withdrawal from Jang, the first task should be to send forward patrols to re-establish contact – otherwise his only source of intelligence would be denied. GOC 4th Division did not agree; he felt that he could not spare any troops other than 4 Garhwal; and they, he said, were not in a fit condition to undertake the task.

I countered that the Chinese could not have reached Jang in strength by that time . . . I took an escort from 4 Garhwal and (accompanied by Anant Pathania and the Commanding Officer of the battalion) went forward towards Jang. From a vantage point about 2,000 feet above Jang village (the latter was not visible) we could observe most of the road from Towang to Jang. There was no sign of movement or Chinese build-up.

The GOC thereupon ordered the Commanding Officer of 4 Garhwal to send a strong patrol to Jang that night to re-establish contact with the enemy and to retrieve his mortars. (This operation, I learnt later, was not entirely successful.)

By the evening of 25 October, the preparation of Se-la defences was well under way and air-drops on Senge had already started. However, there were numerous logistical problems still to be solved, such as shortage of one-ton vehicles, maintenance of the road from Senge to Se-la and others.

The brief winter's day passed quickly as I drove Anant to important landmarks surrounding the pass, pointing out possible enemy approaches and by-passes, but it struck me that I was not succeeding in raising much enthusiasm from him. At the very start I had received the impression that he seemed dispirited and sluggish, as, indeed, the previous quote from my *Summary* suggests. His dejected mood persisted as we continued with our reconnaissance.

Anant Pathania was an officer with a gallant record of service both in the Second World War and in the first Kashmir campaign. Now, at senior age and rank and softened by a cushy job as Director of the National Cadet Corps, he clearly resented the fact that it was his chestful of medal-ribbons that had been the reason for his being catapulted from a comfortable niche in Delhi to a bleak and windswept Himalayan pass to fight a battle under arctic conditions.

Selections for command appointments in NEFA were indeed being made on the basis of past gallantry awards, as I learned on my return to Delhi. Apparently Thapar had been persuaded by naive and half-baked advice that the way to stop the rot in NEFA would be to find battle commanders from among officers holding gallantry awards. Hence the selection of Harbaksh and Pathania; and, in a day or two, a gallant brigadier long past his best years would be uprooted from an undemanding job in Poona and sent across India, up 14,000 feet to Se-la, to replace N.K. Lal in command of 62 Brigade – on the specious rationale that twenty years previously, during the Second World War, he had, as a subedar in the Rajputana Rifles, won the IOM, the IDSM and the French *Croix de Guerre*. Desperation can give birth to crackpot ideas.

In contrast to Anant, Harbaksh Singh was a picture of energy and resolve. He went about his business purposefully, made a wide-casting reconnaissance on his own and, at the end of the day, stoutly proclaimed his confidence in the Se-la position. He felt sure that it would hold out against any attack the Chinese could mount in the near future. A tall, soldierly and inspiring figure, wherever he went the two battalions on the pass (the Sikhs, of which regiment he was Colonel, and the Sikh Light Infantry) greeted him with their traditional rallying cry: *Sat Sri Akal, Naunihal.* His very appearance seemed to straighten their backs, many of which had begun to droop after the rout at Bum-la or the long haul from Tezpur. I recall talking to the subedar major of the Sikh LI after a visit by Harbaksh. The battalion had just arrived on the 14,000 foot pass from the steamy Assam plains. It was beginning to snow and already turning bitterly cold. The men, many still in summer uniforms, were being issued with entrenching tools and warned that they would have to work through the night because, apart from the urgency of the task, their bedding and blankets would not arrive till the next day. It was not the cheeriest of prospects, but if there was any gloom or despondency, I did not see it. I walked up to the subedar major and offered to have some blankets and great coats sent up from the Engineer encampment in Dhirang. The SM acknowledged my offer with a smile and a salute but turned down the offer. He said that I could send the blankets on the morrow; for the present what he really needed were more picks and shovels. Could I arrange for a truckload of engineering tools to be sent up that night, instead of the blankets?

Dusk was falling when we arrived back at Se-la top, where we met 'Nandi' Lal, the Brigade Commander. After the retreat from Towang he also seemed depressed and despairing. It would be easy to sneer at his mood, but in all truth his predicament at that moment was not an enviable one. He too had only recently been removed from the plains and sent to the high mountain ranges and he was clearly not in the best physical condition. During the retreat from Towang the rate of the Chinese follow-up from Bum-la had dismayed him; he must surely have wondered if the troops and defences on the pass could be made ready before the first onslaught was upon them.

While we were having the inevitable mug of sweet

glutinous beverage the Indian *jawan* concocts from tea leaves and condensed milk, Mohinder Pathania took me aside and said that Anant did not seem at all happy at the prospect of having to live at such an altitude and was considering locating his Divisional HQ in the valley below, at Dhirang. He obviously needed a little morale-boosting, Mohinder added.

We bundled Anant into a jeep and drove downhill to a roadside Engineer camp about two kilometres from Se-la. On the darkening horizon below us we could just discern the silhouette of Senge spur, partly flagged in mist. We were informed that a few sorties of Dakotas had para- and free-dropped their loads, most of which appeared to have been retrieved.

I spoke at length to Anant about the tactical and logistical potential of the Senge-Se-la complex and stressed that the camp we were at was the ideal place for his Divisional HQ. 'You can direct the battle from here as well as keep an eye on the stocking-up process. So long as you remain here, sitting astride this road, no one is going to retreat beyond this point. You establish yourself here, Anant, and we will send you all your requirements,' I assured him. I cautioned him to secure the heights overlooking the passes he held, such as Kya-la and Poshing-la. Although this is standard practice in mountain warfare, I had noticed that Nandi Lal had failed to observe it at Se-la, till I reproached him for his neglect.

We found Anant a suite of rooms in the Engineers' camp and left him there, and that is where I thought his HQ would remain. Neither Corps nor Divisional HQ ever informed Army HQ (as far as I am aware) that after Kaul's return to Tezpur, Anant had pleaded high-altitude headaches and asked for permission to move Divisional HQ down to the Border Roads Camp at Dhirang. Astonishingly, permission was granted, whereupon Anant moved into the comfortable Border Roads camp 20 km away, in the valley below, where he made no attempt to site his HQ tactically. Furthermore, he held back 65 Brigade, earmarked for the main defences at Senge, and located it in Dhirang valley to protect his HQ. Not only was his force thus split in two, one half of it was disposed in a tactically indefensible location (which, at the first sign of battle on 17 November, was hastily abandoned by both commander and troops as they fled helter-skelter southwards over Manda pass).

Mohinder and I flew back to Tezpur with Harbaksh on the morning of 26 October. At the last minute Niranjan reluctantly joined our party; it appeared that Thapar was again visiting Tezpur that day and had especially asked to meet him.

HQ IV Corps was a hum of activity, a marked contrast to the sullen and lethargic setting of two days previously. The newly posted Brigadier in charge of administration had arrived and I was glad to greet him. Inder Verma was an old friend, wise and imperturbable, who would, I felt sure, have a moderating influence on the high-drama atmosphere of Corps HQ. I also met Hoshiar Singh, IOM, IDSM, *Croix de Guerre*, the commander-designate of 62 Brigade on Se-la, who was to take over from Nandi Lal. Thapar's command reshuffles based on the valour-factor were being swiftly implemented, I reflected. However, I was glad to see this experienced soldier, with a reputation as a down-to-earth tactician, heading for the front. As I would have expected, he was cool and unfazed by the sudden change in fortune; but alas, it was last time I was to meet him.

Thapar arrived in the early afternoon. Before he could be whisked away by Bogey Sen, I gave him a brief account of the progress of the defences on Se-la. He was well pleased with my report and felt more reassured about the Kameng front. He then dismayed me with the news that Kaul would, if declared fit by the medical authorities, soon be returning to IV Corps and that the present command arrangement was only a stop-gap. I could not hold back from exclaiming that yet another change in command would have an unsettling effect on the troops on Se-la. I described the stimulating impact that Harbaksh's presence had had on the troops on the pass, but all to little effect. Thapar said that the decision had already been taken and the PM's approval obtained. He implied that he had been overruled on the command arrangement.

When I asked if I could stay on in Tezpur for a day or two, Thapar did not consent; he wanted me to return to Delhi with him that evening. He said that the government had sanctioned the raising of a number of new divisions as well as the import of arms and equipment needed for them; this would require co-ordination by the DMO. Furthermore, the government had asked for a paper on immediate strategic plans to meet the Chinese challenge. This also was to be prepared by the DMO as top priority.

Having an hour or so at my disposal, I sought out Inder Verma and enlisted his help in trying to find out if any information had been received about escapees from the Namka-chu front. My guess was that most of them would come southward to the border hamlet of Bleting, and thence through Tashigong to the Darranga area. As Colonel of the 9th Gorkhas, I was particularly anxious for news of 1/9 GR. The Border Road HQ in Eastern Bhutan, at Dewangiri, had reported the arrival of a few stragglers but no details were available. I requested Inder to keep me posted after my return to Delhi.

Back at my office on 27 October I set about acquainting myself with developments during my absence. There was a message from Jogindar Singh, Chief of Staff at Simla: Daulet Singh and he planned to pay a visit to Army HQ for urgent consultations and would like to be briefed by the DMO on the overall operational picture. As I was by then out of touch with events in Ladakh, I went to the Ops Room to be updated.

On 20 October strong Chinese forces had attacked the posts on the upper Chip Chap valley. Fortunately our troops there, (unlike the hapless 7 Brigade at the Namka-chu), had been given the option of withdrawing (as recounted earlier) and many sapper and infantry personnel were able to fall back on Daulet Beg Oldi. From the isolated and surrounded Galwan post, of course, no one escaped. The Chinese followed our withdrawing troops to the very doorstep of Daulet Beg Oldi but refrained from assaulting the post, presumably because it lay outside their 1960 claim line. The airstrip could no longer be used, however, and the post commander decided to withdraw down the valley of the Chip Chap, in a wide westerly arc via Thoise. Well over a hundred personnel escaped along this route.

The next day the enemy switched their offensive to southern Ladakh, their main targets being Sirijap and Yalu on the north shore of Lake Panggong. The Gorkhas at

Sirijap fought it out to the end, holding the enemy off long enough to allow Yalu post to withdraw across the lake in an Engineer storm boat. The Gorkhas were all either killed or captured (the post commander was later awarded the *Param Vir Chakra*). One unconfirmed report had it that light tanks had supported the attack on Sirijap.

After a pause the Chinese launched further attacks on Chang-la, Jara-la and Demchok at the eastern extremity of our line. Stout resistance was offered by each post and casualties were inflicted on the enemy, but in the face of repeated attacks supported by artillery they were withdrawn. The Demchok garrison pulled back to Fukche. This concluded the first phase of the Chinese offensive in Ladakh.

My staff then briefed me about follow-up actions they had taken on the Army Chief's decisions at HQ IV Corps on 23 October. The day after returning from Tezpur, Thapar had met Menon and, after strong resistance from the Defence Minister, had virtually forced the decision to switch divisions from the Punjab to the eastern front. (In fact it was the PM to whom the matter had had to be referred and who had given the decision.) Since then the following moves were under way:

(a) 17 Infantry Division (with two of its brigades) were being moved from Ambala to the Siliguri corridor;

(b) 20 Infantry Division in the Ranchi-Ramgarh area was being made up to three brigades by inclusion of 202 Brigade from Calcutta and sent up to Sikkim.

(These two divisions were to operate directly under HQ Eastern Command till HQ XXXIII Corps could move down from Shillong to Siliguri to take over the Sikkim-Siliguri-West-Bhutan front under Command HQ. Harbaksh was given command of XXXIII Corps and Umrao posted as Master General of Ordnance at Army HQ in an existing vacancy.)

(c) 2 Infantry Division was already being raised and would soon have two brigades under command — 5 and 11 (of the old 4th Division) — with responsibility for eastern NEFA (Subansiri, Siang and Lohit FD).

(d) HQ 3 Infantry Division was immediately to be raised for Ladakh, with three brigades under command — 114 (with four battalions) at Chushul, 70 (with two, supported by a troop of armoured cars) in the Dungti-Chumatang area north of Chushul, and 163 Brigade (with two battalions) ordered to move from Kashmir valley to Leh for its close defence.

It was obvious to me at once that after the withdrawal from Demchok the position of Chushul had become extremely vulnerable, because its maintenance was dependent entirely on the airfield and on the road from Dungti, both now under direct enemy threat. As I recorded in the *Summary*:

Both these [airfield and road] would lie exposed to Chinese interference from the moment hostilities opened: the airfield was within mortar range of Spanggur; the road to Dungti ran parallel and very close to the heights of the Rezang-la feature, all of which could be easily occupied by the Chinese. Furthermore, Dungti itself was threatened by attack from the south-east (along the Demchok road) so that the road between Chushul and Dungti would be unusable as a line of communication once hostilities were resumed.

As no porters or animals were available for maintenance of Chushul over the mule-track from Leh, it was obvious that Chushul garrison would be besieged (and isolated) from the opening phase of battle, unsupportable by reserves, reinforcements or supplies. However gallantly the garrison might resist, the end would be inevitable – when their ammunition ran out the troops would have to pull out as best as they could over the mountains, leaving behind tanks, artillery, vehicles and all heavy baggage . . . I recommended that 114 Brigade be pulled back to Tangse-Darbuk, where it could be logistically maintained.

Chushul was potentially another Towang: it could be easily by-passed and its troops entrapped. I directed my staff to prepare a brief appreciation of the Chushul situation so that I could discuss the problem with Daulet and Jogindar when they visited my Ops Room the next day.

The consensus among my staff in MO Directorate was that in switching 17th and 20th Divisions to the eastern front at that stage we had reacted too hastily, because we had committed our only reserves before the Chinese operational design could be clearly discerned. This criticism was valid, but only to an extent. The threat from Pakistan in the Punjab was not as great as that from China in the Siliguri corridor and the north Assam plains – and possibly,

Sikkim and Bhutan, as the Chinese claimed the whole or parts of these two Himalayan monarchies as either belonging to Tibet or being part of the Tibetan Buddhist heritage. I therefore felt justified in confirming the moves of 17th and 20th Divisions to the east at top priority.

I went to see Jogi Dhillon as soon as he was available and gave him an account of my visit to Tezpur and Se-la. He in turn brought me up to date on the stockpiling programme for Se-la which, he said, was proceeding well, the weather over Se-la having remained clear. He expected to have at least two first lines worth of ammunition and supplies for two brigades stocked at Senge by 15 November. He also informed me that in my absence the Chief had put up a paper to the government asking for the sanction of six new divisions (together with a complement of army and corps troops). These signified an overall increase in manpower of a quarter-million, plus an extra 25,000 vehicles.

When I asked him what was the basis on which the complement of six divisions had been calculated (since the DMO had not yet had an opportunity for making a fresh strategic survey) he replied that six divisions were asked for merely as a first instalment for immediate raising, in order to be combat-ready for large-scale Himalayan operations by December 1963. The Chief, he said, wanted the DMO to prepare a long-term strategic appreciation and make a forecast of the total forces we would require in order to meet future threats from China and Pakistan.

There was a message from the Chief's MA waiting for me at my office saying that I was to see the Defence Minister right away. I took along a map of Se-la marked with the new dispositions of our defences. Ushered in to the Minister's office without the customary wait in the ante-room, I found Menon alone at his desk looking somewhat impatient, as though I had been long expected. He gave me a brief, judgmental glance and then relaxed his usually unrelenting countenance into the vestige of a smile.

'It's good to see you back, Palit,' he said, offering me a cup of tea, and bade me sit down. The anodyne words of welcome and the unwontedly cordial manner of his greeting remain firmly imprinted in my memory. I gave him an account of the situation on the Towang front. I described the withdrawal of the Towang garrison to Jang and Se-la and, spreading my map on his desk, pointed out 4th Division's proposed deployment on the pass. I expected him to ask for more details on the withdrawal to and build-up at Se-la, but he made no comment. He gazed at the map and, after a while, asked me for my opinion about our chances of stopping further Chinese advances – and where. I told him that wherever we could support our deployment with logistical backing, our troops would give a good account of themselves. I added that although it would be rash to predict that we would stop the Chinese at any place beyond the reach of a motorable road, our resistance would stiffen as the Chinese came further down from the crestline. For instance, the latest news was that our troops on the Lohit sector had had to pull back from the border at Kibithoo but had held the enemy near Walong. I assured him that on the two most likely approaches (through Se-la and Sikkim) if the two divisions now being positioned there (the 4th and 20th) could be stored up with sufficient stocks of supplies and munitions, the enemy's advance would be held. I added that although I had not yet had an opportunity of seeing Mullik about the latest intelligence, my own estimate was that 4 Infantry Division would be well dug-in and stocked for battle before the Chinese could mount a set piece attack. Regarding 20th Division, even then moving up to Sikkim, I had not yet received any detailed reports on their progress, but since the road system in that region was more functional on our side of the border than on the Tibetan, I did not harbour any apprehensions.

We discussed the situation in Ladakh for a few minutes and then, just as I rose to take my leave, he abruptly asked, 'Do you think we ought to bring back retired generals to take charge of the war?'

The question was as unexpected as it was loaded and he had asked it with a sly look on his face. I realised at once what he was alluding to. There had been a deal of talk as well as suggestions in the press that the government should recall Thimayya and Thorat to service to take command of the army. I pretended to misunderstand his meaning and replied that in times of war it was always open to the government to recall retired officers from the reserve list.

'I was talking about *generals*,' he snapped. 'They say we need some retired generals to fight the Chinese.'

I knew what he wanted me to say, but I was not about to act as his feed man. I told him guardedly that the Chief of the Army Staff would be the best person to advise him on that aspect and he let it pass. He then said that in future he would like me to give him a personal report on the operational situation from time to time – but of course that was the last time I saw him as Minister of Defence.

In the afternoon I had a long session with Thapar. He told me that the government had given the defence forces a new task: to contain the Chinese aggression and then to evict them from all occupied territories. He said that he had put up a paper to the Defence Minister asking for sanction to raise, as a first instalment, six new divisions during 1963 including procurement of the requisite arms and equipment, if necessary from abroad. These, he assured me, would be approved. What he required of me was a strategic appreciation of the situation for the future conduct of the war against the Chinese. He wanted this in three or four days because he intended to discuss it with the Minister and follow it up with a more detailed proposal for expansion and procurement during 1964–5.

I asked if the PM or the Defence Minister had given him a revised assessment of Chinese aims. Thapar said that the government assumed that the Chinese would attempt to press on with their invasion, even down to the plains, but other than that no political or military assessment had been forthcoming, either from the Intelligence Bureau or from the Ministry.

The government's fear of an invasion of the Assam plains, Thapar said, was based not so much on an intelligence appreciation as on ominous official pronouncements from Peking since the morning of 20 October. Within hours of the launching of the Chinese offensive at the Namka-chu, Peking had broadcast lengthy (and obviously pre-drafted) statements for local and international effect, claiming that it was the Indians that had launched 'large-scale and all-out' attacks on the Chinese and that Chinese 'frontier guards had been compelled to strike back in self-defence'. In the process they had issued the warning that Chinese forces would no longer respect the 'limits of the illegal McMahon Line': a warning that our External Affairs Ministry interpreted as an explicit threat to extend operations to the rest of NEFA and even to the north bank of the Brahmaputra (shown as Chinese territory on their maps).

Thapar also informed me of the government's proposal to ask western countries, particularly the United States, Britain and the Commonwealth (from whom there had been an immediate and genuine wave of sympathy following the Chinese invasion) for immediate deliveries of arms, ammunition and equipment. Furthermore, he said that the United States had at last accorded recognition to the McMahon Line, clearly a great concession on their part in view of their repeated refusals to do so in the past. The General Staff was to make an assessment of our principal military requirements. He said that for the present he would charge Jogi Dhillon with the responsibility of co-ordinating a 'shopping list' for the United States and Britain because he wanted the DMO to be free to give all his attention to operational matters.

I told Thapar that I would have to make quite a few operational and policy assumptions for a long-term appreciation of the nature he had indicated and in order to save time it would be best if I obtained his approval on these assumptions before I started on the paper. I said that I would like to think about the matter and return to seek his approval later in the evening.

I held a discussion with the senior MO staff on the political and military factors to be considered and how we were going to project the conduct-of-war paper to the government. The assumptions we would make were:

(a) The Chinese would probably not violate the neutrality of Nepal, Burma, Pakistan or Bhutan while pursuing their war against India. (This precluded any threat to our eastern border or the Himalayas between Uttar Pradesh and Sikkim.)

(b) It was unlikely that China would receive much military or economic aid from Russia in improving its logistical capacity in Tibet.

(c) The government of India would sanction the raising of

six divisions in 1963 and ten in 1964, with further requirements in 1965 and later, if necessary; weapons and equipment for these new raisings would be procured from abroad if the Director-General of Ordnance Factories was unable to supply them.

(*d*) The *actual* threat from China would have priority over the *potential* threat from Pakistan throughout the period covered by this paper. (We felt that Pakistani opportunism would be held in check during the period we received military and other forms of aid from the United States and the western nations of the Commonwealth.)

I asked my staff to make a forecast of the future logistical potential of the PLA in Tibet. For this purpose we would have to take into account completion of the Sining–Lhasa railway. At the same time we would also have to consider the enemy's lengthening lines of communication through the Himalayan belt as they forced their way south of the crestline with regular formations and troops.

When I went to see Thapar later in the evening he approved the assumptions we had listed, except in the case of (d) – clearly something the DMO should have thought of himself. He stipulated that the defence of Jammu and Kashmir was to receive equal priority with defence against the Chinese, not only for political reasons but also to safeguard our vital line of communication with Ladakh. I asked him whether in his personal opinion the Chinese would attempt to carry the war into the north Indian plains. He mulled over the question for a while, but did not give me a direct reply. He said that as far as he could make out, the general opinion in the government was that they might, but no single individual, neither the DIB nor the Foreign Secretary, was willing to commit himself to a firm answer. For the present the army would just have to plan on a worst-case basis.

On my way back from the Chief's office, seeing the white (in-office) light over the DIB's door, I looked in for a moment to obtain the latest intelligence. Mullik told me that he had positive information from his 'forward posts' that enemy reinforcements were still being sent to the NEFA front from Tibet, mainly to the Towang and Walong sectors, although there had been reports of movement on the Siang and Subansiri borders too. Furthermore, a road from Bum-la to Towang was being constructed at a rapid pace. As the area north of Towang was comparatively quite level and unforested, the road would, he estimated, be ready to take vehicular traffic in three or four weeks. There had been some snowfall at Bum-la already, but the pass was normally negotiable well into December or even January. Mullik had predicted that the Chinese would attempt to achieve as much as possible of their geographical aim before the end of December, because after that logistical maintenance could not be carried out except by yaks, ponies and porters. He would not be specific about Chinese political aims in the sub-continent. When I asked him what would be Chinese capacity for stockpiling supplies and munitions in Tibet during 1964-5 and subsequently, he was not able to give me an estimate, although he promised to try to obtain it from other sources (presumably meaning the CIA).

It was Mullik who first gave me the information that Kaul had been declared fit by the medical specialist and would be leaving for Tezpur in a day or two. In his opinion this was a serious misjudgment on the part of the Defence Ministry. Mullik had positive information that after his misadventure at Sing Jang and his hasty retreat from the Namaka-chu, Kaul had become something of a joke in IV Corps and officers of 4th Division had lost confidence in him as an operational commander. I heard all this with some foreboding.

MO Directorate still did not possess sufficient operational and logistical information to begin work on our appreciation; my staff and I both considered that an assessment based on purely military factors, without politico-economic content or evaluation, would be largely useless. If we meant to undertake something more than just emotive make-believe, we had to know more about China's logistical potential in Tibet during the next few years. Having failed to obtain such political or economic intelligence from Mullik, I rang up N.B. Menon (of the China desk at the Foreign Ministry) and asked him for a meeting. When he learned what I wanted from him, he at once agreed and went on to suggest that he, Dr Gopal (Director of the Ministry's Historical Section) and I should form an informal lunch club and meet once or twice a week to pool information. This, in fact, turned out to be a very useful discussion platform while it lasted. N.B. and Gopal were good friends, both high-calibre officials, scholarly and well-informed on China affairs. Gopal, reputedly, had had much to do with shaping our border policy in the north and, in a later terminology, would be described as something of a hawk on border questions. Analytical and articulate, he brightened our discussions with a gift of puckish merriment, something of a contrast to the quiet, considered officer from the China desk. Together they made a good two-man team; it seemed that the very economy of Menon's responses owed something to the generosity of Gopal's. Their joint contribution to MO Directorate's quest for information was useful, though short-lived.

It was not till late in the evening that I found time to ring up our Regimental Training Centre at Dehra Dun to inform the Commandant, Colonel A.K. Mitra, of the impending surge of 1/9 GR 'refugees' expected at Dewangiri and Darranga. I discussed with him the possibility of sending a regimental reception group by rail to Rangia to facilitate collection of 9 GR refugees as a first step towards reraising the battalion. I told him that my wife had already begun scouring the larger stores and shops in Delhi, collecting welfare items such as blankets, towels and toilet requirements, besides clothing and footwear, all of which our officers and *jawans* would sorely need after their harrowing journey across Bhutan's high wildernesses. Mitra undertook to keep in touch with my wife to progress welfare matters.

When I called at Bijji Kaul's house on my way home that evening I found him still in bed and, for a change, unattended by cabinet ministers and army brass. Looking pale and drawn but full of himself as ever, he told me that Nehru and Menon had both been consulting him at bedside meetings on strategic policy. His advice, predictably, had been that there must be an immediate and considerable increase in the strength of the armed forces, mainly the army, and furthermore, in order to equip new divisions the PM should address a personal appeal to all friendly nations, particularly the United States, Britain and the Commonwealth, for immediate arms aid. Bijji said that

Nehru, despite his frequently expressed disapproval of arms aid, agreed at once and had followed up his resolve by sending the Cabinet Secretary, Sucha Singh Khera, to collect from the bedridden Kaul a list of urgently needed arms and equipment. Bijji said that he had hastily drawn up a list and Khera had taken it to Galbraith, the US Ambassador in Delhi. I shuddered at the thought of the confusion his sickbed interference would cause!

Nor had Bijji confined himself to these banal and unimaginative counsels. He said that he had gone on to offer the PM (who was also the Foreign Minister) advice on diplomatic measures to be taken. Nehru presumably found no difficulty in rejecting Bijji's somewhat naive suggestion that India forge an alliance with the United States and Taiwan to create a joint front against communist China, but part at least of Kaul's advice – to seek US army and air force intervention in case of further Chinese attacks – must have remained in the PM's mind.

The next day Thapar called me to attend an operational discussion with the GOC-in-C Western Command. From the moment I entered the Chief's office I sensed an air of hostility in the normally suave and debonair Daulet Singh. Thapar had obviously told him about the DMO's criticism of his plans for the defence of Chushul and Daulet had not taken kindly to an implied censure from a junior.

A weakness in Daulet's normally equable temperament was a grouchy touchiness about his lack of operational service. If Bijji Kaul's war experience were limited, Daulet had none at all. He had served in a horsed cavalry regiment before the war and hence not taken part in operations on the North-West Frontier. He spent the Second World War in extra-regimental employment, much of it with non-operational units of the princely state forces. Even after independence, he took part neither in the Kashmir war nor in the Hyderabad operations. With that background, he was predictably sensitive to his shortcoming and was easily roused to petulance if this lack of direct experience were ever implied, however remotely. Thapar had once or twice in my presence done just that, but if Daulet had to stomach this irritation from his Chief, he was not going to take even a hint of it from a DMO.

When I began to point out on the map the strategic weakness of the Chushul defences, Daulet rudely turned away from me and addressed the Chief, saying abruptly that there was no danger to Chushul. He was sure that the Chinese would, as on the Chip Chap and Demchok fronts, halt their offensive at their claim line (which ran to the east of Chushul). Even if they did launch an attack, he was certain that his forces would hold out. There was no need for the DMO to get excited about the fate of Chushul, he managed to convey. Not to be lightly cast aside, I told Thapar (perhaps more forcefully than I had needed to) that it was incumbent on us to act on the assumption that the Chinese would continue with their offensive, because that was what the government had determined. In any case, we could not for a second time bank on Chinese goodwill, but must prepare to meet their offensive, in which event our defences at Chushul were untactically sited. The brigade there would be quickly neutralised because the Chinese would sever its exposed line of communication, isolate the garrison and make straight for Leh along the Indus valley road. I added that at Chushul the potential for disaster was graver even than that which had existed at Towang. We must take the decision now to pull back from Chushul and concentrate our forces for the defence of Leh.

Thapar obviously agreed with me, but sensing a growing undercurrent of resentment he ended the discussion and indicated that I could leave. Later in the day, when I had occasion to go to his office again, he harked back to the Chushul argument and said that although I was right about its tactical weakness, he felt certain that the Chinese would not proceed beyond their claim line; he had therefore not overruled Daulet Singh on his defence plan.

A DMO could not sustain an argument against that, but he could wonder that a Chief would stake so much on a personal evaluation that was in fact outside his remit, especially when a previous evaluation had proved so disastrously wrong.

In the event, Thapar and Daulet turned out to be right: the Chinese did not proceed beyond their claim line and my point was never put to the test. In the process I had made an implacable enemy of the Army Commander, as Joginder, his Chief of Staff, informed me later. This was a matter of some regret to me because I liked Daulet Singh as a person and had admired him for his staunchness on many past occasions in withstanding provocative pressures from Army HQ.

Since this is a personal memoir rather than a chronicle of the war it would be inappropriate to record in detail all the events that unfolded during the period between the first Chinese offensive and the unilateral ceasefire a month later. One has a fear of wearying the reader with a narration of routine, or by hammering away at self-evident procedures. Thus, instead of reciting a liturgy of General Staff activities I will confine my record to those aspects that might be of particular interest, or were characteristic of the gaucherie with which the contingencies of war were handled, both by the politicians and by the General Staff.

As I have already had occasion to remark, investigation of problems and issues remains superficial in a system in which higher direction of affairs is arrogated by a small cabal – the system that prevailed in South Block at that time. On border questions the PM's policy-making coterie moved from decision to decision without benefit of staff analysis and advice. Even more remarkably, as the situation on the border deteriorated from stray incidents to armed confrontation and finally to war, the decision-making cell in the government grew not larger but smaller and, consequently, not more but less accountable. Before the Dhola incident it was at the PM's meetings, attended by the Defence Minister, the foreign, defence and army staffs – with all proceedings faithfully recorded – that decisions were taken; subsequently it was the Defence Minister who each morning, as a matter of routine, held informal meetings on the war situation. Decisions of the utmost consequence were taken at these meetings, sometimes even without reference to the peripatetic PM, and executive orders were often passed on verbally. If minutes or other records were kept by Sarin, they never came to light, then or later, so that MO archives for that period, based on assumption or hearsay, remained haphazard and lacked authenticity. Crucial decisions such as whether or not to launch an operation against the Chinese at Thag-la, or even a tactical one such as where to hold the enemy on the Namka-chu front, were taken without benefit of integrated (civilian and military) staff scrutiny and advice. Few authoritarian systems could have spawned a more exclusive policy-making apparatus.

The trauma of Namka-chu wrested a small concession from this oracular regime: the Prime Minister directed the Cabinet Secretary, Sucha Singh Khera, to form a Cabinet Secretary's Committee, consisting of senior bureaucrats from the key ministries, to function as an *ad hoc* advisory body on the conduct of the war. I recall that Khera's committee attracted the services of a number of bright young minds from the IAS such as K. Subrahmaniam, Sounderajan and Bannerjee, but I wonder if best use was made of them by the hierarchical and prickly-pompous Cabinet Secretary (whom I found to be more mindful of form and formality than of the substance of a commission, though it is possible that my opinion of him was unduly influenced by a limited but unfortunate personal experience of the man).

It seemed to me that Khera was never able to shake off the cloak of fantasy that the decision-makers in South Block had wrapped around themselves in the aftermath of Namka-chu. Bewildered by the immensity of the disaster, and unwilling to ascribe it to their own naive and inept decisions, the instinctive reflex was to clutch at alibi-making: an attempt to restore a self-image. Looking back across the years, it seems to me that within a few days of the disaster reality was successfully exchanged for fantasy. The whole border episode was misinterpreted in the light of self-serving interests: a treacherous neighbour had taken advantage of the peace-loving Indians by launching a surprise attack on its border posts with massive forces; our troops had fought valiantly but were eventually overrun by overwhelming enemy forces; thereupon, the whole country had rallied behind the government in a united surge of patriotic fervour (true) and India had gained the sympathy of the world (only partly true – our many non-aligned friends had not been markedly commiserating); the country would now face up to the challenge and prepare to throw the enemy back.

Parliament had already acquiesced in this make-believe by affirming 'the resolve of the Indian people to drive out the aggressor from the sacred soil of India'.

This fantastical projection of border developments served to camouflage the actual truth: that India had been unnecessarily provocative in both Ladakh and the Thag-la regions, but its military initiatives had been no more than hollow posturings; the troops sent up to the high frontiers to execute them had been despairingly under-strength, under-armed, under-provisioned and, in many cases, under inept military leadership. The result was that, when the time was ripe, the Chinese found no difficulty in rudely slapping them back from the border. That was the stark reality that no one seemed prepared to face.

Although the General Staff was more realistic in its attitude to the border defeats, clearly we also had need of psychological restoration, which took the form of the 'Conduct of War' paper that I was required to prepare for the Chief – a grandiose projection of war-planning for the eviction of the Chinese and an extravagant estimate of requirements in manpower, munitions and maintenance over a period of years. It was a projection of strategic intent on a grand scale, one that the limited economy of the country was unlikely ever to sustain.

On 1 November we heard the news that Nehru had taken over the Ministry of Defence; Menon was appointed Minister of Defence Production. The Prime Minister had taken this step because of pressure from parliament, both from the Opposition as well as from his own party. The arrangement lasted only a few days; the common demand was for Menon to be sacked from the cabinet. A few days later, when it was made clear to Nehru by his own Congress Party that even his resignation would be acceptable were he to continue to shield Menon, he finally gave in and Krishna Menon's ministerial career came to an end.

On the morning of 3 November Thapar rang up to say that the Defence Minister (Nehru) wanted to address the Chiefs of Staff and the principal staff officers of the three services. I decided to arrange for the talk to be held in the Ops Room, which could just accommodate the requisite number of chairs. When Pandit Nehru arrived I asked for permission to take notes of his address, which he granted. He spoke for about an hour and I managed to scribble down the salient points he made.

The Prime Minister looked composed, showing no sign of the anguish and bitterness he must have felt at the collapse of his foreign policy and the army's disastrous reverses. He spoke unhurriedly, in a quiet voice and with a minimum of gesture. He expressed the government's determination to defeat the Chinese and warned that we must be prepared for further aggressive moves and a deeper invasion of Indian territory, although logistical difficulties would place a limit on the extent of the enemy's thrusts. He promised the government's support in building up the armed forces to meet the challenge – even if it had 'to spend a thousand crores' to procure arms and equipment. The people would accept the burden, he said. My notes recorded his words:

There it is: we are in for it. In spite of the dangers, it is a good thing, in that it is stiffening the backs of our people, bringing harmony and promoting national integration – all stirred by the crisis. . . .

The backyard of the country will produce the morale and the effort. Your particular job therefore is fighting and preparing to fight. You can tell us how to do it, but war is too serious a matter to be left only to the generals and the maps (*sic*). We must face this together. I will give you all the help; I want yours.

It would have been unnatural not to expect the PM to attempt to justify the enormity of the miscalculation at the Namka-chu:

Before this [the Chinese attack on 20 October] we had discussed this problem with our military chiefs. We knew that they [the Chinese] were collecting forces but we did not have an idea of the massiveness of their preparation. We thought we could push them back. Then we heard that they were stronger than we thought, but we still had no idea of their massiveness. The question then arose whether we should defend Dhola or the other side of the river. This depended on the military chiefs – I only said we must offer resistance, but military appraisal of the situation must be made by the commanders on the spot. There is no sense in their annihilating themselves. All our decisions must be military – e.g. Towang . . . you were the best to judge whether it should have been held or not. Our broad strategy must be governed by political factors, but detailed strategy – and tactics especially – have to be judged by military considerations. . . .

No one expected the Prime Minister to make a clarion call to battle; he was addressing the military bureaucracy, not commanders or troops. Nor was it remarkable that he drew attention to the fact that the disastrous decision to fight at Namka-chu had been military and not political, for that was what Mullik and Menon must have repeatedly told him. (Perhaps they believed it themselves, the meeting at Tezpur on 17 October notwithstanding.) What was reprehensible, in my opinion, was the misplacing of cause and emphasis in his analysis of the catastrophe in Kameng. It was not correct that the Chinese had massed unduly large forces at Thag-la, or that their presence had come as a surprise to us. Mullik had provided sufficient intelligence to indicate that the Chinese had at most two regiments (brigades) supported by artillery and mortars at Thag-la and one more opposite Bum-la. There was no lapse on his part there. Where intelligence had gone awry – and the government was naive to accept it – was to arrogate the role of evaluator and to assume that the Chinese would not go to war on the border issue. Finally, it was not the 'massiveness' of Chinese forces that caused the debacle, but the strengthelessness of ours. We had placed men and weapons in adequate numbers, but without the ammunition or provisions to keep them going – and it is this that determines the fighting potential of a body of soldiers. We had sent a brigade to Namka-chu, sufficient strength to withstand an attack by two Chinese regiments, but only if they were given the weapons, the ammunition and the entrenching tools. Without them even five brigades would not have been enough. It is this central point that seemed still to elude the Prime Minister.

On 4 November I received a message from Sarin to say that the Cabinet Secretary would like the Army Chief to brief his committee on the 'Conduct of War' paper at its next meeting. Predictably, Thapar refused to be lured into a bureaucratic catechism on future war strategy, but when Khera insisted, the Chief directed me to represent him at the meeting, cautioning me against discussing details of facts and figures about future force projections.

At the meeting Khera, after an unseemly display of rudeness to a junior, was persuaded by Sarin that the DMO was indeed competent to speak on behalf of his Chief on matters of strategy. According to the *Summary:*

I represented the COAS at the Cabinet Secretary's Committee, at which were present various Secretaries of the Government of India (or their representatives), the Chief of Naval Staff and the Vice Chief of Air Staff. I gave a brief *resumé* of the Army's planning during the past two years, starting with the Chiefs of Staff paper of Jan 1961, its preoccupations with the Pakistani threat and the 'Foreseeable Future' paper prepared by the General Staff. . . . I stressed that the course of future operations, both Chinese and ours, would be guided largely by logistical capabilities, and that our strategic aim, both long-range and immediate, must be conditioned by the following two considerations:
(a) In the immediate future, the Chinese, having built up their logistical 'fat' for the past 5–7 years, held a temporary advantage over us as far as fighting in the border areas was concerned.
(b) In the larger perspective, we, who were fighting from the administrative base of our own country, held the overall advantage compared to Chinese forces, whose administrative base was 2,000–4,000 miles from their major 'fronts'.
The main recommendation of my paper was that in the next phase of operations, we should attempt to regain the initiative from the enemy and stop 'reacting' to his moves. . . . We should contain the offensive with our existing deployment and build up reserves for an integrated defensive strategy, so that we could deal firmly with a major (enemy) thrust instead of merely conforming to his diversionary attacks. I explained that whereas the Chinese might continue with their attacks in Kameng and Walong Sectors, the main danger to India and the only major offensive feasible during the coming winter (based on logistical calculations) was an attack through the Chumbi Valley (west of Bhutan). We must, at all events, prepare against that contingency.
I informed the Committee that the strategic purpose of the General Staff appreciation that I was at that time preparing was the eviction of the Chinese from our territory. I informed them that that paper was not yet complete.

Today, thirty years later, this strategic overview will seem archaic, naive even, but we were then closer to the Second

World War in time and outlook than we were to notions
of international restraints and the political complexities of
the 1970s and 1980s. We still regarded warfare in the
absolute, decisive terms and wider strategic horizons of the
1940s. Concepts such as limited wars, superpower
management of local conflicts, proxy wars and coercive
diplomacy had not yet modified the perception that decision
was the goal of war. It was left to the Chinese to point
the way to subtleties of contemporary political and strategic
manoeuvres.

After a cursory discussion of my paper, Khera took up
the next item on the agenda – the impending flow of arms
aid from abroad. He told us in dramatic fashion that US
air force cargo planes were even at that moment lining up
at NATO bases to be loaded with arms for India and that
the first consignments were expected to arrive in a matter
of hours. He wanted to know from Army HQ how quickly
the new weapons could be sent up to the front lines. I
replied that I did not know the answer to that, but would
let him have it later in the day. However, I volunteered
the information that I had discussed the matter informally
with Army Commander Sen, who had agreed that the
Belgian (*Fabrique Nationale*) types of weapons from NATO
should be issued to the troops in the plains rather than to
those at the front, where there was neither the opportunity
nor the facilities to train and practise with new weapons.
What the frontline troops most urgently needed, I said,
were additional light machine-guns of the type they were
familiar with; I had therefore recommended doubling the
scale of these weapons to two per section. They would be
taken from troops in the rear, who could then be rearmed
with incoming aid consignments.

Clearly this did not accord with the Cabinet Secretary's
fancy-built conjectures of the latest western arms being
rushed from the international airports to the front line. He
said that the United States and Britain had moved exceedingly
speedily to send us arms to fight the Chinese. It would be
something of an anti-climax now for us to send them to
troops in the rear instead of rushing them to the battalions
in battle. The donor countries would feel that we had been
unduly alarmist and that they had-been unnecessarily put

upon. It took Sarin and me quite some time to convince Khera that matters of arms-management were best left to the army to decide. (In the end we decided to rush a certain proportion of the newly arrived arms to those forward areas where arrangements for conversion training could be arranged.)

Being no longer required, I left the meeting at this point. Sarin came outside with me for a moment. He wanted me to have a word with Deputy Secretary Sounderajan about the list of requirements of arms and ammunition being prepared by Army HQ for the US Embassy. He said that Colonel Curtis, the American Military Attaché, had pointed out some gross anomalies in the list that had been sent him. Quoting one instance, Sarin said that 'high priority' had been accorded to the supply of a number of regiments of heavy mortars (I forgot exactly how many) and ninety first line scales of ammunition for each. Curtis had worked out that if they were to act according to this, it would take fifty-five Liberty ships to transport this item alone – and, taking into account our port facilities, would probably take three months to unload. Sarin asked me to look into it and added that a high-powered military aid mission under a US general was arriving in a few days; we should ensure that no such ridiculous demands were made on them.[2]

Later, checking the lists with Sounderajan and Colonel Curtis, I found that indeed there had been instances of reckless over-bidding. I told the Colonel that there had been a mistake; and I arranged for all future lists of demands to be checked by MO Directorate staff before being sent to the US Embassy or to any other outside source.

After this Sarin established the practice of calling me over to his office, or to his home in Tughlak Crescent, at the end of each day for an exchange of views and information. This arrangement worked well while it lasted, because we had always got on well together. I had known Harish Sarin since the time of the first Kashmir war, when he was Defence Minister Baldev Singh's Private Secretary. Shortly afterwards when I perforce had to do a stint in SD Directorate, he had been Deputy Secretary (GS) and we had quickly established a rapport. By then he was inured to the defence culture and had even acquired expertise in matters that were prescriptively military in character. I well remember that in one or two contended cases when the General Staff had put up an ill or hastily considered proposal, Sarin was able to prevail over senior military officers, much to their discomfiture, by using valid military arguments against them. These experiences had given him a tendency to self-assertion, but he was totally free of arrogance or pomposity; and he was that rarity among the old imperial bureaucracy: a liberal and progressive civil servant. By the time Menon came to the Defence Ministry, Sarin had, by virtue of his sharp intellect and accumulated experience, become an acknowledged expert in the Ministry. Relations between Menon and Pulla Reddy being what they were, Sarin's position had become virtually that of Defence Secretary.

During the past two years I had been aware that Sarin was proving to be something of a hawk on the border question, particularly the NEFA border, perhaps because he had been swayed by Kaul's forceful neo-professionalism into accepting him too glibly at face value. Certainly during the build-up to the Namka-chu episode, he had been a firm advocate of taking offensive action at Thag-la. The sudden and awesome revelation of the extent of our weakness had, I felt, somewhat shaken his faith in the professional competence of Thapar, Bogey Sen and even Kaul, and it could have been one reason why he sought to check out views and opinions with the DMO.

One of the concerns that were exercising his mind was the threat to Chushul. Unbeknown to me, Mullik had passed on to Sarin the episode about the meeting with Thapar and Daulet and my doubts about the security of Chushul and Leh. I explained it all again to Sarin on a hastily drawn pencil sketch. He soon grasped the problem and rang up Mullik on the secrophone to suggest that he apprise the PM about the Army Chief's insouciant attitude to what appeared to be an imminent threat. He added that 114 Brigade should be withdrawn from Chushul before it was isolated and cut off. Mullik agreed but suggested that the DMO accompany him to explain the situation to the PM on a map. Harish consulted me about this and we agreed that it would be highly improper for me to do so.

If I intended to see the PM, it was incumbent on me that I first inform Thapar and I was reluctant to do that. In the end Mullik said that he would see the PM by himself.

Presumably as a result of Mullik's initiative in the matter, a decision of sorts was taken. Thapar informed me next morning that he had issued orders for the evacuation of Chushul. Yet, the entry in my diary for the next day reads: 'Chief vetoes proposal to pull 114 Brigade out.' I do not recollect the exact circumstances of this on-again-off-again alternation but the reason could have been that Thapar, despite his own stipulations about Kashmir, suddenly decided to take a risk in the valley and despatched first one and then two infantry brigades from Kashmir to Ladakh, one (70 Infantry Brigade) to sit astride the main road at Dungti and the other (163 Infantry Brigade) to strengthen the close defence of Leh. He had already ordered the raising of a new divisional HQ at Leh (HQ 3 Infantry Division) to command all the forces in Ladakh.

Another matter on which Sarin consulted me was possible senior appointments. The CGS's chair lay unfilled and Sarin felt that the PM, now actively in the defence chair, might want to make one or two senior command changes. I told him that there had been too many command changes since the crisis began and more of the same would have an unsettling effect on the army. In any case, nothing that we could do now would affect the coming battles, except adversely. There was only one suggestion that I could give him. I said that Lucknow was too far from the actual theatre of operation for the GOC-in-C to exercise his influence. Bogey Sen, whom I had consulted on this point, would not agree to setting up a Tactical Command HQ at Shillong or Gauhati as I had suggested. This was an opportunity, I pointed out, of artfully removing Bogey Sen from the operational chain without his losing face. We could establish a Field Army HQ at Gauhati directly under Army HQ, to co-ordinate IV and XXXIII Corps battles. I suggested calling it a re-raised HQ XIV Army and appointing Kaul in command, and I suggested Sam Manekshaw (then Commandant of the Staff College) for command of IV Corps. I felt that Moti Sagar, whom Sarin had mentioned as a possible candidate for promotion to command, would be better employed as CGS.

Command appointments were, of course, beyond the remit of a DMO. I had expressed my views purely on a personal basis because Sarin had asked for them. On the other hand the reorganisation of the field command system was very much an operational matter, so I prepared a paper on the creation of a Field Army HQ for the Chief's consideration, but before I could formally process it we were again embroiled in a crisis.

One matter in which I was not successful in dissuading Sarin from overreacting was the question of honours and awards for the border battles. I do not know whether Sarin had consulted Kumaramangalam, the Adjutant General, but he told me that the government wanted an early announcement of a list of officers and men who were to be given gallantry awards for the Namka-chu, Ladakh and Bum-la battles. To me this sounded very much a Menon-ish misdirection. I advised against acting too hastily, arguing that in unmitigated disasters like those that we had suffered, when most actions ended in headlong rout or, at best, forced withdrawal, gallantry awards were not normally given on an immediate basis – if only because formal citations were not easy to compile due to lack of witnesses. Our troops had resisted staunchly at both places and inflicted casualties on the enemy, but many of those who could vouch for specific actions were either killed or taken prisoner. Furthermore, the fate of many would-be recipients was unknown; if taken prisoner, their deportment as prisoners-of-war would have to be taken into account. Lastly, should too many of the hastily awarded medals turn out to have been inappropriate, the whole system of honours and awards would be devalued. Sarin, however, was adamant that the morale of the country would be more easily sustained if the government were to announce a list of gallantry awards to indicate how bravely our soldiers had fought. I could not move him from that misconception. Indeed, he said, HQ IV and XV Corps (Kashmir front) had, under government requirement, already forwarded citations. He asked me if I would read through them, a request I politely declined, shocked by the implied subterfuge. On 11 November the first list of awards was announced over All India Radio. Some were well deserved, like the subedar of the Sikh regiment who had stayed behind at his post and taken a heavy toll of the enemy at Bum-la before being killed (and seen to be killed), but as I had anticipated, there were 'duds' too, and some of the recipients were themselves surprised when they read their citations. What is even more lamentable is that when our prisoners returned from captivity and eye-witness accounts of heroism, sacrifice and death became available, only a small number among them received official recognition for their gallantry. Too many medals had already been given to the survivors for the real heroes to be fittingly rewarded.

Meanwhile, my wife was at last ready to take off for Assam with a team of helpers (including A.K. Mitra from the regimental centre and my niece Abha Chaudhuri, who had recently married into the Regiment). Sarin had obtained government sanction for an air force Dakota to be placed at my wife's disposal as an emergency welfare measure. She had collected a large quantity of clothing, toiletries and other gifts from trading establishments. When we received information that the fugitives from Namka-chu had begun arriving at Darranga, my wife, with A.K. and Abha, set off with a plane-load of goodies. They visited Tezpur, New Misamari, Tamalpur (near Dewangiri in south-eastern Bhutan) and other collecting posts and rendered whatever assistance they could to 9 GR and other personnel.

As a matter of general interest I include a brief description of the Gorkhas' battle at Dhola, as given to my wife by some of the survivors. At Namka-chu, it will be recalled, 1/9 Gorkhas (with only two companies available at that time) was the only battalion to have been tactically sited, deployed as they were on high ground some 200 metres up the spur from the riverline. The ground was hard and rocky, at places frozen. No entrenching tools were available, so trenches could not be dug; neither was there any barbed wire to erect obstacles. The few anti-personnel mines air-dropped at Tsangdhar had still not reached the battalion. In the circumstances, the only defences they had been able to construct on the open mountain-side were low *sangars*, stone walls built with whatever flint and shingle they could collect from the surrounding wilderness. There was, of course, no form of overhead cover except an occasional salvaged parachute draped over the stonework. Thus, despite its tactical siting, the Battalion's positon was virtually indefensible. Furthermore, on the previous evening the Battalion had received orders to march to Tsangle and had been preparing to move the very next morning.

At dawn on 20 October, after a sharp barrage that lasted about an hour, the Chinese launched their offensive – not across the riverline, as expected, but from the flanks and the rear, and not in any regular assault formation. They crept up nullahs and other dead ground, infiltrated as near as possible, and then charged the Gorkha positions, firing their automatic rifles as they came. The Battalion inflicted some casualties on the enemy but had only enough ammunition to hold the attackers for one-and-a-half to two hours. Thereafter, their magazines empty, the survivors were hastily organised in small groups and ordered to make their escape uphill, at first toward Tsangdhar, then veering left toward Karpo-la. After some five or six days of trekking over the cold and barren complex of Bhutanese ridges they arrived at Bleting (on the Towang–Bhutan border south of Lumla), whence they took the mule-track to the monastery town of Tashigong. Here they were kindly received but disarmed by the Bhutanese before being allowed to proceed further south to India.

In this connection I would like, as an aside, to narrate the dilemma with which I was faced regarding the 'incident of the abandoned CO'. Lieutenant Colonel Balwant Singh Ahluwalia was the able and assertive commanding officer of 1/9 Gorkhas. During the battle he had been shot through the right shoulder and was in considerable pain. When the evacuation started he was at first carried pick-a-back up the Tsangdhar slope, but he found the process unbearably painful. Major Anant Singh Charak, his second-in-command, ordered a halt and had a makeshift stretcher constructed with a couple of rifles and a blanket. Rearguards were still engaging the enemy; the sound of intermittent firing was a warning to keep moving if they wished to escape. Hurriedly they laid their CO on the improvised stretcher and started off again. Up and down the ridges they carried him, as best they could, but the going was mercilessly rough and

slippery, there being no sign of a track anywhere. Finally
Balwant, no longer able to bear the pain and discomfort
of the jolting passage, asked to be set down and left behind.
At that time the party was still near enough to the scene
of battle to be within the of enemy patrols pursuing our troops.

Charak held a brief discussion with others of the group;
then, his decision made, he had the CO's stretcher laid
out on a prominent spur. He stuck a rifle into the ground
by its bayonet and, further to attract attention, draped
Balwant's turban over the butt of the rifle. They left him
a water-bottle, said their sad farewells and went on their way.

After my wife's visit to Assam, Balwant's father rang me
up in Delhi one day, in considerable agitation, and asked
to meet me. My wife and I called at his house that evening.
Balwant's wife, Bai, remained calm and composed throughout;
his father was not so restrained and accused the Battalion
of abandoning its CO. He thought that it was callous and
unvaliant of Charak and his officers to have left their
wounded commanding officer, with no attendant, to face
an uncertain fate. He hoped that I would take action
against those who had been so derelict in their duty.

I told him that I had already conducted an unofficial
regimental inquiry into the episode. The facts were that
Charak had been determined to carry his wounded CO
back with him, but the latter had finally ordered to be set
down. At Charak's instigation, one of the riflemen had
volunteered to stay behind with Balwant, but only till he
sighted the enemy coming their way; he insisted that after
that he should escape, to avoid being taken prisoner.

I explained to the bereaved parent, who was certain that
his son had been left to die a lingering death, that Balwant's
only chance of survival was to be given early surgical
attention, which would have been impossible during the
eight to ten days of flight that the escaping party faced.
(It was unlikely that he would have survived the rough
journey across the wilds of Bhutan without food or water.)
I also added that I could not expect any officer, or any
other rank, to offer himself for capture by the enemy. I
had accordingly given my opinion, that Charak's decision
was in no way reprehensible. We consoled Balwant's father
and wife as best we could, ourselves uncertain what kind

of treatment Indian wounded would receive at Chinese hands.

It later turned out that the 'abandonment' was the best thing that could have happened to Balwant. He was picked up by the Chinese, given field medical treatment on the spot, carried on a stretcher up to Thag-la, thence to Le and by ambulance to Tsona Dzong, where he received surgical treatment. All this we learned from him when he returned from prisoner-of-war camp the next year, his wound healed.

On 5 November the Chief sent the Western and Eastern Army Commanders to my Ops Room for a briefing on the general situation. Daulet, still nursing his resentment, spoke not a word to me nor did he ask a question. After he left, Bogey stayed behind and we talked about the stocking programme at Se-la which, he told me, was going well, carried out almost entirely by air.

I still could not persuade Bogey Sen to establish a Tactical Command HQ in north Assam, so I tentatively broached the possibility of establishing a Field Army HQ to command the operations in the north. I told him briefly of the appreciation I was making for the Chief and pointed out the advantages that would accrue from a Field Army HQ on the eastern front. As far as I recollect Bogey was noncommittal about the proposal, but he did not oppose it.

Situation Reports from IV Corps indicated that the Chinese were very active on the northern flank of Se-la. As the DMI had not prepared an intelligence appreciation, I rang up Mullik and asked to be briefed by him about enemy movements so that I could discern some sort of pattern from the random information sent in by our patrols.

The DIB had recently effected a reorganisation of his field agents in Kameng. During the Namka-chu episode I had passed on to him complaints from 7 Brigade and 4th Division that there was a lack of liaison between the IB and the army in the matter of field intelligence. Consequently, after the fall of Towang, Mullik had made a hurried redistribution of his field personnel. Each infantry battalion was allotted one of his intelligence agents and a senior intelligence official was attached to brigade and higher HQs. This was a generous gesture on his part because, inevitably, although army units thereafter received field intelligence earlier than they had before, reports from the field took longer to reach the DIB because they had to go through army channels and procedures.

Mullik gave me a quick run-through of the latest enemy information. He said that the Chinese appeared to have been working round the clock to push a motorable road through to Towang. Although the terrain between Towang and Bum-la was in places flat, and more open than on the lower monsoon slopes of India, it was not as level or as good going as the Tibetan plateau north of the watershed. Our agents had reported that considerable blasting of rock faces was being carried out in the region. Mullik's estimate was that the road would not be through before the end of November, by when there would be only about a month's campaigning time left before the passes and the countryside were liable to become snowbound. (In the event, the first convoy of vehicles was seen parked in Towang on 10 November, testifying to a truly prodigious feat of road engineering.)

Mullik said that the Chinese had not waited for the completion of the road to start their pressure tactics against the Se-la position. Patrols sent out by 62 Brigade had reported constant foot and yak-borne traffic eastward along the north bank of the Towang-chu, moving towards Tse-la and the high Mago region. This was obviously an attempt to encircle Se-la from the far north, with the aim of moving down through Poshing-la and severing the main road between Dhirang and Bomdila. Our patrols from Se-la had at times clashed with the enemy north on the Towang-chu track, but they nearly always came off second best, which was not very reassuring to hear.

Similar movements, but on a smaller scale, had also been reported south-west of the Se-la massif, between the pass itself and the jagged, forbidding ridge that marks the border with eastern Bhutan. Mullik looked increasingly dispirited as he recounted these developments. He said that although I had anticipated these moves by the enemy, he was doubtful if our forces would be able to neutralise them with any degree of success. Our newly deployed troops, he said, were neither physically nor mentally attuned to high altitude operations.

That was, of course, true. From the days of 7 Brigade's move to Kameng three years previously, our troops had been unable to carry out any collective training; even individual training was spasmodic, owing to the numerous calls on the men. Furthermore, all the new brigades that now formed part of 4 Infantry Division had been sent up from the plains, unacclimatised and untrained in high-altitude operations. On the other hand, for the first time we would be operating from a position of logistical strength. We planned to stock Se-la on the basis of one month's self-maintenance. If defences on Se-la-Senge were tactically sited, with pickets on all the dominating heights, I did not envisage the Chinese capturing that stronghold in the brief period before the winter bore down on them; after that we would have nearly six months to make further defensive preparations. As for Chinese forces moving round by the northern or southern by-pass routes, it was they whose logistics capacity would become threatened – so long as Se-la held out.

I was not then aware, as I have mentioned before, that in fact there was only one brigade (albeit of four battalions) on Se-la. Anant Pathania had pulled his Tactical HQ back and located it in the valley of Dhirang, where he had also retained (for his own protection) most of the second brigade (65) that we had earmarked for Senge. IV Corps had never informed us of this decision to split the Se-la-Senge troops into two separate defensive sectors nearly 20 km apart. I would certainly have moved strongly to get that decision reversed, especially as 65 Brigade had been deployed in an untactical, indefensible location at the bottom of Dhirang valley.

Mullik urged me to seek Thapar's permission to make a protracted visit to IV Corps and 4th Division. He felt that Bijji Kaul knew and liked me well enough to allow me to act as an unofficial 'activist' on matters of terrain and tactics. He argued that I would be better employed as a local rallying point in Kameng than as DMO in Delhi. I agreed with him, but I said that it was not for me to advise Thapar to take this course. If he, Mullik, were to persuade him, I would take off for Kameng and Se-la at the first opportunity. I undertook to send a personal letter to Kaul obliquely hinting at such a possibility.

Later in the day Mullik rang me up and said that he had met Thapar and Wadalia in the corridor and talked to them about his suggestion that Palit be sent temporarily to IV Corps with authority to advise both Corps and Divisional Commanders on operational plans and preparations. He said that Thapar seemed to accept the proposal and that I would probably receive instructions the next day.

On the following day the Deputy Chief (Wadalia), the CGS-designate (Moti Sagar), the AG (Kumaramangalam) the QMG (Kochar) and John Lal from the Defence Ministry came to the Ops Room for an operational briefing. After it was over, Wadalia asked me to stay behind for a word, at the end of which I could understand why Thapar had not followed through on the DIB's suggestion.

Of all the senior officers (the KCIOs from Sandhurst) the amiable, polo-playing Wadalia was the least high-reaching or ambitious. Dignified and aloof, he preferred to be a bystander rather than a participant, his ambition limited to (and his mind preoccupied with) owning and managing a horse-breeding farm after retirement. Not overly intellectual, he was nobody's fool either – a respectable and revered lightweight in the army hierarchy.

As he was not given to exaggeration or sensationalism, he must have felt strongly to pass an oblique censure on the DMO. He told me that he had received complaints from all three Army Commanders that the DMO needed 'bringing down a peg or two'. They had asserted that I had got above myself and become swollen-headed and arrogant.

I was somewhat taken aback. I told Wadalia that I had been aware of the hostility of some of my seniors (certainly of that of the Western Army Commander). I thought that that was probably because I had always given my frank opinion on their operational plans, sometimes amounting to criticism, but I was sure that I had done so with due respect for rank and seniority. I did not think I had ever stepped beyond the bounds of military propriety. I asked him if he had told the Army Chief about the Army Commanders' complaints and, if so, what was the Chief's reaction? He replied that yes, he had indeed informed the Chief, who had not totally upheld the Army Commanders' censures. The Chief felt that the DMO was sometimes too forthright and forceful but not necessarily discourteous. At the same time the Chief had told him to warn me about the Army Commanders' comments – for my own good, because those same general officers would eventually play a large part in the shaping of my future career. Characteristically, Wadalia added that I was not to take this was a rebuke from him, but just a warning.

I cast my mind back a few days, to the occasion when Muchu Chaudhuri had called at my office and bluntly asked to be given a job 'in the war'. He had said that at his HQ in Poona he felt left out of the mainstream. His war experience should be better utilised. I had said that I quite agreed that so far he had merely had to watch from the sidelines, but I apprised him about the plans then afoot to mobilise for a major war against China and the key role that logistical preparation would play in those plans. I said that Southern Command was inherently the administrative base of the Indian Army and that his would be a crucial role if we fought a full-scale war against China. I did not sound very convincing (even to myself) and Muchu shrugged off my mealy-mouthed cajolery with a gesture of annoyance. He said that he wanted a positive idea from me, not 'bloody condescension'. When he persisted with his need for a war-related appointment I told him (not entirely in jest) that as the senior among the three Army Commanders' there could only be one job for him here in Delhi, and it was beyond my remit to do anything about that. He pretended to laugh that off, but I could see that he was not well pleased. I wondered if he regarded that attempt at badinage as arrogance in a DMO.

I would certainly not have ventured into such raillery had I known of the clandestine moves then afoot to have Thapar replaced. To this day I am not certain where it started, but I first got an inkling of it when I accompanied Sarin to Parliament House as a back-up team to a long statement the PM was going to make about the war. From listening to comments made by members of the press, bureaucrats and others I gathered that General Srinagesh (the Chief before Thimayya) was being considered for recall to service; another name so mentioned was that of General Thorat. Unfortunately, the brief entries in my diary are cryptic allusions that after thirty years no longer recall my meaning: 'Move to oust Thapar; Rao lobbying on behalf of Bijji; advice to Rao; Kumaramangalam's two-hour interview with CR; President interviewed Niranjan.' I remember admonishing Rao (a GSO-I in MO), but not much more.

On the morning of 7 November, Kaul rang me up from Tezpur, pleading to be allotted one more division. When I told him firmly that he had more troops than he could logistically support, he continued to argue and importune, eventually scaling his bid down to 'just one more brigade'. He said that the Chinese had moved forward strongly from Towang and were by-passing Se-la in large numbers. He expected them to put in a major attack on Bomdila from the north and, perhaps, even at Tenga valley. I told him that as long as Se-la held out there was no question of a major attack anywhere else (that is, a sustained offensive supported by mortars and artillery). I told him that what he must aim to do was to turn the tables on the enemy by disrupting their supply columns skirting Se-la. If he could do that with success, the Chinese would have to fall back on Towang. I said that these should be the twin pillars of the Kameng defensive plan: to hold Se-la at all cost and to disrupt the enemy's supply columns. It is extraordinary that even at this time he made no mention of the change of location of HQ 4th Division and 65 Brigade to Dhirang; whether this omission was by design or mere coincidence, I cannot be sure.

Thapar had called a principal staff officers' meeting to discuss the second part of my draft paper, the part dealing with the offensive phase (in which we would be carrying the war into Tibet, after having contained a Chinese invasion of Assam and Bengal). The plan would hinge on logistics, hence the presence of the PSOs. Before the others arrived, I went privately to Thapar's office, by-passing the MA's ante-room, and told him about Kaul's telephone call. I said that we would have to be very firm in not committing any more troops to the mountains until we had constructed a logistical base and line to maintain them. Furthermore, we needed to build up a force for the defence of the plains, in case the Chinese broke through. I stressed that if IV Corps could not hold the Chinese in Kameng it would not be for want of brigades. Thapar agreed. After a moment's thought he said, 'Monty, I think it is about time we paid another visit to Tezpur.' I said that I would arrange for an aircraft to take us the very next day.

In the evening when I returned to my office I found a message from Sarin to suggest that we meet at his house at 7.30 p.m. When I arrived I found Mullik waiting as well. In a few minutes Sarin joined us. He wanted me to brief them on the first (defensive) phase of Army HQ's strategic forecast. After I had run through the various steps we were planning, including force transfers from the west, Mullik told me that I could count on taking a greater risk in the west (the Pakistan front) and move more divisions to Assam. The United States, he said, had tipped us the wink that they would hold the Pakistanis in check and not let them make any belligerent moves as long as we were under threat of invasion by China. The Foreign Ministry, he said, had that same evening issued a note to that effect.

I said that I would have to reconsider the deployment of formations in view of this new development; for the present I would plan to move one more division – 27th Infantry Division – from the Punjab to the Eastern front. (In the event we transferred both 5 and 27 Divisions, though by the time both moves were completed a ceasefire had come into force.)

Mullik then told us that the PM had called him that afternoon and told him that he had heard through political and administrative channels that commanders and troops on the NEFA front were in a demoralised frame of mind. He was greatly concerned and wanted the DIB to pay a visit to Assam for a personal assessment. Mullik said that he would leave in a day or two. He asked me if I had received any information about 4th Division's morale.

The only definite opinion I could give him was that Anant Pathania was a doubtful element. I described his lack of enthusiasm on the occasion of his first visit to Se-la. I had then judged him to be out of condition, both mentally and physically. I did not think he was the man for that key defensive command. If only the two Pathanias could have been switched! It was too late for that of course, but I said that I would, even at this stage, rather have the command of 4th Division lie vacant, in temporary charge of Hoshiar Singh, than have a reluctant and disheartened GOC. As for Kaul, his deportment, I said, was always unpredictable, not because of lack of fortitude but because of his volatile and inconstant nature. I related to them my wife's experience the day she had visited Corps HQ while on her welfare mission. She had found Bijji surrounded by a crowd of admiring war correspondents from Britain and the United States. Riding on a high, he had struck a 'Rommel-like pose' for the cameramen and described, with dramatic embellishments, how he would deal with any Chinese who attempted to cross the Se-la range. Yet, when having tea with my wife later in the afternoon, his conversation had been one long jeremiad, a dejected and defeatist listing of deficiencies and grievances and assertions that the Chinese would carry everything before them. I told Mullik about Kaul's telephone call to me that very morning pleading for yet more troops and added that he would have to judge for himself whether Kaul would stand up to the responsibilities of a defensive battle against a determined enemy.

I clearly recall Pritpal Singh's earthy comment when I informed MO staff at the morning meeting next day about the DIB's mission. 'I am afraid,' Pritpal said, 'IV Corps and 4th Division have got the wind up. The rumour goes that both GOsC are planning to do a bunk if the Chinese attack in strength!' I had always suspected that we had a parlous set-up in Kameng but I had never heard it so bluntly expressed. I questioned Pritpal about his information and was assured that his was no gossipy comment.

Sen was to visit Delhi on 9 December. I felt that I should take the opportunity to tackle him about the morale of IV Corps. He might have been lacking in strategic and logistical grasp but the one thing he was known to possess was resolution in adversity, as he had amply proved in Burma against the Japanese and in the first Kashmir war. I rang him up in Lucknow and, as before, invited him to breakfast upon arrival in Delhi the next morning.

When he visited my house on the morning of the ninth Bogey told me that he had not had any information about low morale in Kaul's command. Such a negative report was, however, of not much reassurance; his staff was not alert on these matters because there was little staff-level contact between the two HQs. Anyway, I wheedled a promise out of Bogey that if there were an attack in strength at Se-la, he would fly down to Tezpur and 'hold Bijji's hand'. That was the best I could do to ease my misgivings about Se-la – and I still did not know that there was only one brigade up there.

Meanwhile, Thapar paid a quick visit to Tezpur on 8 November. I should have gone with him, but as the PM had sent word that he wanted me to make a presentation of the 'Conduct of War' paper, I had to stay behind to put the final touches to the strategic appreciation. I drove with the Chief to Palam to discuss the latest reinforcement proposals for NEFA and I impressed upon him that these reinforcements should remain Army HQ reserve and not be made available to Corps or even Command for the immediate battle. I said that all that Bijji needed to be given at that stage was one more brigade.

Thapar had taken no major decisions while he was at Tezpur. On 9 November, after the breakfast discussion at my house, Sen was summoned for a meeting in the Ops Room. As the *Summary* recorded:

The COAS held a conference in Operations Room on 9 Nov which was attended by the GOC-in-C Eastern Command, the CGS-designate (Lt Gen Moti Sagar), the Offg CGS, the Adjutant General and myself. The main point of discussion was the IV Corps demand for two more divisions. I explained the General Staff thinking on the subject – that instead of committing any more formations to operations, we should build up reserves in the area to meet a major enemy offensive (into the plains sector) when it was mounted. Even logistically, it would be out of the question to maintain a larger force in IV Corps during the next few weeks. The existing logistical cover was inadequate even for the forces then deployed.

In my opinion IV Corps had made an over-estimate of enemy capabilities. My appreciation was that the Chinese could not logistically maintain a three-divisional offensive in NEFA in the immediate future, even if the Bum-la-Towang road were completed.

After some discussion with the GOC-in-C Eastern Command, the COAS decided that in view of the fact that one brigade had recently been allocated to IV Corps in addition to its previous orbat (82 Brigade from Rajasthan) only one more brigade would be so allocated and that also from Eastern Command's own resources (192 Brigade from Nagaland). At the same time, Army HQ reserve in the Siliguri Sector, 17 Division, was to be made up to a three-brigade division by inducting 112 Infantry Brigade Group from Ahmedabad.

Mullik returned from Assam the next day and asked to see me. He told me that he had found Bijji Kaul depressed, convinced that he had been given a hopeless task. He seemed to have resigned himself to defeat, to the extent that he was taking no precaution to counter the Chinese threat via Poshing-la or the southern encirclement of Se-la (southward, to Nyukmadong). Furthermore, there was widespread deterioration in the morale of the troops, the main reasons being first, that junior officers and the men in the ranks greatly resented Kaul's return to IV Corps, the more so because he had replaced the much respected Harbaksh Singh; second, exaggerated accounts about the prowess of Chinese troops were being spread by refugees from the Namka-chu battle, with wild rumours about their superior weapons, mass-attack tactics and fighting capability, building them up to the image of supermen, something like the British and Indian soldiers' awed regard for the Japanese soldiers after their defeats in Malaya, Burma and the Arakan in the Second World War.

Mullik said that he had not yet made his report to the PM. Clearly he did not relish the task of disillusioning Nehru about the command capabilities of his favourite soldier. He had the moral courage to try to persuade Nehru to replace Kaul but, as I have mentioned before, he was too much of a subordinate to like doing it. He may have tried, I do not know; but Kaul was not recalled.

On 11 November there were two alarming messages from IV Corps. They reported 'an imminent attack on Se-la' and 'a tightening ring around Walong', as though these eventualities had not been foreseen or provided for. I took the signals to Mullik and asked him for the enemy's build-up figures. My *Summary* records:

By 8 Nov, the Chinese were reported to have concentrated about 2,000 troops in the Towang salient. A force of 200 had crossed south of Towang river and had moved down towards the Bhutan border (at Nyimsang-la). Activity north of Towang indicated that a new road link from Bum-la to Towang was under construction. It was also becoming obvious that the enemy had been active on the northern flank of the Se-la position. Parties had been seen moving east along the track Rho-Meling. No frontal contact [with Se-la defences] had been established.

In the Walong sector, the enemy put in three attacks against our positions on 7 and 8 Nov and shelled our defences with mortars and 'direct firing guns'. They were obviously building up to the north of our positions as well as trying to outflank the brigade sector from the west in attempts to establish their positions on the heights on the left (which rose to over 13,000 feet). Patrol skirmishes were frequent with casualties on both sides.

Compared with the figures of enemy strengths published later, those quoted above (obtained from the Intelligence Bureau) seem very low. It is not unusual for hindsight and history to exaggerate enemy strengths, especially after a disastrous defeat, but my impression remains that between 9 and 19 November the Chinese strength had increased to about two regiments (brigades) forward of Towang; this is probably why they made little attempt at a frontal attack on the Se-la defences.

Although the news from Walong was alarming, it was not fraught with strategic disaster. We had a strong five-battalion brigade under a stalwart commander and, although the entire force was maintained by a fleet of Otter light aircraft dependent on a single landing-strip, there was no prospect of a serious threat even if the brigade were pushed back. The earthquake and floods of 1951 had left the Walong-Hayuliang valley cut off from the rest of India and there was not even a mule-track along which the enemy could follow up in strength. The Rima-Walong approach in Lohit FD was a minor threat at best.

Meanwhile, HQ 2 Infantry Division had been raised in eastern Assam (GOC, Mohinder Pathania) with 5 Infantry Brigade (formerly of 4th Division) in Subansiri, Siang and

Western Lohit FDs, guarding minor approaches; 11 Infantry Brigade (also formerly of 4th Division) in Walong; and 181 Infantry Brigade (arriving from southern Assam and Tripura) to face the border with Burma.

In Sikkim 20 Infantry Division had been made up to strength with three brigades. 17 Infantry Division (from Ambala) was concentrating in the Siliguri corridor but at first had only two brigades under command. These two divisions were allotted to HQ XXXIII Corps, which moved from Shillong to Siliguri to take over the Sikkim-West Bhutan front. Harbaksh Singh was appointed GOC.

For the next two days I remained preoccupied with the 'Conduct of War' paper. The Cabinet Secretary's Committee had postponed the discussion on my paper to 16 November because the PM wanted to attend the briefing and had asked for an estimate of the total force necessary for the second phase: eviction of the Chinese from Indian territory. I sent my draft paper to the new CGS, Lieutenant General Moti Sagar, on 15 November but by then the battle at Walong had reached a decisive stage and the committee's meeting had to be indefinitely postponed.

The battle of Walong intensified on 12 November when the Chinese established themselves on a dominating 4,000 metre feature to the north-east codenamed 'Yellow Pimple' – a feature that should, by all tactical precedents, have been occupied by our own troops. Bijji Kaul (who was present at the battle that day) ordered a battalion attack to recapture 'Yellow Pimple'. The battalion attack on 14 November succeeded in occupying part of the feature, at a cost of thirty casualties, but before a second assault could be attempted, the enemy launched a determined offensive all along the northern perimeter, supported by artillery and rockets. Kaul, who had returned to Tezpur the previous day, flew in again on learning that the forward positions were being overrun. It was not until mortar bombs began to fall on the airstrip that the Corps and Divisional Commanders left the scene of battle.

My *Summary* describes the closing stages of the battle of Walong:

By 1100 hours, the forward positions were being overrun by

'superior enemy numbers and firepower'. At the same time, mortar shells had begun to fall on the airstrip. The Corps Commander (and GOC 2 Division) 'informed' 11 Brigade Commander 'to hold on to your present position to the best of your ability. If the position becomes untenable you [are] to take up an alternative position and man it to the best of your ability. In the event that also became untenable you [are] to continue to take up [a] series [of] lay back positions and keep delaying the enemy. ....'

By the afternoon, 11 Brigade had begun to pull out, withdrawing along the un-reconnoitered track on the west bank of the great bend of the Lohit river. All heavy arms and equipment, including wireless sets, were abandoned. Contact with Brigade Headquarters and its units was lost at 1330 hours. Thereafter, 11 Brigade ceased to be an effective fighting formation.

One battalion of this brigade, 3/3 Gorkha Rifles, had been deployed on the east bank of the Lohit, opposite Walong. The only bridge across the river was a single-rope 'flying fox' type of bridge, by which only one person at a time could cross. After the battle started, 3/3 GR became isolated on the east bank. Only a small portion of this battalion was eventually able to get back to Hayuliang, returning cross-country through extremely difficult and unsurveyed terrain on the left bank of the Lohit. These parties suffered incredible hardships, followed closely as they were by the pursuing Chinese.

On the morning of 17 November we received a signal message from Kaul in which he sounded so desperate as to be almost demented. After giving us details of the battle of Walong and warning us of the extreme gravity of the situation, Bijji pushed all circumspection aside and starkly asked for foreign military intervention to save the situation. The text of the message is quoted in my *Summary:*

. . . if these requirements and their logistics are beyond our resources and if more time is going to elapse before we receive imported mountain artillery, 120 mm mortars, .30 medium machine guns, helicopters and Caribous and other equipment . . . it is my duty to urge that the enemy threat is now so great and his overall strength is so superior that you should ask the highest authorities to get such foreign armed forces to come to our aid as are willing, without which, as I have said before and which reiterate, it seems beyond the capacity of our armed forces to stem the tide of the superior Chinese forces which he has and will continue to concentrate against us to our disadvantage. . . .

I took the message to Moti and the two of us walked over to Thapar's office. The Chief's first remark was, 'Bijji has finally lost his mind. He expects us to invite the Americans to fight our battles! We'll have to show this to the PM.'

Nehru supervised the Defence Ministry from his office in the External Affairs Ministry. Although this was only a corridor further down the building, it was often that much more difficult to seek him out there, but on this occasion Thapar did not wait to observe formality. We marched straight into the Prime Minister's office, where fortunately we found him alone.

After Thapar and I had briefed Nehru on the situation at Walong, Thapar showed him Kaul's signal. The PM studied the signal for a while, then asked me to call up the Cabinet Secretary and arrange for a meeting of his committee. I put through telephone calls from the office of the PM's Private Secretary, then hurried back to our Ops Room to arrange to host the assembly there.

The meeting began with a briefing by the DMO on the situation on the Walong front, pointing out details of the battle on the wall-map. When I had done, Thapar told me to go to his secretariat and arrange for an aircraft to fly us immediately to Tezpur and Chabua. Before I left the meeting I handed the Chief a manuscript note I had drawn up as a hurried operational brief in case the PM wished to be informed about the General Staff's overall appreciation of the situation.

## NOTES

1. Krishna Menon would often resort to subterfuge to uphold his theory. Y.D. Gundevia, then Commonwealth Secretary, records one such occasion in his memoirs, *Outside the Archives*. According to him, some time in the first week of October (about the time we in Army HQ were proposing to switch forces from the western frontier to Assam and north Bengal) Menon floated a rumour that he had knowledge of 'heavy Pakistani troop movements in the vicinity of Murree'. No such intelligence had been received by the Foreign Ministry or the Intelligence Bureau. It was Gundevia who, at an emergency conference

with Menon, the Indian High Commissioner in Pakistan, the Defence Secretary and the Chief of Intelligence Mullik, succeeded in scotching this clearly contrived alarm.

2. A 'shopping list' was drawn up by the DCGS for the Ministry of Defence and presented to missions sent out by the United States and Britain in the first week of November. While an examination of this list was being carried out in detail, both countries took action to fly out certain essential and immediate requirements of arms and equipment which started arriving in India from 4 November.

# 9
# DEBACLE IN KAMENG

Our journey to NEFA on 17 November culminated in an evening of greater portent than we could have imagined. The Army Chief set out from Delhi hoping that his presence at the battlefront would inspire a demoralised Corps Commander and help him make fresh plans to meet the sudden threat arising from the fall of Walong. Things did not turn out that way. Events can be dominated only by those who have a clear set of goals. We had not yet formed ours. Even the information about the disposition of our own forces was, incredible as it may seem, both inadequate and misleading. In the circumstances, our presence failed to influence the battle for Kameng; on the contrary, it was we who were overwhelmed by the events.

Thapar and I were the only passengers in the Super-Constellation the IAF had placed at our disposal. Our diminutive presence in that cavernous aircraft seemed to accentuate the almost palpable air of gloom around us. I took a seat a few rows behind Thapar, but as soon as we were airborne he beckoned to me to go and to sit by his side. He looked frail and distraught and I perceived that he would need support and incitement to accomplish the task he had undertaken. Although not decisive by habit, he was not always a ditherer. He could be authoritative, but at that moment he seemed to lack the will to be so.

I resolved to take it upon myself to prop up his flagging resolution.

I told him that if the attack on Walong presaged another general offensive by the Chinese, he would have to be very firm with both Bogey Sen and Bijji Kaul. The former had been too reckless in the Namka-chu affair; the latter seemed to have become wildly alarmist. I added that he should be prepared to restrain the one and sustain the other. I also forewarned him that since he had decided personally to oversee the IV Corps battle, his very presence would render him accountable for the outcome, so if Sen or Kaul failed to respond to the crisis he must not hesitate to remove either or both, and, if necessary, assume command himself. This was obtrusive advice from a junior, but Thapar seemed not to resent a younger man's presumptuousness. He nodded his head, placed a hand on my arm and said: 'I am glad you are with me, Monty. We will see this through.'

After a few moments he asked me what I thought of Muchu (General Chaudhuri) and how he would fit in as Chief. That was a sad moment, because I realised at once that he had the possibility of his own dismissal or resignation in mind. The question was unexpected and awkward to answer, and I made a noncommittal reply. To cover the awkwardness I told him, in lighter vein, about Muchu's request to me a few weeks previously for a 'job' in Delhi. That, at least, brought a smile to Thapar's face.

Thapar then said that he had been thinking about Kaul's signal. Would we have to ask for armed intervention by the United States or Britain? I assured him that the situation was nothing like as desperate as Kaul had painted in his alarming signal. I took out a copy of the note I had earlier given Thapar in the Ops Room and went through its contents as a confidence-building measure.

The note was a summary of MO Directorate's operational survey following the first Chinese offensive. The General Staff appreciation was that even if a second Chinese offensive resulted in further advances in Ladakh, it would still not pose a threat either to Kashmir or to the Punjab, because the Chinese potential for war in Ladakh was limited to trans-border operations; even Leh would probably be out of their reach, particularly if a part of the garrison at

Chushul managed to withdraw across Chang-la in time. In NEFA, an advance down the Lohit river at Walong would also not constitute a serious national threat (despite Kaul's panicky signal after the fall of Walong). As for Kameng, we felt confident of the Se-la defences holding out. Even if Chinese foot-columns by-passed them and laid siege to Dhirang and Bomdila, Se-la would hold out long enough for the winter's snow to take the punch out of the Chinese offensive. Our confidence was based on the firm plans we had made for the build-up and stocking at Se-la. As I recorded in my *Summary:*

Own Dispositions and Build-up.

When I had last discussed operational plans with HQ IV Corps (on 25 October) the intention had been to concentrate the greater part of 4th Division in the Se-la-Senge area, with a brigade defensive position at Bomdila. Logistical difficulties, particularly a grave shortage of one-ton vehicles, as mentioned before, obstructed a speedy forward concentration of 4th Division. . . . However, the position on 17 November was not unsatisfactory – because two brigades, with a total of about seven battalions, with supporting arms and weapons, had by then been concentrated in the Se-la-Senge defensive sector.·. . .

Detailed dispositions of IV Corps forces for the Kameng battle, on 17 November, was as follows:

(a) *Se-la-Senge Area* – 62 and 65 Brigades, with a total of seven infantry battalions (including covering troops); HQ 4th Division;

(b) *Dhirang* – Rear HQ 4th Division; two infantry companies; one field battery (eight guns); DGBR (Border Roads) elements; administrative echelons.

(c) *Bomdila* – 48 Brigade, with two battalions; on 16 November, one battalion was sent to Thembang, with one company further forward; one squadron of tanks; one field battery.

(d) *Misamari* – 67 Brigade, with two battalions, awaiting induction to Kameng.

(e) *Daranga* –181 Brigade, with three battalions and a squadron of tanks.

(f) *Tezpur* – HQ IV Corps.

In addition, a considerable force of Border Roads Engineer units (four field companies, eight construction companies, eight pioneer companies and others) were in support of 4th Division at that time.

It will be seen that for the main battle, two brigades had been located in the Senge-Se-la defences (with rations stocked for twelve days). Although our positions elsewhere in Kameng were somewhat thin on the ground, only infiltrating or outflanking attacks on a small scale could be mounted against them. (The northern route from Meling-Mago-Lap-Valley-Tse-la-Poshing-la to Bomdi-la was a difficult track, about ten days march through uninhabited areas, over which no sizeable force could be logistically maintained.)

The information available to the DMO on 17 November was, in fact, inaccurate, even if not to such an extent that it was gravely deceptive. What had happened was that Anant Pathania had pleaded altitude sickness and asked permission to move his Tactical HQ down to the bottom of the range, to Dhirang (see Chapter 8). Kaul having okayed this pusillanimous proposition, Pathania not only quit the Se-la area but also compromised its defence plans by holding back most of the second brigade (65 Infantry Brigade) at Dhirang. He sent up only one of its battalions; the rest of the brigade he kept down at the bottom of the valley for the security of his own HQ. (He had meanwhile sent for his Main HQ, till then located at Tezpur, to join him in Dhirang.) This redisposition effectively split 4th Division into three separate defensive localities instead of just the two that I had envisaged. Furthermore, one of his three positions, at the bottom of a valley, was untactically located. Not only that: officers and men of HQ 4th Division had not even bothered to dig any trenches or erect any form of defences, preferring to live in the comfortable Border Roads huts and neat lines of tents.

Nevertheless Se-la-Senge still constituted a formidable defensive locality. 62 Infantry Brigade, with five infantry battalions and adequate artillery, mortar and engineer support, and stocked for a twelve-day battle, could reasonably be expected to withstand an assault by a weak enemy division, which is the most that the Chinese could be expected to concentrate at Jang.

As for Bomdila, a move had been made, even if at the last minute, to safeguard it against the threat from the north via Lap valley and Poshing-la (where there had already been an unsuccessful patrol skirmish with a strong enemy column). On the morning of 16 November a battalion had been sent to Thembang, a village on the ridge north of Bomdila, and a company towards Poshing-la.

On arrival at Tezpur airfield Thapar and I were met by Sen and Sibal. Sen informed Thapar that earlier that day the Chinese had opened their second offensive by launching an attack on Se-la; a battle was even then in progress. On hearing this Thapar decided to cancel his onward journey to Chabua and remain at Tezpur. He sent a wireless message recalling Kaul to Corps HQ immediately.

Herding us all into his staff car for the trip to Corps HQ, Sen began to recount details of the Chinese attack. Starting in the morning, he said, a motley force of Chinese in various kinds of garb, including some in Mompa costumes, had moved up from Jang and launched a series of assaults against 4 Garhwal Rifles, who were deployed at Nuranang,[1] forward of Se-la, as the covering troops of the main defences. The Garhwalis had repulsed four successive attempts to overrun their positions, inflicting considerable casualties on the Chinese. Sen then added that the latest information was that GOC 4th Division had ordered the battalion to withdraw from Nuranang.

I was astounded. I turned toward Sen and asked: 'Why were they withdrawn? If the Garhwalis have repulsed four attacks by the Chinese surely they should remain at their post?'

Sen did not look too pleased at my interruption and replied with bad grace that I would have to ask GOC 4th Division if I wanted an answer to my question. Not to be put off, I said that withdrawal by the Garhwalis would mean that our troops would break contact with the enemy, who could then build up for an attack on the main position without interference. I urged Sen to issue orders to cancel the withdrawal of the covering troops battalions.

'It is not for me to interfere in IV Corps' battles,' Sen said, somewhat pompously.

'Not even in the absence of the Corps Commander?' I asked, but he ignored my question. Thapar chose to remain silent.

By that time we had arrived at Corps HQ where we were met by the BGS, K.K. Singh, who told us that information had just been received that the fighting had spread to Bomdila. 5 Guards, the battalion at Thembang, had reported over the wireless that they had been surrounded

by a Chinese force coming in from the north and had
asked for permission to withdraw; permission had been
granted by the Brigade Commander.

I could scarcely believe what we were being told. None
of the commanders seemed to have the heart for a fight.
As soon as we were secluded in the Corps Ops Room, I
remarked to Thapar: 'Everyone seems to be withdrawing!
As far as I can make out the Guards have not even been
attacked, and yet they are being pulled out of battle. Their
withdrawal will mean that the road from Bomdila to Dhirang
will be exposed to the enemy who would then be free to
disrupt 4th Division's line of communication at will. This
is a disastrous decision.'

At this point Sen told K.K. Singh that he was no longer
required and dismissed him, an extraordinary precedent, I
thought, in the BGS's own Ops Room. When K.K. left, I
leaned forward in my chair to confront Sen: 'Sir, I hope
you will reverse at least *this* decision. And if it is too late
to stop the withdrawal, 48 Brigade Commander must be
ordered to re-establish a position on Thembang ridge with
fresh troops; or, at least, to position troops somewhere on
the lower slopes of that ridge – to deny the enemy easy
access to the main Towang road.'

'I have already told you, Monty, it is *not* my job to
interfere in the Corps' or the Division's battles,' he replied
coldly. I was taken aback by the obstinate and negative
attitude he had adopted. It was the very reverse of my
expectations of him.

'On the contrary,' I persisted, 'in the absence of the
Corps Commander you, by your very presence, are responsible
for the corps' battle. It has reached a critical stage and it
is for you to assume command.' Bogey Sen looked down
at his shoes and said nothing.

I could not hold back an exclamation of impatience and,
turning to Thapar, I said, 'Sir, please take over the battle.
The Army Commander disclaims that responsibility.'

Thapar reacted at once. He seemed to shake himself out
of a reverie. 'A-ho,' he replied in Punjabi, and looked at
me inquiringly. My first suggestion was that we recall the
BGS to the Ops Room.

I realised that this was my chance to impel Thapar to

action. I advised him that we should place 48 Brigade in
Bomdila under direct command of Corps HQ, because the
Divisional Commander at Senge must not be made to look
back over his shoulder. All his attention must be riveted
on the Se-la battle.

Thapar agreed with me. K.K., however, intervened to
point out that the Divisional Commander was not up at
Se-la; he had relocated himself at Dhirang. It was then
that I first learned about Pathania's plea to be allowed to
move down from Senge because of persistent headaches
and Kaul's assent to this inglorious defection. This was
another blow to my diminishing confidence in IV Corps'
operational ethos.

At this juncture GOC 4th Division came through on the
line from Dhirang. Speaking to the BGS, he reported that
groups of Chinese had come round the left flank of the
Se-la defences. Pathania feared that the enemy would
probably attempt to sever the road between Senge and
Dhirang. He also said that 'the Dhirang–Bomdila road had
been cut' by the enemy and that he was finding it difficult
to contact HQ 48 Brigade on the telephone. He asked for
permission to withdraw 4 Infantry Division.

When K.K. passed the message to me I took it upon
myself to tell him firmly to say 'no' to the withdrawal, but
to keep Pathania waiting on the line. Bogey Sen interrupted
to say that in his opinion we should give Pathania permission
to withdraw.

Ignoring Sen's remark, I turned to Thapar and again
asked him to assume command of the battle. I told him
about Pathania's abject plea to withdraw 4th Division just
because the Chinese were working round his flank, a
possibility that had been clearly anticipated and provided
for. I said that the defence plans for Kameng would collapse
around us unless he took a firm grip on the situation. As
I recorded in the *Summary:*

I emphatically pointed out that:
(a) the Se-la–Senge sector was one of the strongest natural
defensive positions in NEFA;
(b) we had a sizeable force, stocked for battle, deployed in this sector;
(c) as far as I knew, all possible encircling moves by the enemy

had been foreseen and plans must have been drawn up to meet
such contingencies;

(*d*) a withdrawal into Dhirang Valley (down 40 km of a steep,
narrow and winding road) would be untactical and could only
end in a rout;

(*e*) no alternative positions had been prepared, not as far as we knew.

In these circumstances, I pointed out that withdrawal from
Se-la could only result in the loss of Kameng FD without a fight
and the disintegration of 4 Infantry Division. This must not be
allowed to happen.

A withdrawal is the most intricate, demoralising and
high-risk manoeuvre of war: intricate, because it necessitates
the pre-selection, preparation and occupation of a series of
fall-back positions in the rear through which frontline troops
successively pull back after breaking contact with a pursuing
enemy; demoralising, because a move-back is seldom a
preferred choice but enforced on a weaker force by a
superior enemy; and high-risk because the meticulous
synchronisation of each leap-frog movement can fail, resulting
in disaster — especially when running down a steep
mountain-side chased by an enemy from overlooking heights.

Thapar saw that clearly, while Sen appeared to be
speaking about the withdrawal of 4th Division as an abstract
notion, blind to the realities of the situation. Unfortunately,
instead of firmly ordering Pathania to stay and fight, Thapar
began a discussion with Sen, trying to persuade him in a
guarded way that 4th Division must be 'advised' to stick
it out on Se-la. When I tried impatiently to intervene,
Thapar held up his hand to restrain me.

Ignoring my attempts at interruption, Sen told Thapar
that permission *must* be given for the withdrawal. 'If 4
Infantry Division can make a clean break now,' he said,
'it will have a chance of getting away intact.'

Before Thapar could be influenced by this specious
argument I asked the Army Commander what the Division's
operational role was: to fight the enemy at Se-la or to keep
itself intact? I had not consciously intended sarcasm, but
Sen obviously resented my question. Thapar began to
intervene between us, but before he could say anything I
firmly asserted that there could be no question of allowing
Pathania to pull back from Se-la. The attack at Nuranang

had been a minor one and was repulsed by a battalion of infantry. What was the reason for withdrawing?

More discussion followed between Thapar and Sen and, of course, they got nowhere. Meanwhile K.K. was holding the line to GOC 4th Division, though I did not know if Anand Pathania was still there at the other end. While I was attempting again to break into the Thapar-Sen dialogue, Bijji Kaul arrived from Chabua.

A Bijji entrance was seldom undramatic. He bounced in with a jaunty step, his uniform somewhat crumpled, and wearing on his head that popularly approved hallmark of active duty, a sort of khaki Gandhi cap made from an ordnance-issue woollen scarf. He succeeded in creating a picture he obviously meant to create: a warrior just back from the wars (which, to give him his due, was not entirely counterfeit).

Without waiting for preliminaries, Kaul launched into a dramatised blow-by-blow account of events subsequent to the fall of Walong and the part he had played in them: details of 11 Infantry Brigade's withdrawal along both banks of the Lohit; supply-dropping missions for the withdrawing troops; 'rescue' missions by helicopter, in one of which Kaul had personally landed 'amidst sporadic enemy fire' and offered to evacuate the Brigade Commander (a quite unprofessional procedure, in my opinion, because the brigade would have been left in the lurch without a commander. The Brigade Commander, stout-heartedly, declined the offer).

Every time I tried to interrupt Kaul to bring him to the business at hand, he would take off on a description of some other hair-raising episode of the Lohit battle, jumping up and down excitedly at the wall-map. Nor did Thapar and Sen try to stop this slapstick recital. Eventually, unable to contain myself, I walked over to where Kaul stood by the map and gripped his arm.

'Bijji-bhai,' I said firmly, 'forget Walong, the crisis is in Kameng. Your Fourth Division is collapsing.'

'What?' he exclaimed, suddenly alarmed. 'What are you talking about?'

Briefly I gave him the news from Se-la and described the situation in 4th Division. I said that though a number of Chinese attacks on Nuranang had been repeatedly repulsed, Pathania had panicked and was asking for permission to withdraw. I explained that without previously prepared plans a withdrawal was impossible; there was no alternative except to fight it out at Se-la. In any case, we had foreseen all the likely Chinese moves and provided the resources to deal with them. Se-la would hold out, I assured him, but no one had yet said 'no' to Pathania's request to pull back. I was waiting for the Corps Commander to do so, I added.

At this point Thapar called me over and, for whatever reason, directed me to go to the main office and put through an urgent call to Army HQ to ensure that the move of 82 Infantry Brigade (being sent to Chabua from Rajasthan, as reinforcement for 2 Infantry Division) was carried out by air and not by rail. Perhaps the real reason for this was, that embarrassed by an over-assertive DMO, he was getting rid of him from the assembly. I cannot say that I reproached him for his action. Casting my mind back to the proceedings in the Corps Ops Room that evening, I realised that I had ill-used both form and formality and, however great the provocation, a wiser man might have handled the situation more effectively.

I chose to go to Inder Verma's office to put through my call. Seated at his desk waiting for it to come through, I described the infuriating charade that was being played out in the Ops Room. I said that I could never have believed that men in responsible positions could be so weak-willed and irresolute at a time of battle crisis. As for Anant Pathania, it had come as a shock to be told that the old warrior was asking for permission to run away even before battle was engaged.

It was then that I learned that in fact Anant Pathania had, the previous day, rung up the BGS and desperately begged to be allowed to move his HQ even further away from the front, either to Tenga valley or even as far back as Foothills Camp. When refused this request, he had still gone ahead with plans to decamp, and had surreptitiously sent a staff officer from his HQ, a Major Umat, to reconnoitre a new location for his Divisional HQ in Tenga valley, where Umat had been promptly placed under arrest by Colonel Shamsher Singh, logistical staff officer of 4th Division.

I must have sat at Inder's desk for about twenty minutes, letting the tension that had built up in me unwind, when K.K. Singh came in looking for me. With a somewhat derisive smile on his face he flung a copy of a signal on the desk in front of me and said, 'So much for your advice on Se-la.'

I picked up the signal. It was an operational message from Corps HQ to 4th Division granting it permission to withdraw. I was stunned and scandalised — but also driven to rage.

'Who has authorised the withdrawal?' I asked K.K. curtly. He replied that I had better take that up with the Corps Commander and left the room. I turned to Inder, the one person in Corps HQ to whom I felt I could turn for help, and asked him if he could stop transmission of the message. This was not his job, but since he was himself from the Corps of Signals, it would be easy for him to bend the rules. Decisive as ever, he promptly replied that that should not be too difficult. Because of the high mountain ranges that intervened, he explained, wireless traffic from Tezpur to Dhirang had to be relayed through Bomdila. He would do his best to get through to 48 Brigade and have the message cancelled, quoting my authority, to which I agreed.

Picking up the message sheet from the desk I walked back to the Ops Room. At the door I met Kaul coming out. I stopped him, showed him the signal and asked who had authorised it. For the first time in our relationship I felt a sudden spark of hostility between us. He hesitated for a moment, then mumbled, 'Ask the Army Commander,' and went on his way.

Assuming that what Kaul meant was that Sen had ordered the withdrawal, I went straight up to Thapar who was sitting in his chair, staring vacantly at the wall-map. I thrust the message at him and asked, 'Do you realise, Sir, that the Army Commander has given 4th Division permission to withdraw from Se-la?' He looked up at me, startled, uncomprehending; it was obvious that this was news to him.

Sen was in the next chair, talking to his BGS. I raised my voice and asked Thapar how it was that when the

Corps Commander was present in his HQ the Army Commander was issuing operational orders – whereas in the former's absence he had refused to shoulder any responsibility.

Sen turned towards us. He looked at me, puzzled, and asked what I was talking about. When I told him about the message he replied firmly that he definitely had not issued any orders for a withdrawal.

I did not waste any further time trying to trace the source of that ignominious order. I addressed Thapar, perhaps somewhat overdramatically (this is quoted from my *Summary*):

. . . we could never face the nation if 12,000 troops, supported by artillery and mortars and stocked for battle, 'ran away' without even facing the enemy. I told him that in my opinion 4th Division was in a position to withstand an attack in strength by the Chinese. . . . After some discussion [the COAS] directed that the withdrawal order be cancelled.

I went back to consult Inder Verma, who confirmed that he had got through to HQ 48 Brigade in Bomdila and prevented the message from being relayed to HQ 4th Infantry Division. The message was then withdrawn and, at about 9 p.m., Kaul issued a second signal ordering 4th Division 'to remain at Se-la and to fight it out to the best of its ability and withdraw only if its position became untenable.'[2]

It was past 9.30 p.m. when I returned to the Ops Room. By then I had become aware of a general feeling of antagonism towards me from everyone except Thapar. Sen affected to ignore me whenever possible, but that I could well understand: my forthrightness had at times verged on rudeness.

When Bijji Kaul returned to the Ops Room, I cornered him near the wall-map and said that it was time to give some thought to 48 Brigade, which also seemed to be giving way to panic. I explained that the first priority would be to re-establish troops on Thembang ridge during the hours of darkness. I picked up the phone and asked to be connected to the Brigade Commander at Bomdila. When

Gurbux Singh came on the line, I handed the set to Kaul but stood at his elbow, determined to ensure that firm orders were passed. As recorded in the *Summary*:

By this time, GOC IV Corps, having been apprised of the withdrawal from Thembang which had exposed the Dhirang road to enemy action, had been able to get through to 48 Brigade Commander on the telephone. The latter stated that no contact had been established with 5 Guards after their withdrawal began (nor was contact established later, as the battalion had virtually 'disintegrated'). In the meanwhile, Chinese infiltrators were reported to have cut the road between Bomdila and Dhirang. GOC IV Corps ordered 48 Brigade Commander to clear the road-block but the latter said that it was 'too dark to send out a counter-attack force!' and in any case he did not want to deplete Bomdila's defences any further. However, GOC IV Corps ordered him to send out a fighting patrol immediately, to attempt to clear the road-block, which could not (he added) have been established in strength. In any event, he ordered that the road be patrolled to gain information of enemy moves. He also informed Commander 48 Brigade that he was ordering two battalions of 67 Brigade to move from Misamari to Bomdila during the night, so that these reinforcements would be available to him sometime next morning. (The Commander of 67 Brigade had already gone forward for a reconnaissance of Bomdila and Dhirang. He was at that moment in Dhirang.)

Later in the evening, 48 Brigade Commander, on being asked about the progress of the road-clearing operation, said that the patrol which had gone out had been pinned down by 'defensive fire' on the outskirts of Bomdila and had been unable to proceed further. He reported that the enemy were then within 400 yards of the forward positions of Bomdila' defences.

At about 10 p.m. Kaul suggested to the Chief and the Army Commander that they repair to the Corps Commander's hut, a short distance away across the central courtyard, for dinner. He also invited Sibal and me. Before going in to dinner I called at Inder Verma's office and asked him to try and get GOC 4th Division on the line and connect him to the Corps Commander's residence.

Seated for dinner, I thought it might restore the flagging morale around the table if I passed on some of the heartening tidbits of gossip I had picked up while sitting in Verma's office. I said that Brigadier Hoshiar Singh was reported to have expressed satisfaction with the state of the defence at Se-la and was confident of holding out against even a strong Chinese attack. The defences were tactically sited and the troops well dug-in; there were adequate stocks of reserve ammunition and supplies, distributed down to units. His only problem was not having up-to-date maps – of which there was a dire lack all round – although he had partly made up for this by wide-ranging patrolling and reconnaissance.

My little 'pep talk' was received in silence while dinner was being served. When the mess orderlies had withdrawn, Sen again asserted, in a lugubrious tone, that the only course open was for the Division to withdraw from Se-la but when I asked him where they were to withdraw to, he did not answer. Thapar remained silent. I felt sure that he disagreed with Sen, but I think his mind and will had been numbed by the events of the evening.

The telephone rang while we were still at dinner. I hurried to the desk and picked it up. Recognising Pathania's voice I shouted across the room to Kaul, saying that his Divisional Commander was on the line. While waiting for him I identified myself to Pathania and said that the Corps Commander wanted to speak to him. Fearing that the connection might be broken before Kaul could take the line, I added: 'Anant, there is to be *no* withdrawal. The Corps Commander will tell you that himself.'

While waiting for Bijji to come to the telephone, I asked Pathania whether there had yet been a frontal attack on the Se-la position. Pathania said no, there had not, but the Chinese seemed to be active all around him at Dhirang and between Dhirang and Bomdila.

At this point Kaul took the line from me and a drawn-out conversation ensued. There was much reference back and forth to Thapar, who for once was definite that there was to be no withdrawal. At last Bijji Kaul gave his subordinate commander orders for battle – in words which will surely remain a classic *double entendre* in our military history books. I recorded in the *Summary*:

'*Achchha*, Anant,' Bijji said in Hindi, 'For tonight you hang on

318 / WAR IN HIGH HIMALAYA

to your defences.' Then, in English he added: 'Have another chat with me in the morning!' How far that unconventional enjoinment would stand up as an imperative to a jittery subordinate to stay and fight, I need not comment upon – but it was too late to do anything about it.

At 11 p.m. Thapar and I left for the Circuit House in Tezpur where we had been lodged. As he had not brought an ADC with him, I went in to his suite of rooms to ensure that he lacked nothing. As I was leaving, he asked me to stay a while and talk to him.

When he emerged from the dressing-room in his pyjamas, he went to the bed and lay down, inviting me to sit by his side. After a while he asked me if I thought Pathania would obey orders. I replied that he had not been given firm orders to remain at his post. In case Thapar had not overheard Kaul, I repeated Kaul's exact words. Thapar remained quiet, gazing up at the ceiling. To make him feel better I said that I did not think Hoshiar Singh would quit, unless given a direct order by Pathania; even then, he might still decide to remain at Se-la. He was experienced enough in infantry tactics to realise that a withdrawal in those circumstances could only end in disaster.

I had left instructions to be awakened early in the morning. When the orderly brought me a cup of tea at 5.30 a.m. he told me that Thapar was already up and about and had asked to see me. I hurriedly slipped on my dressing-gown and, taking the tea-tray with me, I went to his room.

Thapar looked careworn and haggard. Almost the first thing he asked me was whether I thought 4th Division positions on Se-la would be able to hold out, to which I replied, 'Yes, Sir, if they choose to fight it out and if General Sen will let them. It will take a strong effort to dislodge them – and I don't believe the Chinese can produce that effort before the passes are snowed up.' I suggested that he order Bogey Sen back to his HQ at Lucknow but Thapar made no comment on this.

Instead he asked me whether Kaul would be able to conduct the corps battle resolutely, to which I had no difficulty in answering 'No.' I said that the Corps Commander appeared to be under great stress, possibly as a result of his demoralising experience on the Namka-chu riverline, followed by a debilitating illness. I recommended that he be sent back to Army HQ as CGS. If the PM would not agree to recalling Kaul, I suggested that we create the Field Army HQ I had spoken to him about (XIV Army) and push Kaul upstairs to command it. I cautioned however that Kaul must not be ousted from IV Corps without a replacement, otherwise it would again fall to Sen to assume charge in Tezpur, and that would be even more disastrous. I added that a fresh, vigorous commander was needed in Tezpur. Since Harbaksh was already spoken for (he had been appointed GOC XXXIII Corps) I suggested the name of Major General 'Sam' Manekshaw.

'Bijji won't stand for that,' Thapar said, as I had expected. 'You know that he instituted an inquiry against Sam last year and would have had him out of the army if he could. No, I don't think he will be acceptable to Kaul.' [3]

'Leave that to me, Sir,' I replied. 'I will talk to the Corps Commander. I am off to Corps HQ now, but I shall be back within the hour.'

At about 6.30 I borrowed Thapar's staff car and drove off to Corps HQ, to Kaul's residence. I found him lying in bed in his pyjamas, but wide awake. He looked up at me, smiled somewhat sheepishly, almost guiltily, and gave me his dreadful news. As I recorded it:

### 4th Division's withdrawal

At about 0700 hours next morning [18 Nov] I went to see the Corps Commander. He informed me that the Brigade Major of 62 Brigade [on Se-la] in an earlier telephone conversation with a Corps Staff Officer, had 'let the cat out of the bag', by stating that one of the forward battalions occupying the Se-la defensive sector had been withdrawn during the night; subsequently, after an attack on the 1 Sikh positions that battalion had also been withdrawn.

The Corps Commander then informed me that he had contacted GOC 4th Division at 0630 hours; the latter informed the Corps Commander that he was closing down his headquarters at Dhirang Dzong, because of the Chinese threat, and was moving – though he could not state what his destination was to be. Thereafter,

Corps HQ was not able to contact either 4th Division or any of the formations or units in the whole Se-la-Senge-Dhirang Sector, either by wireless or by telephone.

It would be a long time before the world would learn the true story about the sequence of chicken-hearted directions from Pathania that finally decided Hoshiar Singh to abandon the defences of Se-la. It was not until many years later, when corps and unit histories, personal memoirs and other documents began to be published, that one learned about the full extent of the disaster caused by one man's faintheartedness. That blot on the honour of the Indian Army has not been erased to this day.

At the time my reaction was a mixture of stunned disbelief and anger that once again it was the generals and commanders who had so wretchedly betrayed the young officers and men of our army. I had little doubt that the 'withdrawal' from Se-la would degenerate into an uncontrollable rout and in the process the slaughter could be great. As for those who would be taken prisoner, none of us knew what kind of enemy the Chinese would prove to be. (In the aftermath of investigations, although only a few instances of mass atrocities were proven, it was obvious that in the absence of any statutory code of conduct, the treatment of prisoners by their Chinese captors depended upon individuals and circumstances. There were occasions when surrendering troops, with their hands in the air in the traditional gesture of surrender, were ruthlessly gunned down and then individually finished off to ensure there would be no witnesses, their personal possessions looted. There were also occasions when Chinese officers went out of their way to redress reported cases of maltreatment and even returned looted property to their owners).

When I asked Kaul if he had any plans to face the new situation, he replied that he intended to go up to Bomdila and reorganise its defences. He said that Gurbux Singh had that morning reported that the enemy seemed to have broken contact during the night. The previous night's reports from the trenches that the Chinese had closed to within 400 yards of the forward defended localities, Gurbux added, had proved exaggerated. The road-block between Bomdila and Dhirang was, however, still in place. Kaul said that he would go up to Bomdila and ensure that its defences were sound.

It was typical of Kaul to want to escape from his HQ and its implied command accountability, and dash off towards the front to undertake some imagined feat of derring-do. I advised him not to leave his HQ without informing the Army Chief, adding that more than the defence of Kameng was now at stake. The Chief, I said, would issue operational instructions later in the morning.

I took the opportunity of informing Kaul about the Chief's intention to raise a HQ XIV Army to command IV and XXXIII Corps and to co-ordinate battles in the plains sector, from the Siliguri corridor to the Brahmaputra valley. I said that he, Kaul, would be the obvious choice for the new command, but he would have to accept Manekshaw if the latter were appointed GOC IV Corps, which was the Chief's intention. Kaul reacted predictably, saying that on no account would he tolerate Manekshaw as a subordinate. I had come prepared with my ploy. I told him that if he persisted with his objection Thapar would probably appoint Manekshaw CGS. That prospect, I well knew, would unsettle Kaul's self-confidence, and I was right. Kaul meekly agreed to taking on Manekshaw as a subordinate commander.

Leaving the Corps Commander's shack I went to the main Corps HQ offices to see if I could obtain more information. The only person I found at his desk was Lieutenant Colonel 'Vir' Vohra (formerly of my Regiment, then serving on the General Staff at Corps HQ). Vohra confirmed that HQ 62 Brigade (on Se-la-Senge) had gone off the air and had almost certainly abandoned their wireless sets before withdrawing, because not one set had opened up or responded during the past few hours – not from Se-la, not from Senge, not from Dhirang. Total silence reigned within the wireless and telecommunications network of 4 Infantry Division. There could be no doubt that everybody was on the run. 4 Infantry Division had ceased to exist.

The implications of the catastrophe appalled me more than I can describe. I took the fall of Se-la not only as a national calamity but also as a personal grief, for I had staked much by persisting with my advice to defend Se-la, against opposition from both Corps and Command HQ; and I realised that the abandonment of Se-la would in time be blamed on its 'tactical unsuitability'.

Needing to hide the depth of my despair, I went and sat in the staff car and sent the driver to 'A' mess for a cup of tea. Although I felt almost stupefied by the tragedy, I had to sort out in my mind the likely consequences in terms of enemy threats to the plains sector. I was aware not only that I would have to suggest a clear and firm line of action to Thapar but also prod him to take charge at Corps HQ.

I found myself in some doubt about whether we ought to continue to defend Bomdila or to withdraw 48 Infantry Brigade to Misamari in anticipation of fighting a defensive battle in the plains. I decided that it was too late to plan a tactical withdrawal unrehearsed; that could also turn into a rout. It would be best to muster a separate force for the defence of the plains sector.

I drove back to the Circuit House and found Bogey Sen and his BGS already there. Sen was still advising Thapar to order the withdrawal of 4 Infantry Division from Se-la.

'Four Infantry Division,' I informed them, 'has pulled out without orders and without offering battle. Some time between midnight and this morning our forces ran away from Se-la, Senge and Dhirang. They seem to have abandoned all their wireless sets because there has been no further contact with any formation or unit thereafter.'

Thapar and Sen both looked stunned. Both had in their days commanded this famous Second World War infantry division and although it was a completely reconstructed formation that had ended up in Senge-Se-la-Dhirang, there must have been a degree of personal tragedy in this news for both of them.

I turned to Thapar and said that we must get to Corps HQ soon and plan to prepare Assam valley for defence. I added that it would probably take the Chinese at least four days to build up for a formal invasion of the plains. On the other hand they might follow up their success by immediately sending infiltration parties to Udalguri, Rangia and Misamari.

We arrived at the Corps Ops Room at about 8 a.m.
Kaul opened the proceedings by recounting the events of
the previous night. As recorded in the *Summary:*

General Kaul informed us that there had been some delay in
despatching the two battalions of 67 Brigade from Misamari to
Bomdila the previous night (owing to difficulties in marshalling
the necessary vehicles and to traffic congestion on the road) but
that leading elements ought to reach Bomdila by mid-day and
the main body by early afternoon. He felt that as the enemy at
Bomdila could not be in any great strength, our defences ought
to be able to hold out . . . particularly in view of the fact that
strong reinforcements would be reaching them shortly.

As for the main body of 4th Division, Kaul expected that the
two brigades from Se-la and Senge were withdrawing towards
Dhirang, clearing road-blocks on the way; they would, it was
estimated, eventually join up with the Dhirang garrison and then
fight their way back together to Bomdila. There had, however,
been no contact with any wireless set in 4th Division and the
possibility of a rout could not be overlooked.

[As it later transpired, the 'withdrawal' from Se-la-Senge was
not carried out as an operation of war. It was a panicky flight,
and the Chinese took every tactical advantage to pursue and
shoot down our troops from the heights above. As for Divisional
Headquarters and the Dhirang garrison, having met some opposition
on the Bomdila road, they decided to bolt for home – escaping
southwards over the Manda-la Pass into the Kalakthang district
and thence to the plains.]

At about 1100 hours, Corps Commander again contacted 48
Brigade Commander on the telephone and was told that the
road-clearing column had still not left Bomdila, because the tanks
and the infantry had not yet 'married up'. General Kaul ordered
the Brigade Commander again to send the column out immediately
and warned the latter that if there were any further delay in
obeying his orders and carrying out this vital task he would
remove him from his command. [This column, it was later learnt,
did not start until 1230 hours, by which time the enemy, though
still in small numbers, were infiltrating towards the outskirts of
Bomdila.]

Meanwhile, I had advised COAS and GOC-in-C that the time
had come to make plans for the defence of Assam. We must, I
said, foresee the possibility of the Chinese capturing Bomdila, in
which case the whole of the Misamari-Charduar-Tezpur area
would be threatened. At the same time, a smaller enemy thrust

from Walong must also be expected after a period of build-up.

GOC-in-C Eastern Command said that he had no more troops left and therefore he could not make any plans. I argued that the Chinese threat to the plains would not materialise immediately and that we would be given a brief respite during which we could reorganise and, if necessary, send further reinforcements from the Punjab. An argument ensued between General Sen and me, which the COAS cut short by directing me to work out an outline plan for discussion between him, the GOC-in-C and the Corps Commander.

The events of that day remain vividly implanted in my memory. There was a nightmarish quality about the proceedings in the Corps Ops Room. The three senior commanders held a number of discussions in which opinions gyrated freely but were seldom to the point. In the midst of the most acute military crisis the nation had faced in centuries, none seemed able to stretch his strategic horizon to take in the full significance of the situation. Instead, they kept moving round and round in circles of futile argument.

I told Thapar that before I could produce an outline plan as a basis for discussion we had to consider moving more forces from the rest of India to the Brahmaputra valley. When I found that I could not rouse him to a decision I took it upon myself to send a message to Western Command ordering the immediate airlift of 5 Infantry Division and the rail move of 63 Cavalry (Stuart tanks) to Misamari. I also ordered 82 Infantry Brigade to Chabua to reinforce Mohinder Pathania's 2nd Division (located between Margherita and Ledo).

While I was writing down a few notes to produce an outline plan for the Chief, I overheard the latter ask Kaul to arrange for a helicopter. Greatly alarmed, I asked the Chief why he wanted a helicopter. He replied that he had decided to visit Bomdila with the Corps Commander. I protested strongly against this 'hasty decision'. I argued that there was little the Army Chief could do in a brigade headquarters, whereas he was needed at Corps HQ, which 'must be manned at this critical stage of battle'. Any number of operational problems, I added, might crop up: a threat down the Lohit river from Walong; 4 Infantry Division's future operations, should we make contact with it; and orders to 67 Brigade if it became involved in a battle in Tenga valley before it reached Bomdila. All these might require co-ordination and decision at Corps HQ.

'Bogey is here, Monty,' Thapar said, 'You and he can cope with the situation.'

'I could not get General Sen to give a decision last evening, Sir,' I replied. I hated to say it openly, but I added, 'Both the Army and the Corps Commanders lost control of the situation last night and that, I believe, was the main reason for the premature withdrawal from Se-la. I really think you should remain here.'

It saddened me to see Bogey Sen hang his head down. He seemed to accept my censure and it was a matter of great anguish to me that the reproach had to come from one who, from the day he joined his regiment as a second-lieutenant, had received from Sen nothing but kindness and consideration. I think he may have come to realise by then that he had not measured up to his responsibilities. That was certainly my estimate of my own role, but then I was only a staff officer, whose function was not to take decisions but to provide the material and the advice for those on whose shoulders that responsibility rested. And of the three men who were thus accountable, the least effective during the past twenty-four hours had been, in my opinion, Bogey Sen.

I finally managed to dissuade both general officers from going to Bomdila, whereupon Thapar asked me if I had put anything down on paper about the defence of Assam. I said that I would have something for him as soon as possible. Leading a reluctant Kaul to a far corner of the room, I sat down with him to make a hurried assessment of the forces available in Assam and to indicate guidelines for action.

Quoting again from *Summary*:

(a) We could count on the following forces for operations in the immediate future:

(i) *North of the Brahmaputra*

181 Brigade, with a squadron of armour in area Daranga;

A composite 48/67 Brigade (after the battle of Bomdila) in the Misamari area;

Stragglers from 4th Division [which I still hoped would fight their way back via Bomdila];

5 Brigade deployed in Subansiri and Siang;

A garrison of 4,000–5,000 mixed combatants (Border Roads personnel, engineers and rear-parties) who could be organised into resistance groups.

(ii) *South of the Brahmaputra*

23rd Division with one brigade but with virtually no supporting arms, arriving in the Jorhat area in 4–7 days;

2nd Division, with remnants of 11 Brigade but without heavy equipment or supporting arms; 192 Brigade and 82 Brigade would be joining this division in 2–4 days, but without supporting arms or adequate logistical backing;

A number of Assam Rifles and police battalions from Nagaland.

(iii) *Reinforcements*

If one more division could be spared from the Punjab, it could be concentrated by rail and air in the Gauhati area in 10–15 days.

(*b*) It was obvious that close control and coordination between north and south bank operations would be vital; and this could no longer be exercised by IV Corps Headquarters.

(*c*) North bank operations could be conducted in two ways:

    (i) fight a series of delaying actions westwards, backing up towards the Siliguri corridor;

    (ii) fight down to the river and then cross south and join up with south bank forces.

(*d*) South bank operations must aim towards denying the oil fields from falling into enemy hands and then join up with north bank forces, or disintegrate into resistance groups in Assam.

(*e*) For these operations, a field Army Headquarters must be established at once, on an *ad hoc* basis, in Gauhati.

(I should point out that there was an inadvertent omission from the list in sub-paragraph (*a*) (i) above: 5 Infantry Division, which was to fly in soon from the Punjab, was not mentioned. In fact the first troops began landing at Misamari the next day, that is to say on 19 November.)

After jotting down the above points Kaul and I went to the BGS's office to inquire whether there was any fresh information about 4th Division's movements. When we learned that there had still been no contact, Kaul announced that he would go up in a helicopter and make an air reconnaissance of the Senge-Dhirang area to observe the progress of the troops moving down the road from Se-la.

This time I made no attempt to dissuade him from his escapade. I returned to the Ops Room to brief Thapar and Sen on the points I had jotted down. I found them sitting dejectedly on chairs drawn up near the map, staring at it silently, as though waiting for the oracle on the wall to provide a solution to their problems. I managed to break into their reverie only after my second or third attempt.

I informed Thapar about the orders I had issued on his behalf regarding the move of 5 Infantry Division to Misamari and I obtained his *post facto* approval. I then said that our first concern was to make plans to oppose the Chinese should they break through to Foothills Camp. Sen interrupted me at this stage to reassert that nothing could be done: he had no troops available. I told him that we had enough troops on the north bank to meet Chinese raiding parties, which is all that they would be for the next few days. Furthermore, our forces could be kept supplied with ammunition and food almost indefinitely, whereas the Chinese forces would not be logistically integrated this side of next summer. 'There is plenty we can do – and *will* do,' I said, addressing Sen. I was aware that I might have been overstating my case, but I was determined that I should more than match the Army Commander's despondency before it drove Thapar to a like hopelessness.

To my astoundment Bogey Sen turned to Thapar and said: 'Sir, there is no option left for us but to ask for a ceasefire!'

'What!' I blurted out, 'Surrender?'

'If it comes to that, I suppose, yes,' he replied.

'Never! What are you talking about, Bogey?' I said, unconsciously reverting to a familiarity from an earlier time. 'If the Chinese come down into the plains, that's the time to get our own back on them – not put our hands up!'

I looked at Thapar and thought I sensed support, but he said nothing. Just then – it was about 3.30 p.m. – news came through from Bomdila that its defences were under attack and that a company of 1 Sikh Light Infantry manning the forward defence location had suffered some casualties. I took the telephone and asked to be put through to Brigadier Gurbux Singh, but no one in Brigade HQ could tell me where he was. He had not been seen for the past hour or more.

328 / WAR IN HIGH HIMALAYA

The Army Chief decided to return to Delhi immediately. I asked for permission to stay on in Tezpur and saw, with gratitude and not a little surprise, Bogey Sen nod his head in agreement. Thapar would not countenance any such thing. He said that he needed me with him to discuss my outline plan on the flight home. I then suggested waiting for the Corps Commander's return. When I telephoned the BGS to inquire about Bijji's whereabout I learned that Kaul had not gone out on a helicopter reconnaissance, as he had announced, but by road to Misamari. When Thapar insisted on immediate departure, I asked for a few minutes to make a call and told the corps staff to try and get Brigadier Gurbux Singh on the line again. As I wrote in the *Summary:*

Just before we left, BGS IV Corps was able to get through to 48 Brigade Headquarters again, but said that the Brigade Commander still could not be found. The situation in Bomdila was confused, as the enemy seemed to have overrun the forward defences. Leading elements of two battalions (67 Brigade) had begun to arrive in Bomdila, but the main body was still near Tenga Valley.

I took the telephone from the BGS. Lieutenant Colonel Bhupinder Singh, Commander 22 Mountain Regiment, Artillery, was speaking at the other end. I asked him if he had a knowledge of the rough disposition of the troops; he said that he was in the picture. I told him that I was the DMO, Army Headquarters, and that I authorised him to assume command of 48 Brigade in the absence of the Brigade Commander and to organise resistance in Bomdila or in Tenga Valley to the best of his ability, including in his plans the two battalions of 67 Brigade which were coming under his command. He acknowledged my message and stated that he would do his best.

At the airfield, I informed Corps Commander of the action I had taken. Shortly thereafter, we took off for Delhi.

Kaul had joined us soon after we arrived at the airport. He said that he had appointed Brigadier Madhav Rajwade, MC (Chief Engineer at Corps HQ) to command the troops at Foothills Camp, with instructions to collect as many stragglers and camp details as he could find and organise a defensive position. His aim would be to stop or delay an enemy advance on Misamari. Kaul intended to go back to Foothills after seeing off the Army Chief.

I tried to take him to one side in order to impress upon him the importance of getting his staff to draw up operational and logistical plans and issue orders for the defence of Brahmaputra valley, but he was too eager to air his own views to have any time to listen to mine. Just before we boarded the aircraft I enumerated for him his corps' order of battle on the south bank and stressed that he had sufficient forces there – logistically supported by a large, well-stocked supply and ordnance base at Gauhati – to foil any Chinese attempt to cross the Brahmaputra (a threat that, in my estimation, was unlikely to develop for another seven to ten days).

Thapar had not given a decision on the two alternatives I had listed in my notes, that is, whether north bank forces would fight delaying actions to fall back towards the Siliguri corridor (whence the eventual general offensive must originate) or would withdraw southwards across the Brahmaputra. Apprehensive of the security of the railway line from Udalguri to Siliguri (the main logistical line from India) I took the decision myself and told Kaul that while south bank forces would remain where they were, north bank forces, if pressed, would fall back westwards, first on the Udalguri–Rangia line and then to Goalpara. Kaul had brought none of his General Staff with him, so I hastily thrust my own notes into his hands, but as far as I am aware he subsequently made no attempt to draw up any coherent plan for the defence of the Brahmaputra valley. Instead, as we learned later, he rushed up to Misamari and Foothills Camps after seeing off the Chief. When he learned that the enemy were advancing from Tenga valley toward Chacko, he decided to return to Corps HQ and make plans to evacuate Tezpur.[4]

Once more we were the only passengers in a huge Super-Constellation. This voyage found us overset not only by gloom but also by anxiety and alarm. Taking a seat across the aisle from Thapar I took out my note-book and hastily jotted down from memory the points I had noted in the paper I had handed to Kaul. Before I could ask Thapar whether he was ready to discuss the outline plan for Assam, he beckoned to me to move closer and sit on the armrest of his seat. There were tears rolling down his cheeks. When I went to sit by him, he clasped my hand and we sat thus for a few moments, silently communicating to each other by touch our common misery. Later, this is what I recorded in my *Summary:*

In the aircraft, returning to Delhi, the Chief had a long and intimate discussion with me. He was most distressed about the 'major disaster' that had befallen the Indian Army – the withdrawal of 4th Division even before facing the main enemy attack and the consequent loss of Kameng Frontier Division. He sought my advice, not only as his Staff Officer but as a confidant.

As for operational advice, I discussed the outline plans, as I had roughly drawn them up, for the continued defence of our territory (as detailed in paragraph 313 above). He asked me to make out an *aide memoire* for his briefing of the Prime Minister, which I did on a loose sheet of paper.

As for personal matters, I advised him to the best of my capacity as a comparatively junior officer and a younger man, in the belief that my counsel was both objective and appropriate.

I was subsequently severely criticised by Bijji Kaul and others for having overreacted to the circumstances as they presented themselves to me. Perhaps their criticism was justified, but I do not think that it was just the passing drama of the moment that moved me, as my critics hinted. I was particularly castigated for misadvising Thapar during the journey to Delhi. I shall therefore describe in detail what transpired.

After he had composed himself somewhat, Thapar asked me whether it would be best for him 'to step down'. When I did not reply for a moment or two, he went on to add: 'I consulted Bijji this morning. He was emphatic that there was no call for me to resign – and that I must not think of taking such a step. Now I am not so sure; and I would like your frank opinion.'

I had in fact anticipated his question and had thought out a reply. Still sitting on the arm of his chair, I said: 'Sir, all of us – the PM, the government, Army HQ and the generals in the field – all must shoulder the blame for the operational trap into which we led ourselves. Our forces could *not* have stopped the Chinese at the Namka-Chu or at the Chip Chap or at Walong and should never have been sent there for that purpose. But the fact remains that at all these places the army did its best and made the enemy pay a price for their gains. Only at Se-la have we betrayed our trust. There, where we *could* have stopped them, we ran away without fighting – and the tragedy is that the betrayal came not from the troops but from the generals in command.

'You have asked me for a frank opinion. I think that all three generals – Pathania, Kaul and Sen – would be deemed remiss in battle; but you were also there. You *elected* to be present at Corps HQ – and you did not succeed in preventing Pathania's defection. So, my answer is 'Yes'. I think it appropriate that you should accept the responsibility for the disaster at Se-la. If I were you, I would go straight to the Prime Minister when we arrive at Delhi, explain frankly what happened and why, and offer my resignation. I hope that he will not accept it; but as Chief you have to take all of the blame on your shoulders.'

It was a poignant moment. I felt sure that Thapar would accept my advice; he had probably made up his mind already. At the same time, I was well aware that the important thing at the moment was not the question of his resignation but the planning and reorganisation of resources for the battle on the plains, should the Chinese press on with their offensive as the government had forecast.

I advised Thapar that when he went to the Prime Minister he should take with him a plan of immediate defence measures in the Bengal and Assam plains. He listened to what I had to say about north and south bank operations and asked me to write out an *aide memoire* for him. During a brief stopover at Lucknow for refuelling, while Thapar descended on to the tarmac to take the air, I copied out the salient points from my notes on a loose sheet of paper – including the recommendation to raise HQ XIV Army – and recommendations for the change-around of commanders.

After he had glanced through my handwritten notes, Thapar asked me who I thought he should recommend to the PM to succeed him, Muchu Chaudhuri or Thorat. I had not given this matter any thought, and I fear that mindlessly I gave him the wrong answer. Perhaps because I did not know Thorat well, I replied that I did not consider it advisable to bring back a retired general officer as the next Chief. I added that I did not think that 'it would go down well in the army', an expression of prejudice rather than a remark sustainable by either logic or precept.

'Yes,' Thapar mused, 'after his successes in Hyderabad and Goa, Muchu has acquired a "halo of victory". Yes, I think it should be Muchu.' I do not know whether it was Thapar's recommendation that eventually decided the PM to select General Chaudhuri as a replacement, but if it was I do not think I rendered a great service to the Indian Army by my thoughtless comment. What army leadership needed at that juncture, to jolt it out of the compliant and irresolute ways into which it had sunk, was a firm, mentally secure and self-reliant Chief to inspire professional intrepidity and determination. During his three years as Chief, Chaudhuri was not able to meet that requirement.

We arrived at Palam airport soon after 9 p.m. When I saw Thapar into his waiting car, it was a sad moment. He grasped my hand, thanked me for my support and said that he would seek an immediate appointment with the Prime Minister. He then told me to keep him informed on news about 4th Division and Bomdila. I could not find words to express the sympathy I felt for him. Instead, I could only voice the hope that in case the PM accepted his resignation, ' : would offer his services to the country in some other capacity, in or out of the army. He said that he would do that, thanked me again and left.

I drove to Sarin's house from the airport, but before beginning to brief him on the day's disastrous events I telephoned the Ops Room, to be told that HQ IV Corps had reported the fall of Bomdila. There was no information about 48 and 67 infantry Brigades. The Corps Commander, it appeared, had again gone forward towards Foothills Camp, intending to organise a defensive line somewhere in the vicinity of Chako. There had been no contact with 4th Division.

I recounted to Sarin the bizarre chain of events and non-events of the previous twenty-four hours: the abandonment of Se-la, Anant Pathania's shameful *sauve qui peut* decree at Dhirang and the confusion attending the defence of Bomdila. I told him about Sen's totally negative attitude at moments of crisis and about the ignominy of his ultimate advice to Thapar on 18 November, that we ask the Chinese for a ceasefire; about Kaul's vagrant method of command and his failure to inspire Pathania to stay at his post and fight; and about Thapar's lack of firmness, even though he alone of the three generals had at times reacted professionally to tactical crises. I then told him about my conversation with Thapar on the aircraft and added that perhaps even at that moment Thapar was at the PM's house offering his resignation. Sarin said that in his opinion my advice to Thapar had been correct and justifiable.

I also enumerated for Sarin the forces available on the north bank and the general military situation in Assam valley. I described the operational plan I had suggested to Bijji Kaul and the overall strategic report I had recorded for Thapar to take to the PM, emphasising the need for establishing a Field Army HQ in Shillong and, even more, the need to remove Bogey Sen from responsibility for further operations.

Regarding the strategic options in Assam — whether to fight back westwards towards the Siliguri corridor or to fight on in Assam valley using the south bank as a base for operations — we argued on the merits and demerits of each. Where I had been undecided before, I had by then become firmly of the opinion that, if not for purely military reasons, from the point of view of the morale of the army (and indeed of the whole nation) even a temporary abandonment of Assam valley, which the first course would inevitably entail, would be devastating and would shatter the whole fabric of national unity.

Sarin was generally in agreement, but was not entirely convinced that a Field Army HQ would be necessary to command the three divisions that were all that we could send into the valley. I argued that eventually the Siliguri sector (XXXIII Corps) would also have to be placed under Assam Command (Lucknow was too remote to co-ordinate operations in north Bengal and Assam), even if the GOC-in-C were replaced.

I also impressed upon Sarin that if the fighting spread to the Assam plains, there would be no choice other than to commit the air force, both for ground support roles and for interdiction missions in the mountains and on the Tibetan plateau, even if such an extention of the war resulted in Chinese bombers attacking some of our cities. The overall advantage in using the air arm, I said, would lie heavily with us. Sarin replied that we would use our air force only if we could ensure adequate air defence of our north Indian cities. He then mused, as if thinking aloud, that perhaps we might seek the help of the US or British air forces. When I remarked that we could hardly do that with any justification when we had kept our own fighters grounded, he did not reply.

I left him with these thoughts and went home to a late but welcome dinner.

## NOTES

1. This was the battalion that I had met when I accompanied Anant Pathania on a reconnaissance of Se-la area on 25 October. Nuranang was about midway between Se-la and Jang, at a point where the winding valley narrows considerably.

2. What I did not know then was that earlier that day, when Pathania had telephoned Kaul suggesting a possible withdrawal from Se-la, Kaul had given the responsibility for that decision to Pathania himself. 'I leave it to you,' he had said, 'I will approve whatever you decide.' This was told me by Colonel Shamsher Singh, then AA&QMG 4th Division, who had overheard the Corps Commander's telephone conversation.

3. The mutual dislike between Kaul and Major General 'Sam' Manekshaw was common knowledge in the army. In 1961, after Kaul was appointed CGS, he initiated a senior level inquiry against Manekshaw (then Commandant of the Staff College) based on reports from several sources, including the Intelligence Bureau, about his anti-national prejudices and pronouncements and his excessive pro-British bias. There were too many plausible instances for the accusations to be shrugged off. Kaul openly delighted in pursuing the matter. Finally, a high-level court of inquiry – Army Commander Daulet Singh, Corps Commander Bikram Singh and Adjutant General Kumaramangalam – dismissed the charges, mainly because (it is only fair to record) the Director of the Intelligence Bureau, when called for his evidence, refused to give it, saying that his office could not, by established practice, be expected to give evidence. Since then Manekshaw had remained at his former post, ignored by Army HQ when a vacancy

to corps commander's rank became available (he was senior to Harbaksh). Thereafter he was superceded also by Moti Sagar, years his junior in service.

4. Since the decision to abandon Tezpur led to much panic, confusion and subsequent recriminations, I would like to assert emphatically that this step was not taken with the Chief's consent. Kaul did not record the truth when he wrote in his book *The Untold Story* (p. 420): 'The decision to move the Corps Headquarters from Tezpur to Gauhati was reached in mutual consultation between me, Lieutenant General Sen and General Thapar. This move was carried out on 20th afternoon.' Thapar left Tezpur at 5.30 p.m. on 18 November. Till then the move of Corps HQ to the south bank had not arisen. He never met Kaul again as Army Chief because he tendered his resignation personally to the Prime Minister later the same evening.

# 10

# UNILATERAL CEASEFIRE

On the morning of 19 November I tried to telephone Bijji Kaul but he proved as elusive as ever; no one in his HQ could tell me where he was. What was evident, however, was that Kaul had not issued any orders for organising defences or delaying positions on the north bank. The only fresh information HQ IV Corps could give me was that there had been a number of 'encounters' between the enemy and our troops south of Chako, on the road to Foothills Camp. (I interpreted that as meaning that the Chinese were ambushing and shooting up Gurbux Singh's 48 Brigade retreating from Bomdila). An alarming rumour had spread during the night that a Chinese force had been sighted on the road just north of Foothills. Although this subsequently proved baseless it probably started the panic that quickly moved up the chain and, later in the day, stampeded Corps HQ into abandoning the north bank and making a run for Gauhati.

The morning newspapers announced the fall of Se-la and Bomdila in chilling headlines. Reading through the depressing account, my thoughts inevitably turned to the people of Assam. With what fearfulness, I wondered, would those in Gauhati and Shillong read the morning's news that day? What a shock it must be for the Assamese to be suddenly informed that the great Indian Army, which had arrived with such pomp and privilege to protect them three years earlier and which had so imperiously set about its ways in NEFA and Assam, had now been rudely hurled back by the Chinese and that the enemy was even now on their doorstep. Who would defend Assam now? Or had India abandoned the north-east region to a future under Chinese arms? I wondered whether there would be panic in the cities and how it would all end. Not for another twenty-four hours would I learn of the ultimate infamy of the Indian Army and its abdication from the fray.

I went early to my office, to await a call from Thapar. He rang up at 9 a.m. and asked me to arrange an operational conference in MO Directorate which, he said, the Defence Minister (Nehru) would be attending. He added that Daulet Singh and his Chief of Staff, Jogindar Singh, were in Delhi and that I was to send a message inviting them also.

Having made the necessary arrangements, I glanced through the signal messages from Western Command to catch up on news from Ladakh. The situation in the north-west was reassuring. On 18 November the Chinese had captured the heights east of Chushul but they had suffered heavily in the process, especially at Rezang-la which overlooked the Chushul plain from the north-east. Whether for that reason or because the defences around the airstrip lay outside the Chinese claim, Chushul itself had not been attacked. I knew that the defences there had been adequately prepared, even though digging trenches in the frozen ground was a herculean task (the average altitude of the Chushul plain was about 4,200 metres: over 14,000 feet). There was a stout-hearted brigadier in command — 'Tappy' Raina, who had been one of my Assistant Military Secretaries when I was in MS Branch — and I felt certain that if the Chinese attacked Chushul they would find it a hard nut to crack. The danger, of course, was that they might outflank and isolate 114 Brigade and make for Leh along the Indus valley road.

At about 10 o'clock General Muchu Chaudhuri telephoned from Poona, complaining that his HQ was not being kept in the picture about the war situation and that he was obliged to rely on the *Times of India* for all his news. He had a few unkind things to say about the DMI, and to pacify him I gave him a brief account of the events in NEFA and Ladakh.

Chaudhuri then asked me to obtain the Chief's permission for him to visit Delhi within a day or two. I agreed to do that, and then added that he would probably be sent for anyway and that he should have a bag packed in case he had to move at short notice. There was a silence; then he asked, 'Do you realise what you are saying?'

'Yes, Sir, I do. I think you should hold yourself in readiness.'

Another silence; then: 'Well if I do get there, Monty, I'll have to lean heavily on you. Can you tell me any more at present?'

I said, 'No,' but that I would ring him up after I had had a word with Thapar.

At 10.30 Thapar, Wadalia, Daulet Singh, Moti Sagar (the new CGS) and Jogindar Singh (Daulet's Chief of Staff) came to the Ops Room. Nehru and Sarin could not attend because at the last minute the PM had decided to go to Parliament House, taking Sarin with him. This was unfortunate because I foresaw that a purely military discussion would be more likely to arrive at the wrong conclusion, and that is precisely what happened.

Moti Sagar had assumed his appointment only the day before, so he let me conduct the conference. I started off by recounting the events leading to the fall of Kameng and briefly described the plan I had suggested to Kaul and Thapar: hold the enemy on the north bank as long as possible and then withdraw across the Brahmaputra to the general area of Jorhat-Nowgong-Gauhati. I said that within the next twenty-four or forty-eight hours 5 Infantry Division would complete its fly-in to Tezpur and although at first it would be without artillery and other heavy equipment, including vehicles, it would still be better equipped than the leading Chinese elements. 23 Infantry Division, with about six battalions (but no artillery) would, at the same time, be arriving from Nagaland as a reserve for IV Corps. I also described the continuing build-up of our forces in the Siliguri sector and briefly touched upon my proposal to carve out a new theatre of operations in the region between Siliguri and Gauhati under a Field Army HQ.

I could not have sounded very convincing because Thapar

did not support my suggestions. Instead, he wanted IV Corps to withdraw westwards from both north and south bank in Assam and organise a firm defensive zone in the Siliguri plains, under Eastern Command. I countered that, whereas evacuating Tezpur and the north bank had some merit, there was absolutely no reason to abandon the south bank. With nearly three divisions available (after the completion of 5th Division's fly-in) and a strong logistical base at Gauhati, we could not only defend Assam but even plan a limited offensive against the Chinese – and that, I argued, could best be directed by a Field Army HQ located in Shillong or Gauhati.

No one agreed with me, although Moti Sagar nodded his head once or twice in support. Daulet (still openly hostile) firmly counselled evacuation from Assam, and that was how it stood when the conference broke up: no firm decision was taken.[1] (I did not raise the question of replacing Sen, hoping to take up the matter later with the Chief alone.)

Thapar asked me to walk back with him to his office. On the way he told me that he had not recommended the replacement of Bogey Sen because he was not yet sure whether he was staying on as Chief. If his resignation were accepted he would leave his recommendation for his successor in the form of a handing-over note.

I told him in passing that I had drafted a brief report of the events of 17 and 18 November at Tezpur and that I would send it to him for his approval. He hesitated for a few seconds but finally agreed that indeed we should keep a record of the sequence of events during the crisis period, written from the Army HQ point of view.

Before leaving Thapar's office I made one more attempt to convince him that we could and must defend southern Assam, not only from the military point of view but also because of political and social considerations. I said that if we were to withdraw from the south bank we would literally be deserting the Assamese people, for which they would never forgive us. It was even possible, I added, that parts of Assam would be lost to India for ever whether or not the Chinese crossed the Brahmaputra, because the Pakistanis might decide to share in the spoils of war and occupy the Garo and Jaintia hills or even the whole south bank including the oil wells of Digboi.

Thapar sat silently for a long while. The burden, I could see, was almost too much for him. Eventually, he replied, 'I told the PM last night that I might have to withdraw from Assam and he seemed to accept it. But I agree with you – it would be an unimaginable disaster. I'll think it over.'

When I returned to my office I found Moti Sagar waiting for me. I told him about my talk with Thapar and also about my recommendations to have Bogey Sen replaced and for Manekshaw to take command of IV Corps while Kaul was promoted to a Field Army command. Moti (who had till then been the Military Secretary) smiled enigmatically and said that while I was creating jobs for others I ought to think a little about holding on to my own job. He said that rumours had reached MS Branch about my recommendation to sack Sen, in consequence of which some of the PSOs – in particular Kumaramangalam, the Adjutant General – were out for my blood. Moti added that the 'KCIOs Club' (the Sandhurst-trained senior officers) felt threatened and they blamed me for battering at their citadel.

I had not known Moti well but what little I had seen of him I had always regarded highly. Intelligent, self-effacing and quiet-spoken, he had a reputation for straight-dealing and fairness, and he wore his integrity around him like a cloak. During the next twelve months I got to know him well and to regard him as a firm but kindly superior and a good friend. I realised at the time that Moti was giving me a friendly hint to be more restrained and I took note of it, but it is difficult to act contrary to one's nature.

I showed Moti Sagar my report on the sequence of events at HQ IV Corps on 17 and 18 November (Appendix 'A'). Jogi Dhillon, the DCGS, walked into my office at that moment and he also read the report. They both commented that it contained such damning evidence that I ought to obtain the Chief's remarks on it. In their opinion my report virtually accused the whole chain of command, from the Army Chief down to the Divisional Commander, of grave, impeachable misconduct, from non-performance to dereliction of duty. I told them that the report was intended for MO files, not for general dissemination, and that I had so informed the Chief. I also said that when it was completed

I intended to ask him to countersign it as an endorsement of authenticity.

After snatching a hurried lunch at home I went to Sarin's house to tell him what had transpired at the morning conference. I sounded greatly downhearted, so he began by reassuring me about Assam and said that the government 'would never capitulate', meaning that Assam would not be abandoned. The irony was that even at that very moment the Home Ministry, unknown to Army HQ and the Defence Ministry, was sending out orders to evacuate officials from Tezpur and other cities and to initiate a scorched earth policy, including the destruction of the Digboi oil fields and all the power plants in the valley. The Director-General of Civil Defence was ordered to Gauhati and Tezpur to organise the evacuation of central government officials, leaving the Assamese and their government to fend for themselves.

Sarin asked me if I had been able to discover what Kaul's plans were. I replied that Kaul was still absent from his HQ but I knew that he had issued no orders for a protracted defence of the plains sector. I added that once a government decision was taken to defend Assam, I would ensure that Army HQ would arrogate that responsibility. We would move 5 Infantry Division from the Misamari area to the south bank where, together with 2 Infantry Division and an *ad hoc* division from Nagaland, IV Corps would be re-formed.

I again stressed the need for allowing the IAF to be committed to battle to provide air support for the ground forces but Sarin was still chary of committing the air arm to a ground-support role before we had ensured air cover for north Indian cities. When I insisted, he said that he would speak to Nehru once again on the subject.

I returned to my office and drafted a paper on the situation in Assam for the Cabinet Secretary's Committee. Thereafter I went to the CGS's office, hoping to obtain Moti's permission to send a warning order to IV Corps for the move of 5th and 2nd Divisions to the south bank to forestall the government's decision to fight on in Assam, but neither Thapar nor Moti were in their offices. While I was debating in my mind whether to send the message on my own responsibility, a call came from John Lall (Joint Secretary in the Defence Ministry, in charge of air force matters), summoning me to an immediate meeting with Sarin. I hastened to Lall's office and we then walked over to Sarin's.

Sarin did not waste time on preliminaries or explanations. As we entered his office he handed us a sheet of paper and asked us to offer our comments on it. The document was a letter in draft from Prime Minister Nehru to President Kennedy of the United States. I do not now recollect what the opening paragraph was but my diary records what the second contained: in it the PM was pleading for 'the active participation of the US Air Force' for the defence of India. The specific request was for 'twelve squadrons of F-104 fighters and two squadrons of B-57 bombers'.

After we had read the draft, Sarin told us that he expected the PM to sign the letter the same day. All he wanted to ensure was that the number of squadrons he had asked for in the letter was approximately what we would require. When I asked whether he had consulted the Air Chief, Sarin replied that he was not authorised to consult anyone else: the only persons who knew about the contents of the draft letter other than the PM and himself were the Foreign Secretary and, now, we two. The matter must not be divulged to anyone else, he cautioned us.

Lall and I had a brief discussion on the Air Force's requirements but neither of us knew whether airfields and infrastructural facilities in Assam or north Bengal were adequate for the advanced types of aircraft we were asking for. However, we agreed that since the Pakistani Air Force deployed both F-104s and B-57s, and their military infrastructure was not known to be greatly in advance of ours, we would be justified in asking for these aircraft. The only element we might have lacked was surveillance radars, but those could be flown in at the same time as the squadrons themselves. As for the number of squadrons required, we were not competent to make a comment, especially as the IAF's fighter and bomber squadrons had still not been used in the war.

I do not recall my reaction at that time to the contents of the letter. Although Sarin had, the previous evening, speculatively mused on the possibility of asking for British or American help in providing air cover, I had not for a moment imagined that Prime Minister Nehru, the architect of India's non-alignment policy, would ask for actual intervention by US forces, a course of action that could be seen in no other light than that of entering into a form of military alliance. Sarin's disclosure had therefore come as a considerable surprise. However, I was not in any way dismayed by it – as many were later when, after considerable attempts at dissemblance by the government, the fact of the appeal to President Kennedy for armed intervention was ambiguously acknowledged. The Director of Military Operations, at a desperate stage of a war that seemed to be moving along a course of escalating disasters, could only welcome the proposal of obtaining military help, whatever its source. One would have preferred it not to take the form of actual intervention by the armed forces of another country; on the other hand, in the present crisis any other form of aid would have taken days or even weeks to be effective.

Before leaving Sarin's office I asked him if the PM had issued instructions for the defence of Assam. I was amazed to learn that there was still some hesitation in taking this all-important decision. Nehru, it appeared, wished to consult Home Minister Shastri before making up his mind. There was little I could do except control my increasing impatience while the threat to Assam grew hourly (as it seemed at the time).

When I arrived back at my office I learned that Thapar was leaving the army 'on grounds of ill health' and that Muchu Chaudhuri was to officiate as Chief of Army Staff in the rank of lieutenant general. I later discovered what had actually transpired. Cabinet Secretary Khera had called on Thapar with a message from Nehru that instead of pursuing the resignation issue the government would prefer him to retire for health reasons. Thapar did not deserve this unworthy, unnecessary and unbecoming duplicity but accepted it like the loyal subordinate he was. As for Muchu's appointment, it appeared that there was a considerable lobby, both civilian and military, against him in Delhi. The PM therefore took an unseemly, vacillating and counterproductive middle course and granted him officiating status only, withholding for the time being his due promotion to the rank of general.[2]

I tried several times to seek an appointment with Thapar, both to obtain his approval of my report on the Se-la fiasco and to bid him goodbye, but he remained closeted with a succession of visitors. His Military Assistant, Colonel Chandhorkar, advised me to postpone my request for an appointment till the next morning.

In the evening Sarin telephoned to say that I was required to represent Army HQ at a cabinet committee meeting at 10 p.m. to discuss Assam. The entry in my diary for that incident is brief and cryptic: 'I declined to attend.' I do not recollect why I should have conducted myself so presumptuously but I think what caused me to stay away was an unwillingness to have to state before the committee Thapar's last expressed view on Assam (to abandon it). Before I did that I wanted a chance to convince Chaudhuri to take a more positive course of action. Be that as it may, the next morning I learned that the Cabinet Secretary's Committee had also shied away from taking a positive decision on Assam.

On reaching the office next morning I was told that the DIB, Mullik, wished to see me urgently. I walked down the corridor and found him closeted with his two deputies, Hooja and Balbir Singh. Mullik wished to speak to me alone and suggested that we go to the Ops Room in MO Directorate. Once there he asked me to show him on the map the army's plans for the defence of Assam. He said that he had been greatly concerned ever since he had received information that HQ IV Corps had evacuated Tezpur, without in any way co-ordinating the withdrawal with the civilian authorities. The army, he said, seemed to have given in to panic and the Home Ministry had contributed to the chaos by issuing orders for the civilian staff to quit Tezpur. Mullik wanted to know whether the army intended to make a stand or surrender Assam to the Chinese. If the latter, he would not allow it. He had made up his mind to mobilise a large contingent of armed police from neighbouring states and to organise a resistance movement in the Brahmaputra valley rather than hand Assam to the enemy on a plate.

In place of his normal self-controlled and well-regulated demeanour there was a hint of agitation and tension about him, which in no way diminished when I told him that I had failed to get the Army Chief or Sarin to take a decision to stand firm in Assam. I recounted the inconclusive proceedings of the previous day's operational conference and my unsuccessful attempt to persuade Thapar to change his mind. He was quite taken aback when I quoted Thapar as saying that the PM seemed to have accepted his proposal to abandon Assam.

'Never!' Mullik said vehemently. 'I will speak to the Prime Minister. If the army won't fight, the police will. Are you sure the army will pull out of Assam altogether?'

I replied that till then there had been no sign of anyone wanting to take a firm decision either way. I commented, however, that if it were true that Kaul had left the north bank – about which we in Army HQ had no information – paradoxically, that might portend well. Since it was inconceivable that he would, without Army HQ permission, pull out altogether from Assam, Kaul must have decided to move to the south bank to organise its defence. There was hope for us yet, I added wryly.

I walked back with Mullik to his office. Hooja and Balbir had left. Mullik called them on his intercom and issued instructions for a number of armed police battalions to be sent from Madhya Pradesh, Bihar and other states to Assam, adding that he would ask the PM's permission personally to organise a resistance movement there. He put down the telephone, smiled quizzically and said: 'You should be coming with us, Palit. We could use someone like you. Shall I ask the PM for your services?'

I replied that as the CGS was new to his job and as we had an officiating Chief who had yet to take up his appointment, it would be out of the question for the DMO to leave Army HQ at that juncture. I was greatly flattered by Mullik's compliment but did not allow myself to be swayed by it.

Chandhorkar rang up to say that Thapar had decided not to come to the office because General Chaudhuri was to be appointed officiating COAS from that very morning. He added that Chaudhuri had in fact already arrived and would, later in the morning, walk over to my office to be briefed on the war situation.

Meanwhile, I had been called by Sarin to meet the team from the Pentagon led by Brigadier General Kelly, who had brought with him about ten army and army-airforce officers of the ranks of major and lieutenant colonel. They were all in olive green fatigue uniform, (each with his name printed on a white strip of cloth stitched above the right breast pocket: an affectation that I had not come across before).

I briefly recounted for them the course of the campaigns in Ladakh and NEFA, glossing over the debacle at Se-la. I was unable to answer questions on likely Chinese moves because till that morning (21 November) there had been no report of any enemy advance into the north Brahmaputra plains. I did not pass on the news Mullik had given me (that IV Corps was withdrawing across the Brahmaputra) because I did not think the United States would be willing to send arms and equipment if they learned that we were a fleeing army. When cross-questioned on details of the pull-out from Se-la I said that we had not received any details of that battle yet. Understandably, Kelly expressed amazement at the lack of information available in the office of the Chief of Operations and I did not blame him. I was glad when the session ended: it is not pleasant for a DMO to have to be evasive at an operational briefing.

Chaudhuri and Daulet Singh came to my office shortly after midday. Chaudhuri grumbled about having to *officiate* as Chief of the Army Staff and to have to continue in the rank of lieutenant general. It was the Cabinet Secretary who had informed him of this slight and he was obviously put out by it.

Daulet left after a quick visit to the Ops Room and I proceeded to give the officiating Chief a brief review of the operations in NEFA, not withholding from him the shameful story of Se-la and IV Corps' 'unauthorised' withdrawal from the north bank. Chaudhuri was visibly shaken and said that he had no idea that it had been such a total disaster. When he asked what orders we had since issued to IV Corps, I told him about the operational conference the day before and the continuing hesitation over Assam. Pensively, he walked over to sit facing me at my desk and asked me for advice on what his first action should be as officiating Chief. I replied without hesitation that he should immediately issue orders for the regrouping of IV Corps in the Gauhati-Nowgong-Jorhat area, incorporating 2, 5 and 23 Infantry Divisions and any other troops available in Assam. I said that he had no need to consult the government. It was within the army's sphere of responsibility to plan the defence of the country without seeking government approval at each step. I also told him about my suggestion of creating a new Field Command HQ, in the Siliguri-Assam theatre, to be entrusted with the task of the defence of Assam and north Bengal. We would of course need government sanction for this. I then informed him of my firm conviction that Bogey Sen was incapable of exercising operational command at army or theatre level.

Muchu Chaudhuri was uncharacteristically subdued, displaying little of his customary aggressive (or flippant) manner. He mused over my advice as if trying to make up his mind and, hesitatingly, told me to draft out a signal along the lines I had indicated but not to send it till I had his approval. He agreed that a definite order should be issued but said that he would think over my draft before making up his mind. He also directed me to produce a formal paper on long-range plans for the defence of the Assam-Bengal plains. He said that since the government had been informed by Thapar that he intended to abandon Assam he was obliged to refer the matter to the Defence Ministry. Meanwhile, I was to be ready with plans for the destruction of all heavy installations and ammunition, food and other stocks in Gauhati.

Chaudhuri asked me about the MO paper on 'Conduct of the War Against China' which Thapar had mentioned to him. I handed him a copy but cautioned him that most of the calculations on the Chinese logistical potential in Tibet were more in the nature of informed guesses than estimates based on hard intelligence. The paper was a first attempt at future planning. I suggested that he set up a separate planning cell, preferably under the Chiefs of Staff, whose sole concern would be future war plans. The DMO, I said, was too tied down with day-to-day operational responsibilities to follow up all the loose ends of intelligence and logistical planning, details of which would require a separate staff to compile. Chaudhuri took the paper from me but made no comment.

After Chaudhuri left my room I drafted a signal for Eastern Command ordering the holding of the main approaches through the mountains of NEFA to the Brahmaputra valley. I stressed that there would be 'no further withdrawal anywhere'. 5 and 192 Infantry Brigades had already been permitted by HQ IV Corps to withdraw to the plains, but in Subansiri and Siang Frontier Divisions that process would take some days to be completed and we could stop it if we took prompt action. (I did not know then the extent of the disaster that had befallen the troops deployed near the McMahon Line in these two frontier districts.)

In the afternoon I took the draft signal and a script of my Assam-North Bengal scheme to Chaudhuri. I found him in conversation with General Cariappa (the first Indian C-in-C after independence; later promoted to field marshal). After an exchange of pleasantries Cariappa said that he had glanced through my 'Conduct of War' paper and complimented me on it. Chaudhuri said that he had not read it but our first task should be to avoid offering further provocation to the Chinese. Cariappa made no further comment but he seemed not to be overpleased at Muchu's remark. The important thing for me was that Chaudhuri authorised despatch of the signal to Eastern Command ordering IV Corps to stand firm and not carry out any more withdrawals. At last a decision had been taken that in effect enjoined IV Corps to defend Assam. I hurried back to my office and despatched the message. As far as I can recall Army HQ still had not officially been informed about IV Corps' plan to abandon Tezpur, although in fact at that very moment all military personnel were on the move – all, that is, except the Corps Commander himself and his BGS (who stayed behind, as we later learned). I had wanted to include in the signal specific orders for the regrouping of the three divisions in Assam but Chaudhuri would not allow that. He said that we would consult the government before issuing detailed operational instructions for Assam.

The next morning brought startling news. The headlines in the papers announced that the Chinese had ordered a unilateral ceasefire on all fronts, and a total withdrawal from NEFA starting on 1 December. This was a subtle and astute move that no one in India had anticipated. Nor were we able to fathom its full significance for a long time.

I rang up the Ops Room to instruct the duty officer to call a conference of MO-1 Staff before the offices opened. The newspapers had mentioned several constraints and conditions attached to the Chinese communiqué and I wanted to mark them on a map for the information of the CGS and the officiating Chief as soon as they reached their offices.

The Chinese statement, which had in fact been communicated to our Chargé d'Affaires in Peking by the Chinese Prime Minister as early as the night of 19 November, clearly made a distinction between the eastern and western sectors. In NEFA the withdrawal would be to positions 20 km behind the line of actual control *as it existed in November 1959.* In other words, they would relinquish areas in NEFA that were claimed by India. In the western sector, however, they would withdraw only to a line 20 km behind the line *as it existed on the day the Chinese invasion began.* Marking these lines on the map, I wondered if this were another indirect Chinese way of telling us that they were prepared to forego their claim in NEFA if we abandoned ours in the Aksai Chin.

The CGS came into my office just as I finished marking the map. I showed him the withdrawal lines and proposed that we should plan to start pushing our troops back into NEFA in the wake of the Chinese pull-out, though at one remove from the Chinese rear parties. Moti Sagar said that the officiating Chief and he were to attend a cabinet committee meeting in Khera's room to discuss the implications of the ceasefire but, as far as he could make out, Muchu Chudhuri was not in favour of moving our troops back into NEFA. We would have to wait till after the Cabinet Secretary's conference before issuing orders.

Before Moti left my office I asked him to countersign the two-page report I had written on 'Events Leading to the Loss of Se-la and Bomdila'. I had not been able to meet Thapar to ask him to authenticate my narrative, so I was anxious at least to have it on record that I had written it in the immediate aftermath of the debacle and not with the judgment of hindsight. As far as I knew no one had kept a record of those events, either at Army or Corps HQ, so I was aware that my report would be important source material when an official account of the operations came to be written. Moti agreed to countersign my report (as shown in Appendix A):

In accordance with Brigadier DK Palit's desire for me to certify having seen the above note in draft form on 20 November 1962 and in the present form on 21 November 1962, I do so. I cannot certify to the accuracy or otherwise of the statement made above.

*Signed:* Moti Sagar, Lieutenant General
CGS
21 November 1962
(MOTI SAGAR)

When Moti returned from Khera's meeting he sent for me and passed on the government's decision on operations in NEFA. He said that Muchu had had his way. Khera had wanted the army to move back into NEFA but Chaudhuri had insisted that troops would not operate forward of the plains. MO Directorate was required to send a signal addressed to all formations down to brigades that there would be no re-entry of troops into NEFA. They were to remain vigilant and continue normal patrolling but stay south of the Inner Line.

I hesitated to issue these instructions. If our troops were prevented from moving into NEFA, we would be completely out of touch with the enemy. Even if the civilian administration re-established itself in Bomdila they could not be expected to give us accurate information about enemy preparations for another offensive. Or were we accepting Chinese declarations at face value?

I told Moti that I had informally checked with the Ministry of External Affairs, N.B. Menon, who had confirmed that the provisions of the Chinese ceasefire did not forbid the occupation of NEFA except in a 20 km zone next to the border. Moti agreed with me that it was essential for our troops to be ordered to reoccupy areas up to Towang, Limeking and Walong; so together we went to tackle Chaudhuri.

Moti Sagar spoke at length about the undesirability of leaving NEFA totally unoccupied, for both tactical and administrative reasons, but we could not convince the officiating Chief. He strongly rejected our arguments and forbade any move into NEFA, saying that he could not risk a backlash. He directed that our forces be ordered to hold defensive localities well south of the Inner Line, at places such as Misamari, Charduar and Lakhimpur in north Assam. When I suggested that we ought to consult the government before we decided to leave NEFA unoccupied, Chaudhuri hesitated for a moment and then, somewhat unconvincingly, said that he had already done so and the government had agreed that Bomdila, Ziro, Along and Daporijo need not be reoccupied.

It is embarassing to record this but I instinctively knew that Chaudhuri had just made that up (and this would not be the only time he would make convenient of-the-cuff statements circumventing the truth). I had already come to the conclusion that Muchu Chaudhuri's great concern at that time was not, as it should have been, to take a firm grip on the army and rebuild its shattered morale, but to avoid taking any operational step that might provoke the enemy and thus stir up trouble for himself. Having witnessed his predecessor virtually sacked in an operational crisis, and having then seen that crisis miraculously abate, he was not going to take any risk that might recreate it and jeopardise his confirmaion as Army Chief. His insecurity was never very far from the surface.

My reference to a 'shattered' army may come as a surprise to some readers. In subsequent years, after the trauma of our dishonour had begun to heal, it became fashionable to argue in self-justification that it was not the entire Indian Army but only a small proportion of it that had suffered a humiliating defeat. It was pointed out that on fronts other than Se-la the Indian Army had lived up to its traditions, fought hard for as long as it was possible and taken a heavy toll of the enemy before being overwhelmed by superior numbers. No disgrace, it was asserted, accrued from the battles at Namka-chu or Walong; as for the defence of Rezang-la, that episode would be recorded as one of the most heroic in our military history.[3]

That, as far as it goes, is true, but it will not serve as an alibi. Certainly the Kumaonis at Rezang-la, and the Gorkhas, Rajputs and others at Dhola, offered valiant resistance in the face of hopeless odds and inevitable disaster, but the bravery and the self-sacrifice of the men and junior leaders are not what we are talking about. They did indeed fight hard, against impossible odds and even after the reverses of November most battalions would still have gone into battle to fight on under their colours, as they have always done. It was not they but the high command that failed to stand up to the test; it virtually folded. If the fighting had continued on 20 November, I feel sure that there would have been few left among the top ranks who could, or would, have effectively directed the army in war or led army corps into battle. It will be the task of some future historian or sociologist to determine the cause of that disintegration but the truth is (at least as I saw it) that after the run-back from the borders the army became virtually leaderless. In Delhi, Thapar (and Chaudhuri after him) lacked the inspiration and the will to withstand a defeat and regroup the army for war. Bogey Sen in Eastern Command was ineffectual, little more than a cipher. At IV Corps Kaul must at last have come to terms with his ineptitude for field command, even if only subconsciously, as evident from his frequent and prolonged absences from Corps headquarters.[4] So far as is known, despite the General Staff's suggested plan handed to him by the DMO he made no effort to recover from the shock of the disasters in central Kameng and to regroup for battle. In Western Command the system, by and large, held firm but even Daulet, normally stable and self-reliant, quit his Command HQ at the height of the crisis and rushed down to Delhi, where he remained overlong and appeared to show no anxiety to return to his post. Moreover, he had done little to recast plans for the defence of the western (Pakistan) front.

It was the worst of times for the Indian Army, a time to hang down our heads in shame. (Colleagues at the office confided to me that they shrank from going into town and appearing in public in uniform.) Fortunately for our *amour propre*, the community at large was never told the whole truth about the debacle. Government handouts to the press painted the picture of a valiant Indian Army stabbed in the back by a supposedly friendly neighbour and then, after offering fierce resistance, overwhelmed by massed Chinese forces equipped with superior weapons. *The Statesman* was so misinformed that it described the retreat from Se-la as a 'planned withdrawal . . . that would surely be regarded by future historians as a great page in military history.' The government ensured that the public was left unaware of the dishonour attached to the defeat. The shame that *we* felt was self-imposed – but none the less acute for that.

Jangu Satarawalla came to my office to share a sandwich lunch and to discuss details about expansion plans for the army. Inevitably the conversation turned to a post-mortem on the war and the reasons for the sudden and shocking collapse of the forces at Se-la and Bomdila. It would be comforting to believe that the Chinese defeated us because they enjoyed greater logistical facilities and were thus able to sustain larger forces in battle than the Indians; that their automatic rifles were decisively superior to our obsolescent .303 bolt-action Lee-Enfields; or that their guerrilla tactics proved superior to our conventional methods. These were the excuses, but they were only half-truths.

Logistical disadvantage was not something that the Chinese had manoeuvred us into; it was of our own makirg and arose out of our own purblindness. Like tactics, logistics must be treated in terms of the arithmetics of space and movement, not taken for granted as a natural concomitant of troop deployment. There was no conscious effort at any level to make calculated estimates of the distances of lines at which we could logistically support, successively, divisional, brigade and battalion battles. In Eastern Command the General Officer Commanding-in-Chief not only lacked firsthand knowledge of the terrain where he sent his troops to do battle, he seemed to be ignorant of the constraints of military logistics. In Delhi, the General Staff too often blindly accepted assurances by the Intelligence Bureau and the government, assurances that tended to make logistics irrelevant.

As regards weaponry, too much has been made of the fact that the Chinese had better weapons than our troops. It is my opinion that the superiority of Chinese weapons was not so marked that it could account for our abject defeats. The fact is that our main weapons were never deployed for battle. At no place except Se-la was the Indian Army able to bring to bear on the enemy the weight of its range of weaponry – and on that occasion the weapons were never used, they were surrendered without a fight. The small arms with the infantry were used with effect as long as the ammunition lasted but we catered for no logistics of replenishment, so that when ammunition ran out or when the enemy's heavier weapons appeared, our troops could only run away or, be mown down.

Reports that it was by 'guerrilla tactics' and 'massed attacks' that the Chinese gained their victories do not bear close scrutiny either. In any case, the two terms are mutually exclusive; one uses either the hit-and-run tactics of the guerrilla or the mass tactics of attrition, not both in the same setting at the same time. The fact is that our troops lacked training, acclimatisation and endurance. Even those who had been in the high mountains since their first induction into NEFA in 1959–60 had been given no opportunity during those three years to train in mountain tactics or harden themselves against high-altitude demands. Preoccupation with administrative chores such as basha-building and routine line of communication duties kept them confined in camps, untrained and unacquainted with the surrounding terrain, so that when the fighting started our troops tended to remain track-bound, unadventurous and slow-footed. The Chinese were repeatedly able to get the better of them in patrol actions and cross-country movement, misguidedly described by the press as 'guerrilla' warfare. As for their alleged 'massed attacks', there were no reports of these from the troops who actually fought the Chinese. The figures of Chinese strengths were greatly exaggerated in the aftermath of defeat. In my estimate, their forces in Kameng totalled less than ours.

At the risk of being repetitious I must again assert that the main responsibility for the disasters of 1962 lies squarely on the shoulders of the high command and their staffs, for their unawareness or disregard of operational and logistical constraints on the Himalayan front, for their failure to impress on the politicians the impossibility of the operational tasks demanded of them, and, above all, for their insensitivity to the plight of the officers and men in the battalions witlessly pushed up into the high mountains – insufficiently armed, clothed or provisioned – at the mercy of an enemy well-prepared for war.

In the evening I was inundated with calls from the Chief requiring me to write a number of papers on operational matters. First, I was asked to prepare a brief for the Prime Minister describing the situation in Assam and the General Staff plan for the defence of the south bank. I wrote out one in long-hand and took it to Chaudhuri, but he had already changed his mind. His 'new concept' was that the troops would stay where they were on the north bank but they would be given no operational task other than 'watch and ward'. We were to make no plans for the defence of Assam. I argued that we must have a contingency plan in case the fighting started again, but Chaudhuri had closed his mind on the subject: there would be no more fighting, period. He directed me to write a note accordingly, armed with which we were to attend a meeting in the PM's room later that night. I was also to bring with me a revised paper on a defence plan for Sikkim and the Siliguri corridor.

Letting the office staff go home early, I took my papers home and began work on the operational plans Chaudhuri wanted, my wife doing the typing. I waited till nearly midnight for a call from the Chief, but it never materialised.

Next morning I went to see the CGS to express my concern at Chaudhuri's negative attitude in refusing to make contingency plans for further operations. I said that IV Corps was in a state of near disintegration and unless we gave it a firm plan to work on, its cohesion and fighting potential would be totally eroded. How could we ignore operational realities?

While I was still talking to Moti, Chaudhuri came into the room and announced that the British Chief of the Imperial General Staff, General Sir Richard Hull, was due to arrive in Delhi that evening. He asked me for a detailed paper describing our plans for the defence of the Assam plains. He asked me, with a straight face, why I had no such plan ready! 'The CIGS will want to know what defensive measures we are taking in case the fighting is resumed,' he said. 'Get on with it, DMO. I want to see it before I leave for lunch.' Meekly I replied that such a paper had been put into his hands the day before. I added that I would send him a second copy immediately. When I turned to leave the room Moti tipped a wink at me.

A half-hour later Muchu Chaudhuri breezed into my office and handed me a sheet of paper on which he had written down a territorial redistribution of infantry divisions. It must have taken him all of five minutes thus to relocate the order of battle of the Indian Army. I noted that he had allotted 20 and 27 Infantry Divisions to Sikkim. I commented that we could not take away the only division remaining on the Pakistani front without the permission of the government. Chaudhuri brushed aside my objection with an impatient wave of his hand and said that he had discussed his proposals with the Defence Minister. The government, he said, had agreed to his proposal that the army be absolved of responsibility for defence against Pakistan, except in Kashmir.

This was a startling development. Mr Chavan, formerly Chief Minister of Maharashtra, had recently arrived in Delhi to take charge of the Defence Ministry. Nehru had specially chosen him because of his reputation as a forceful administrator. In his quiet, unassuming way he soon made his presence felt in the Ministry but at the beginning of his tenure he seemed to have fallen unduly under the spell of Muchu Chaudhuri's forceful personality.

With his previous experience limited to state administration, Chavan had come to Delhi unfamiliar with defence policy and organisation. It was natural for him to lean heavily on the only person among the military hierarchy with whom he had dealt before. In course of time he would see through Chaudhuri's egotistic nature and shallow judgments, but in his first few weeks he allowed himself to be beguiled by the latter's misleading aura of professionalism. There can be no other explanation for the sudden abdication of defence responsibility for the border with Pakistan, whatever guarantees the Americans or the British might have given.

I argued that we had a sufficient number of divisions in the east: two in the Siliguri corridor and three in Assam. In my opinion that was enough to defeat a Chinese venture into the plains 'sectors. I said that it would make more sense to leave 27th Division in the Punjab but move HQ XI Corps from the Punjab to Assam to take over from HQ IV Corps.

'No,' Chaudhuri replied sharply. 'I want Bijji to sweat it out there. I don't want to heap his woes on H.B.'[5]

I made no comment.

'You know I have my knife into Bijji, don't you?' he asked. 'But then you are a pal of his, I suppose.'

Again, I refrained from making any comment and Chaudhuri walked out of the room.

In the evening the CGS invited me to share a pot of tea with him in his office. I ventured an opinion that Muchu Chaudhuri was not in the habit of studying the papers that were put up to him, preferring to rely on intuition or preconceptions, or whatever. He issued orders based on off-the-cuff decisions that often did not stand up to scrutiny. I cited the example of his unthought-out plan for the random redeployment of the field forces and of the successive and contradictory directions on defence plans for Assam. Moti smiled and said that we would have to put up with the Chief's idiosyncrasies. It would be up to us, the General Staff, to ensure that orders issuing from his office were sound and practicable. This might involve uneasy moments at first, but he felt certain that Chaudhuri would gradually settle down to his new responsibilities. At the moment, Moti added, the Chief was apprehensive about his standing with the government and that might have unsettled him temporarily.

Moti informed me that Chaudhuri had spoken to him about plans to expand Military Operations Directorate. He wanted a major general as DMO, with two brigadiers as deputies under him, one for future planning and the other for day-to-day operational management. I commented that this was another instance of Muchu's thoughtless reaction to a problem. The whole point of my proposal for a new cell for future planning was to move it out of Army HQ and transfer it to the Chiefs of Staff Committee, where it

could more effectively function in tandem with the Joint
Planning Committee. Saddling a DMO with it, however
much his rank was upgraded, was not the solution. Moti
said that I should send him my suggestions in the form
of a note so that he could discuss it with the Chief.

Just before I left for home that night Bijji Kaul rang
up from Tezpur. When I remarked about his long absences
from Corps HQ, he said that he had felt the compulsion
to go out and look for Anant Pathania and 'rescue' him
from his tramp across the hills. Why he felt so compelled
he did not say. That evening he had at last found Anant
and flown him back to Corps HQ. When he finished
recounting his long saga about hair-raising flights over the
hills and valleys of NEFA, I cautioned him about his too
frequent sorties out of Tezpur. I told him that the impression
was gaining ground that he preferred to fight brigade
battles, leaving the command of the corps to his staff.
Perhaps I exaggerated, but he needed to be warned.

On 23 November I was requisitioned for the whole day
by Harish Sarin to prepare a series of papers for the
National Defence Council which Nehru had formed after
our reverses. The Council consisted of prominent Indians
not in government service, including one or two retired
generals. It was to hold its first meeting in the next two
or three days. One of the papers that was specifically
required was an assessment of the army's will and capacity
to continue with the war. When we discussed the matter,
I gave Sarin my personal view that the first priority should
be to find the right man to inspire and rebuild the army.
The implication was obvious but I did not voice it explicitly.
I assured him that at the unit level officers and men could
be relied on to give of their best, but they needed to rebuild
their confidence in the generals. I confessed that after my
recent experience in Tezpur my opinion could well be
unduly alarmist. I suggested that he seek a more objective
view than mine. In fact, I said, it should be the Defence
Council that should address itself to this crucial matter.
Sarin replied that he wanted an Army HQ assessment and
since the Chief and the CGS were both new on the scene,

the DMO's opinion would be the most relevant. The American and British teams were certain to interrogate him on this subject. I replied that I would know what to say to a foreign military mission but offering an opinion to our own government implied a different kind of responsibility. We left it at that and though I prepared a series of factual documents for the council's meeting, I did not venture one on the state of the army.

On 24 November I was placed at the disposal of two high-level foreign military delegations, one led by General Sir Richard Hull, Britain's top soldier, and the other by General Paul Adams, Commander of the US Strike Command. Their staff officers came to my Ops Room for a briefing in the morning. Brigadier General Johnson of the United States asked some penetrating questions about our Kameng battles and our forced retreat to the plains. He also wanted to know my opinion about the army's capability to repulse a renewed Chinese offensive. I replied that although the Chinese might make some gains on the north bank of the Brahmaputra, we were confident of defeating any attempt to cross over to the south bank or to force the Siliguri corridor in north Bengal. When asked about the imbalances in our force structure, I handed the general a copy of our 'Army of the Foreseeable Future' paper, which he said he would study and link up with India's 'shopping list' for arms and equipment.

Next day, while I was busy making arrangements for the visit of Generals Hull and Adams to Siliguri, Chaudhuri again came into my room. He said that he had been directed by the Prime Minister to meet Biju Patnaik (Chief Minister of Orissa), but as he was busy with the visiting generals he wanted me to go in his place. Patnaik had been given some special task connected with resistance movements, he explained, and I was required to fill him in on all that was happening in Assam. Chaudhuri added that he knew Patnaik and warned me to be careful of what I said. I replied that I had heard much about Patnaik, none of it to his discredit, but what concerned me more was the number of guerrilla and resistance movements being launched without any co-ordination by the General Staff or the Ministry of Defence: Mullik's police resistance movement in Assam, rumours of a Tibetan guerrilla force being organised by the government, and now Patnaik.

'That's why I am sending you, Monty,' Chaudhuri said, contradicting himself. 'You will know how to handle it.'

I had met Biju Patnaik and his brother George many years ago when I was a schoolboy on holiday in Cuttack when my father had been posted there. The brothers were then at Ravenshaw College, where George, as the district cycling champion, was something of a schoolboys' hero. In later life it was Biju who became the more famous of the two. He started life as a contractual entrepreneur and political activist. He was also a daring air pilot and during Indonesia's war of independence he flew many crucial missions in support of that country's struggle against the Dutch. Thereafter he became the proprietor of Air Kalinga, a mainly charter airline which, among other tasks, had often undertaken hazardous air-drop missions for isolated Assam Rifles posts in NEFA which the IAF refused to undertake because of safety regulations. Nehru was reportedly well disposed toward him and looked upon him as a go-getter and a troubleshooter. At one time, just after Menon's dismissal, the rumour had been that Nehru was going to bring Patnaik to Delhi as Defence Minister.

After we had probed and identified each other from the past, Patnaik told me that he wanted an accurate assessment of the army's morale, its operational capability and its plans in Assam. He had been to Tezpur with Home Minister Shastri, he said, and had seen the army visibly disintegrating. The PM had now put him on the job to assess the army's organic solidity.

I told Muchu what I wanted,' he said, 'but he seemed very hazy. I suppose that is why he sent you. Now tell me what is going on. Can we stop the Chinese?'

I assured him that the officers and men in the field were reliable and staunch; they would obey orders. Of that there was no doubt in my mind. Whether or not we could stop the Chinese would depend upon the kind of orders they were given. I told him that his experience in Tezpur should not unduly colour his conclusions. There was no need to doubt the fighting capability of the army. What needed to be provided was professional and stout-heared generalship.

He did not take me up on the obvious implication of my statement. Instead he said, 'You are too optimistic, Palit. I am informed that the army will require new arms and equipment before it can be effective.'

I said that it was true the Indian Army required to be modernised but that was a separate issue altogether. With what we had we could take on the Pakistanis anywhere, and also the Chinese on the lower heights. What we could not do was to fight the Chinese on the crestline of the Himalayas, not because we did not have the arms but because we did not have the logistical potential – as yet. We discussed the subject for a while but I am not sure that my advocacy increased his confidence in the army's fighting potential.

We had established a rapport by then and I ventured to ask him about his own role in the war, but he gave away nothing. All he said was that the PM had entrusted him with a special task. It was much later that I learned from a reliable source that Patnaik became closely involved in the CIA operations based at Chaubatia in Orissa, from where, reportedly, U-2 flights and the air-dropping of arms to Khampa rebels in Tibet were carried out.

Walking back from Patnaik's office, I found the corridors of the Ministry filled with Americans in uniform, walking in and out of offices. Their presence created an air of bustle and business that pervaded the atmosphere in South Block. 'They are really taking over,' I recorded in my diary. 'We have been instructed to give the Americans all the information they ask for.'

Surendra Singh of MO-IV had been visited by a Lieutenant Colonel Allen of General Adam's planning staff who had assured him that the Americans would help India raise fifty new divisions within three years, enough to evict the Chinese from Tibet. We would receive all the co-operation and military aid we needed from the Pentagon. Allen had implied that the Americans and the Indians would thenceforth be allies against the Chinese.

On the morning of 25 November I flew with Generals Hull and Adams in the former's comfortably appointed Comet, a converted airliner. I had once met Dick Hull in England, at the house of his sister Barbara Swinburn, wife of General Henry Swinburn who had been my boss as Military Secretary in 1946. Hull invited me to sit with him and Adams at his special table and the two generals questioned me at length about the recent campaign. I observed that whereas Hull interested himself in the general course of the operations, and the personalities involved, Adams was more interested in the particularities of high-altitude warfare: the performance of weapons and equipment, casualty evacuation and treatment, the fatigue factor in the mountains and ration scales. He gave me a thoroughly business-like grilling. Unfortunately, I was unable to give him adequate information on some aspects, it being too soon after the event for us to have received feedback from units. He occasionally sent for his two main staff officers, Colonels Allen (planning) and Cardenhas (intelligence) to take notes of what I said. He was entirely professional.

Arriving at Bagdogra, we were met by Bogey Sen and Harbaksh Singh (Army and Corps Commanders) and taken to an improvised map room, where Harbaksh gave the visitors a briefing on the situation on the Sikkim–Chumbi border, including his plans and troop dispositions. He proposed to commit both his divisions on that border to guard the two main approaches from the Chumbi area, across Jelep-la and Nathu-la, and that left him nothing for his left (northern) flank. When asked how he would counter a possible back-door threat from Khamba Dzong via north Sikkim, he nonchalantly stated that it would not worry him if the Chinese severed his line of communication; he would rely on built-up stocks and airlifts, as he had planned to do at Se-la. It was an unnecessary display of over-confidence, made the more conspicuous by Bogey Sen interrupting him to criticise the rashness of his proposal. There was in fact no situational correlation between Se-la and the Sikkim heights and I agreed with Sen's criticism. Unfortunately, the argument turned somewhat acrimonious with neither side attempting to conceal their mutual antipathy. It was not till Krishen Sibal whispered in Bogey's ear that there were foreign VIPs present, that the unseemly argument died down.

I have mentioned this incident because it had an amusing

sequel. In the car driving up to Gangtok, General Adams asked me to clarify the rank structure in the Indian Army. Was there, he asked, just the one rank for all senior generals, somewhat like the new Chinese PLA system? When I appeared nonplussed at his question, he elaborated: 'Well, in Delhi we met your Army Chief and he is a three-star general. Here the Army and Corps Commanders both have the same three-star rank – and neither seems to have authority over the other. How are orders issued and obeyed?' It took much tactful explanation to convince him that a normal and logical chain of command did indeed operate in the Indian Army. At the same time I explained that the only peculiarity of the Indian Army rank structure was that lieutenant generals came in two grades, Army Command grade and Corps Command (or PSO) grade, with different scales of pay. The latter addressed the former as 'Sir'. (This oddity was caused by the government's paranoid and totally illogical fear of creating more than one four-star general.)

The purpose of the trip to Gangtok and beyond was to give our visitors a feel of road conditions in the mountains and for them to call on the Sikkim government. It had rained persistently for the past two days, so they went through the whole gamut of hill-road calamities: landslides, displaced boulders rolling down from mountain tops, lines of vehicles stuck axle-deep in the mire. Consequently there was no time to visit Nathu-la or Jelep-la.

I noticed that Adams and his staff officers often stopped near groups of soldiers to talk to the men, or to check details such as convoy arrangements, ammunition stocks and even the mechanical functioning of rifle bolts and machine-gun parts. I was therefore much gratified when, at the end of the drive, Paul Adams remarked to me: 'Well, Brigadier, I've seen the convoy discipline of this outfit, their care of arms and their camouflage drill; I've checked their field works and I've spoken with junior officers. I'd be quite content to see one of my divisions as well organised and disposed on the ground.' That was not an inconsiderable compliment from the top land forces commander of the United States

Cardenhas sought me out at the reception held at the

Indian Residence in Ganglok to discuss the possibility of inspiring a local guerrilla movement in the mountains of Sikkim. He had learned that a very large proportion of the inhabitants were ethnic Nepalis, including many Gorkhas (which I had not realised till then) and would form an excellent recruiting base. The United States, he said, would willingly arm and equip them and even send training advisers if we so desired. I took him to General Sen and we held a brief discussion on the subject. Sen told me to take the matter up with our host, I. Bahadur Singh, the Government of India Resident. When I spoke to Bahadur Singh and inquired if I could discuss the subject with the Sikkim government, he took me to the Maharajkumar of Sikkim who was at the party, saying that he was the best person to promote the idea.

I had known the Maharajkumar in the 1950s when, as an honorary officer of the 8th Gorkhas, he used to make periodic visits to the Gorkha centres in Dehra Dun. Although he appeared somewhat reserved on first acquaintance, he was in reality cheerful and easily approachable. (In later years, when I joined the governing body of my old school, St Paul's in Darjeeling, I became quite friendly with him and his Maharani, the former Hope Cook.)

The Maharajkumar, Cardenhas and I discussed the feasibility of starting a resistance movement in the mountain ranges dividing eastern Sikkim and the Chumbi valley. The Prince was enthusiastic and promised all support from the Maharaja's government. He said that both Gorkha and Lepcha subjects of his state would prove good mountain fighters, although they would require to be given training and firearms. When Cardenhas suggested that we record concrete proposals, I closed the discussion because I did not want yet another guerrilla operation launched before a co-ordinating authority had been established in Delhi. I told Cardenhas that we would take further action only after discussing the matter with the Director of the Intelligence Bureau.

It was late when we arrived back at Bagdogra. As we were billeted in widely dispersed areas (owing to a general shortage of accommodation), I became separated from the rest of the party. Next morning, when I arrived at the airfield at the time Sen had given me, I found to my astonishment that the CIGS's Comet had already left for Tezpur. I was informed that Sen had herded the visiting generals into the aircraft as soon as they had arrived and given the order for the aircraft to take off without waiting for the DMO. I had to sit the day out at Bagdogra airfield. In the evening, when the aircraft returned from Tezpur to pick me up before proceeding to Delhi, Hull and Adams both asked me why I had not gone with them. 'General Chaudhuri told us that you would be the one to give us an objective account of the battle, so we were surprised to hear that you were not accompanying us.' I made no comment. During the return flight Brigadier Newton-Dunn, the British Military Adviser, spoke to me about the briefing in Tezpur and described it as an 'embarassing experience'. Generals Sen and Kaul 'had their claws out', as he put it, and the account of the Kameng campaign was 'sketchy and often contradictory'. According to Newton-Dunn, while Kaul talked about a fighting withdrawal from Se-la, Sen described it as a 'hurried retreat ending in a shambles'.

On 28 November I accompanied Hull and Adams on a visit to Ladakh, this time flying in one of the American C-130 super-transport planes the US Air Force had sent us on loan in early November. The day was overcast but windless. Flying over Lahoul and the Zanskar range, the view was a dramatic vista of snow-covered peaks, ridges and valleys spread out beneath us like a carpet of white, like a sand model cast in snow.

We circled over Chushul first and went on to Leh, but there also it was decided not to risk a landing, the American pilots not having had any previous experience of making a touchdown at such a high altitude. We were back in Delhi early, well before the luncheon hour.

Cardenhas used the opportunity of a free afternoon to hold a meeting with MO staff on organising a guerrilla movement in Sikkim. He suggested locating an operating base at Hashimara with separate groups for Sikkim and western and eastern Bhutan. It was obvious that what he was considering was not so much a resistance movement as a conventional commando organisation to raid enemy territory in Tibet, operating from a base in north Bengal.

This is not what we had envisaged when we had discussed the subject in Gangtok. I took Cardenhas to Mullik's office, where we held another discussion. Mullik too was not over-enthusiastic about the idea of a commando-type organisation, especially when Cardenhas spoke about operating 'ahead of the Indian Army, even into Tibet', mentioning 'freeing Tibet' as a possible objective. Mullik balked at all this, pointing out the international implications of such a project. The meeting ended inconclusively. When we were leaving Mullik asked Cardenhas to stay behind. (No deal was ever struck about commando or guerrilla operations but I understood that Cardenhas thereafter became a regular visitor to the DIB's office, confirming my supposition that he was probably an officer of the CIA.)

Chaudhuri telephoned to inform me that Bijji Kaul had put in his papers and was being posted temporarily in command of XI Corps in the Punjab, pending retirement. He also informed me that, as HQ Eastern Command would have to assume direct responsibility for the defence of Assam, he intended to visit Bogey Sen in Lucknow the next day in order to tie-up IV Corps' plans. When I asked him if he would like me to prepare an *aide memoire* on the situation in Assam, he said there was no need for any briefs or notes: 'I am completely in the picture. I shall discuss the matter with Bogey and issue directions.' He added that in case hostilities started again he intended to 'bring in the air'.

I had become accustomed to his off-the-cuff decisions and his psychological need to pretend to ignore his staff, so I did not think it necessary to point out to him that the air arm was not under his command and the decision to use it was not for him to take. If he were circumventing procedure, I told myself, at least it was for the right cause. We could always sort out the protocol when the time came.

Just before I left for home Sarin rang up to say that we would not be working together any longer because there was going to be a new order in the Defence Ministry. P.V.R. Rao had replaced Pulla Reddy as Secretary and one of his first acts had been to take personal charge of General Staff matters. Sarin was being sent to another section of the Ministry. He added the information that T.T. Krishnamachari, Minister of Finance, had been nominated by the PM to lead a delegation to Britain and the United States to press our calls for military and other aid.

## NOTES

1. It transpired that Kaul did not wait for instructions from Army HQ. His sensationalised statements – that the Chinese were streaming down from the mountains and that we could expect paratroops to land in north Assam at any moment – served to create panic in Tezpur town and in the tea gardens. By the next day there was a chaotic exodus along the roads leading westwards and southwards to cross the river by bridge or ferry. Kaul ordered all military units, including HQ IV Corps and the Border Roads Organisation, to evacuate to Gauhati – thus clogging up the roads even more effectively.
2. Mullik later told me that there had been a considerable lobby against Chaudhuri's appointment, both at Army HQ and in the ministries, because his conduct during and after the Goa operation had raised a number of eyebrows. Shastri (the Home Minister) had also been looking at his record as Military Governor of Hyderabad after the takeover of that state in 1948. Eventually, on Mullik's recommendation, Nehru agreed to instal Muchu in the Chief's chair but, for the time being, in his Army Commander's rank of lieutenant general – in my opinion a weak and counterproductive decision.
3. When moves were at last permitted into the forward area months later, the party that went up to Rezang-la found the Kumaoni troops that fought there under Major Shaitan Singh frozen in their battle positions, still holding their weapons in their trenches. The extent of Chinese casualties was much in evidence in the frozen waste around them.
4. As described in his book *The Untold Story*, Kaul spent much of 21 and 22 November flying about in a helicopter, searching the foothills north of Udalguri on a self-imposed mission to find the fleeing GOC of 4 Infantry Division. On 22 November he at last located Pathania near Kalakthang and brought him back to Tezpur.
5. Lieutenant General Henderson-Brooks, GOC XI Corps in the Punjab.

# 11
# THE PRICE OF DEFEAT

It was inevitable that the humiliation of our defeat would in time be sharpened by disillusionments; one of the most poignant of these was the lack of sympathy from Afro-Asian nations in the aftermath of our plight. Except for President Nasser of Egypt (who subsequently masterminded the favourable Colombo proposals) the vast majority of non-aligned leaders pointedly failed to appreciate India's viewpoint. Some urged unsought advice on New Delhi to accept Peking's proposals. The Russians, while not censorious, were not markedly supportive either. It was the western powers, particularly Britain and the United States, who were spontaneous in their sympathy and rushed to our help with offers of arms and other aid. They despatched high-powered missions to Delhi. Averell Harriman and General Paul Adams came from the United States and Duncan Sandys (Commonwealth Minister) and General Hull (CIGS) from Britain, closely followed by Admiral of the Fleet Lord Louis Mountbatten, Chief of the UK Defence Staff.

Because of my operational preoccupations I had been only vaguely aware of these background developments. I was therefore somewhat surprised when on 30 November Chaudhuri told me to drop everything and place myself at the disposal of the Ministry of External Affairs as army adviser for bilateral negotiations with Pakistan on the Kashmir problem. The same afternoon I was called to a preliminary meeting by Y.D. Gundevia, the Commonwealth Secretary, an occasion that marked the beginning of a warm and rewarding friendship which lasted many years, first as colleagues in government and, later, well into our respective retirements.

Yezdi Gundevia, a member of the Indian Civil Service and a few years my senior, was one of those rare and happy beings who combine professional pre-eminence with an irrepressible sense of fun. Blessed with an abundance of commonsense, his drollish manner enabled him to demolish pomposity or censor presumption with equal ease, and without giving offence. Small in stature, he had a thin, sensitive face which became framed in laughter-lines whenever he smiled – and that was often – while the eyes themselves never lost their faint look of pleasantry, even when he found the company tedious or the conversation commonplace. He was a tonic to associate with.

After filling me in with an account of Duncan Sandys' heavy-handed shuttle diplomacy between Islamabad and Delhi, Gundevia went on to say that Nehru, normally a hardliner on Kashmir, had at last been arm-twisted into agreeing to start negotiations with President Ayub Khan on a settlement of the Kashmir problem. According to US Ambassador Galbraith, President Kennedy would be able more easily to obtain Congressional approval for aid to India if we were to arrive at an understanding with Pakistan. In a way we were being made to pay the price of defeat, Gundevia added, but he had always been convinced that the best solution to the Kashmir problem would be its partition. The occasion had now presented itself. It was all very well to propound abstract theories and long legal arguments, he said, but he was convinced that there would never be a solution in Kashmir other than by force of arms or by a sharing of territory. Since we had abjured the first (and probably would never be able to enforce it anyway) there was no alternative but to accept the second. In any case, the fifteen-year old Ceasefire Line had made partition a virtual *fait accompli*.

Mountbatten, who later joined the Sandys mission,

suggested independence for Kashmir valley, a gratuitous
piece of advice that was quickly picked up by Bakshi
Ghulam Mohammed, Chief Minister of Kashmir, who
proposed 'internationalisation' (as if that were significantly
different). Yezdi's view was that all that was just so much
shadow-boxing. He was sure that India and Pakistan both
privately conceded that partition was inevitable in the long
run. He had no doubt that Pandit Nehru could wheedle
parliament into agreement, though it might be more difficult
for President Ayub to persuade the Pakistanis. In order to
make partition acceptable to Ayub it would be necessary
for India to suggest an adjustment of the Ceasefire Line
decidedly in favour of Pakistan.

At my suggestion we walked over to the MO Directorate
Ops Room to study the geography of the Ceasefire Line.
As the ceasefire had been abruptly imposed in the middle
of a war on the basis of actual troop deployments on 31
December 1948, the Line was an arbitrary alignment, not
everywhere based on geographical or tactical logic. After I
had briefly described our defensive sectors on the map,
Yezdi left it to me to redraw the line on a rational basis
-- giving a little here, taking a little there, but giving a lot
more than taking. 'I should suggest a number of alternative
lines on the map,' he said, 'and in a day or two we could
discuss them in some detail.' The only restrictions he placed
on me were that no part of Srinagar valley and no Dogri
area was to be compromised.

Walking back to his office, he suddenly turned to me
and asked: 'What is the best alignment for a border in
mountainous terrain?'

'Along the top of a range of mountains,' I replied, without
pausing to think.

'Wrong', said Gundevia, twinkling a smile at me. 'What
good is that for siting defences? If you think it out you
will see that a border aligned along the crest of a ridge
creates problems for both sides. Neither can occupy the
top, yet in order to site their defences both sides will try
to get up as close as possible to the crestline, resulting in
an eyeball-to-eyeball confrontation with all the attendant
tension. Isn't that what you have been doing on the
McMahon Line? Is that a good arrangement? Wouldn't it

be wiser to align a border along a riverline or a valley, with the two sides occupying the opposing heights, well separated?'

When I thought about it, I realised that he was right. An international border and a defensive position posit conflicting tactical parameters.

Over the next two or three days I worked on the map. Together with Yezdi, we decided on five alternative lines (to give us flexibility in bargaining). The one with the 'maximum give-away' ran as follows: from the north-east (north of Zojila) to Tithwal the border would run along the Kishenganga river; thence southward, cross-country so to speak, over the Kazinag range to the top of the Jhelum gorge just west of Baramulla; southwards from there the line kept west of Gulmarg but gave away the valuable tillages of Poonch, Mendhar and Jhangar. This line conceded to Pakistan some 3,500 sq km of territory more than they held under the ceasefire agreement.

I drafted a written summary of our discussions for the information of the Chief but when I showed it to Gundevia he advised me to tear it up. He wanted no record of our proposals kept in either of our offices. I was to lock the maps up in my safe and brief my boss verbally, he said, not via a file.

It had been decided to open negotiations at ministerial level before holding a summit meeting between Nehru and Ayub. Since it would be a few days before a minister was appointed, I was released to resume my duties as DMO. This was a timely blessing because there were a number of ongoing and interconnecting activities in General Staff Branch that I was anxious to co-ordinate personally.

Chaudhuri had charged me with the task of compiling a summary of events and policies leading up to the Namka-chu episode. What he wanted particularly was a clear allocation of responsibility for the major decisions. I told him that whereas I could cover most of the drama from my records, the period between my departure for Cochin on 8 September to the start of the Chinese offensive on 20 October would have to be allotted to the DCGS, because it was he who had handled operational matters during that period, to the near-total exclusion of the DMO and his directorate. Chaudhuri agreed to get Dhillon to write a report to cover that period.

Fortunately I had already started preparing such a document and had collected the relevant files and reports. I had maintained a handwritten diary of day-to-day events during the crisis, hence I was able quickly to compile my *Summary of Events and Policies*, from which I have quoted so liberally in this book. I handed parts of it to Pritpal Singh, to check whether I had missed out anything important. I also showed a draft copy to Jogi Dhillon. Neither of them offered any comments or suggestions.

Pritpal Singh of MO-1 had accompanied Chaudhuri on the latter's visit to Lucknow. He told me that the Chief had handed out a number of *ad hoc* decisions without benefit of staff examination. For example, he had decided to change the regional command system in eastern India without consulting Air HQ, whose command organisation is, of necessity, co-ordinated with ours. It appeared that during a discussion on command and control of northern border operations, the Eastern Army Commander, General Sen, had supported my suggestion about the abolition of HQ Eastern Command and the raising of a Field Army HQ in Gauhati. His recommendation was that the territories under the existing Eastern Command be reallocated, with everything south of the Ganga to go to HQ Southern Command, the Uttar Pradesh (UP) area to Army HQ, and north Bengal and Assam to the new Field Army HQ. Chaudhuri did not agree. He gave his own decision on the spot: the existing Eastern Command would be renamed Central Command and a new HQ Eastern Command would take over operational responsibility for Sikkim, Bhutan, NEFA and Nagaland. Unaccountably, he located the new headquarters not at Gauhati as I had envisaged, but in Fort William, Calcutta.

Another decision Chaudhuri took during his tour was to cancel a General Staff directive sent by the DMO to Eastern Comand requiring it to prepare an appreciation of possible Chinese threats to eastern UP through Nepal. (At that time there was no plan for force deployment to cover the wide gap between UP Himalay and North Bengal.) When Chaudhuri was told about this he derided the very notion of such a contingency, despite the fact that an age-old trade highway over the Kodari pass connected Lhasa to Kathmandu, whence a three-ton road gave access to the Indian border at Raxaul. Chaudhuri decreed that there was no necessity to consider a threat through Nepal.

He also took a largely untenable decision on guerrilla and commando forces in Sikkim and Bhutan. Without discussing the case with the DIB or the Home Ministry, he issued an arbitrary ruling that these forces would be co-ordinated at Army HQ by a special Director of Operations to be known as DMO 'B', who would function in parallel with the existing DMO.

I found an opportunity of tackling him on these matters when I went to his office to discuss the agenda for a forthcoming Chiefs of Staff Committee meeting (his first). I had included the points mentioned above but when I presented my arguments against the decisions he had taken in Lucknow, Muchu Chaudhuri became visibly irritated.

'The formation of a Command HQ in Calcutta and the threat to India through Nepal have nothing to do with the other Chiefs', he said. 'They are purely army matters – and I have made up my mind. There's nothing more to be said.'

My argument that the organisation of Air Force and Army Commands had to be linked did not impress him; nor did the contention that the Air Force would have a lot to say about a Chinese threat through Nepal. I could not shake him from his obstinacy. He ordered me to delete the items from the agenda. In the process of admonishing his DMO he even brushed aside my arguments in support of two important matters that had long been subjects of dispute between General Thapar and Air Marshal Aspy Engineer.

The first concerned command and control of the surface-to-air guided weapons (SAGWs, as they were then termed) that India had negotiated to procure from Russia and which were expected to arrive in the near future. The Air Force had laid claim to them but under Unni Candeth's tutelage (when he was Director of Artillery) I had convinced General Thapar that SAGWs were an extension of anti-aircraft artillery and were not to be regarded as super-fighters of the IAF. They should primarily be integrated with anti-aircraft defences. Aspy Engineer had, of course, not given way and his hat was still in the ring.

The other point pertained to a General Staff proposal to create an army air corps of helicopters and light aircraft to enable us to manage our own intimate air-support functions such as casualty evacuation, communication flights and artillery spotting. The Ministry of Defence was agreeable but the Air Force had strongly opposed any move to diminish its reach and influence. In this they had the upper hand: the army lacked the resources to provide repair and maintenance cover to any aircraft it might acquire as army equipment.

I explained all this to Chaudhuri and added that we had in fact planned to 'go it alone' as an experiment. Kartar Dubey, whose Border Roads Organisation owned a number of Russian M14 helicopters, had agreed to let the army have a couple of flights to organise our own casualty-evacuation system in Ladakh and NEFA. He had even investigated the possibility of getting the machines maintained 'by the trade' – that is, in the civilian market. I suggested to Chaudhuri that we insist on raising our own air corps with or without an okay from the Air Force.

It was a wasted effort. Chaudhuri had, it seemed to me, made up his mind to veto any proposal put up by his DMO.

'You are just like everybody else, building little empires of your own. On matters of national importance I won't stand for any plotting and intriguing,' he pontificated. 'Let the Air Force have their missiles and withdraw the army air arm proposal. We don't need one.'

When Aspy Engineer met me at the coffee table after the Chiefs of Staff meeting, he smiled sadly at me and asked, 'Getting soft in your old age, Monty?' He obviously rued the lack of fight in an opponent. As a result of this setback it took the army another twenty years before it could raise its own air corps; and the missiles have remained with the Air Force ever since.

On the second day of the Chiefs of Staff Committee meeting Air Commodore Mehta, Deputy Secretary (Military) in the Cabinet Secretariat, passed me the information across the table that the United States had turned down Nehru's request for US Air Force intervention, the main reason being that they expected us to use our own air forces in combat before they could consider committing theirs. Air Commodore Mehta added that in the US view we had greatly overestimated the Chinese air capability in Tibet.

I recall with amusement (and not a little embarrassment) that when Mehta was talking to me Aspy Engineer overheard our conversation. He looked curiously in our direction, but he made no comment. Mehta, unaware that the Air Chief had not been consulted before Nehru's appeal for US air support, made no effort to lower his voice. I tried desperately to send him unspoken signals to shut him up but he blithely continued to give me the rest of the story. Fortunately Engineer considered it more dignified to leave his curiosity unsatisfied than to acknowledge publicly that the Air Chief had been ignored.

On 11 December I was given a pleasant surprise when Bijji Kaul walked into my office. He had just been to see the Chief, who had informed him that his resignation had been accepted. According to Bijji, Chaudhuri had alternately gloated over his discomfiture and patronised him by offering to recommend him for a job in the Ministry, which, needless to add, Bijji politely declined. I was glad to see that he was not in a noticeably downcast frame of mind. Warm and friendly as ever, he said that he had come to bid me goodbye and also to warn me to be careful of Chaudhuri, who had been heard to say that he was planning to get rid of his bull-headed and bumptious DMO. When I made no comment Bijji went on to add that I would have to learn to be more restrained in my opinions and reactions. Without being condemnatory Bijji told me that in his opinion it was mainly my presence and deportment at Tezpur on the fateful night of 17 November that had been the cause of the command convulsions that followed.

'You are too headstrong, Monty,' he said. 'You stir the pot too vigorously – and you have a romantic's values. If you had not accompanied Thapar to Tezpur that afternoon, everything would have been back to normal by now. The Chinese would have gone back to China; Thapar would have remained the Chief; I would still be commanding my corps; and Muchu would have been packing up to proceed on retirement.

There was a trace of bitterness in his voice, but Bijji was not being accusatory so I let it pass, not fully accepting his censure. Before he left he again warned me to be wary of Muchu. I told him that I had already sensed Muchu's hostility and although it disheartened me, it was not in my nature to be compliant. I could only try to be more restrained in future.

I asked him about his personal plans but all he would say was that Nehru had suggested a career abroad for him, in the private sector, and he intended to follow that up. First, however, he was going to take his wife away on a holiday.

On 12 December I handed two copies of my *Summary of Events and Policies* to Chaudhuri. Without even glancing at them he walked over to a wall safe and locked them up.

'I don't want any record of this kept in your office,' he said. 'I hope you haven't kept a copy.'

'Indeed I have,' I replied, firmly meeting his gaze. 'Furthermore, I intend to keep a personal copy too.'

'A personal copy? Why?' he asked. 'What you suggest is highly irregular.'

'Please read my report, Sir,' I requested. 'It is censorious and attributive, and much of what I have written is based on top secret MO Directorate records. Once I leave this office I shall have no access to them. If my report is ever used as an evidential document I must keep a copy to defend it.'

'You are being over-dramatic as usual,' Chaudhuri commented but he did not persist with his injunction. Instead, he asked me to take a seat at his desk as he had a few things to discuss with me informally.

He told me that he was having a 'bit of pother with that fellow Mullik' who was determined that the Intelligence Bureau should retain control of guerrilla operations, although he had asked for an army general to be appointed as director, under his overall charge. 'By the way,' Chaudhuri suddenly asked, 'have you been discussing this with Mullik?'

'Yes, I have,' I replied, 'It was I who suggested that it must be the DIB who co-ordinate all unconventional operations.'

'Wasn't it disloyal of you to express an opinion directly contrary to mine?'

'You have never expressed your opinion to me,' I

countered, not a little indignant myself. 'If you were to discuss operational matters with your DMO before taking decisions, the contradictions would not arise. I would have given you my advice that the army was neither geared nor competent to organise and manage a resistance movement. In fact if an irregular force were to be handled over to us, it would not be long before they became "regularised" and tied to our logistical system and thus lose their native *élan*. No – we could train and operate commandos, but not guerrillas or resistance movements. That is a job essentially for a civilian intelligence agency.'

Chaudhuri thought that over for a while. He appeared displeased but did not counter my argument.

'Oh well,' he conceded, 'he can have the guerrillas if he wants them so badly. Incidentally, he asked me for a major general to help run it but I told him that I had none to spare. Would you like to take it on? If so, I am prepared to send him your name. It would mean an out-of-turn promotion for you.'

I told him that Mullik had already offered me the job and the promotion, but that I had not accepted the offer. It was for my Chief, I said, to make the decision. As far as my own views were concerned, I added, I was quite certain in my mind that there was only one job for a DMO to go on to, and that was the command of a division. Chaudhuri then suddenly changed tack and said that he had been considering replacing the DMI with an officer of the rank of major general. He asked me if I would be interested in the job. I told him that my views remained unaltered.

I have no idea why Chaudhuri should have made these patently guileful offers. We both knew that the Army Section Board No. 1 for my particular group of contemporaries had not been held and although I presumed I would eventually be selected for promotion, the prior approval of the Board was *de rigueur*. An interesting sequel to this episode was a piece of information Mullik gave me a few days later. He said that Chaudhuri had rung him up to tell him that he was thinking of asking Major General Lloyd, a retired DMI from the War Office in London who had come to Delhi with Mountbatten, to take over as DMI in Delhi. Mullik knew how to deal with that bizarre proposal.

On 14 December N.B. Menon of the China desk at the Foreign Ministry rang up to tell me about another of those unexpected moves that the Chinese were in the habit of springing upon us. They had intimated their intention to return all arms and equipment captured by them in NEFA. The material was being collected at Dhirang and they wanted us to make arrangements to take them over at an early date. Menon invited me to his office to discuss this entirely unexpected *démarche* and how we should handle the matter.

We were quite at a loss as to how to regard this move. Our first reaction was that it was an elaborate PR exercise to accentuate India's humiliation. The fact is that we did not really understand the nature of our enemy. For example, their treatment of prisoners-of-war varied greatly. China was not a signatory to the Geneva Convention, yet in some places the Chinese had been meticulously correct in their conduct, while in others they deliberately set out to create ill-will against officers by over-indulging NCOs and men, stressing their under-privileged status in the Indian Army. We had also received reports of grievous atrocities committed by them. A few days previously the Chinese had handed over a batch of wounded prisoners to the Indian Red Cross at Bomdila. Although detailed debriefings came later, word-of-mouth information indicated that the Chinese had at times behaved brutally. Besides indulging in unnecessary massacres of fleeing troops (including the gunning down of Brigadier Hoshiar Singh near the village of Phudung, well to the south of Manda-la) they had on occasions summarily executed disarmed prisoners. At other times they had looted watches, rings and other personal belongings from both the living and the dead. To be entirely fair it must also be recorded that in many cases Chinese officers had investigated and attempted to redress such complaints.

We had good reason therefore to treat this new *démarche* with circumspection, although our caution was to prove unnecessary. Eventually an Indian team went to Dhirang and the Chinese politely handed over large stocks of materiel – arms and ammunition, clothing, equipment and fighting vehicles – all meticulously inventoried with receipts vouchered

in detail.[1] At no time, then or later, did they make any
effort to publicise or in any way exploit this unprecedented
transaction.

Meanwhile MO Directorate was trying to settle down to
normality, but with no marked success. The conduct of
business did not revert to the even tenor of normal staff-work.
On casting my mind back to that period I realise that
under Chaudhuri's chiefship, General Staff procedures were
inexorably eroded. Because it was an endemic of his nature
to disdain counsel, he preferred to take decisions without
benefit of staff examination or advice, on a subjective and
sometimes even whimsical basis; and because Moti Sagar
was unable to hold his Chief on a tight rein he must be
counted as contributing to the partial paralysis of the
General Staff system during that period.

Following the announcement of the ceasefire, Chaudhuri
had issued a number of off-the-cuff, piecemeal orders,
including transfers of divisions. These moves needed to be
co-ordinated and incorporated in new operational instructions
to the Commands. Changed defensive plans for the Punjab
border and Kashmir, reoccupation of the north bank in
Assam, cross-Command reallocation of resources and other
important decisions needed follow-through directives, without
which HQ Commands would be stranded in a policy
vacuum. For example, after the transfer of 5th and 27th
Divisions from the Punjab border to the east, Daulet Singh
had made no new plans to defend the denuded Punjab-Pakistan
border. Moti Sagar approved my proposal that if we had
to meet a sudden Pakistani attack anywhere in the west,
we should plan to yield territory in less crucial places in
order to concentrate available resources to defend the vital
ones. Accordingly, we planned to suggest withdrawing 25
Infantry Division from its deployment in the Mendhar-Poonch
area in order to provide the GOC-in-C Western Command
with a Command reserve for the southern sector of the
Punjab border. Try as he might, Moti could not pin down
Chaudhuri to a decision. For days the Punjab plains lay
exposed to attack from Pakistan. All that Chaudhuri agreed
to do was to put the matter before the Military Affairs
Committee of the National Defence Council (set up by
Nehru after the debacle), as though that *ad hoc* civilian

advisory body had taken over responsibility for the defence of India. When I persisted in badgering him for a decision he told me that he had been discussing these matters with the Defence Minister and that Chavan had directed the Army and Air Chiefs to work out a plan for taking 'joint critical action'. He told me to get the JPC on to it and produce such a plan. Perplexed, I asked him over the telephone if I might come over and obtain clearer instructions. He shut me off with: 'Oh well, don't bother. I suppose I'll have to do it myself!' What 'critical' plan he produced for his Minister he never confided to his DMO.

Another concern was the vagueness that surrounded the army's expansion plan. After the debacle in NEFA the Americans had talked of helping us raise fifty divisions, but I had heard no more about it. At that time Sarin had advised me to make an appreciation of force requirements related to phases of future operations against the Chinese, starting with the defensive phase, followed by operations to regain lost territory and, finally, going on to an invasion of Tibet. The DMO had made such an appreciation and set it within a timetable of equipment availability and logistical capability. (Chaudhuri had been shown a copy soon after his arrival at Army HQ but he probably had not bothered to study it, preferring to make off-hand pronouncements on what he thought expansion targets should be, without relating them to strategic tasks and threat assessments.)

Although Sarin no longer dealt with military operations, I sought him out and told him about the chaos in MO Directorate and the consequent lacuna in our operational management, particularly regarding the defence of the Punjab and the expansion programme. I said that I could not bring Chaudhuri to apply his mind to any appreciation or problem; he did not even study the papers we sent up to him, seeming instead to operate on a basis of reflexes and reactions. His directives for new raisings did not relate to strategic roles or requirements.

Not many people would have wholly accepted so extraordinary an accusation. Presumably Sarin did, because the next day he primed the Defence Minister to ask for a formal and detailed operational briefing in the Ops Room, after which he would discuss strategic tasks and expansion plans for the armed forces. Thus it was that next morning I received a call from Chaudhuri saying that Defence Minister Chavan wanted to visit the Ops Room for an operational conference.

I was not quite certain about the format for the proposed conference. The practice of convening meetings of the PM's Defence Committee of Cabinet and the Defence Minister's Committee had been discarded two or three years previously. The only high-level deliberations (apart from *ad hoc* meetings in the PM's office) were the informal 'morning prayers' in the Defence Ministry (instituted by Krishna Menon) attended by the service Chiefs, senior bureaucrats, the DIB and a representative from the Foreign Ministry. They met in the Defence Minister's room once or twice a week but no formal agenda was prepared; no points were sent to the General Staff for detailed examination. If formal minutes were recorded, I certainly never saw any. In the circumstances I asked Chaudhuri what preparation he would like me to make for the Minister's conference. He replied that there was no need for an agenda or any other formality. He would 'handle it all without any fuss'.

Chavan arrived accompanied by Defence Secretary P.V.R. Rao and the Army Chief. After Chaudhuri had offered the Minister a chair, he pointed toward me and said: 'This is Brigadier Palit, my Director of Operations, Sir. He will give you a briefing on the operational situation.'

It was ill-contrived, to say the least, to toss such a predicament suddenly at a member of one's staff, but my resentment was easily mollified by Chavan's smilingly felicitous remark. Extending his hand toward me he said: 'Oh, I know about Brigadier Palit. When I was appointed Defence Minister the first piece of advice given me in Bombay was that I must read Palit's book on strategy and tactics. I am glad I did. Now, Brigadier, please give me your views on the defence situation on the Chinese front.'

'My *views*, Sir?' I asked, somewhat taken aback.

'Yes, I would like your views on the present defence policy along the northern border.'

I glanced at the Chief. Interpreting his bland impassivity as permission to express my own views, I began with a brief exposition of border deployments and policies subsequent to the ceasefire. In Ladakh there was no great problem since we had withdrawn from Chushul and formed a ring of defences around Leh. Skipping briefly through the central sector I went on to Sikkim and Bhutan, where also there was no controversial issue. When I came to NEFA and Assam I indicated that I harboured some doubts about the measures we had taken. I did not voice any specific criticism but when Chavan pressed me for my opinion on what changes we should make in our policy, I stated that the army must be sent back into NEFA to reoccupy the areas vacated by the Chinese because it was essential to maintain contact with the enemy. I added that at the moment we were operating without 'contact' intelligence. Chinese ceasefire conditions permitted us to move into most of NEFA, I stressed; our restraint was entirely self-imposed – and pointless. It was incongruous, I said, to harbour plans for a future offensive against the Chinese and, at the same time, fight shy of our responsibilities in the mountains.

Chavan then asked me about plans for the defence of Assam. I told him that till then all we had done was to locate brigades at fixed points such as Misamari and Charduar, in a static framework of defence. I suggested instead that both in Assam and in the Siliguri corridor the main reliance should be on a mobile concept of war, for which an adequate and mobile force should be located somewhere centrally. When asked to explain the difference between static and mobile defence, I answered that the former was a rigid, mechanical allocation of troops to the ground that left little room for manoeuvre should the enemy take a course of action other than the one anticipated. I gave him the example of the brigade at Misamari, dug in around the airstrip and hamlet, weighted down with the impedimenta of a defensive locality including three first-line scales of ammunition. If the Chinese came down from the hills, by-passed Misamari and made an encircling move towards Tezpur along the numerous tea-garden roads, the brigade at Misamari would be left high, dry and out of battle. It would have been more useful to give it a mobile task as a striking force, unburdened with surplus materiel and uncommitted to a specific locality. I then went on to recommend that operations in Sikkim, Bhutan, NEFA and the Brahmaputra valley could best be co-ordinated by a Command or Field Army HQ located not in Lucknow but in Assam, at Shillong or Gauhati.

Chavan stepped up and examined the vast expanse of the wall-map, asking questions of detail from Kashmir's Ceasefire Line to the McMahon Line in NEFA. Eventually, he walked to the centre of the map and asked, 'What about this gap between Uttar Pradesh (UP) and north Bengal?'

I glanced at Chaudhuri, wondering whether he would like to take over.

'Actually, Sir,' Chaudhuri said, 'my DMO and I disagree on this point. I'll let him have his say first.'

I explained on the map that the quickest route for a Chinese force in central Tibet to reach the Gangetic plain was over the Kodari pass in north Nepal, through Kathmandu and down the Tribhuvan highway to the plains of Bihar. 'There is not one Indian bayonet located to face the mountain approaches between the Kumaon hills and Darjeeling,' I said. 'The entire length of the Indo-Nepal border is unguarded.'

Chavan thought over this for a while and then asked me what action I would suggest. I said that we should give the responsibility of the Nepal–India border to Eastern (or Central) Command and ask them to make a plan. We would then provide them with the resources to carry out the task. At the same time, the Chiefs of Staff should prepare an emergency joint army-air plan to forestall the occupation of the airfield at Kathmandu if the Chinese made any move to enter Nepal. Diplomatic action to enable such a step should be set in motion from now, I added.

'Have you discussed this with your Chief?'

'No, Minister. The Chief does not anticipate such a threat.'

'He is probably right,' Chavan said. Then, turning to Chaudhuri, he added: 'Still, there is no harm in getting the local authority to examine the problem. I will discuss this with the Prime Minister. Thank you, Palit. That was very useful'.

To my great and pleasant surprise Muchu Chaudhuri called me up later in the day to commend me for my exposition of the operational situation and added that he would speak to the GOC-in-C Eastern Command to prepare an appreciation on the threat through Nepal.

Personally gratifying as the whole episode was for me, I still had not received directives on the two issues that concerned me most: the expansion programme and troop allocations for the defence of the Punjab border. Chavan had not even discussed them. When I tried to tackle Chaudhuri, he parried my queries by saying that he would give his decision in a day or two.

A few days later (when I returned from Rawalpindi after our first series of talks with Pakistan) I sought out Mullik and asked him if he knew what was the government's thinking on the subject of future strategic policy on the northern border. Was it still the government's intention eventually to launch an offensive against the Chinese? Were we to plan for an invasion of the Aksai Chin? I told him that I could not obtain precise information on these matters from the Ministry of Defence.

Mullik replied that he had held an informal discussion with the PM. Nehru, he said, was quite definite that we must 'give the Chinese a licking in Tibet', having correctly assessed the trauma that our defeated forces had suffered. He felt that the Indian Army would cease to exist as a first-class fighting force unless it were allowed to win back its self-esteem. 'We are in a position similar to what Egypt must have been in when the Israelis pushed them back to the Suez Canal in 1956 and the UN had to come to the rescue,' Nehru had said. 'Substitute the Chinese for the Israelis and the unilateral ceasefire for the UN.'

Mullik advised me to prepare estimates of force levels and logistical requirements for the task of a limited invasion of Tibet – in the Chumbi valley or across the NEFA border in Kameng – and to get on with raising the new divisions as fast as we could. He had been reliably informed by a high CIA source that India would be given all the arms and equipment she asked for.

However reassuring that was, my dilemma remained unresolved. I explained to Mullik that an appreciation on future operational tasks could only be undertaken if there were a consensus on policy. That condition was proving elusive since the new Army Chief had taken over. Chaudhuri appeared to be following an operational policy different from that of the Prime Minister, presumably because the Army Chief was determined to avoid taking any action that might be interpreted by the enemy as an aggressive posture. According to him even the reoccupation of Kameng FD, clearly permissible under the Chinese ceasefire terms, would bring the Chinese down from the heights, so he was going to keep his forces south of the Inner Line, out of harm's way.

It could well be, I said, that the Chief was right, but that was not the point. Were his views known to the Prime Minister? Was there a meeting point between military counsel and government policy? We could not follow two divergent directives at the same time – that is, to prepare 'to give the Chinese a licking in Tibet' and, at the same time, cower behind the Inner Line in order to avoid causing them offence.

I also explained that there was more to an expansion programme than just raising divisions and procuring arms and equipment. Without clearcut aims and a planned timescale an expansion programme could become counterproductive. I said that the government needed to give us not only an operational policy but also an approximate forecast of projected events. When were we to switch from one posture to the next – that is, from a defensive to a recovery-of-territory role? The six divisions under raising must be programmed to fit into that plan. Thereafter, in how many years could India hope to move on to a trans-border offensive role? The completion of the estimated order of battle of thirty-six divisions needed for such a role would have to be related to that timescale, otherwise we might find ourselves with a permanently expanded army-in-being standing idle for a number of years, causing a heavy and unnecessary burden on the economy. On the other hand, it could be that the timing of the strategic task would have to be made contingent upon the completion of the expansion programme. In that case a different set of assessments would have to be made: if we switched to the offensive in, say 1968, with thirty-six divisions, would we be able to complete our task in two to three years? Could the period of hostilities be even further shortened if we waited till 1970, depending on Chinese development programmes, resistance movements in Tibet and similar contingencies? We had posed all these questions in the MO appreciation but there was no discussion on the subject. The Ministry of Defence did not even refer the matter to the Foreign Ministry.

Mullik commented that I was overstating the degree of precision the army could expect from the government, but he was sensitive enough to realise that I was trying to say something without being explicitly critical of Chavan and Chaudhuri. He promised to raise these issues with the PM so that Army HQ would be issued with a clear set of directives and strategic requirements.

Shortly afterwards I was again called up by the External Affairs Ministry and thus lost touch with the day-to-day progress of operational matters. It was not until many months later, when a new threat to NEFA was projected by the Intelligence Bureau, that Pritpal Singh of MO-1 showed me the following note from the Foreign Secretary to the Defence Secretary, forwarded to the Army Chief by the Emergency Cabinet Secretariat on 29 January 1963:

PM agrees that: there is no objection in principle to Army Units and Assam Rifles going into NEFA and various points . . . should not move into the disputed areas of Long-ju and Thag-la . . . . As regards Towang . . . preliminary investigations into the possibility of locating some troops in this area may be undertaken . . . . Army's programme . . . should, when it is ready, be cleared with him before it is actually implemented. This programme should, however, be undertaken now in the light of the state of communications. . . .

According to Pritpal, Chaudhuri modified the Prime Minister's policy without informing the Ministry of Defence. He considered a move back into NEFA by the army too provocative a step in the circumstances. Accordingly, Army HQ issued a letter to HQ Eastern Command under the file 'Defence of NEFA' (No. 62718/GS/MO-I of 9 February 1963):

According to the Colombo Conference proposals, which have been accepted by the Government, the Indian Army is free to move up to NEFA/Tibet border. . . . [but]

In accordance with the policy given out by the COAS, we will give battle to the enemy *in the plains* for the present, due to our various difficulties. However, there is a requirement to move up into the areas vacated by us *for training*. . . . In fact it is vital that Assam Rifles move into their posts soon . . . provided it is logistically possible.

Recent operations in this area have brought out clearly our inability to maintain adequately the troops deployed there. No regular Army units will, therefore, be moved up until they can be maintained by land routes. . . . [Emphasis added]

Thus was established the extraordinary precedent that not only did the army undertake an operational policy markedly different from that laid down by the government, but also that the latter remained unaware of that situation.

As regards Nepal, a newly constituted Central Command was subsequently given the task of preparing contingency plans for a small all-arms force to forestall a Chinese occupation of Kathmandu. The Ministry of External Affairs must have taken prompt steps to initiate diplomatic action because in mid-January, when I was temporarily restored to MO Directorate between negotiating rounds in New Delhi and Karachi, the CGS told me that he had received two letters from the head of our Military Mission in Nepal (Major General Pritam Kirpal) suggesting that Army HQ liaise with HQ Royal Nepal Army for defensive plans in case of an attack by China. Kirpal had requested that he be authorised to handle operational planning on behalf of the Indian General Staff, a request we had to turn down if for no other reason than that our Military Attaché in Kathmandu had in the meantime sent us his own separate appreciation in which he deprecated reliance on the Royal Nepal Army! To complicate matters further, we learned that the possibility of a joint defence pact with Nepal was being discussed between the External Affairs Ministry and the Ambassador of Nepal –without reference to the General Staff!

Before I was again switched to the Pakistan talks there was one other episode that merits mention in this memoir because it serves to place in its proper perspective something that acquired exaggerated importance in later years: the unflattering story of the genesis of the Henderson-Brooks Report.

On 18 December, Lieutenant General Henderson-Brooks (GOC XI Corps) came to my office. He said that the Army Chief had appointed him chairman of an Operations Review Committee. His task would be to examine the plans, policies and decisions that led to the outbreak of hostilities against the Chinese. The other member of the board, he informed me, was Brigadier P.S. Bhagat, VC (then Commandant of the Indian Military Academy). I had heard rumours about the proposal to set up such a committee but I was surprised to learn that it had been appointed by Army HQ. I had presumed that it would be appointed by the government and headed by at least a minister or the Cabinet Secretary.

'Prem will be coming to you later to collect all relevant documents,' the general said. 'What I want from you now is a copy of your review of the operations. The Chief has asked me to collect it.'

'H-B', as he was generally known, was a cheerful, easy-going senior officer of the Sandhurst-trained cadre. Like many others of his seniority he had been by-passed for command and staff responsibility during the Second World War because his rank and service would have demanded a senior appointment which the British were unwilling to yield to Indians. Many such officers were of course 'rehabilitated' when India achieved independence and their capabilities were appropriately utilised, but H-B's case was unique. Technically a 'domiciled European', he was in fact a second-generation British expatriate who had in the early 1930s chosen to be counted (and categorised in the Army List) as a King's Commissioned *Indian* officer, albeit in looks, speech and manner he was as English as his hyphenated surname. Although independent India acknowledged no restrictions of race, creed or caste, it was inevitable that he would be treated as a special case. He was given responsibilities appropriate to his seniority but was never in the mainstream; and people whose competence and capability are not recognised either become disaffected or lose interest. H-B lacked ballast.

I told H-B that the Chief must have forgotten that he

had specifically ordered me not to retain a copy of my
review in the Directorate. I suggested that he obtain a
copy from the Chief. I offered him a cup of tea and in
the course of our conversation asked him to give me an
indication of the sort of documents he was seeking, so that
I could have them ready for Bhagat. He replied that he
wanted appreciations of border problems, operational
instructions to the Commands, records of meetings with
Defence and Foreign Ministries and copies of all government
instructions to Army HQ. 'I want to see everything important
that pertains to the formulation and execution of policy
regarding the northern borders,' he said.

After he had gone I went to see the CGS, who confirmed
that the Chief had given H-B permission to ask for any
document on any subject that was relevant to the inquiry.
I told Moti Sagar that I was not entirely happy about
that. I would be glad to hand over any General Staff or
other Army HQ document, but not documents emanating
from the PM's secretariat, the Foreign Office or the Defence
Minister's office. As far as my understanding went I was
only the custodian of these documents, not the arbiter of
their security status. I said that I did not think I possessed
the right to hand them over for investigation by a
comparatively junior lieutenant general of the army.

'The Chief has authorised it,' Moti Sagar said.

'The Chief does not have that authority,' I replied. 'I
am sure that only the PM or the Defence Minister can
authorise the documents in question to be released to a
non-ministerial committee of inquiry.'

'You could be right, but I can't give a ruling on that,'
Moti replied. 'You will have to ask the Chief.'

The Chief was away from his office so on an impulse I
decided to knock at Mullik's door. If anyone could advise
me on the legal niceties about the security of ministerial
documents it had to be him.

After listening to my quandary Mullik confirmed that it
would certainly be reprehensible to hand over high-level
government documents without proper authority. He said
he would find out more about the Review Committee and
let me have a firm answer. True to his word, he rang me
up an hour later to confirm that his advice had been

correct. It would be highly improper to hand governmental policy documents to General Henderson-Brooks' committee.

When Prem Bhagat called later in the day, I told him that whereas he could visit the two MO sections that dealt with Eastern and Western Commands and ask for any document that had emanated from Army HQ, I was not authorised to hand over government files, records or notes.

Prem was an old friend from the days when we were gentlemen-cadets together at the Military Academy, he a year my senior. This day he chose not to display any regard for old acquaintance. He tried to argue, lost his temper and finally resorted to bluster. He accused me of trying to 'shield Krishna Menon'. When I asked him if he, a brigadier, had come here to sit on judgment on a former defence minister he stormed out of my office, saying that he would report my obduracy to the Chief.

Within a few minutes Chaudhuri rang up and issued a peremptory order that I hand over all documents the committee wanted. I replied firmly that I would not like to do that and explained why. Without giving him an opportunity to overrule my objections I told him that I would be happy to transfer the PM's and other ministerial documents to his office and obtain a receipt. It would then be up to him to release them or not, although I warned him that he would lay himself open to censure for a grave breach of prerogative. He thought about that for a minute and then asked me to bring over a few of the documents for him to see.

I selected three or four documents from the files in my cupboard and went to the Chief's office. I showed Chaudhuri the minutes of the PM's conference of November 1961, notes by Foreign Secretary M.L. Desai belligerently advising that we give the Chinese a 'bloody nose' in the Galwan valley, and Sarin's note conveying Minister of Defence Production Raghu Ramaiah's direction to the Army Chief 'to take action for the eviction of the Chinese from the Kameng Frontier Division of NEFA'.

I explained the importance of these and similar documents. There was an insidious move to apportion blame to the army for the decision to wage war at Namka-chu. These documents clearly refuted that imputation and should therefore be placed before an inquiry committee, but not a low-level committee such as the one he had appointed. If he did that, I warned him, not only would he be committing a breach of trust, his action could well serve to dilute the impact of their evidence.

Chaudhuri remained engrossed for a while. I asked him if he would like me to bring the rest of the documents in my keeping and hand them over to him.

'No, they can remain in your care,' he replied. 'I shall have to give H-B a more specific task. Is there any harm in his seeing other documents in MO Directorate?'

I told him that that was up to him but in my opinion it would be inappropriate for a corps commander to sit in inquiry over the previous Army Chief and the Army Commanders, which is what Henderson-Brooks would in effect be doing. I urged him to appoint a retired chief or other senior officer to head the committee. Chaudhuri said he would think it over.

What I consider must have transpired was that he discussed the matter with the Defence Minister and was probably rebuked for the step he had taken. I surmised this only because the next morning the CGS rang me up and said that he had just come from the Chief's office where Chaudhuri had had 'H-B on the mat and torn strips off him'. When I expressed surprise – H-B had done no more than follow his Chief's instructions – Moti said, 'Yes, I agree, but H-B did write me a rather foolish letter, with a copy to the Chief, complaining about obstructionism in GS Branch. That may explain why the Chief was so worked up'.

The government did not wish to institute an inquiry into high-level policies and decisions. So, instead of the committee being upgraded to widen its scope, it remained as originally constituted but its terms of reference were changed. Henderson-Brooks and Bhagat were sent to Tezpur and ordered to confine their inquiry to IV Corps' operations. Furthermore, H-B was directed not to carry out any kind of a witch-hunt or to apportion responsibility for the reverses.

To this day few individuals outside the central cabinet have been given access to the Henderson-Brooks Report. Defence Minister Chavan made a low-key statement about it in parliament, ascribing the reasons for the NEFA debacle to leadership failures in the army and to the tactical mishandling of troops, but excused them by explaining that our forces had fought under severe geographical and tactical handicaps. 'Such initial reverses,' he continued, 'are a part of the tide of war and what matters most is who wins the last battle.' Clearly the purpose of that pompous irrelevance was to divert criticism from the government. In that he succeeded. His statement also served to create the impression that the Henderson-Brooks Report was a definitive review of the whole Sino-Indian confrontation. This was, of course, far from the truth.

Meanwhile Gundevia had again put in a demand for the DMO's services because the first round of talks with Pakistan was about to begin. The cabinet, Gundevia told me, had unhesitatingly approved the Prime Minister's proposal about a partition of Kashmir (though Nehru virtually denied it a few days later in parliament) and we were all set for the talks with Pakistan.

Sardar Swaran Singh, the Minister of Railways, who had previously conducted a series of talks with Pakistan on other territorial disputes, was appointed leader of the delegation for the Indo-Pak talks. From our very first meeting I came under the spell of his calm personality and patent sincerity. A Sikh from the Punjab Congress cadre, kindly, clear-sighted and articulate, there was something Gandhian about him. Because he had the Prime Minister's full confidence he was an eminently suitable choice.

In the third week of December the Minister held his first formal meeting. G. Parthasarathy, recently appointed ambassador to Pakistan, Shankar Prasad, Secretary for Kashmir, R. Chopra and B.L. Sharma (from External Affairs) and, of course, Gundevia, were the other members of the delegation. In an informal briefing Swaran Singh stressed that we must insist on discussing all matters of dispute between the two countries, not solely Kashmir. Furthermore, should Pakistan introduce the issue of a plebiscite, we should firmly point out that free democratic elections in Kashmir had made this irrelevant. A settlement must be made on the basis of partition, not plebiscite – and partition should be decided on a geographical, not communal, basis. After a brief discussion we broke into groups in the adjacent coffee-room in order to establish acquaintances.

At the end of the meeting the Minister asked me to stay behind and discuss lines on the map with him and Gundevia. He also warned me that Pakistan might offer to sign a joint defence pact with India and I was to be prepared to deal with that issue after consulting the Ministry of Defence. When I showed him the five maps marked with five different lines, he asked if I could consider offering a little more of Kashmir valley because Pakistan's acceptance of partition would hinge on how much of the valley we were willing to give up. I offered the obvious objection that defence of Kashmir would become that much more difficult if we were to allow a Pakistani military presence in the valley. It would give them a ready-made base, a springboard for attack.

'Brigadier, we are talking about drawing an international line through Kashmir and not another ceasefire line,' the Minister said. 'There is a difference in hazard between the defence of an international boundary and the defence of a temporary battle-line. Once we agree to accept an Indo-Pak boundary through Kashmir, international law will come into play, with all its inhibitions. Please keep that in mind.'

Gundevia had taught me one lesson in practical geopolitics. Here was another. Clearly my strategic horizon was being expanded.

The impression I received at that first meeting was that although everyone felt the humiliation of going cap-in-hand to Pakistan, there were nuances of approach and expectation within various groups in the delegation. The Minister and Gundevia genuinely wished for a successful outcome, that is, an agreement on an international boundary through Kashmir. The bureaucrats, on the other hand, were hardliners and not in favour of offering a sop to the Pakistanis. That was not surprising because in a socialist-democratic system it is always the bureaucrats who are the conservatives. I felt sure that our officials wanted the talks to fail. Their only concern was that it should be the Pakistanis and not we who called them off. As for the General Staff, Chaudhuri had informed me clearly of the extent of his interest: what was important was not the success or failure of the negotiations, but rather that they should last long enough to cover the period during which our side of the Punjab border was without troops.

When I puzzled over the reference to a joint defence pact, Gundevia explained that the Foreign Office held the view that the Pakistanis might now consider that there was a Chinese threat to their borders also and therefore revive President Ayub's old offer of joint defence with India. I sent a note to the Chief to ask for his instructions. Chaudhuri ridiculed the idea. He walked over to Gundevia's office with me and told him that India should treat any proposal on joint defence with deep suspicion. In any case, he was convinced that the Pakistanis would never take sides with India against China. This was not something that an Army Chief should normally tell the Foreign Office, but he was dramatically proved right on our first evening in Rawalpindi.

The first round of talks started in Rawalpindi on 27 December. Gundevia's parsimony had resulted in our suppliant status in Pakistan being accentuated by the wretched manner of our arrival. To save on travel costs Gundevia had chosen to fly us in a ramshackle Air Force Dakota C-47 hastily converted to passenger service. After a long and tedious flight we disembarked looking dishevelled and disgruntled. We were met by a very dapper Zulfiqar Ali Bhutto, Pakistani Minister of Industries and leader of their delegation, and a line of immaculately dressed officials. To add to our discomfiture they made no attempt or even pretence at welcome, not even with the briefest of speeches. Bhutto was courteous but aloof; some of the officials (particularly the Foreign Secretary, Dehlavi) were just aloof.

While we settled into a large but comfortless colonial-type government guest house, Swaran Singh went to pay a formal call on President Ayub Khan, by whom he was cordially received. The shock was therefore the greater when later that evening we tuned into Pakistan Radio's news broadcast. The announcer exulted in the main item: the Chinese and Pakistan governments had signed an agreement in principle about their common border. According to the agreement a tract of Kashmiri territory to the north-west of Hunza had been given away to China. The timing of the announcement, the fact that neither Bhutto nor Ayub had thought fit to inform Swaran Singh about signing away a part of Kashmir, and vituperative anti-Indian comments in the press next morning combined to aggravate our wrath and mortification. The only saving grace was provided by the Chinese; they stipulated that since Kashmir was disputed territory the agreement would be deemed provisional.

The officials in our delegation advised breaking off the talks immediately and returning to Delhi, but the Sardar and Gundevia remained calm. We discussed other options till well past midnight. In the end the unruffled firmness of the Sardar soothed outraged passions and it was agreed that we would stay.

A plenary session of the two delegations was held next morning, but just after we sat down at table it was interrupted by a presidential summons to the two leaders. Ayub Khan, almost certainly under pressure from the American and British heads of missions (who had that very morning flown in from the capital, Karachi) explained to Swaran Singh that the news release on the agreement with China was not intended as an affront; the mistiming was inadvertent. This was unconvincing, but the Sardar did not demur.

The plenary session was never resumed. Swaran Singh astutely decided to conduct discussions informally with his counterpart, without the baleful influence of Pakistani bureaucrats. During the next two days the ministers met together a number of times, only occasionally helped by their advisers. As military advice was not required during these preliminary phases, Swaran Singh told me to make an effort to seek informal contacts with old army friends and to try to establish a modicum of mutual goodwill.

I called on the Commander-in-Chief of the Pakistani Army, General Mohamed Musa, whom I had known before, and the CGS, Major General Malik Sher Bahadur, who had attended Staff College with me in Quetta. They acceded to my request to be permitted to call on Major General Syed Ghawas, Master General of Ordnance, an old friend from 5/10th Baluch When I called at his home in the evening he and his wife (who normally observed *purdah*) received me warmly. After a most convivial evening, Ghawas arranged for me to motor to Abbotabad the next day to take the salute at a recruits' attestation parade at the Baluch regimental centre.

What struck me as strange was that none of the Pakistani officers I met made the slightest reference to our war with China. I should have thought that the urge to quiz the DMO of one of the belligerents about the details of the fighting would have been professionally irresistible. Yet neither Musa nor Ghawas, with whom I succeeded in re-establishing our former easy informality, nor any other old army friend I met, made any allusion to our border war.

By the time the first round of talks ended on 29 December our team had made headway in the negotiations, owing mainly to the success of discussions between our respective ministers. Bhutto, the young Pakistani Industries Minister, departed from his country's previously intransigent stand on a plebiscite in Kashmir and agreed to consider alternatives, including partition by mutual agreement. He had sidetracked the secretaries' group, although only temporarily.

Bhutto had not at that time acquired the prestige and power of his later years. The officials succeeded in restraining his individual style during the next round of talks held at Delhi in mid-January. Presumably pressurised by them, Bhutto insisted on their attendance at full plenary sessions at which, without retreating from their previous commitments, the Pakistanis inserted new conditions: territorial division should take into consideration 'the composition of the population', control of the river waters and the requirements of defence. The first point, a euphemism for a religious-communal approach, nearly caused a breakdown of the talks but both sides eventually agreed to hold a third round in Karachi in early February 1963.

At the end of the Delhi round Gundevia called us all to his office to warn us that at the Karachi session, which would almost certainly be the key meeting, Pakistan would press arguments on strategic and river water issues to make larger territorial demands. We should anticipate their arguments and be prepared to counter them with our own.

When we arrived at Karachi on 7 February we were more than pleased to learn that, except for Bhutto, the Pakistani delegation had undergone a complete facelift. The Interior and Defence Secretaries had been dropped and the virulent Dehlavi was away abroad. In their place came a batch of bright young men: Agha Shahi, Shafqat and Ashaq (the latter a confidant of President Ayub Khan). There was an air of expectation about them; they were impatient for us to produce a map with a line.

At Pakistan's request the first meeting in Karachi was restricted to officials. The Pakistanis produced the expected arguments but were on the defensive and did not persist with any of their demands, content with merely placing them on record. At the end of the morning Agha Shahi openly asked for a marked map showing our proposed boundary. Gundevia thereupon decided that the matter must at this stage be referred to the respective ministers.

As I wrote in my *Report to the Chief of Army Staff:*

### Discussions on the map
Sardar Swaran Singh consulted his advisers in the evening. We agreed that instead of giving a marked map to Mr Bhutto, the Minister should take with him an unmarked map and only broadly indicate the territorial concessions we were willing to make. It was also agreed that . . . at Ministerial level a 'haggling' posture would be undignified; and that [Swaran Singh] should indicate to Mr Bhutto our 'maximum' line – keeping in reserve, of course, our last concession, the Handwara area (which incidentally, had not been marked on the map and was, in fact, known only to the Sardar, Mr Gundevia and myself).

On the second day, when the two Ministers met unattended by advisers, Sardar Swaran Singh disclosed our 'maximum' concession to Mr Bhutto on an unmarked map. The latter affected to express surprise at the 'minor' nature of the concession, which he described as merely an 'adjustment of the Cease Fire Line', and as such quite unacceptable. Asked to indicate what sort of territorial demand he had in mind, Mr Bhutto proceeded to claim most of J&K, including Jammu, Udhampur, Kishtwar, the Valley and Ladakh, leaving only a small pocket of a few hundred square miles around Kathua for us! Mr Bhutto did not support his 'demand' by reasons or principles, stating in almost as many words that this was more or less an arbitrary claim based on 'the emotional attitude of Pakistanis'. . . .

In spite of this obviously farcical claim, it had become clear by then that Pakistan was more anxious than we that the talks should not be broken off. At subsequent meetings, Sardar Swaran Singh's avuncular personality broke through the younger man's defences sufficiently for the latter to acknowledge, off the record, that Pakistan's claim was unrealistic. Mr Bhutto explained, also off the record, that had our concession included Riasi District, Pakistan's demand would have been pared down to more reasonable limits and, in fact, a partial settlement in the south could have been negotiated, leaving the Valley for a later stage.

Swaran Singh regarded Bhutto's unrealistic overbid as a diplomatic tactic: if later Pakistan agreed to a considerable climbdown from this position, that could suitably impress the American and British lobbyists (while India, on the other hand, obviously could not give away much more). In Gundevia's opinion Bhutto's allusion to Riasi and his 'feeler' about a 'settlement in the south' were definite indications of his eagerness to bargain towards a settlement. In the circumstances we asked for a postponement of further negotiations till a fourth round of meetings in Calcutta in early March, by when the military situation in India would be much more secure than it was when the talks had begun. If we had to pay a price, the forfeit would become smaller the longer we deferred an agreement. We had also been advised by Delhi on the telephone that a deterioration was expected in the internal situation in Pakistan. Ayub's power and prestige had suffered after the agitation in East Bengal, a serious concern not only for the President but also for West Pakistan as a whole, particularly as the second session of the National Assembly was due to begin in Dacca within a few weeks. Furthermore, news of Colonel Aref's coup in Iraq, which had brought about the fall of the Pakistan-supported regime of Brigadier Kassem, had caused ripples of concern at many levels. As Agha Hilaly, Pakistan's High Commissioner in Delhi, confided to me: 'It is difficult for you, Brigadier, with such a permanent and established machinery to run your affairs, to realise how dangerous this sort of coup in a neighbouring country can be to a country like ours.'

Before we assembled in Calcutta in mid-March for the fourth round of talks, Pakistan signed a formal border agreement with China, in disregard of our protests. As though this were not enough to inhibit negotiations, virulent attacks were made on the Indian government, and Prime

Minister Nehru personally, at the National Assembly session in Dacca. Maulana Farid Ahmed likened India's 'eviction' of Muslims to East Pakistan from Tripura to Nazi concentration camp methods: 'Hitler's gas chambers were more merciful than India's atrocities.' Fazal Qadir Chowdhuri, Information Minister in the Pakistani cabinet, called Nehru 'the successor of Hitler'. Even Bhutto, although not abusive in expression, implied that Muslims appointed to high places in India were like Jewish leaders whom Hitler had won over by making them 'honorary aryans'.

At the opening meeting on 12 March Swaran Singh made a long and forceful statement reproving Pakistan for signing a border agreement in Kashmir which disavowed the historic boundary between India and Sinkiang, a flagrant disservice to the sub-continent. He also roundly condemned the intemperate language used on the floor of the House in Dacca, especially in regard to the Indian Prime Minister. Mr Bhutto, very much on the defensive, was apologetic and stated that some of his colleagues in the cabinet were emotional and irresponsible. On the pact with China he offered the usual sop that no affront to India or harm to its cause was intended.

Swaran Singh had decided to ask for a 'long postponement' of the talks but Ambassador Galbraith of the United States dissuaded him from this course because, he warned, even a temporary break now might jeopardise Mr T.T. Krishnamachari's mission, then in Washington to finalise military and other aid to India. Swaran Singh decided on 'spinning out the time' to take in a fifth round in Karachi.

Our return to Delhi witnessed a series of manoeuvrings by the Americans and, for the first time during these talks, the Russians. I sent an account of these diplomatics to the Army Chief in my *Report on the Karachi Talks* dated 27 April 1963.

### US Lobbying

For some weeks prior to the (second) Karachi Conference, Ambassador Galbraith had been maintaining pressure on the Ministry of External Affairs at various levels urging that the time was ripe for the Indian delegate to offer a substantial territorial concession in the Valley. Although no specific formula was mentioned . . . the Ambassador was referring to the north-west corner, the Handwara salient. The Ambassador assured us that if the Pakistanis did not accept this he was prepared to fly to Washington to convince President Kennedy of the genuineness of India's efforts to settle with Pakistan and press for the military aid programme to go through. . . .

The Commonwealth Secretary made it clear, both to the Prime Minister and to the Ambassador, that defence advice was strongly against the Handwara concession. . . .

On Wednesday (17 Apr 63) the Prime Minister called an emergency meeting of the cabinet to obtain the views of his colleagues on the Handwara question. There was considerable discussion but no conclusion was reached.

### Soviet Appreciation

*Meanwhile the Soviet Ambassador in Karachi gave our High Commissioner his appreciation of likely developments. He felt that in spite of US efforts to convince them to the contrary, the Pakistanis would maintain that military aid to India was a direct threat to Pakistan. In fact, he said, Pakistan had already threatened to withdraw from SEATO and CENTO should the United States go through with the aid programme. Therefore, in the absence of an Indo-Pak settlement, the only way the Americans could give this aid to India would be by matching it with increased military aid to Pakistan. The Soviet Ambassador had already received intelligence of the following proposals.*

(a) The USA would give two more wings (72 aircraft) of supersonic (F-104) fighters to Pakistan.

(b) Two warships (type unspecified) would be made available to Pak Navy, with reinforced decking for subsequent conversion to rocket-carrying surface vessels.

(c) A new armoured brigade would be added to the present orbat of Pak Army.

(d) Plans were afoot to earmark missile sites in Pak territory as a US controlled safeguard against invasion. . .

When our High Commissioner confronted the American Ambassador with these 'rumours' of increasing aid to Pakistan . . . the latter emphatically denied them. . . . Our High Commissioner, however, was not entirely convinced.

### Anglo-American 'Intervention'

Before another meeting of the cabinet could take place on Friday (19 Apr 63), our High Commissioner in Karachi arrived with news of an Anglo-American 'proposal' and that caused a considerable stir in the Foreign Ministry. It appears that as early as on 11 Apr 63, the US and UK envoys in Karachi had flown to Dacca to meet Mr Bhutto, and presented a partition proposal for discussion between the two delegates. No such intimation was given to our government, though the US Ambassador in Pakistan, on being asked by our High Commissioner, did produce a draft of the proposal.

Broadly speaking, the Anglo-US proposals stated:

(a) That they recognised the claim of both India and Pakistan for a 'substantial' position in the Valley.

(b) That each must have free access through the Valley to safeguard their strategic interests in the north and north-east.

(c) That the special claims and interests of each in certain specified territories must be recognised – for instance, India's interest in Ladakh and Pakistan's interest in the Chenab basin.

(d) That the people of the Valley should have the rights of local self-government and free movement.

(e) Certain other recommendations regarding economic development of Kashmir, welfare and medical measures.

What the proposal implied was that the Valley should be partitioned, giving a 'substantial' portion to Pakistan; furthermore, Riasi and the Chenab basin should go to Pakistan as 'compensation' for our getting Ladakh; and that there should be a 'soft' international boundary between the two halves of a largely self-governing people in the Valley.

Not only was this far beyond the scope of the concessions we had conveyed to Galbraith, the very fact of this uninvited 'intervention' spelt disaster for the talks. It was obvious that Pakistan, having been given this formula, would use it as a minimum demand. As the proposal was quite unacceptable to India, all that it had succeeded in doing was to ensure that there could now be no hope of reaching a settlement and that the talks were doomed to failure. This was conveyed to Mr Galbraith.

The cabinet's attitude to the talks hardened considerably as a result of this uncalled for interference by US and UK. Not only was their proposal distinctly against Indian interests, their approach showed a degree of 'collusion' with Pakistan. (India was never formally informed of the proposal, which was made only to Pakistan.)

It was nevertheless decided that the Indian team would go through with the talks and not cancel its visit to Karachi.

Mr Nehru wrote a letter to President Kennedy and the British Prime Minister, stating that he had been pained by this manoeuvre. (To the latter he even expressed doubt as to whether any useful purpose could now be served by Mr Krishnamachari's visit to the United Kingdom.)

Between the fourth and fifth rounds of talks I was able to spend a few weeks in my office as DMO, picking up the threads of operational developments. Reports from Mullik's Intelligence Bureau indicated significant military activity in Tibet opposite NEFA, particularly north of Walong in the Rima area and in Tsona Dzong, north of Towang. The Army Chief said that he did not place great reliance on Mullik's reports, but the CGS took note of the possibility of renewed hostilities and he bade me expedite the army's expansion plans. This proved difficult because I could not pin the Army Chief down to a target figure for the number of divisions we were to raise. Furthermore, General Staff reserves of materiel were almost totally exhausted. We would have to await receipts of arms aid from the United States before new raisings could be equipped.

On 1 May I called in Colonel Frazier of the US Military Mission for a discussion on the United States' aid programme, to assess how long it would be before we could begin raising and arming our new divisions. I reminded him of his previous vision of helping us raise fifty new divisions and pointed out that we were still floundering helplessly in the first expansion programme of six divisions.

Frazier brought me up to date with the latest US attitude towards India's defence problems. He said that Washington's new policy was that American aid plans would cater only for a defensive, not an offensive, role for the Indian Army. That decision had been conveyed to the Army Chief by General Kelly. He added that the former had thereupon decided that the Indian Army would build up to a total of twenty-five divisions: sixteen to be deployed on the borders (both western and northern) and nine divisions in 'training and turnover' roles. Frazier was unable to satisfy my curiosity regarding what a 'training and turnover' division signified or on what basis the figure of twenty-five had been decided. I told him that as far as I could see from our files there had been no change in the recent past from our previous expansion plan to aim for a total of sixteen divisions in the first phase. Frazier was quite adamant that Chaudhuri had increased the figure to twenty-five.

When I went to consult the CGS I found that he was as ignorant as I about the Chief's change of expansion targets. Moti Sagar had assumed that Chaudhuri was dealing directly with MO Directorate. He suggested that I clarify the matter as soon as possible with the Chief, but that proved difficult because the latter was too often away from his office. At last on 8 May I was able to corner Chaudhuri. I explained our threat appreciation, based on which we had arrived at an initial expansion plan for sixteen infantry divisions (excluding the Armoured Division, independent infantry brigades and the holding forces in Kashmir and Nagaland). I told him that that was only the initial expansion figure. If the government's directive remained the same as it was in December – that we were to evict the Chinese from disputed areas occupied by them – a long-term planning group would have to work on further expansion plans.

It was disconcerting to realise that although Chaudhuri had heard me out, he had not listened to a thing I had said.

'I have now decided on twenty-one divisions,' he said, looking pleased with himself.

'You mean twenty-five divisions surely,' I remarked, thinking he had merely made a slip of the tongue. 'That's the figure you gave the Americans.'

'Ah, that was before I received Sounderrajan's paper. He has made a convincing plan for a twenty-one division army!' Sounderrajan was a Deputy Secretary in Defence Ministry, a bright young bureaucrat but not directly concerned with operational matters.

I told Chaudhuri that before he committed himself to figures I would like to look at Sounderrajan's paper and scrutinise his workings.

'Don't worry yourself about that,' said the Chief. 'I am handling that side of it. That's what I am best at, you know. Right now I am working on a list of locations and roles for these twenty-one divisions. I shall send my final decision to you.'

I went to see Moti Sagar again to warn him that the Chief's expansion plan was just a game of whimsy, playing at figures without staff examination, and that I was at a loss to know how to handle the situation. In my absence my MO staff had not been given any direction either by him or the Chief, even though the American Military

Mission was leaning heavily on us for our plans. It was clear to me that unless Army HQ took effective control of the expansion plan the American advisers would begin to consider the Indian General Staff incompetent and confused and perhaps have a rethink on their arms aid promises. The only way to bring Chaudhuri to order, I said, would be to have General Kelly prevail upon him to adhere to MO Directorate's expansion figures. I received the CGS' approval for this strategy of indirect approach and told my staff to prepare a fresh plan based on a purely defensive position. The Armoured Division and the forces in Kashmir were not to be included in the target figure.

Before I could progress this move I was recalled by the Ministry of External Affairs for the fifth round of talks. Swaran Singh convened a meeting in his office to decide on the delegation's reactions to possible Pakistani approaches. He anticipated that Bhutto would persist with his territorial *quid pro quo*: in return for the Riasi headwaters of the Chenab he would concede our claims in the north – Kargil and Ladakh. The Minister said that he would himself conduct the discussions, whether on the Chenab basin (river waters issues) or on the division of the valley. He did not intend to make any further advance on his original territorial offer, even if this led to a breakdown of the talks. Nor would he give Bhutto an opportunity of improving upon his offer, which, as it stood, was sufficiently ludicrous for even the Americans to sympathise with India. The aim, he said, was 'to make a success of the breakdown of the talks'.

The concluding paragraphs of my report on the fifth round reads:

On the Chenab Basin our argument was that the Pakistani claim on the waters of the Chenab was fully met by the Indus Waters Treaty and that Pakistan had no *locus standi* in this respect; in fact, the provisions of that treaty specifically forbade a territorial claim being based upon rights of river waters accorded by the Treaty. As for 'ideological' claims, (by which they meant the composition of population) we turned down this argument as a basis for territorial claim because the present population count (as opposed to the 1941 census, which the Pakistanis cited) showed a Dogra majority in Riasi province. . . .

Pakistan's posture was alternatively threatening and appealing, which considerably weakened their position. They were obviously anxious to drag out the negotiations; we made it plain that though we would not oppose a protraction of the talks should the Pak leader desire it, as far as we were concerned the two 'offers' were obviously wide apart and the talks had reached deadlock.

More than ever before, the immaturity of the Pak delegation's arguments and their jejune approach to the problem became handicaps of which even they must have been aware. For instance, Mr Bhutto – in answer to our statement that we had already agreed to 34,000 square miles of J&K territory [that is, Pakistan Occupied Kashmir (POK)] being acceded to them – said that the part of Kashmir occupied by Pak had never been regarded as 'disputed' territory, not even by nations friendly to India; and therefore it was to be assumed that the present negotiations were only limited to Indian occupied Kashmir which was the only 'disputed' part of J&K. In a devastating but entirely polite rejoinder, Sardar Saheb stated that he was surprised to hear this naive theory, because as far as facts went even China, who was a particular friend of Pakistan and inimical to India, had recognised Pakistan Occupied Kashmir as 'disputed' territory, and had therefore insisted that the Sino-Pak Treaty over the border be 'provisional'. Pakistan by agreeing to this 'provisional' clause, had also acknowledged that POK was disputed territory. How could Mr Bhutto now make this unreal statement?

In the final session on Thursday (25 Apr 63), Mr Bhutto was openly pleading for a sixth session. The evening before he had mentioned the possibility of a 'temporary arrangement' (joint administration) in the Valley for a year or so – implying that India, in pursuance of her strategic requirements, might be allowed access to her line of communication in Kashmir, to pursue her 'warlike attitudes' for a specified period. He suggested that in the Delhi session the officials might like to discuss the terms and conditions of this 'temporary arrangement' – meaning some form of joint control in the Valley as an interim measure. Sardar Saheb demurred at first, but on being reminded that each party had agreed to discuss any point brought up by the opposing party, delivered his Karachi *coup de grace:* he said that he would be prepared to consider these 'temporary arrangements' in Kashmir – provided they applied to the whole of J&K State, i.e., including Pakistan Occupied Kashmir. Try as he did, Mr Bhutto could not wriggle out of this. On this note we left Karachi, with the prospects of further talks starting on 14 May 63.

At the Karachi session the negotiations had clearly proved futile but Bhutto had virtually pleaded with Swaran Singh to hold yet another round in Delhi in mid-May and, of course, the latter agreed. According to Gundevia's reasoning the Pakistanis were apprehensive that the western powers would blame them for the breakdown of the talks because they were so unreasonable about the exchange of territory. Bhutto preferred to let the talks drag on because he knew that as long as they continued, there would be no significant flow of arms to India. A sixth round in Delhi would earn Pakistan a few 'bonus points'. To lure the Indian team Bhutto had even begun to drop hints that he might make territorial concessions to improve upon what Gundevia irreverently termed Bhutto's 'kachhua' offer (a 'turtle' offer). It was also possible that Bhutto had been primed by the British or the Americans (or both) that something big was afoot and he must prolong the charade for a while longer.

What the big powers had planned for Delhi was another piece of 'sledgehammer diplomacy' (Gundevia's phrase). A high-powered delegation from Washington led by the Secretary of State, Dean Rusk, two of his Assistant Secretaries of State (Talbot and Manning) and Assistant Secretary of Defence William Bundy was matched by as formidable a team from Britain: Duncan Sandys, as before, Lord Mountbatten and Lord Selkirk, Commissioner-General for South-east Asia. At meetings with Nehru and Chavan they made it clear that unless India came to some sort of an agreement with Pakistan they could not agree to arms aid because they were not prepared to alienate their ally Ayub Khan. They then gave Nehru a letter from President Kennedy in which the latter suggested a way out of the impasse: Pakistan and India should agree on using the good offices of a mediator. Rusk and Sandys, though not always in agreement over the modalities, made a round of calls on cabinet members and other luminaries to persuade them to advise the PM to accept the mediation proposal. It was not necessary. Nehru promptly agreed, certain in his mind that if he displayed enthusiasm for it Ayub Khan would be sure to turn it down.

Perhaps that is what happened; either that or, as Galbraith's account in his book *Ambassador's Journal* implies, Sandys' maladroit handling of the matter prevented its successful outcome. Pakistan was too wary to accept the idea and Bhutto did not raise it when he came to Delhi. All he did was to insist on the demand he had made in Karachi, that we agree to hand over the valley to a joint administration or, alternatively, to 'internationalise' it for a certain period of time and then hold a plebiscite. Swaran Singh was easily able to hold Bhutto at bay and his seemingly interminable arguments dragged out the time.

Just when it seemed that there was no more to be said except to issue a joint statement about the failed talks, Gundevia surprised everyone by introducing a totally unrehearsed matter. He suddenly suggested that it would be a fitting finale if the two sides were to end the communiqué with a No-war Declaration.

Bhutto was plainly taken aback but it did not take him long to recover. He resorted to the line Pakistan had taken every time India had made this offer in the past: Pakistan could not trust a country that settled all her territorial problems by taking the offensive, whether in Hyderabad or in Junagadh or in Kashmir.

That virtually ended the talks. A simple communiqué was agreed upon, to the effect that the ministers had failed to reach an agreement on the Kashmir dispute.

When I resumed duty in MO Directorate after the final Indo-Pak session, I resolved to expedite the expansion programme before the sense of operational urgency following the Chinese invasion lapsed into lethargy. The government had made clear its determination to meet the challenge posed by the Chinese. Mr T.T. Krishnamachari, Minister without portfolio, was appointed to the newly created cabinet post of Minister for Economic and Defence Co-ordination and had already set in motion various measures. The Finance Secretary, Boothalingam, was sent to the United States to sound out the potentialities of arms aid and 'T.T.K.' was to follow in his wake shortly. Clearly, it was not the government but Army HQ that had so far dragged its feet over the expansion programme.

Back in the office I found that I had walked into a minor international embarrassment on the expansion issue, a confusion created by Chaudhuri's quick-changing pronouncements. It appeared that Moti Sagar, who had accompanied the Boothalingam mission to the United States, had made a presentation of our arms requirements at the Pentagon in which he quoted Phase II expansion targets wrongly given him by Chaudhuri (the twenty-one-division plan). The Pentagon, already informed by the Kelly Mission that the Indian Army's plans catered for sixteen divisions, lodged a protest at government level about the exaggerated figures presented by the CGS; whereupon Chaudhuri, instead of explaining the reasons for the misunderstanding, told the Americans that sixteen was the correct figure, thus undermining the CGS's standing.

I remonstrated with Chaudhuri, pointing out that what Moti had projected was in fact the Phase II target. I added that Kelly was aware of the figures of new raisings for each successive phase and it was he who should be made to clear up the misunderstanding. Chaudhuri would not agree. Instead, he decided on the first expedient that came into his head: he would get around the *faux pas* by cutting out Phase II altogether and making do with the sixteen divisions of Phase I. To cover the operational gaps, he intended to allot dual roles to four of the divisions under the sixteen-division plan. The permanent locations of these four divisions would be along the Himalayan border but they would be given alternative roles on the western (Pakistan) front. Chaudhuri said that he would work out an organisational table for these dual role divisions in order to make them suitable for operational roles both in the mountains and on the Punjab plains.

The suggestion was plausible only in the sense that managing the deployments of divisions to meet changing operational needs is an intrinsic part of General Staff tasks. In this case, however, Chaudhuri had overlooked the factor of America's political sensitivity regarding Pakistan. It was not long after he had telephoned General Kelly about his new proposal that Frazier came running to my office, with fresh objections. The Pentagon was aghast at the implication that American arms intended for Indian mountain divisions might be used against Pakistan. Kelly must have conveyed this to Chaudhuri, because he sent for me the next day to tell me (predictably) that he had had a new idea. Instead of the dual role proposal, he would revert to the twenty-one-division plan but with the difference that the five extra divisions planned for Phase II would be raised without US aid. Because of shortages of equipment in India, this signified that the new divisions would be complete only in their infantry components. The supporting arms, such as artillery, engineers and signals, would be made up to no more than one-third of the normal establishment. Furthermore, no army and corps troops (normal operational requirements in the order of battle) would be raised for these five divisions.

I was at a loss to imagine what roles these under-equipped divisions could perform; they would be equally ineffective on the Pakistan front and on the northern borders. My doubts must have been apparent on my face because Chaudhuri impatiently told me that he had decided to transfer responsibility for the expansion programme from the DMO to the Director of Staff Duties. This would leave the DMO free to concentrate on operational matters, he added. Furthermore, presumably to ensure that there would be no more obstructionism from his DMO, he suggested that I might take this opportunity of availing myself of a month's leave, so that I could return to work rested and refreshed.

Chaudhuri's implied dismissal came as no surprise. It had been obvious for some time that he was not at ease in dealing with his DMO, possibly because it was not in my nature to pander without a protest to the eccentricities of a senior. Chaudhuri liked to regard himself as a one-man decision-making service and his staff as suitable adjuncts to admire and formalise his brilliant decisions. Pursuit of this self-image led him away from reality, so that his assessment of problems too often became a ritual in make-believe. Gradually the Army Chief and his DMO become caught up in an odd relationship that neither could take any further. This was a matter of some regret for, like many others, I had built high hopes on the new Army Chief.

Chaudhuri was pitchforked into the Chief's chair at a time of acute crisis in the Indian Army. A senior Sandhurst man and well regarded by the British, he had had a good career during the war both on the staff in North Africa and in command of an armoured regiment in Burma. Having commanded both the Hyderabad and Goa operations, he had acquired a reputation for success – a 'halo of victory', as Thapar had termed it – and many of us had hoped that his tenure as Army Chief would not only restore morale and self-confidence within the service but also help to establish an appropriate position for the army and the General Staff in the governmental system. He had the wit and the eloquence to do this; and there was something hypnotic in his personality. Defence Minister Chavan had fallen under his spell when he first arrived, at a time when the government machinery had been shocked into a state of apathy. A firm and plausible Chaudhuri could have carried through bold reform programmes to overhaul and modernise a creaking, colonial politico-military system. Never before had such an opportunity presented itself and it is doubtful if it ever will again, but Muchu Chaudhuri displayed not an ounce of reforming zeal. Apart from the fact that the government's withholding of his due rank had driven him to an extreme of paranoia, he proved to be shallow of purpose, unable to put his undoubted intelligence to proper use or to keep in touch with the real world. He allowed himself to be propelled by his personal concerns, taking snap (and sometimes conflicting) decisions, divorced from reality. He would not brook staff analysis, perhaps because he subconsciously feared that it might fail to support his off-the-cuff and arbitrary decrees.

When Moti Sagar returned from Washington, I gave him an account of my interview with the Chief. With a rueful I-told-you-so smile he told me not to be too concerned about it and advised me to take up Muchu's offer and go off to Kashmir with my family for a month's holiday. As Yezdi Gundevia had already told me that Chief Minister Bakshi Ghulam Mohammed of Kashmir had accorded me the use of the state guest-houseboat in Srinagar, my wife and children enthusiastically helped me make up my mind.

When I returned to Delhi in early July I was not sure to what degree I would be expected to resume duties as DMO, but the matter was temporarily decided in my favour because the Chief and the CGS were both shortly to visit the United States and Moti insisted that I officiate as CGS during his absence. Since Jogi Dhillon, the Deputy CGS, stood in even greater disfavour with the Chief than I, Chaudhuri agreed.

A few days before the departure of the Chief and the CGS for the States, the DIB issued dire warnings of large-scale forward moves by Chinese forces and a significant build-up in strength, particularly in the Tsona Dzong region, north of Towang, and also at Rima, north of Walong. In order to discuss these moves Chaudhuri came over to the Ops Room with Batra, the DMI. After I had pointed out the area of the reported build-up on the map, Chaudhuri asked Batra for his comments on the DIB's report, whereupon the latter with uncharacteristic confidence affirmed that the new developments did not portray any ominous designs on the part of the Chinese. They were merely administrative moves, he said, not operational. At the same time, he firmly cautioned that should Indian troops re-enter NEFA, the Chinese would definitely react by invading Indian territory again.

What the DMI, who had no independent source of information, based this opinion on I did not ask, but it obviously suited Chaudhuri well. After they left the Ops Room, Pritpal told me that the new GOC IV Corps, Sam Manekshaw, had expressed more or less the same opinion to him in a telephone conversation: that there was no danger of Chinese belligerence as long as we did not go back into NEFA. The Army Chief and the Corps Commander were obviously of one opinion on this matter and clearly Batra was being used as a stooge to support this line. (After Chaudhuri reached Washington the press in India began to carry reports that the Army Chief was playing down the Chinese threat in his talks with Pentagon officials, and the Foreign Secretary felt it necessary to telephone Chaudhuri and warn him not to undermine India's case for arms aid, which had been built up by Biju Patnaik, Boothalingam, T.T.K. and, indeed, President Radhakrishnan himself.)

A day or two after the Chief's departure for America the Deputy Chief, Wadalia, rang up to say that the Defence

Minister wished for another discussion in the Ops Room on the military situation in NEFA. He added that he had been in touch with the Army Chief in Washington and the latter had urged that we must convince the Minister that NEFA was being adequately defended.

'How do we do that, Sir?' I asked. 'We have allowed no troops to go back into NEFA.'

'The Chief wants you to handle it. Somehow, the Minister must be reassured.'

I thought over the monstrous implication of what Wadalia was saying and decided to put my foot firmly down on any such suggestion of prevarication.

'I am sorry, Sir, I cannot do that. I am not prepared to misrepresent the operational situation.'

'Very well,' Wadalia said, after a pause. 'I will brief the Minister myself.'

Wadalia must have telephoned Manekshaw to consult him about his dilemma, because when he came to the Ops Room he had in his hand a list of place-names which he asked me to point out on the map. I did not know what Wadalia had rehearsed, but after Chavan and Defence Secretary P.V.R. Rao arrived he went to the map and described the disposition of our troops, first on the Assam plains (2, 5 and 23 Infantry Divisions) and then, more vaguely, 'elements of the forward brigades' of 5th Division that were supposedly located in Kameng.

As though waiting for his cue, Chavan sat up in his chair, looked at Wadalia and asked about exact strengths and disposition of deployments within Kameng. Fumblingly, Wadalia pointed out Tenga valley, Dhirang valley and an area vaguely north of Bomdila and said that we had sent reconnaissance patrols into those areas. On being questioned for further details, the Deputy Chief said that the troops in question were elements of advance Engineer parties gone forward to reconnoitre and survey the condition of the bridges along the three-ton road to Towang.

Wadalia's attempt at cover-up was so gauche that it bordered on the ludicrous. As I had kept my eyes averted from Chavan's I did not observe his reaction, but after a while, without making a comment, he got up from his chair, thanked Wadalia politely and left. On his return to his office he must have issued orders for Chaudhuri's recall from the United States because within a day or two Muchu was back, earlier than he had been expected.

On Monday 29 July I received a summons from Aspy Engineer, chairman of the Chiefs of Staff, to attend a meeting of the committee to discuss the situation in NEFA. I arrived at the conference room while the intelligence briefing was still in progress. My personal diary records:

Dave (IB) was giving out his estimate – but, taking his cue from the COAS' attitude and remarks, the DMI was paring down all IB estimates of Chinese build-up. The CAS and CNS were obviously on the IB's 'side'; I even sensed a certain play of hostility between the two other Chiefs and ours. I cannot say I blame the former because there was absolutely no grounds on which our DMI could presume to correct facts and figures given by the DIB. . . .

When at last the operational discussion started, the Chairman (Air Chief) asked me whether there was any possibility of the Chinese attacking through NEFA during the monsoons (which had, of course, already started). I replied that though the monsoon was not good campaigning season, the disadvantages lay more with us than with the Chinese, because most of the precipitation took place on the North Assam plains and along the foothills, comparatively little beyond the Bomdila range. . . .

At this the (Army) Chief vehemently interposed to state that he did not agree with me and that he thought I was quite wrong. He seemed unduly excited and annoyed, and went on to reiterate that in his opinion there was no threat to NEFA. I explained that I was stating a fact in answer to a question, not offering an opinion whether there was a threat or not – and the Naval Chief backed me up. . . . COAS displayed such obvious hostility toward me that the Chairman eventually told me that I could withdraw. . . .

On the way back to my office I called on Mullik and told him about Batra's contribution to the intelligence briefing. Mullik smiled in his quiet way and said that Chaudhuri had been feeding Batra intelligence snippets handed out by Lord Louis Mountbatten to the Indian Chiefs of Staff during his recent visit to Delhi. Mullik then showed me recent air photographs of the Tsona Dzong area that clearly indicated the considerable reinforcement activities in Tsona, Trinu, Marmang, Le and Shao: a proliferation of new barracks, dumping sites and networks of vehicle tracks. Mullik said that whatever Mountbatten or Muchu might say, the new Chinese moves had caused a degree of alarm in South Block, one of the reasons for Chaudhuri's recall from America.

When I asked Mullik whether he had been able to find out any more about the conflict of strategic views between the government and Army HQ, he said that as far as the Prime Minister and the Defence Minister were concerned they were not aware of any contradictory policies. I did not tell him about Chaudhuri's instructions to Wadalia about misinforming the Defence Minister on NEFA, but I did say that NEFA was still unoccupied and that Army HQ had issued no orders for either 5th or 2nd Division to move back into the hills. Mullik asked me what were my views and those of the CGS on the question of tactical realities in NEFA. Would we be able to defeat a Chinese offensive in NEFA? I replied that because we had wasted eight months, if the Chinese attacked in the near future we would be at a disadvantage in north Kameng, yet even without plans and preparations and simply with the troops and resources now at our disposal, I felt sure that we could prevent the enemy from crossing the Manda-la-Bomdila range. In any event, we should confront him and not allow him a free run through NEFA.

Late in the evening Chaudhuri sent for me in his office and directed me to prepare a summary of the new Chinese threat as assessed by the Chiefs of Staff Committee earlier in the day. He then began to read out from jottings he had made on a piece of paper, considerably toning down the Intelligence Bureau's facts and figures as given out at the Chiefs meeting. When I began to take down verbatim what he was reading out, he stopped me and told me that he wanted me, as secretary to the COS Committee, to draft the intelligence appreciation as part of the minutes of the meeting – in other words, he was asking me to fudge the records to suit his interpretation of the threat.

When I left the Chief's room I went to Moti Sagar and protested against Chaudhuri's attempt to make me falsify the minutes. I told him that I was not going to be a party to the hoax. The CGS agreed with me and told me not to take any further action in the matter; he would intervene with the Chief. If any intelligence 'sugar-coating' was to be done, he said, it must be the DMI's job, not the DMO's.

I heard no more about the incident, probably because it was overtaken by events. The next morning Chaudhuri rang me up to say that he wanted to be briefed in the Ops Room on NEFA. When he arrived, the first thing he asked me was whether a small force from 5th Division could be deployed and maintained in the Tenga-valley-Bomdila area. I realised that he was under pressure from the Ministry to do something in NEFA, so I was careful in my assessment. I replied that a brigade group – and possibly even two brigades – could be built up in the Tenga-Bomdila area and be adequately maintained by the two roads that connected Tezpur with Bomdila (the new three-ton road via Balakpung, along the Barelli valley, and the old one-ton road over the Chaku range). Between them they should be able to produce a total capacity of 100 tons per day. Chaudhuri thought that over but was not convinced. He decided to pay a visit to HQ Eastern Command and IV Corps and he wanted Deputy Air Chief Arjun Singh to accompany him.

At a conference at the newly established HQ Eastern Command in Fort William, Calcutta, the Chief gave a watered-down version of the Chinese build-up opposite NEFA. He then announced the government's decision that in case of renewed hostilities the IAF would be used in the offensive role 'right up to but not including Lhasa'. He said that he had invited Arjun Singh to accompany him to HQ IV Corps so that he could make a preliminary assessment of operational tasks on the NEFA front.

Clearly the main purpose of the briefing conference at Corps HQ on 2 August was to downgrade both the IB's assessment of threat and the government's concern about a renewed Chinese offensive. Manekshaw supported that aim by categorically stating that the recent forward concentration of the Chinese was purely for administrative purposes, not for an offensive across the McMahon Line. He claimed that by dumping stocks forward the Chinese were 'saving petrol'. He added confidently, 'They will attack only if they are given a reason – like last year. And this time they will come in with a force of three divisions.'

Manekshaw's estimate was that to face such an onslaught he would require five brigades in Bomdila-Tenga-Chako and this he could not muster at that time. 'We must therefore give them no cause for an offensive, gentlemen,' he pontificated, 'because were they to come in now I should lose more territory than my distinguished predecessor!'

A talk with my old friend Inder Verma, still the brigadier in charge of administration, confirmed my suspicion that Manekshaw had dressed up an intelligence picture to support his resolve to stay out of NEFA. It could not have been only a coincidence that the Chief entirely agreed with his views.

During a break in the discussion I sought out the Chief in the Corps Commander's office and gave him my opinion: that the corps intelligence appreciation was contradictory. His estimate of the Chinese build-up was greater than the DMI's and exceeded even that of the Intelligence Bureau. What, then, made him confident that there was no threat? What did he mean by 'administrative purposes'?

Manekshaw left the room at this stage, but try as I might I could not persuade Chaudhuri to enforce the government's policy and order GOC IV Corps to send troops up the hill to Bomdila. The meeting at Corps HQ served to reinforce his resolve not to offer any provocation to the Chinese.

On my return to Delhi I gave Moti Sagar an account of the conference in Tezpur and told him of my suspicion that the Corps Commander – with not a little help from the Army Chief – was 'cooking up facts and figures' to suit his own preconceptions. Moti merely smiled and replied, 'A lot of people seem to be doing that.' Then, teasingly he added, 'Meanwhile, I have had a complaint about you, Monty. I don't think you are very popular in IV Corps HQ, but I can't say that I hold you to blame.'

On 6 August Chaudhuri sent for me and said that he wished to consult me on a subject which I was to treat as entirely personal and confidential and not discuss it even with the CGS. He said that there was a move 'among the civilians' to prove that in the face of a growing threat of a renewed Chinese offensive, the army had made no plans or preparations for defence. He had therefore written a paper to refute the allegation and he wished me to read and comment on it.

I read the Chief's paper and found it to be more or less a repetition of the Chaudhuri-Manekshaw theme: there was no threat of a Chinese offensive; their build-up on the NEFA border was a measure to get around administrative difficulties and to save petrol. He offered a muddled explanation to justify IV Corps' static defence concept in north Assam. (The latter appeared to be an attempt to rebut a specific criticism by someone in the Ministry.)

I discussed the paper with Chaudhuri the next morning and told him, as forcefully as was seemly, that it was not for an Army Chief to minimise threats projected by both the Intelligence Bureau and the government. If he persisted in doing so he would be laying himself open to criticism, even if there were no Chinese attack. I added that Army HQ's refusal to reoccupy NEFA would mean giving the Chinese a free run through Kameng – and that was a negative, almost defeatist, policy. If the Chinese were allowed to occupy NEFA they could embark on a road-building programme to facilitate an unopposed advance right down to the edge of the plains. They could build up a forward base in Dhirang for an attack on north Assam, a course that we must deny them at all cost. We had to oppose an enemy move into NEFA, even if all we could achieve were harassing operations. I also reiterated what I had told him before, that Manekshaw's plan of siting static and heavily encumbered brigades to defend Charduar, Misamari and Tamalpur (on the Bhutan border) would not prevent an enemy advance into the plains. The Chinese would merely isolate and move around our static areas. Army HQ should insist that IV Corps' plan be changed to one of co-ordinated defences along the Bomdila-Manda-la ridge and, in the plains sector, a more aggressive plan for counteroffensives and mobile defence by 2, 5 and 23 Infantry Divisions. I again urged him to send for Manekshaw and order him to move troops up to Bomdila.

Chaudhuri did send for Manekshaw but the outcome of his visit was totally unexpected. What transpired between them before Moti Sagar and I were summoned to the

418 / WAR IN HIGH HIMALAYA

Chief's office I do not know, but when the CGS and I went in Chaudhuri told us that he had solved the problem about having to move troops into NEFA. Manekshaw, he said, would send one of the brigades of 5th Division into Tenga valley for jungle and mountain training; the DMO could then send a note to the Ministry to inform the government that we had deployed troops for the defence of Kameng Frontier Division.

Suspecting some kind of machination, I asked for details of the brigade's plans. In addition to carrying out a training programme, would the brigade occupy fixed defences at Bomdila? Or was it to be given a mobile, harassing mission? Neither, it seemed. It appeared that all that Manekshaw was planning to do was to move three infantry battalions of 5th Division into Tenga valley to carry out individual training, with no artillery or other support; the men were to carry only pouch ammunition.

'We don't have to give the government any details,' the Chief told me. 'I merely want you to inform the Ministry that we are sending a brigade up for the defence of Bomdila.' With that we were dismissed.

When Moti and I returned to the CGS' office I could no longer hold back my anger. I told him that the Chief and his Corps Commander were deliberately setting out to deceive the government on a vital operational matter and in the process dragging us into the plot. I urged that we report the attempted chicanery to the government. I added that we could not stretch our personal loyalty to the Chief to the point of betrayal of the country's security.

Moti asked me to sit down and telephoned his Military Assistant to order a pot of tea.

'Calm down, Monty,' he said. 'I know you are right, but do *you* think the country's security is at stake? Do you believe that the Chinese are about to drive into NEFA?'

'The government has accepted the DIB's assessment. How can we have a different operational policy from the government?'

'You have not answered my question,' he said. 'Do *you* personally believe that we are about to be attacked?'

I thought over the question and decided that I was not really convinced that an attack was imminent.

'No, Sir, I don't,' I replied, 'but it does not alter the fact that the Chief is intending to deceive the government on operational policy.'

'Yes, I see that,' Moti said, 'and we must not allow that to happen. We can dissuade him, but there is no need to make a report to the government against the Chief. If we had believed that an attack were likely, that would be a different matter. As it is, it is a hypothetical situation.'

And we left it at that. I did not send a false operational report to the Ministry of Defence; how Moti Sagar dealt with the situation he never told me.

August turned to September and there was no move by the Chinese to re-enter Kameng. The forward concentrations along the NEFA–Tibet border continued to pose a potential threat, but the invasion scare gradually died down. In his book *The Chinese Betrayal*, Mullik makes no reference to the threat, and the Chinese have never given any explanation for the build-up of their troops during those weeks. At the time, however, the threat of a second Chinese invasion seemed both real and imminent. I have included the episode in this chronicle because it affords an illustration of the sort of malpractice that becomes possible when the machinery of government includes defective systems.

It is likely that in their interpretation of Chinese intentions Chaudhuri and Manekshaw were right and the rest of us wrong. The Chinese could well have been planning a punitive offensive, to be launched only if the Indian Army again adopted an aggressive posture; in which case Manekshaw's restraint did indeed serve to defuse a dangerous situation. It could also be argued that if the Army Chief and his Corps Commander were right in their intelligence assessment, their deception of Government was justified in the interests of national security. As far as I recall it was October (or even later) before 5 Infantry Division was deployed in Bomdila and the Tenga valley. Till then Kameng Frontier Division remained virtually defenceless and the government was kept in ignorance of that fact.

I left Army Headquarters in December 1963 to take command of 23 Infantry Division, a part of IV Corps, in Assam. Manekshaw had by then left to become the Army Commander. The new GOC IV Corps lost no time in pushing brigades of 5th and 23rd Divisions up into the mountains of Kameng. The tactical vacuum was filled at last, but it would be a long time before the deceit practised by an Army Chief ceased to trouble my mind.

For a young and irate brigadier, the baseness of that episode had focused on the duplicity of general officers. It was only later, when I thought about it more analytically, that I perceived that the system was as much at fault as the individuals. Deliberate and successful deception on vital operational matters can be possible only in an official mandate that enforces a separation of the civilian bureaucracy from the services staff. The Indian system is unique in this respect; there is no regular interface between the civilian and the military in the machinery of government. In the Pentagon or the Ministry of Defence in Britain, for example, service headquarters and their staffs are integral parts, whereas under the Indian system a distance is maintained between the Ministry and Army HQ; the latter is not a part of government. There is not a man in uniform working in the policy sections of the Ministry of Defence; the civilian bureaucracy, in its day-to-day functioning, has little physical or mental contact with the General Staff. There is no intimacy of shared thought and information; the prospect of detecting subterfuge is therefore minimal.

At the Ministry of Defence in Britain the rapport and inter-communication between the principal staff officers and their civilian colleagues is often as close as that which exists between PSOs and the theatre commanders. The likelihood of a CGS suggesting a major misrepresentation, and a distant field commander agreeing to it, is so remote that it can be discounted. In the Indian system the service Chiefs and their headquarters are distant from, and often resentful of, civilian bureaucrats in the Ministry. There is little contact between them except at infrequent, formal conferences. It is essential that this system undergo reform if we are to assure ourselves of corporate integrity in defence matters.

Organic segregation of the service Chiefs from the government not only serves to diminish their status and performance, it also results in denying politicians the counsel of military professionals – as was evident during the years covered by this memoir. Apart from an occasional meeting in the Prime Minister's or Defence Minister's office, the only contact between the service Chiefs and the country's decision-makers occurred when tney met the Defence Minister as single-service Commanders-in-Chief (rather than as Chiefs of Staff, despite their formal but misleading designation). In the absence of familiar exchanges between civilian bureaucrats and the General Staff, the influence of one upon the other was ritualistic and mechanical, not innate and pervasive. The situation is unchanged to this day.

Another dangerous by-product of the system is that because the three services operate outside the reach of the Ministry's co-ordinating influence, they remain isolated from each other. A Chiefs of Staff Committee exists but it is denied governmental authority. That derives only from the Minister or the civilian bureaucrats. The committee therefore restricts its deliberations mainly to routine matters that do not require government approval. If government (including financial) authority is needed on any issue, the service Chiefs tend to enter into individual relations with the Minister, not as a Chiefs of Staff body; thus, it is the Minister who effectually arrogates the role of a Chief of Defence Staff.

Not being part of government, and isolated from the other services, a service Chief is denied awareness of the critical determinant for formulating defence policy: the interrelation between threat perceptions, policy constraints, force structure and economic realities. His view of defence policy is a worm's-eye view and therefore simplistic and lacking in intellectual perspective.

It is not my purpose here to suggest that the bizarre mistakes made during the course of the confrontation with China could have been avoided had there existed a more integrated defence management system in South Block Secretariat. That would be far from the truth. The fact is that the manner and method in which everyone, from the Prime Minister, the Defence Minister and their bureaucracies to the General Staff and the commanders in the field, dealt with issues of national security and border policy were naive and amateurish — and inadequate to cope with the subtlety and sophistication of Chinese diplomacy. Failure of our border policy was inherent in a situation of Chinese intransigence over the Aksai Chin and Nehru's refusal to negotiate territorial compromise, but disaster was avoidable. Even the Intelligence Bureau's finding that the Chinese would not go to war to assert their border rights was proved largely correct – until they were pushed too far. Chinese restraint in Daulet Beg Oldi in May 1962 and later in the Galwan valley bears out Mullik's theory to a degree. What appears to have altered China's policy from containment to punitive conquest was almost certainly the Indian government's aggressive handling of the situation on the Namka-chu, combined with its gross misappreciation of the Indian Army's potential to wage war at Himalayan heights. Clearly it was these factors that led to the disasters in Kameng; and they could have been avoided had the organisation of government allowed for the practice of close consultation between the politicians, the civilian bureaucrats and the services staff. When an emergency arises, it is not enough for the Chiefs and their principal staff officers to send long notes on equipment shortages to the Ministers and the bureaucrats. The state of the armed forces and their fitness or otherwise for war must be under constant examination in an integrated machinery of government. Only then will problems be viewed in long-term perspective instead of being dealt with piecemeal as they arise.

## NOTE

1. The Chinese did not, however, return transport vehicles or any of the earth-moving and other Engineer equipment.

# EPILOGUE

In the aftermath of the Himalayan debacle, the Nehru government at last conceded that however great the urgency of national development, the armed forces must never again be neglected. President Radhakrishnan described the decision in typical fashion 'Military weakness has been a temptation; a little military strength may be a deterrent.' The Finance Ministry loosened its purse strings to promote a five-year Defence Plan, the main objectives of which were: a considerable expansion of the armed forces (raising the total to over a million); modernisation of weapons and equipment; greater self-sufficiency in defence production; and the creation of an operational infrastructure along the northern borders. In order to meet chronic shortages of foreign exchange, the government even agreed to compromise on its policy of abjuring military aid and accepted both credit and outright grants from the United States, the industrialised Commonwealth nations and the Soviet Union (though in the event the sum total of aid received from western sources did not amount to much over $80 million).

The Indian Army eventually increased in strength to more than 21 divisions; and the IAF to 45 squadrons. At the same time, organisational reforms were undertaken to improve the operational functioning of units and formations, and rigorous and imaginative training methods were introduced, aimed at providing high-altitude and jungle warfare capabilities. All the appropriate mechanistic moves were made; and yet, in the wars that were fought in 1965 and 1971, it became obvious that not much had changed in terms of governmental management of war and the quality of Indian generalship. Communication between political leaders and the military was still an *ad hoc* function on a single-service basis, with little or no inter-service co-ordination. In 1965, the army virtually went to war on its own and, lacking a coherent strategic doctrine, it very nearly met with disaster. In the actual conduct of operations, although officers and men in the field fought well, the high command failed to harness their operational potential to maximum strategic effect. Tried and tested operational plans were thoughtlessly discarded in favour of picaresque deployments of armour under a so-called 'strategy of attrition'. Only the high performance of a brigade of under-gunned tanks in the Khem Karan area and the stubborn staunchness of a GOC-in-C stopped a panicky Army Chief from throwing in the towel, abandoning the Amritsar sector to the enemy and withdrawing behind the River Beas. And finally, at the moment of our greatest advantage the Army Chief's non-comprehension of the intricacies of long-range logistics deprived India of a decisive victory.

In 1965 Muchu Chaudhuri was still the Chief of Army Staff. He later described his role in that war while delivering a National Security Lecture organised by the United Services Institute. He said that after the Rann-of-Cutch skirmishes with Pakistani forces in the spring of 1965, he had held several discussions with the Prime Minister (Shastri) and the Defence Minister (Chavan) about the possibility of a full-scale war with Pakistan – and 'the necessary sanction was obtained', presumably meaning that he had obtained government's approval of war plans; but neither he nor the Minister thought to keep the other two service chiefs informed. Still the high flyer trapezing from swing to swing, Chaudhuri by-passed the Chiefs of Staff Committee, the JPC and the JIC and decided to act entirely on his own. Air Chief Marshal P.C. Lal DFC, Vice Air Chief at the time, later commented:[1]

General Chaudhuri speaks with satisfaction of the freedom with which views were expressed at his informal meetings with the

Prime Minister and the Defence Minister, and the speed with which decisions were taken. It comes through clearly from his statements that he treated the whole business as his personal affair, or at any rate that of the Army's alone, with the Air Force as a passive spectator and the Navy out of it altogether. He ignored the basic concepts of our higher defence organisation. . . . The origin of this disease can be traced to pre-independence days. . . .

It was not until a crisis developed in the Chhamb sector of the Jammu front that:

On the afternoon of 1 September, General Chaudhuri burst into the office of the Defence Minister – who was discussing plans for the modernisation of the Air Force with the Air Chief – and demanded air support for his beleagured forces.[2]

Chaudhuri's actions as a loner were characteristic, but prime responsibility for permitting infractions of accepted practice clearly lay with the government. By continuing to keep the service Chiefs and their headquarters out of the government, it effectively undermined the process of routine in-house consultation with the military as a corporate whole. In the circumstances the only contact possible was with individual Chiefs on a one-to-one basis, and that also without benefit of staff analysis; Chaudhuri was able to corner the market because the other two Chiefs were, by nature, not so pushy. In this respect there had been no reform in politico-military procedures as a result of experiences in the Chinese war.

The Navy and the Air Force were not the only ones Chaudhuri disdained to heed; intelligence reports received like treatment. The DIB's assessments had earlier confirmed that Pakistan had raised a second armoured division by surreptitiously using equipment earmarked as 'reserve' by the American administrators of military aid. Chaudhuri refused to credit the report. He felt sure that Pakistan possessed only one armoured division, deployed in the northern (Sialkot) sector, and he suddenly decided, contrary to all previous plans and overruling the protests of the Western GOC-in-C, Harbakhsh Singh, to relocate India's only armoured division from the Jullunder area to the

Jammu Sector in the north – thus leaving the road to Delhi exposed to a Pakistani armoured thrust from the west and south-west.

In fact the Intelligence Bureau had got it right. Pakistan had indeed raised a second armoured division and secretly positioned it on the Khem Karan front whence, on 7 September, the Pakistanis launched a major offensive. The first momentum of the armoured attack overran many of our forward defences and it looked as though the Pakistanis would achieve a major breakthrough. The Corps Commander's unnecessarily alarmist report put Chaudhuri in a panic. He rushed from Delhi to Harbaksh's HQ in the Punjab and ordered him to abandon the Amritsar salient and pull back behind the Beas – just the *coup* that Pakistan must have hoped for; but this time Harbaksh was adamant and refused to comply. He told Chaudhuri that he would not accept a verbal order on such a crucial issue. Instead, he went forward to the threatened sector to see things for himself. What Chaudhuri did about issuing a written order when he got back to Delhi is not known, but the crisis passed the next day when the out-gunned Centurions and Shermans of Theograj's 2nd Independent Armoured Brigade and the recoilless 106 mm guns of 4 Mountain Division played havoc with the Patton tanks of Pakistan's armoured division in one of the great tactical victories of the war.

Finally, it was Chaudhuri's misreading of the dynamics of battle-logistics that caused the crowning blunder of the war. Logistics in modern war entail not only provision and resupply of materiel but also General Staff management of the process to ensure balanced replenishment according to battle forecasts. At the commencement of hostilities in early September 1965, the forward movement of materiel from central ordnance depots was set in automatic motion, without regard to the fact that the expenditure of items such as ammunition would clearly vary from sector to sector and must be assessed according to the intensity and scale of the fighting. Inevitably, non-intensive sectors became choked with relays of ammunition trains clogging up the railway's marshalling yards, whereas sectors in the thick of the fighting were running short and clamouring for resupply.

A General Staff study after the war ascertained that in overall terms only about 14–20 percent of the Indian Army's ammunition stocks had been used up; large dumps of unused ammunition were lying in sectors where the fighting had not been intensive. Relocation of these misdirected stocks would not have been a major problem. (The figures are from memory and reflect averages for all types of ammunition.) On the other hand, in Pakistan (where not only were the stocks smaller but there was also no significant industrial capacity for indigenous production) nearly 80 per cent of ammunition stocks had actually been expended. Taking into account *their* distribution irregularities, the Pakistan Army could not have continued to fight at high-intensity scales for much longer.

This was the logistical situation on both sides when, on or about 20 September, the Prime Minister summoned the Army Chief for a meeting in his room. Also present which was L.P. Singh (Shastri's old Home Secretary). Shastri told Chaudhuri that the Security Council had been calling persistently for a ceasefire and that Pakistan had indicated that it would accede to the UN's demands. More sensitive to the need for consulting the military than had been his predecessor, Shastri wished to consult the army before accepting a ceasefire proposal. He asked his Army Chief whether India could expect to gain marked territorial or strategic advantage if the war continued for a few days longer. If the answer were yes, he would hold off the Security Council for a while.

It was not Chaudhuri's practice to consult his staff. As usual, he gave an off-the-cuff answer, informing the Prime Minister that the army was coming to the end of its ammunition holdings and could not sustain the fighting for much longer. Chaudhuri advised acceptance of the ceasefire proposal.

There were echoes here of 1962. Chaudhuri had probably not fully recovered from the shock of the near disaster at Khem Karan and was unwilling to take any risks. An easy option had been suggested by the Prime Minister, and he jumped at it. Instead of victory the war ended in a stalemate that enabled both sides to claim victory.

Higher direction of war was as haphazard and immature

in 1965 as it had been abject in 1962. One of the requirements of a commanding general is that he must be able correctly to determine what kind of war and under what doctrine his forces should fight. For the first time a Prime Minister had given the Army Chief permission to mount an offensive into Pakistani territory in the event of an invasion of Kashmir. Instead of pursuing his objective through a war of movement, Chaudhuri chose to play safe and decided on a war of attrition. His strategic plan was to make a number of limited advances into Pakistani territory on a wide front and then dig in, in the hope that the enemy would wear himself down in a series of counter-attacks. Instead, the Pakistanis exploited India's surrender of the initiative by mounting their own grand offensive.

Attrition, as I have had occasion to comment before, is more an anti-strategy than a strategy. The only circumstance in which one may be justified in using it as a preferred choice is when one enjoys marked weapons superiority over the other side. This was not the case in 1965. On the contrary, it was the Pakistani Army which was a half generation (if not more) ahead of the Indian Army in weaponry, particularly in armour and artillery. Clearly they would hold the advantage over us in a slogging-match and, indeed, it should have been our determination to avoid attrition at all cost. As it was, what saved us in the Punjab was the high performance of our men and, most particularly, of our young officers. It was their courage and fortitude that turned a timid and sterile plan in our favour.

Ironically, the only aspect of attrition in which we eventually did hold the advantage was in logistics. We had worn the enemy down to near-exhaustion of his ammunition stocks, but the advantage was mindlessly thrown away by an impetuous and unthinking Army Chief.

The ensuing stalemate notwithstanding, myths were soon created about the brilliant handling of forces by our high command and the great victory that India had won. Fortunately, myths can sometimes have a useful function. They serve to draw a veil across the murkier sides of history that would be demoralising if the whole truth were known. It is just as well that in 1965 (as in 1962) the ranks of the army remained unaware of the bungling and faintheartedness at the top. Their achievements in battle did much to wipe out the stigma of 1962 and to restore the self-esteem of the army.

Six years later the Indian Army faced its biggest challenge since Independence – the war that established Bangladesh.

The image of that campaign remains in our minds as a glorious undertaking, superbly executed; a massive but rapid thrust deep into enemy territory, using the tactics of manoeuvre and mobility, to liberate the East Bengalis before the United States could intervene on Pakistan's behalf. That was the image that endured. One would have thought that that was one time when the services of the myth-makers would not have been needed. One would have been wrong; the reality did not match the image.

Although Mrs Gandhi resolutely faced the political crisis throughout the summer months of 1971, she was unable effectively to use the military as an instrument of policy. She failed to save the people of East Pakistan from a prolonged period of misery, degradation, murder and rapine; and she failed to stop millions of refugees from crossing into India to escape the Pakistani terror campaign, imposing an unacceptable burden on our economy. She failed in all these things because in April 1971 she unquestioningly accepted Manekshaw's opinion that the army was not then in a fit state to undertake military operations.

In his book *The Liberation of Bangladesh*, Major General Sukhwant Singh (Deputy Director of Military Operations in 1971) states that Manekshaw's reason for abdicating his responsibility in April 1971 was that the army 'was not well attuned to re-orient operational plans rapidly at such short notice, nor had it the wherewithal to conduct operations without the administration's infrastructural backing . . . Manekshaw wanted to lead a victorious army and not a hastily committed rabble.'

Manekshaw's opinion of the Indian Army (assuming that it was correctly reported by the author) is a withering, and surely undeserved, indictment of the officers and men who had by their steadfastness in the 1965 war redeemed their high reputation after the humiliation of 1962. More than that, it is also a severe self-indictment, because by then Manekshaw had been Army Chief for two years. Why had he allowed the army to run down to being a 'rabble'? Why had the contingency of a confrontation on East Pakistan not been foreseen and plans prepared? The army had benefited greatly from the Five Year 'Roll On' plans for several past years. Why then should it in an emergency find itself 'short by 360 different types of units?', as Manekshaw reported?

Mrs Gandhi's acceptance of Manekshaw's unsustainable personal opinion of the army's unpreparedness for war demonstrates the weakness of the Indian governmental system. The disjunction between the political and the military ensured that the Prime Minister's reliance on and supervision of the military depended upon her occasional contact with one individual, not routine familiarity with a headquarters or a General Staff body of opinion. Without such a basis of familiarity or personal knowledge there was no way for her to refute the Army Chief's disclaimer. Instead, she turned away from the armed forces and handed over the defence problem in the east to paramilitary command. It was not the army but the Home Ministry's Border Security Force that went boldly forward into military confrontation with the Pakistani Army. Together with the guerrillas of the Bengali *Mukti Bahini*, the BSF was made responsible for all military operations along the frontier during the first few months. The army's abdication was near total.

Under Manekshaw's over-cautious command it took the Indian Army nearly nine months to be ready for war against a beleaguered and inferior fighting force. It was a respite the Pakistanis used to some advantage, building up their defences, laying in stocks of ammunition and organising the newly forming command structure for war. Time was on their side, and they were given nine months of it.

According to Sukhwant Singh the main strategic considerations that decided Manekshaw against a military commitment in May were: firstly, the army's divisions were disposed mostly facing the west (against Pakistan) and the north (China) and it would take a considerable time to build up a force large enough to engage the two or three divisions that Pakistan had recently sent to its eastern wing; secondly, the timing was wrong, because the only period during which troops facing the Chinese could be redeployed for operations in the east would be the winter months, when the Himalayan passes became snowbound.

A counsel of fears indeed. Pakistan had begun to reinforce its eastern wing only *after* the 'crackdown' of 25 March, and that had been limited by the need to airlift troops all the way via Colombo. The two divisions that were flown to Dacca had to leave behind their armour, artillery and other heavy equipment; thus the Pakistani forces in the eastern wing constituted mainly an infantry force. Against them, even starting from scratch, India could have concentrated four or five divisions from Assam and north India in ten to twelve days at the most (including armour and artillery). The Indian Railways had given ample proof of its capability to manage such moves – both in 1961 and in 1965

As for the conceptual threat from China, Sukhwant Singh mentions in his book – and was supported by intelligence estimates at the time – that there was no sign of a Chinese build-up or other activity during the summer of 1971. Indeed, the risk of even token Chinese interference was low. Moreover, the Indian General Staff must surely have anticipated the need to move troops from one front to another in order to achieve a balance of forces in case of a war on two fronts. Force levels and dispositions are not determined on a rigid mathematical basis of single-purpose divisions.

It was strictly negative advice; and it is surprising that Mrs Gandhi accepted it. A rapid concentration followed by a swift, surgical operation against under-equipped and over-extended Pakistani forces would have saved the people of Bangladesh nine months of deprivation, terror and misery – and prevented the panic-stricken flight of ten million refugees to India. It is on record that the divisional commander in Silchar – GOC 54 Infantry Division – when urged by Mrs Gandhi in June 1971 to give his frank and personal estimate of the possibility of a successful strike at that time, replied that if he were to receive orders at that moment he would be in Dacca within a week. He was certain that Pakistani forces opposing him at that juncture could be quickly overwhelmed.

In the aftermath of the Bangladesh war the whole nation was justly proud of the performance of the armed forces, particularly the army. It was assumed by all, even by those of us who covered the campaign for the press, that the spectacular dash for Dacca had been planned from the start. Since neither the government nor the services headquarters have ever revealed the truth, the myth has been perpetuated.

The truth is quite different. Nothing so bold or decisive was ever envisaged by the military high command. Even after nine months of meticulous preparation, including building up a massive force surrounding East Pakistan, all that the Army Chief planned to execute was a cautious, limited advance across East Pakistan's border to occupy a narrow strip of territory (to support Mrs Gandhi's intention of setting up a government of Free Bangladesh in East Pakistani territory). It was not until the sixth day of the war, 8 December, by when the forces on the ground had demonstrated the magic touch that swiftly took them deep inside enemy territory, by-passing strong-points, that Manekshaw decided to issue the order to go for Dacca.

The facts were revealed for the first time in ex-DMO Sukhwant Singh's account of the war. According to him the task given to the three army corps in the field were to advance across the border in limited depth, capturing Pakistani strongholds – Chalna, Khulna, Hilli and others in the west; Comilla, Chittagong in the east. There was no mention of Dacca or the 'liberation of Bangladesh'. The aim of the Indian offensive was not enlarged to include Dacca till the sixth day of the war, by which date the troops on the ground had worked their way deep into East Bengal, proving that even in that land of innumerable river obstacles they could exploit rapidly forward. On the eastern front, a rapid thrust towards Brahmanbari by General Sagat Singh (the same whose Para Brigade made a dash for Goa in 1961) first offered hopes of a decisive victory.

Sukhwant's history of the war only *implied* that Dacca had never been Manekshaw's objective. It was the late Air Chief Marshal P.C. Lal's autobiography that set the seal of authenticity on the matter. The Air Chief recorded in

*My Years with the IAF:*

Here, I must clarify one doubt which had existed in my mind, and also in the minds of others, as to what the objectives of the 1971 war were. As defined by the Chiefs of Staff and by each respective Service Chief, it was to gain as much ground as possible in the east, to neutralise the Pakistani forces then to the extent we could and establish a base, as it were, for a possible state of Bangladesh. . . . We did intend, however, that the people of East Pakistan should determine their own future to the extent possible. And it was for this purpose that a base had to be established for them in the east. The possibility that the Pakistani forces in East Pakistan would collapse altogether, as they did, that Dacca would fall and that the whole country would be available to the leaders of the freedom movement in East Pakistan, was not considered something that was likely to happen. *Caution dictated that the people commanding in the East should work to limited objectives.* . . . [Emphasis added]

In the face of subsequent euphoric myths and claims that grew up around the Indian Army's achievements, it seems almost iconoclastic to lay bare the truth: that the military plan in 1971 was, in fact, almost a carbon copy of Chaudhuri's cautious moves in 1965 – that is, based on a war of attrition on a wide front, and with limited play-safe objectives. Strangely, the one proposal offered by Eastern Command that could have resulted in a war of mobility and manoeuvre was vetoed by Manekshaw during the planning stage. Eastern Command had suggested a determined push southward from the IV Corps sector (Shillong), along a route on which there was only one major river to cross and one built-up area to overcome. It was both the shortest and the quickest road to Dacca, but Manekshaw would not countenance it; to clinch matters he moved IV Corps from the (northern) Shillong-Tezpur sector to the eastern front, to take over at Tripura. In its place he left a static line-of-communication headquarters with just one brigade under its command. As far as Manekshaw's view of the battle went, the northern thrust was a non-starter; but fate often serves up its own brand of perversity. In the event, it was this static headquarters in the north, with its lone infantry brigade, that broke through to Dacca and delivered the *coup de grâce*.

We have enjoyed twenty years of peace since 1971, the longest period since independence, but in the all-important matter of civilian-military interaction there has been no move forward. The wars of 1965 and 1971 did not inspire any reform in this respect and there has been virtually no effort made to establish a system with an in-built interface between the politicians and the service heads (except by accident, as happened for a while when General Sundarji was Army Chief and Arun Singh Minister of State). The ministries and the military continue to remain on different sides of the divide.

The potential weakness of that dichotomy is the lack of a common yardstick for the assessment of each other's views and advice. Not only is there no effectual dialogue between the government and the military, the lack of a common staff denies to both a shared investigative base, so that even the infrequent meetings between them become *ad hoc* occasions, subject to bureaucratic trauma in times of crisis. If their deliberations were to be based on a wider groundwork of shared staff analyses, the likelihood of the government issuing operational orders against the advice of the professionals – as happened in 1962 – or of a single individual being permitted to exercise an absolute veto overriding national compulsions – as was the case in 1971 – would be greatly diminished.

The British-Indian imperial system had neither the need nor the facility for an interface between politicians (in Whitehall) and the military headquarters (in Delhi). Independent India does, but successive governments since independence have mindlessly continued to follow the British procedure. Neither service Chiefs nor ministerial bureaucrats have ever pressed for an overhaul of the system, perhaps because both regard the consequences of such reform as a threat to their self-interest.

On the other hand, it must be recorded that in the matter of generalship and service professionalism, the war of 1971 clearly demonstrated that they had passed the nadir of incompetence and were at last coming into their own.

In the army a new generation of officers, more keenly vocational than their British-Indian predecessors, had by then risen to high field command. The generals directing battles displayed skill and proficiency of an order that began to build up a new confidence within the service. Corps and divisional commanders on the eastern front, once given loose rein, were often decisive, innovative and inspiring. For the first time since independence tactical direction at higher levels matched the high performance of officers and men doing battle in the field.

By the time of the Bangladesh war the older, cautious – almost fogeyish – senior officers had been weeded out and replaced by those trained in India and with a greater commitment to professionalism. The basis of officer recruitment had been gradually widened, breaking down old class barriers and prejudices. Whatever the sociological reason behind the phenomenon, newly commissioned officers – often from a lower income group than their seniors – took their profession seriously. Of social graces and personal interests there may have been less evidence, but they were undoubtedly more professional. And in the matter of leading their troops into battle, they in no way detracted from the old British-Indian tradition.

Even in the planning and management of war the high command in Delhi displayed, for the first time, a mastery of military-bureaucratic techniques. Whatever the inhibition that restrained him from a timely military response, once Manekshaw took up the task of preparing the army for war, he set about it with an unrivalled talent in military culture. He was the first Indian-trained officer to become Army Chief and unlike many of his Sandhurst-trained seniors he had spent his career mastering the mechanics of his vocation: he was a finely turned professional. For the first time the three services planned and performed in unison – and much of that credit also goes to Manekshaw, for he was Chairman of the Chiefs of Staff at the time. The conduct of operations was greatly facilitated by the planning and foresight that had preceded it, operationally and logistically. The changeover from a cautious, limited objective to a decisive thrust at Dacca did not cause the smallest hold-up or hesitation – so much so that none of the local commanders ever realised that the whole aim of the war had suddenly been enlarged. In retrospect it would not be incorrect to say that the Bangladesh war was something of a turning point for Indian Army officers; from the relaxed amateurism of a leftover cult of the old imperial army, they were elevated to the determined professionalism of technology, weapons and tactics.

## NOTES

1. Air Chief Marshal P.C. Lal, DFC, *My Years with the IAF*, p. 162.
2. Ibid., p. 163.

# Appendix

## EVENTS LEADING TO THE LOSS OF
## SE LA AND BOMDI LA

I record below the sequence of events connected with 4 Infantry Division's activities on 17 and 18 November 1962, based on notes made by us on the return journey from Tezpur on 18 November 1962.

COAS and I arrived at Tezpur at approximately 1730 hours on 17 November 1962 and were met by GOC-in-C and BGS Eastern Command. (GOC IV Corps was away at Headquarters 2 Infantry Division.)

On the way to Corps Headquarters GOC-in-C informed us that 4 Garhwal, covering troops for Sela, had repulsed four attacks that morning, but that GOC 4 Division was withdrawing them. As this would mean losing contact with the enemy, who could them build up unhampered for the attack on the main position, I urged the GOC-in-C to stop this rearward move, but he refused saying it was not for him to interfere in IV Corps' battles, even in the absence of the Corps Commander.

On arrival at Corps Headquarters, we were given the information that 5 Guards of 48 Infantry Brigade, who were occupying a position at Thenbang (on a ridge North of the valley that lies just North of Bomdi La) had reported that they were 'surrounded' by the enemy, and had been given permission by 48 Infantry Brigade Commander to withdraw. This action would mean exposing the Bomdi La – Se La route to the enemy, and thus cutting 4 Infantry Division's Line of Control – a disastrous decision. In fact a road block between Bomdi La and Dhirang was already reported – though unconfirmed. I urged GOC-in-C to at least reverse *this* decision, and in fact, order 48 Infantry Brigade to counter-attack and, if not recapture Thenbang, at least to hold the slopes North of the Line of Control in order to protect it. GOC-in-C again refused to interfere. I tried to get his BGS to plead with him to change his mind, stating that in any case the GOC-in-C, in the absence of GOC IV Corps, must assume command at this critical stage in the battle; this also was of no avail. I then turned to COAS and asked him 'to take over the battle,' and save the situation, arguing that in an operational emergency leading to disaster, more 'protocol' had no place.

The Chief thereupon discussed the matter with GOC-in-C, when BGS IV Corps informed us that GOC 4 Division (who was at Bhirang Diong) reported that the enemy had cut the road near him. He felt that the road between Se La and Sengi any also be cut, and asked permission to withdraw!

I emphatically stated that a force equivalent to two infantry brigades, holding one of the finest natural defensive positions in NEFA, must not be allowed to withdraw without a fight. We had planned for all contingencies such as outflanking moves and road-blocks. These could be not be met and countered with the large force in Se La – Senge. The Chief also felt the same. GOC-in-C counselled withdrawal, on the grounds that a 'clean break' night mean that the Division would get away 'in tact'. I asked whether the aim of 4 Infantry Division was to fight the enemy or to preserve itself intact. I urged him again and again to say a definite 'No' to 4 Infantry Division, but he was adamant that only the IV Corps Commander could issue such an order and that we must await his arrival. Even my plea that every minute counted (re these two decisions being given – Thembang and Sela) was of no avail. Only further discussions resulted.

At about 1830 or 1900 hours, GOC IV Corps arrived, having been present at the battle of and the withdrawal from, Walong. A good half-hour was taken up with discussions of East NEFA, in spite of my repeatedly reminding them of the urgency of the 4 Infantry Division's decisions.

At this juncture, I was directed by COAS to telephone Army Headquarters and find out if Headquarters 82 Infantry Brigade (for Chabua) were flying or coming by train, and if the latter, to ensure that it was changed to a move by air. This involved my absence from the room for about 20–25 minutes. When I returned, BGS IV Corps informed me that permission had been granted to 4 Infantry Division to withdraw (even before facing a possible enemy attack).

When I remonstrated with GOC IV Corps regarding this 'infamous' decision, he told me that GOC-in-C had ordered it. I then went to Chief and pleaded that he intervene in this matter. I stated that we could never face the nation if 12,000 men with 36 guns, stocked with rations and ammunition for battle, 'ran away' without a fight. Chief reacted instantly and consulted GOC-in-C and GOC. GOC IV Corps then issued another signal which ordered Commander 4 Infantry Division to stay and fight it out to the best of his ability and withdraw only when his position 'became untenable.'

GOC IV Corps also ordered 48 Brigade Commander to clear

the road block, on the telephone. There was much demurring regarding it being dark, and the Bomdi La defences. GOC ordered him again, but added to me as an aside that he had little hope of it being carried out. Later in the evening 48 Brigade Commander reported that he had tried to send out a patrol but it had been 'pinned down by enemy D.F.'

After dinner, GOC 4 Corps again rang up GOC 4 Division, and after much discussion (and reference to the COAS) he ordered 4 Division to hold its defences during the night and to have another 'chat' with him in the morning before he withdrew.

At 0700 hours in the morning, GOC IV Corps informed me that BM of 42 Infantry Brigade, in a telephone conversation with GSO1 IV Corps, had inadvertently 'let the cat out of the bag' by saying that the battalion occupying defences on the Rya La gap in had been withdrawn the previous night and that after an attack on the 1 Sikhs at 0400 hours, the latter had also withdrawn. GOC 4 Division had also stated that he intended closing down and moving his Headquarters, though he did not then know where. After that there was no other communication with Headquarters 4 Infantry Division or any part of that formation. Not one wireless message from it was picked up by Signals monitors.

The above is a record of facts. My opinion is that when GOC 4 Division first asked for permission to withdraw, in the early evening of 17 November 1962, if he had been given an immediate and clear order that he shall *not* withdraw, 4 Infantry Division would, in all likelihood, have stood and fought instead of pulling out of Se La, and eventually NEFA, in a disorganized retreat.

Brig
DMO
November 1962
(D.K. PALIT)
Sd/-

# INDEX

and, 13-18;
collapse of at Bomdila, and
Se-la, causes of, 310-12, 353-55;
commander's morale fall of,
309-10;
composition of, 8-9;
debacle in NEFA, causes, 237-
39, 304-34;
decline in Kameng, causes,
305-30;
defence situation, 381-83,
during Krishna Menon's tenure,
238-39;
evolution of, factor influenced,
4-7;
expansion plan for, 83-84;
move to NEFA, 350-51;
new weapon to, discussion
about, 282;
operational policy of, in Ladakh,
91-99;
operations for the defence of
Assam, 325-26;
and Pakistan Army, a
comparison, 428;
position at Namka-Chu and
NEFA, 158, 183-84, 216-18;
preparation to face Chinese
aggression, 160-62;
preparation to invade Goa,
127-28;
rank structure of, 363;
reaction towards Chinese
activities, 166-67;
recruitment in, by caste, 9-11;
reforms in, 8-9;
role of, in: Indo-Pak War, 424-
28;
liberation of Bangladesh, 429-
36;
Second World War, 11-12;
strength, increase in, 423-24;
withdrawal from Se-La, 318-19
Corps: IV, 289;
dispositions of, 306-07;
messages from, 298-99;
XXXIII, 264;
company at Tsangle, 217
Divisions, Infantry

2nd, 264, 299, 341, 347;
3rd, 264;
4th, 200;
move to Sikkim, 47;
in NEFA, 47, 90;
operational task, 211;
position of in Se-la, 318;
in Tejpur, 48, 186-87;
withdrawal of, from Se-la, 322;
5th, 324, 338, 341, 347, 379;
17th, 117, 131-32, 135, 151-52;
moves to Siliguri, 264;
20th, 264, 300;
23rd, 338, 347;
in Nagaland, 148;
27th, 379;
moves to Sikkim, 356;
54th, 431
Brigades, Armoured
2nd Independent, 426
Brigades, Infantry
5th, 47, 348;
7th, 164, 199, 205, 227;
destruction of, 240;
move to Kameng, 291;
at Namka-Chu, 206;
in NEFA, 51-67;
in Towang, 58, 189;
11th, 47, 312;
48th, 151-53;
to Misamari, 242, 322;
at Mollem, 153;
62nd, 197, 290;
63rd, 152;
65th, 233;
67th, 325;
82nd, 313, 324;
moves to Chabua, 313;
192nd, 348;
Brigade, Para:
at Panjim, 153
Army, Madras, 7
Army, Tsar in Afghanistan, 23
Ashaq, 397
Aspy, Air Marshal, 134, 373
Assam, Cabinet Committee
meeting to discuss, 344;
defence plan for, 382;
police battalions for, 345

North East Frontier Agency
(NEFA), 38, 44, 46, 62;
new threats to, 385-86;
reorganisation of command in,
245-50;
situation in, 411-12

Operation *Leghorn*, 200;
preparation for, 201, 203-24
Operation *Onkar*, 108, 159, 186-87;
policy pattern of, 186-94;
reaction to, 183
Operation *Polo*, 118
Operational Review Committee,
task of, 388-89
Operation *Vijay*, 111;
developments, 111-18;
plan on map, 142-43;
troops for, 143

Palit, Brig DK, 48, 49, 50, 65, 86,
87, 123, 256, 373, 374, 391;
appointment of as DMO, 75-77;
assessment about new threats
from China, 415-19;
briefs Nehru about situation in
Towang, 246-47;
comments about Chiefs of Staffs
paper, 82-83;
Conversation of with:
Anant Pathania, 316;
Gen Chaudhuri, 376-77;
Defence Minister YB Chavan,
381-82;
Gen Hull, 362;
as Deputy Military Secretary,
68;
discussion with CGS about
Chinese notes, 164-65;
efforts to keep up morale of
Indian officers, 307-10;
experiences in Khinzemane and
Towang, 48-50;
Harish Sarin's association with,
282-87;
letter to Gen Kaul, 203;
master plan for the army, 83-84;
meets: Gen Kaul, 120, 272;
Biju Patnaik, 355-56;

Gen Chaudhuri, 113, 115;
Col Frazier, 402;
Maj Gen Joginder Dhillon,
197-202, 266;
Krishna Menon, 53, 266-68;
Mullik, 169, 170, 204-05, 295;
Nehru, 179-80;
Niranjan Prasad, 186-88;
Swaran Singh, 394;
Gen Thapar, 268-69, 270;
Gen Wadalia, 292-93;
moves to Se-La, 49;
as officiating CGS, 411;
opinion of, Anant Pathania,
295-96;
plans for crash training
programmes, 56;
posting of, as Deputy Military
Secretary, recounts events that
caused decline of Indian army,
331-34
relations with:
Gen Kaul, 157-58;
Mullik, 163;
Gen Thimayya, 79
reports on Indo-Pak talks on
Kashmir, 397-98;
suggestions to protect Ladakh,
159;
suggestions to Gen Thapar,
339-40;
summary of events and policies
during Chinese oppression,
178-79;
Gen Thapar, conversation with,
130-31, 304-05;
transfer of, from NEFA to Army
HQ, 68;
views on Gen Chaudhuri's
expansion plan, 402;
views about increase in
production of arms, 87-88;
visits Buddhist monastery,
63-64;
welfare measures by the wife of,
286-88;
with team from Pentagon, 346
Panchsheel Agreement, 43
Parthasarathy, G, 392